Languages of the Law in Early Medieval England

Languages of the Law in Early Medieval England

Essays in Memory of Lisi Oliver

EDITED BY

Stefan Jurasinski and
Andrew Rabin

PEETERS
LEUVEN – PARIS – BRISTOL, CT
2019

A catalogue record for this book is available from the Library of Congress.

ISBN 978-90-429-3979-0
eISBN 978-90-429-3980-6
D/2019/0602/85

Table of Contents

Acknowledgements

The editors have incurred a number of debts in the preparation of this volume. Most importantly, we would like to thank the contributors for both their efforts and their patience during the editorial process. Special thanks are due to Wallace Johnson and Susannah Brietz Monta for offering such lovely and personal tributes that capture so well part of what made Lisi so remarkable. We are grateful to the English Department at Louisiana State University at Baton Rouge, and to Bim Oliver and the entire Oliver family, for their insight and assistance as we prepared this volume. The work of all who have participated in the development of this book as anonymous referees or consultants at various stages of its development is gratefully acknowledged; particular thanks are due to Levi Roach, who shed his anonymity and offered some very helpful suggestions. We owe much to Kees Dekker, who guided the typescript swiftly through the process of review and production. The book is better for the many suggestions offered by Kees and members of the editorial board. Finally, we are deeply grateful to our own families for tolerating us, both as we compiled this volume and during all those times in the past when Lisi would call and we'd be off on another adventure...

Contributors

Rebecca BRACKMANN is an associate professor in the Department of Literature and Language at Lincoln Memorial University.

Rolf H. BREMMER Jr. is a professor emeritus in the Department of English at the University of Leiden.

Kristen CARELLA is an associate professor in the Department of English of Assumption College.

Charles DONAHUE, Jr. is the Paul A. Freund Professor of Law at the Harvard University Law School.

Daniela FRUSCIONE is a researcher at Goethe Universität Frankfurt am Main.

Jay Paul GATES is an associate professor in the Department of English at the John Jay College of Criminal Justice.

Paul HYAMS is professor emeritus in the Department of History at Cornell University.

Wallace JOHNSON is former Special Assistant to the President of the United States and retired Assistant Attorney General at the U.S. Department of Justice.

Stefan JURASINSKI is a professor in the Department of English at The College at Brockport, State University of New York.

Simon KEYNES is the Elrington and Bosworth Professor of Anglo-Saxon in the Department of Anglo-Saxon, Norse, and Celtic at Cambridge University.

Nicole MARAFIOTI is an associate professor in the Department of History at Trinity University.

Susannah Brietz MONTA is the John Cardinal O'Hara, C.S.C., and Glynn Family Honors Associate Professor in the Department of English at the University of Notre Dame.

Han NIJDAM is a faculty member in the Department of Linguistics of the Frisian Academy of the Royal Netherlands Academy of Arts and Sciences.

David PORTER is a professor in the Department of English at Southern University.

Andrew RABIN is a professor in the Department of English at the University of Louisville.

Elaine TREHARNE is the Roberta Bowman Denning Professor of Humanities in the Department of English at Stanford University.

Abbreviations

EDITIONS AND SCHOLARSHIP

DMLBS:	*Dictionary of Medieval Latin from British Sources*
DOE:	*Dictionary of Old English,* University of Toronto, ed. Angus Cameron *et al.*
EETS:	Early English Text Society
EHR:	*English Historical Review*
JEGP:	*Journal of English and Germanic Philology*
Liebermann, *Gesetze*:	Felix Liebermann, *Die Gesetze der Angelsachsen*, 3 vols. Halle, 1903-1916.
OED:	*Oxford English Dictionary*
Oliver, *Beginnings*:	Lisi Oliver, *The Beginnings of English Law*. Toronto, 2002.
Oliver, *Body Legal*:	Lisi Oliver, *The Body Legal in Barbarian Law.* Toronto, 2011.
S:	charter indexing number from Peter Sawyer, *Anglo-Saxon Charters: An Annotated List and Bibliography*. London, 1963.
Whitelock, *EHD*:	Dorothy Whitelock, *English Historical Documents v. I: c. 500-1042*, 2nd ed. London, 1979.
Wormald, *Making*:	Patrick Wormald, *The Making of English Law: King Alfred to the Twelfth Century*, vol. I. Oxford, 1999.

ABBREVIATIONS OF INDIVIDUAL LAW CODES

Note: when kings are mentioned in the text, their names appear in roman font. However, when the reference is to their legislation, the titles are italicized.

Af.	*Alfred*
Abt.	*Æthelberht*

I Atr.	*I Æthelred*
II Atr.	*II Æthelred*
III Atr.	*III Æthelred*
IV Atr.	*IV Æthelred*
V Atr.	*V Æthelred*
VI Atr.	*VI Æthelred*
VII Atr.	*VII Æthelred*
VIII Atr.	*VIII Æthelred*
I As.	*I Æthelstan*
II As.	*II Æthelstan*
IV As.	*IV Æthelstan*
VI As.	*VI Æthelstan*
I Cn.	*I Cnut*
II Cn.	*II Cnut*
I Eg.	*I Edgar*
II Eg.	*II Edgar*
III Eg.	*III Edgar*
I Em.	*I Edmund*
II Em.	*II Edmund*
I Ew.	*I Edward*
II Ew.	*II Edward*
EGu.	*Edward-Guthrum*
Hl.	*Hlothere and Eadric*
Rect.	*Rectitudines Singularum Personarum*
AGu.	*Treaty of Alfred and Guthrum*
Wi.	*Wihtræd*

Introduction

Stefan Jurasinski and Andrew Rabin

The scholarly work of Lisi Oliver requires no *apologia*. If anything, it seems, like a UFO, to necessitate some sort of accounting, resembling as it did so little of the work that emerged within the humanities, and even within her own field, over the past several decades. Whence came these odd and wonderful books whose narrator delightedly zigzags from the minutiae of Indo-European etymologies to the subtypes of fractured skulls? And how did these wild rides through the densest of technicalities remain so consistently and profoundly absorbing? In an era that has long paid lip service to "interdisciplinarity," Oliver's work stands out as something of a monument to what may be achieved by indifference to the compartmentalization that came to govern academic life only in the last century and a half. Are Oliver's publications the work of a linguist, a specialist in literature, or a historian? We can be glad that Oliver seemed never to be much troubled by these kinds of questions. Her work offers important lessons to all of us wrestling with the challenges facing the contemporary humanities.

From the outset of her career, Oliver seems to have been exceptionally fortunate in both her choice of subject matter and her method of approach. While other doctoral students were sweating to squeeze blood from turnips already wrung dry by generations of commentators, Oliver found herself preparing (to immediate acclaim even before revision as a monograph) the first book-length study of what may fairly be called one of the most important collections of texts in Old English. How this goldmine was left for Oliver's private perusal is a long, sad story worth telling both for its lessons in all the things that can go wrong in the reception of an important body of primary texts and for the light it sheds on the nature and magnitude of Oliver's achievement.

The subject of Oliver's doctoral dissertation was, of course, the laws issued in Old English in the kingdom of Kent between the baptism of King Æthelberht in 597 and the accession of Wihtræd in 695.[1] That these texts are available to us at all is a miracle in itself. The earliest of these—the laws issued by Æthelberht—is also the earliest text of any sort available in Old English, antedating even Caedmon's Hymn, which Bede attributes to a cowherd-turned-poet living c. 680. Yet they survive uniquely in a manuscript prepared more than half a millenium after their promulgation. Like most medieval manuscripts,

[1] Lisi Oliver, *The Language of the Early English Laws* (PhD dissertation, Harvard University, 1995).

it is a witness to the damage that can be done by human inattention over several centuries, having been once dropped in the Thames.

Only decades ago, it was possible even in book-length surveys of Old English prose for scholars to take little or no notice of the laws of early Kent. That they should be so ignored owes much to the fact that, in the centuries following their initial reception, the Kentish laws were rarely approached without scholars' first donning the blinders of their academic disciplines. In spite of being uniquely positioned to comment on these texts given the demands of their sometimes unusual syntax and morphology, specialists in the Old English language and its literature for the most part were content to dwell on other materials.[2] Æthelberht's laws also constitute the earliest example of legislation in English and thus may quite legitimately be described one of the primary points of origin for written English law itself. (Certainly the text was understood as such by Bede and by King Alfred.) But their being written in Old English, along with the widely held view that English legal history did not begin in earnest until the Constitutions of Clarendon issued during the reign of Henry II, rendered them irrelevant to the chronology of English institutions. The bold title Oliver gave her first monograph—*The Beginnings of English Law*—was intended to bring home the full significance of what she had done in bridging centuries of scholarly neglect and myopia.

In editing these texts anew and elucidating their relationship to developments in seventh-century England, Oliver helped to initiate the most broad-based and serious reappraisal of Anglo-Saxon law in nearly a century. The academic study of Old English legislation in general was prone to long periods of stagnancy not long after this corpus came to light through the combined labors of William Lambarde, a justice of the peace and ultimately Master in the High Court of Chancery during the reign of Elizabeth I, and the rather more obscure but no less important Laurence Nowell.[3] (Their *Archaionomia,* the *editio princeps* of pre-Conquest royal legislation, did not take notice of the laws of Kent.) The neglect this corpus would suffer is evident in the fact that, when William Blackstone some two centuries later would turn his attention to the Anglo-Saxon laws, he did so through the edition of David Wilkins—which remained, in most respects, that of Lambarde and Nowell. Though the academic study of early English

---

[2] A sense of the prevailing views before Oliver's time is apparent in Stanley Greenfield and Daniel G. Calder's *New Critical History of Old English Literature* (New York: New York University Press, 1986), 108-9. While this text, intended to orient advanced undergraduate and graduate students within the range of writing that survives in Old English, does include some discussion of the Kentish laws and says nothing erroneous, consideration of these texts extends no further than a couple of pages and serves as little more than a brief prologue to remarks on Alfredian and later works of legislative prose.

[3] On the career of Lambarde, see Wilbur Dunkel, *Willam Lambarde, Elizabethan Jurist: 1536-1601* (New Brunswick: Rutgers University Press, 1965).

law had hardly begun, already the corpus of Anglo-Saxon legislation was beginning to drift out of view.

The more exacting editorial methods that accompanied the rise of comparative philology in the early nineteenth century bore promise for a renewal of scholarly inquiry. But these methods came regrettably twinned with Romanticism, often at its worst. Thus the scholars most able to read the language of Anglo-Saxon legislation could not resist chasing its contents into the ether of some supposed *urgermanisches* system of laws that had predated the advent of writing on parchment among the continental *Germani*. The Anglo-Saxon laws became important, not so much for what they revealed about the conditions of their time, but for the light they might shed into the mists of Germanic prehistory. Frederic William Maitland may have shuddered at the excesses of this movement. But his jointly-authored *History of English Law*, the source through which readers would learn the subject for the next century, put the Anglo-Saxon laws right back where they had been when they emerged as a field of academic study—as an odd little prelude to the emergence of English common law. Illustrative of their fate is Maitland's placing the chapter of his *History* devoted to Anglo-Saxon law in the hands of Frederick Pollock. The result, it is fair to say, is little more than a tour of then-fashionable German thinking on the subject for Anglophone readers.

The work of Maitland's contemporary and friend Felix Liebermann, who did more than any scholar of any period to set the study of these texts on the proper footing, still left more to be done. Liebermann's *Gesetze der Angelsachsen* remains, over a century after its publication, the standard edition in which these texts appear, and deservedly so. Yet its being the supreme fulfillment of German scholarship of the nineteenth century was, in many ways, its undoing for the twentieth. An edition whose three volumes constitute a maze of intricate commentary, full of cross-references that leave one perpetually wondering whether some crucial note might have been missed, it did little to stimulate further interest in the subject. The scholarly environment from which it emerged, populated by men of leisure such as Liebermann himself, would suffer a terrible blow with the First World War, with any residue being wiped clean by the second.[4] The rebuilding of Europe in the aftermath of the latter gave a new prominence to

[4] On the effects of World War I on the intellectual atmosphere of Europe, see, e.g., Hugh Kenner, *The Pound Era* (Berkeley: University of California Press, 1971), 382-3: "The guns of August, and September, and October, the guns of 52 interminable blood-drenched months, destroyed morale, destroyed a generation, destroyed Europe. Everything afterward seems provisional. [...] By the mid-1920s a massive triviality, a failure of will on a truly forbidding scale, was allowing English culture to lapse into shapes characterized by childishness, self-indulgence, utter predictability." For an overview of Liebermann's career, see Andrew Rabin, "Felix Liebermann and *Die Gesetze der Angelsachsen*," in Stefan Jurasinski, Lisi Oliver, and Andrew Rabin, eds., *English Law Before Magna Carta* (Leiden: Brill, 2010), 1-8.

American universities, and American students' interest in learning foreign languages did not often (understandably enough) extend to German. For the most part, Liebermann's *Gesetze* moldered for decades on bookshelves. The saddest testimony to this book's fate, and to the cheapness of nineteenth-century printing, is that few original editions of the book now survive intact in academic libraries; the pages of those that do will sometimes tear and even crumble when touched.

Intended as a definitive critical edition, the *Gesetze* instead became, like the texts edited therein, a monument to the past, containing a world of scholarly exchanges frozen in amber and less intelligible with the passing of each decade. Its dominance meant that all contributions to the study of Anglo-Saxon law would involve double acts of recovery. Making sense of the crabbed prose of Old English legislation involved resuming debates with scholars deceased for in some cases 150 years, products of a world almost as foreign to educated persons of the late twentieth and early twenty-first centuries as the Middle Ages themselves.

Few scholars were as well positioned to take up this challenge as Lisi Oliver, who kept until the end of her life a collection of binders in which the entirety of Liebermann's *Gesetze* was photocopied. Born in Frankfurt, Oliver remained throughout her life a fluent speaker of German. She also brought to the study of these materials a restless and all-encompassing curiosity. And some knowledge of everything, as it turned out, was what would be needed in the first edition of the Kentish laws to appear in a century, as understanding these texts involves deep knowledge not only of early medieval history and of earlier Germanic languages, but also of matters such as agriculture and human physiology.

One enthusiastic reader of Oliver's dissertation was Patrick Wormald, whose *Making of English Law* (1999), still the dominant study of early English legislation nearly two decades after its appearance, defers to her judgments about the language and provenance of the Kentish laws.[5] Once reshaped into her first monograph, the book assumed a pronouncedly different form. That the laws of Kent were edited anew alongside an accurate English translation, and with thorough commentary and historical background, was an achievement in itself. But these texts were also for the first time made available with an accessibility appropriate to their importance. The gifts of a great teacher are evident throughout the book, which combines tremendous methodological rigor with a warmth and humor often sorely lacking in works of scholarship. Not many books devoted to Anglo-Saxon prose could boast the readership gained by *The Beginnings of English Law*; effectively, she had delivered this text back to the Anglophone world,

[5] In his *Making of English Law*, Wormald found the grammar and overall organization of Æthelberht's laws "illuminated as never before" (95 n. 332) by Oliver's dissertation.

answering in some respects Maitland's lament upon the publication of Liebermann's *Gesetze*: "We have lost the Anglo-Saxon laws."[6]

Oliver's publications in the years after the appearance of her monograph reflect a new object on her intellectual horizon that perhaps could only have been discernible after writing *Beginnings*. The latter had struck a great blow against the theretofore orthodox view that Æthelberht's laws represented vernacular mimicry of laws issued at roughly the same time in Francia. But refuting such arguments led Oliver into a deeper awareness of these so-called *leges barbarorum*. Of particular interest were the injury tariffs that figure so prominently in both Kentish and Frankish legislation, lists of injuries and appropriate compensations that had long been seen as one of the characteristic features of post-Roman legislation. Unlike the provenance of the Kentish laws, the injury legislation of early Western Europe did not lack for commentators. Yet Oliver was probably the first to put to these texts a brilliant new series of questions. Might early medical knowledge, otherwise unattested, be buried in the ways in which these texts assigned value to teeth, nails, and bones? When distinct legal traditions grant different compensation amounts to the same injuries, does their doing so suggest ways in which maps of bodily perception might be reconstructed for the kingdoms of early medieval Europe? In time reflections on these and other matters led to her 2011 monograph, *The Body Legal and Barbarian Law*. Written while Oliver was the recipient of a year-long fellowship from the National Institutes of Health, the book is an exhilarating performance in which Oliver's characteristic gifts are most fully apparent. While the book resists attempts at categorization, it may be said to have recovered some of the better qualities of the comparative philology ascendant in Liebermann's day, which was similarly all-encompassing in its range of interests, and which sought nothing less than to rebuild from literary and other fragments the most intimate perceptions of average people in the early Middle Ages. No specialist in early medieval law had done anything this ambitious in many decades.

In the decade that followed, Oliver's attention shifted to the *domboc* (or "book of judgments") issued by Alfred the Great in the last years of his reign. Her final publications show the depth of her reflection on this text as she applied to it the insights gained from prior work on early Western European laws. Her last year saw her awarded both a year-long fellowship from the American Council of Learned Societies (for work on a collaborative edition of the *domboc*) and the title of "Distinguished Research Master," the highest awarded to faculty at her home institution.

The essays collected in this volume testify to the range of Lisi's interests, the broad influence of her scholarship, and—what certainly would have been most important to

6 Frederic William Maitland, "The Laws of the Anglo-Saxons," *The Quarterly Review* 200 (1904): 139-57, at 157.

her—the many friendships she developed along the way. The first group of essays focuses on the texts that most fascinated Lisi throughout her career, the pre-ninth century laws of Kent and Wessex. Charles Donahue's magisterial discussion of clauses 72-7 in the laws of Æthelberht builds on Lisi's work in *The Beginnings of English Law* to shed light on both the legal status of women in seventh-century Kent and on the potential usefulness—or lack thereof—early royal legislation may have had in judicial dispute resolution. Stefan Jurasinski turns from the laws of Æthelberht to those of Wihtræd and Ine in order to examine the relationship between royal legislation and episcopal decree, and in so doing to question how those distinctions have been understood both by medieval readers and modern scholars. Kristen Carella's chapter offers innovative readings of the *Dialogue of Ecgberht* and the Legatine Capitulary of 786 as a means of challenging the critical consensus that Kent and Wessex were the only early Anglo-Saxon kingdoms from which written law survives. Lastly, Nicole Marafioti considers how the issues examined in this first section—the question of applicability, the relationship between the sacred and the secular, and the role of law in the creation of cultural identity—all come to shape the most wide-ranging of early Anglo-Saxon legal texts, the laws of Alfred the Great.

Lisi's work was characterized, not only by scholarly rigor, but also by a strong commitment to the value of comparative study and a careful consideration of issues of methodology. These facets of her work are highlighted by the contributors in the second section of this volume. Thus, Daniela Fruscione pairs the Kentish laws with continental sources to see what such texts can reveal about the nature of women's migration in the early medieval period. In a similar vein, Han Nijdam expands on Lisi's work in *The Body Legal and Barbarian Law* to examine what might be learned about early medieval ethnic identity from the Old Frisian injury tariffs. Paul Hyams, in contrast, ranges not across cultures but time periods and genres with a facility reminiscent of Lisi herself to provide a compelling new account of the nature of servitude in Anglo-Saxon England. Finally, Elaine Treharne brings problems of comparison and methodology to the fore with a forceful argument for the centrality of paleography to the study of early medieval textual, and especially legal, culture.

Lisi's scholarship was enlivened by her recognition that the range of genres that constituted "law" in Anglo-Saxon England were not limited to royal legislation. As was also true of her friend and mentor Patrick Wormald, her scholarship was notable for her willingness to consider the evidence of charters, glossaries, literature, and other genres too often dismissed by more traditional legal historians. The essays in the third section take up questions of genre in order to develop a broader understanding of the full range of early English legal composition. In the section's first piece, Rolf Bremmer considers the intersection between Old English literature and law through a detailed discussion of the proverbial content of early English royal legislation. Simon Keynes then explores the connections between the making of law, the issuing of charters, and the recording of litigation in his fascinating account of the so-called "Cuckhamsley Chirograph." In the final essay, David Porter examines the evidence for Anglo-Saxon legal practice that can be derived from the Old English glossaries, a corpus of texts that served as one of Lisi's primary intellectual preoccupations for much of her career.

The influence of early law and Lisi's scholarship on it is the focus of the essays that round out this collection. The section begins in the eleventh century with a discussion by Andrew Rabin of the reception of early Kentish law by later Anglo-Saxon legislators, in particular Archbishop Wulfstan of York. Jay Gates moves into the post-Conquest period with an analysis of Old English legal vocabulary in the great twelfth-century Latin compilation *Quadripartitus.* The final two essays in the volume consider the importance of early law to the sixteenth- and seventeenth-century antiquaries who both made possible the recovery of early English textual culture and laid the groundwork for the modern study of pre-Conquest law. Rebecca Brackmann's account of the changing depictions of Cnut—from Viking invader to lovesick lawmaker—provides a valuable case study in the ways in which early medieval kingship was received and adapted by later generations. Finally, Susannah Brietz Monta tracks the early modern perceptions of King Alfred in order to better understand how the idealized lawgiver of the medieval past provided a model for those seeking to create a new law for the Reformation present.

These essays are offered in memory of a gifted scholar who did more than perhaps most Anglo-Saxonists of her generation to bridge distinctions between academic disciplines and to establish new networks of scholarly exchange. Her doing so was not part of some academic project but the spontaneous product of an enthusiasm in which others could not help but be carried along. She could be (and should be) praised for her extraordinary generosity to students and colleagues, for her captivating presentations at conferences (always delivered *extempore*), for her fierce intellectual independence and immunity to faddish thinking. Along with these qualities, however, what made knowing Lisi such a great gift was the testimony of her life and work to the importance of having fun with what you do and of not taking things too seriously. Reflecting on how we might attain these virtues, though a worthy pursuit, will only get us so far; the *cure* for their opposites may sometimes be found in reading Lisi's books.

A Bibliography of Works by Lisi Oliver

Books and Monographs

2011. *The Body Legal in Barbarian Law*. Toronto: University of Toronto Press.

2002. *The Beginnings of English Law*. Toronto: University of Toronto Press.

Articles

2014. "Genital Mutilation in Germanic Law," *Capital and Corporal Punishment in Anglo-Saxon England*, ed. Nicole Marafioti and Jay Gates (Woodbridge: Boydell), pp. 48-73.

2012. "Documentary Culture and the Making of English Law," *Cambridge History of Early Medieval English Literature, 500-1150*, ed. Clare Lees (Cambridge: Cambridge University Press), pp. 499-529.

"466. Sens, Musés de Sens (Trésor de la Cathédral) [Prou 158]," *Anglo-Saxon Manuscripts in Microfiche Facsimile*. (Tempe, ACMRS).

2011. With Susannah Brietz Monta. "Spenser, Wolfram and the Reformation of Despair," *Journal of Literary Onomastics* 1: 9-28.

2010. "Preface." *English Law before Magna Carta: Felix Liebermann and* Die Gesetze der Angelsachsen, ed. Stefan Jurasinski, Lisi Oliver and Andrew Rabin (Leiden: Brill).
With Maria Mahoney. "Ecclesiastic anatomies of late Antiquity." *Rhetorics of Bodily Disease and Health in Medieval and Early Modern England*, ed. Jennifer C. Vaught (Aldershot: Ashgate), 25-42.

"Æthelberht and Alfred's Two Skulls." *Heroic Age*. 14: np. (on-line publication)

2009. "Protecting the Body in Early Anglo-Saxon England," in *Peace and Protection in the Medieval West*, ed. T. B. Lambert and David Rollason. (Toronto: Pontifical Institute for Medieval Studies), 60-77.

"Royal and Ecclesiastical Law in Seventh-Century Kent," *Essays in Memory of Patrick Wormald*, ed. Catherine Karkov and David Pelteret (Aldershot: Ashgate), 97-114.

2008. "Sick-Maintenance in Anglo-Saxon Law." *Journal of English and Germanic Philology* 107: 319-42.

"Æthelberht's *fedesl* Revisited," *Notes and Queries* 55: 125-6.

2006. "*Lex Talionis* in Barbarian Law," *Journal of Indo-European Studies* 52: 197-218.

2003. "Who was Æthelberht's *læt*?," in *Confrontation in Late Antiquity*, ed. Linda Hall. (Cambridge: Orchard Academic Press), pp. 153-66.

1998. "Irish Influence on Orthographic Practice in Early Kent," *North-West European Language Evolution* 33: 93-113.

"Towards Freeing a Slave in Germanic law," in *Mír Curad, Papers presented to Calvert Watkins*, ed. Jasanoff, Melchert and Oliver, (Innsbruck: Innsbrucker Beiträge zur Sprachwissenschaft), pp. 549-60.

"*Cyninges fedesl*: The Feeding of the King in Æthelberht §12," *Anglo-Saxon England* 8: 59-75.

1996. "Spilled Wine and Lost Sovereignty in Chretien's *Perceval*," *Neuphilologische Mitteilungen* 97: 91-102.

1995. "Three Final Vowels and Their Relevance in Dating Early Anglo-Saxon Laws," in *Harvard Working Papers in Linguistics* 4: 163-78.

1994. "Irish Influence in Early Anglo-Saxon Orthographic Practice," in *Proceedings of the Harvard Celtic Colloquium* 14: 115-31.

1993. "Linguistic Methodology in Comparative Law," in *Harvard Working Papers in Linguistics* 3:109-126.

"Forced and Unforced Rape in Early Irish Law," in *Proceedings of the Harvard Celtic Colloquium* 13: 93-106.

1992. "The Origin of Old Irish Resonant Geminates and MacNeill's Law," in *Proceedings of the Harvard Celtic Colloquium* 12: 93-109.

1977-1985. Various articles on dramaturgy and music history in *Opera Company of Boston News* and *Opera Guide*, publications of the Opera Company of Boston.

Edited Collections

2010. Co-Editor (with Stefan Jurasinski and Andrew Rabin). *English Law Before Magna Carta: Felix Liebermann and* Die Gesetze der Angelsachsen (Leiden: Brill).

2008. *Selected Writings of Calvert Watkins, vol. 3* (Innsbruck: Innsbrucker Beiträge zur Sprachwissenschaft).

1998. Co-editor (with J. Jasanoff and H. Craig Melchert): *Mír Curad, Papers presented to Calvert Watkins* (Innsbruck: Innsbrucker Beiträge zur Sprachwissenschaft).

1994. *Selected Writings of Calvert Watkins, vols. 1 and 2* (Innsbruck: Innsbrucker Beiträge zur Sprachwissenschaft).

Our Lisi

Susannah Brietz Monta

On a humid Louisiana spring day, my toddler son bounced around a playground, introducing people he loved to his little friends. He flung a pudgy finger in my direction: "This is my mommy!" With a radiant smile he turned to my husband: "This is my daddy!" For a moment, he hesitated, puzzled. Then the furrow across his tiny brow relaxed: "And this is my Lisi!"

Many are the academic tributes to Lisi Oliver's formidable intellectual accomplishments; her scholarly legacy richly deserves these accolades. The essays in this volume constitute a special celebration of her work. But to my children, who came to know her during my eight years as her colleague at Louisiana State University, she was more than an academic superstar. We did not own her, of course; she was not *our* Lisi. But with the tendency of young children to lead from the heart, my son recognized what I had never articulated. A professional relationship, forged of crawfish and circumstance, had grown into one of the most cherished friendships in our lives. When Lisi began playing with my kids at their music school's annual family concert, her choice of instrument may have slightly puzzled the school's directors. (Have you ever heard Bach's "Jesu, Joy of Man's Desiring" played by classical strings — and ukulele?) But those concerts were a natural outgrowth of her generous involvement with our family. My children grieved for her as for a beloved aunt, cousin, or the dearest of friends. (It would have been important to her that I not say "grandmother.") They cheerfully volunteered at our local city-wide celebration of cycling in her honor; they have roared with laughter as they repeat our family's many in-jokes with her, determined to keep them alive; and they light candles for her at their Catholic school, insisting that the priest, who never met her, remember her in his prayers.

She left many material traces in our lives, witnesses to her all-encompassing friendship. My minivan bears the scars of her attempts to drive it, when she took my young sons to the movies in the days just after my daughter was born. On a wall in our garage, one of her many bicycle helmets hangs: she rode with us every spring, and she'd tired of hauling a helmet back and forth between Baton Rouge and our new home in South Bend, Indiana. In my closet are shoes she gave me: rather improbably, despite a seven-inch height difference, we wore the same size. When my daughter plays soccer, she drinks water from a sports cup Lisi gave her. My older son's love of women's basketball began under her tutelage; he still watches games beneath a purple-and-gold LSU banner. My younger son trusted her enough to make her the first audience for his creative writing, reading aloud from a treasured notebook while she listened and punctuated his hesitant offerings with enthusiastic exclamations. Lisi's fondness of large stray dogs was legendary in Baton Rouge. Her first canine rescue, a black Rottweiler-Labrador mix named Sadie, was adopted six months after my first son was born and became his best friend, despite outweighing him by roughly eighty pounds for much of his childhood. My dog, who is a tenth the size of her last adoptee, a mastiff named Pilot, has been emboldened by a little metal, bad-ass collar she sent him. In my linen closet are the old sheets and towels Lisi and I took every spring to the International Medieval Congress in Kalamazoo, Michigan, in an attempt to make the spartan Western Michigan University dorm rooms civilized enough to house people who were no longer twenty-one (but who occasionally behaved as if they were).

Deeper still are the intangible traces she left. I arrived at LSU at age twenty-eight, terribly unsure of myself, despite the fact that I'd evidently persuaded my future colleagues that I belonged in the tenure-track position they'd entrusted to me. Lisi had enough confidence for the two of us; she simply assumed that I would succeed as a teacher, scholar, and colleague, and willed me forward. I rode her wave of optimism, as so many of us did. Somehow she managed to talk with me about the academy, tenure pressures, teaching challenges, and budgetary crises in ways that were completely, often hilariously frank, and yet stubbornly hopeful. She harbored no illusions, and she had no cynicism. Despite openly acknowledging evidence to the contrary, she, like Julian of Norwich, trusted that all shall be well, and all manner of thing shall be well.

Her personality was woven of verve, bravery, honesty, and a deep joy in all she undertook, from cycling, music, sports fandom, and dog adoption to early English law and Indo-European linguistics. She harnessed all of her intelligence and energy to bring the many virtues of friendship to academe. Lisi was extravagant with her friendship; she bestowed it with cheerful abandon. Somehow you think a heart that big will just keep beating. And maybe in some ways it does. I hear echoes of her humor in my children's good-natured teasing of me and each other. I catch snatches of her easy-going charm, and her down-to-earth reproaches to ivory-tower hauteur, in the students and colleagues she's mentored over the years. Her warmth and fearsome intelligence are reflected in the welcoming, supportive, distinguished LSU Department of English, a department for which she worked so hard and was so proud to represent. Her innovative work on early English law revived a field that is now known both for its scholarly insights and its tight-knit community. Her scholarship's intellectual repercussions, as well as her collegial way of working and networking, will endure.

What she gave us, friends and colleagues alike, was love. And love, as Solomon knew, is as strong as death. Those of us in this volume are privileged to have known her, to have been among those on whom she lavished her friendship. And we will honor her by the way we teach, study, play, write, laugh, sing, and love.

Good night, sweet friend. And flights of angels sing thee to thy rest.

A Tribute to Elisabeth "Lisi" Oliver

Wallace Johnson

I am delighted to contribute a brief note to this commemorative book of essays—contemplated in life but much more significant in death. Not only a brilliant scholar, Lisi was also a generous, loyal friend and, she would no doubt have added, a pretty good Ukelele player.

I first connected with Lisi many years ago due to our joint interest in early laws of the British Isles—she a linguist and scholar, me a devoted student of those early laws, but trained in an entirely different discipline as a lawyer. I was interested in the origin of specific intent in the emergence of the community crime of murder within the early laws of the British Isles. Her scholarly publications, *The Beginning of English Law, the Body Legal in Barbarian Law*, and her contribution in *Capital and Corporal Punishment in Anglo-Saxon England*, ensured we were meant to cross paths sometime, and sooner for me turned out to be much better than later. Our conversations by phone and over the Internet and then in person were wide ranging and deep; certainly much broader than the limited focus we shared concerning crime and punishment.

Though her position was in a department of English, Lisi was very much a student of early English law. Before Lisi began publishing her work, the study of these laws had generally been left to linguists and philologists since so much is yet to be understood about their composition and meaning. Few had taken on the challenge of explaining the manner in which an early king and his counselors might use the law to unify a people of varied needs and interests, as was certainly the case for seventh-century England. Influence from Rome had begun to affect an island already Christian with significant influence from Ireland as well. And that is where Lisi's passion resided and where much of her scholarship concentrated.

Lisi had the rare characteristic of being a "connecter." She networked better than almost anybody could! I am sure that an academic schooled in psychology could explain *why* but she put people and interests together instinctively and in a way that left everyone at ease. Something that came so easily to her is so hard for so many others. Once she had a sense of a person's background, interests and personality, she immediately made sure to put him or her in touch with others who shared them, and she did this more capably than any computer program could operate.

The roadmap to our friendship began with emails. Telephone calls followed, then links from her to others with like academic interests, and ultimately meetings at the

Medieval Institute in Kalamazoo. We talked about a joint book project comparing the fourteenth-century trials of the Knights Templar to political show trials in 1930s Russia and during the Nixon years. (Our discussions of the book were cut short by her demise.) I found myself acting as an external reader of her collaborative edition of Alfred's *domboc* and involved in other ways in a variety of independent projects which she stimulated in her unique way with scholars who shared our interests.

One might wonder how a practicing attorney like me with a bent toward legal history could find so much worth discussing with a linguist like Lisi. I begin by observing it was all due to Lisi and her energy. To best understand this, one must ask: How does the study of ancient language overlap so necessarily with the study of law and governance? An example of how that worked may be seen in how we worked together on her last book.

In the years immediately preceding her passing, Lisi and Stefan Jurasinski neared completion of a newly edited version of a key legal text which, though not nearly as celebrated, it is of comparable importance to Magna Carta. As the three of us worked together reading text, the two scholars argued over the meaning of early English words while I sought to interpret the text culturally. I listened to the arguments over linguistic and philological questions and offered insight into what the early medieval author sought to do and how he likely governed in the historical context of those times. The interchange brought to life the meaning of the law and the manner in which king and counselor sought to unite and govern an emerging nation composed of disparate, previously warring, peoples. The effort was both productive and, for me, great fun.

Many contributors to this collection joined at table with Lisi at "The Law Dinner" customarily held during the Medieval Institute at Kalamazoo. Lisi was a magnet for all scholars and academics with an interest in early medieval law whether professional or amateur. It was a group including both senior academics as well as those just coming along and entering academia. All would join together, socializing while discussing the complexity of the academic world in which each lived with all the overlaps so common inside a small, albeit global, "family." I was privileged to have joined them and gained a glimpse into this community of which Lisi was such an integral part.

She will be missed by so many people who knew and were affected by her in life. These essays serve as a tribute to her memory but they are much more than that. This volume is a contribution to the scholarship she so enjoyed and to which she gave so much. Future generations will get a glimpse of her as they enjoy the essays all are about to read. Thank you, Lisi, for this and all else you have done now for the many future generations of scholars, not just the few who you actually touched.

I. English Law Before the Viking Age

The Status of Women in the Laws of Æthelberht

Charles Donahue, Jr.

I had the pleasure, indeed the honor, to serve on Lisi Oliver's dissertation committee. Her edition of Æthelberht's so-called "code"[1] convinced me, and, far more important, the Harvard Linguistics Department, that the document contained archaisms that could not have been known to any speaker of Old English after the reform of the language in the late ninth century. Our sole witness of the document, therefore, a manuscript of the early twelfth century, is likely to reflect a text that was created in the late sixth or early seventh century, and is almost certainly not a forgery.[2]

I claim no expertise either in Old English or in Anglo-Saxon law. I have, however, used Oliver's edition of the document to introduce courses in both English and Continental European legal history for more than twenty years.[3] The students find the text fascinating, particularly its provisions about women. The results of our struggles to make sense of the text are recorded below.

As do all early legal documents, the text assumes that the reader knows a great deal that the modern reader does not know. It also reflects a society that is obviously very different from our own. The question is whether we can, without anachronism, provide some of the unstated context from what the document does state.

Three words of caution before we begin: First, many have studied Æthelberht's laws in the context of other post-Roman laws of roughly the same period. I make reference to these occasionally, but only with extreme caution. The early sixth-century Burgundian Law, for example, seems at times to be dealing with institutions that have parallels in Æthelberht's laws.[4] Comparison, however, of a document that probably dates from the late sixth or early seventh century with one that almost certainly dates from the early sixth, of one written in England where we can see no traces of Roman law with one written in Burgundy where the influence of Roman law and Latin ideas is pretty obvious, with one that is written in a West Germanic dialect with one that is written in vulgar

---

[1] The word "code" has many misleading connotations. I will not use it.

[2] Lisi Oliver, "The Language of the Early English Laws," Ph.D. dissertation, Harvard University, 1996.

[3] Oliver, *Beginnings*, 60-81. In what follows I accept Oliver's text and numbering without comment or specific page reference. The older, and until Oliver the standard, edition is Liebermann *Gesetze*, I:1-8.

[4] *Leges Burgundionum*, ed. L. R. von Salis, MGH Leges nationum Germanicarum 2.1 (Hannover: Hahn, 1892).

Latin and which purports to be product of a people who spoke a quite distant cousin of West Germanic is, to say the least, dangerous.

Second, there is no evidence that Æthelberht's laws were ever applied to the resolution of actual disputes in seventh-century Kent. Indeed, there is no evidence that any of the extensive Anglo-Saxon laws was ever directly applied to the resolution of any disputes in the Anglo-Saxon period. We have records of some 200 disputes from the entire Anglo-Saxon period. Not a single one of them cites any provision of the Anglo-Saxon laws even where there is a provision that is relevant and would, almost certainly, have been available to the participants in the dispute.[5] The Anglo-Saxon laws are a cultural product of Anglo-Saxons. They were not used as law in the way that we use law.

Third (and related to the second), I have considerable skepticism that the amounts of the compensation payments given any place in the document bear any relationship to what actually got paid. Granted the poverty of the society, of which more below, the amounts seem very high. There is, however, considerable evidence that the relationship of the numbers to each other has been developed with some care.

Clause 72 of Æthelberht's laws reads: *Gif friwif locbore leswæs hwæt gedeþ, XXX sciłł gebete*. Virtually every word in this clause is problematic; let us proceed from what seems to be the less problematic to the more. The syntactical pattern follows that of a substantial majority of the clauses in the document: if someone does something, that person shall pay a *bot* (a word normally translated as "compensation payment"), which is then specified either by a specific amount or a multiple of something. In this case if we extend *sciłł* to *scillingas*, *scillinga*, or *scillingum* (all three are found with, it would seem, no real difference in meaning), we can translate the apodosis of the conditional as "let [the person named in the protasis] make a compensation payment of 30 shillings." There may be reasons for not so translating it, but the pattern of the text gives us this translation as a first approximation.

The subject of the protasis is *friwif*, a compound of *freo* and *wif*. The word *wif* occurs in c. 31, where it pretty clearly means "wife," in the modern English sense, though *cwynan* occurs in c. 78, where it also seems to have the same meaning. Not much later Old English, however, used *wif* in ways that did not necessarily indicate marital status, just as the modern German cognate *Weib* does not necessarily indicate marital status. Hence, we should hesitate to assume that the use of *wif* here says anything about the woman's marital status. It may be a generic for a female human being. It probably is normally limited to women who are mature.[6]

[5] See Patrick Wormald, "A Handlist of Anglo-Saxon Lawsuits," *Anglo-Saxon England* 17 (1988): 247-81; but cf. Tom Lambert, *Law and Order in Anglo-Saxon England* (Oxford: Oxford University Press, 2017), where it is argued that early English laws were not without some practical effects.

[6] See the extensive list of usages given in *An Anglo-Saxon Dictionary*, ed. Joseph Bosworth and T. Northcote Toller (Oxford: Clarendon, 1898), s.v.

This woman is "free." We are probably safe in assuming that that means that she is not a slave (*ðeow*, *þeow*; c. 82, 83). That it means that she is not an *esne* (c. 78-80) is not clear. That it means that she is not a *læt* (c. 27) is probable but not certain. That she is the female equivalent of the *friman*, who occurs several times in the document (e.g., c. 28, 29, 31, 73), seems likely, although "female equivalent" in this context may be an oxymoron if not a contradiction in terms.[7]

This *friwif* is also *locbore*. The adjective is probably intended to be restrictive, that is to say that this provision is intended to apply only to those who meet this qualification. The problem is that *loc* in Old English, like "lock" in Modern English, has two quite different meanings: it is what you open with a key, and it is what you have on your head, unless you are bald. That the latter meaning in modern English is usually in the plural unless a small portion of the hair is intended might lead us in the direction of the first meaning, but we cannot be sure that this usage goes back to Æthelberht's time. The *bore* part of the compound is clearly derived from *beran*. Hence, we should translate "lock-bearing," even if we have not decided what kind of locks the *friwif* is bearing.

We probably should try to decide; it is likely to make a difference. Liebermann thought that it referred to hair, and on the basis of other Germanic sources, posited that unmarried women in Æthelberht's Kent wore their hair down, and that they wore it up when they married.[8] Hence, *locbore* was a sign of marital status, that the *friwif* was unmarried. There are two rather fundamental problems with this interpretation. The first is that comparative evidence about hair-styles is not particularly powerful. The one thing that we know about both men's and women's hair-styles comparatively is that there is a great variety of them and that they change. To say that we are ill-informed about women's hair-styles in Æthelberht's Kent is greatly to exaggerate the state of our knowledge. The second problem is more a logical problem. Whether a woman is wearing her hair up or down she is still "lock-bearing." It is, of course, possible that an idiomatic usage could develop that defies the literal meaning of the phrase, but it is not easy to see how this happened. We need not, however, abandon the idea that the phrase has something to do with hair. If one has to do a lot of physical work, long hair gets in the way. It is possible that *locbore* is a mark of class. Women who were expected to work in the fields in Æthelberht's Kent may have worn their hair very short. That the "friwif" is "locbore" may tell us that she is a woman who was not expected to do a lot of physical work; hence, that she was of relatively high status. This seems a more plausible suggestion than anything that has to do with wearing the hair up or down.

---

[7] But see c. 73.

[8] Liebermann, *Gesetze* III:13. Liebermann was certainly not the first to think that "loc" referred to hair. Bosworth offered a Latin translation of the protasis of c. 72 in the 1838 edition of the *Dictionary*: *si libera mulier capillata inhonesti quidquam fecerit*. Joseph Bosworth, *A Dictionary of the Anglo-Saxon Language* (London: Longman, 1838), s.v. "leswe, lyswe."

Of course, *locbore* may have nothing to do with hair. Sometime ago Christine Fell suggested that if we think about the other meaning of "lock" we may come up with a woman who was in charge of the locks, a trusted servant perhaps, or even the mistress of the house, someone who had access, perhaps sole access, to those things that were kept under lock and key.[9] Fell would have us conjure up an image of a medieval chatelaine with a bunch of keys hanging from her girdle. That image does not, however, fit well with our *friwif*. She is not carrying the keys, at least not literally; she is carrying the locks. And what is hanging from her girdle would make her look more like Marley's ghost than the romantic images that we have of the medieval chatelaine. We can avoid the awkwardness of the image, to some extent, if we assume that the locks in question are padlocks. Padlocks have been found in southern English archaeological sites from a not much later time.[10] We still have to wonder, however, why the *friwif* is lugging around the locks rather than the keys. If the *friwif* is carrying the keys rather than the locks, why does the text not describe her as "key-bearing"? *Cægbora* is a compound that is, in fact, recorded in Old English, admittedly much later.[11]

We have learned more about economic conditions in Æthelberht's Kent since Fell wrote. As measured against the standards of later Anglo-Saxon England, to say nothing of the twelfth century, Æthelberht's society was very poor, and technologically unsophisticated.[12] Æthelberht himself might have been able to afford someone, man or woman, to look after what he kept under lock and key. It is hard to imagine that anyone else, even someone of the eorl class, could have afforded to have such a servant. This law is not limited to someone in the household of the king, and the implausibility of there being many or any such people in other households makes for a strong argument against Fell's position. It does not destroy it, however. We have seen that a *wif* may not be a married woman, but that does not mean that she was not a married woman. She could be the wife of the master of the household. That, however, leads directly into the problem of what she was doing that requires a compensation payment.

Leswæs hwæt gedeþ; "Does some *leswæs*." *Gedeþ* is unproblematic. *Hwæt* actually helps, because it tells us that there is probably a range of offenses that fall within the category. *Leswæs* is a real problem. This is the only occurrence of the word with this spelling in

---

9 Christine Fell, "A "friwif locbore" Revisited," *Anglo-Saxon England* 13 (1984): 157-66.

10 Robin Fleming, personal communication.

11 See Christine Rauer, "The *Old English Martyrology* and Anglo-Saxon Glosses," in *Latinity and Identity in Anglo-Saxon Literature*, ed. Rebecca Stephenson and Emily Thornbury (Toronto: University of Toronto Press, 2016), 73-92, at 84.

12 For a general introduction to just how poor the society was, see Robin Fleming, *Britain after Rome: The Fall and Rise, 400-1070* (London: Allen Lane, 2010).

the Old English Corpus.[13] It is commonly accepted that the same word, spelled differently, occurs in c. 9: *Gif cyning æt mannes ham drincæþ 7 ðær man lyswæs hwæt gedo, twibote gebete.* Notice the same *hwæt* here, reinforcing the notion that this it is not one specific offense but a category of offenses.

The etymology of *leswæs/lyswæs* is not helpful.[14] The same or related words do, however, appear in the Old English Corpus. In the *Andreas*, l. 1219 *lyswe larsmeoðas* seems to mean "corrupt counselors"; in *Maxims I*, 188 *Lot sceal mid lyswe, list mid gedefum* seems to mean "Cunning goes with corruption; craft with what is right"; in the medical book known as Bald's Leechbook" *micge lyswen* seems to mean "purulent urine." A rather wide semantic range, with meanings all of which suggest "evil" may, if we focus on the medical meaning, imply something that is not only corrupt but also repulsive.

That *leswæs/lyswæs* is something narrower than just "evil" is suggested by the fact that the payment for it in c. 72 is specific. If we start, with c. 9, the temptation is to think that something sexual is meant. After all, what can happen when a bunch of guys who probably owe their position to their athletic prowess are drinking? We are well aware today of what can happen when members of the college football team have been drinking. This particular modern analogy may not be anachronistic. If c. 9 is speaking of some kind of sexual offense, then c. 72 probably is too.[15]

If we start with c. 72 and assume that we are dealing with a responsible person who is in charge of locks, then the range of possible offenses becomes quite different. The way such a person can betray his or her master is by embezzling from what is under lock and key or by allowing someone else to steal from it. The range of possible offenses is broad, but they all involve a breach of trust of some sort. "Does something seriously dishonest," as Oliver translates it, seems about right. When, however, we go back and apply the same translation to c. 9, it seems odd. I suppose there are things that can happen when the king is drinking with his buddies that are "seriously dishonest," such as someone filching the purse of a man who is too drunk to notice, but that is certainly not the first thing one thinks about in such situations.

Certainty is not possible. Indeed, with so many degrees of freedom even a probabilistic statement of what c. 72 might mean seems dangerous. Nonetheless, the balance of

---

[13] I used the online edition of the Corpus, produced by the Dictionary of Old English Project at the University of Toronto, available by subscription.

[14] F. Holthausen, *Altenglisches etymomologisches Wörterbuch* (Heidelberg: Winter, 1963), s.v. "lysu."

[15] Liebermann was cautious. He thought that "lyswæs" in c. 9 was synonymous with "yfel" in c. 8, and refused to specify what it meant in c. 72. He did, however, posit there that the person who was to pay the 30 shillings was not the woman but the man who held her "mund." *Gesetze*, III: 5, 13. Thirteen years earlier, he supplied *der Schänder* in his translation after *büsse* ("gebete"), suggesting that the offense was probably sexual and the person who made the payment was the man with whom the "friwif" committed the offense. *Gesetze*, I:5.

probabilities seems to suggest that what c. 72 means is: "If an upper-class woman commits some sexual offense, let her make amends by paying 30 shillings."

This is, of course, to reject Liebermann's suggestion that it is some man who makes the payment. The reason for rejecting this suggestion is that there is no place else in the document where the subject shifts from protasis to apodosis without an indication that the subject has changed.[16] The one possible exception is c. 83: *Gif þeow stelep, II gelde gebete.* This may mean that the master of the slave pays the two-fold compensation, but this is not certain. We need to make the further assumption that Anglo-Saxon slaves, like Roman, technically did not own anything. That may or may not be true of Anglo-Saxon slaves in Æthelberht's time. Even Roman slaves might have property of which they were in charge; the same may have been true of Anglo-Saxon slaves in Æthelberht's time. Clause 82 also seems to assume that the offending slave is capable of making a payment.

If, however, we interpret c. 72 as requiring a payment by the *friwif*, that immediately raises the question to whom is she to make it. That the payment is owed to the king as a kind of fine seems unlikely because elsewhere in the document it is always specified if a payment is to be made to the king. The only alternative would seem to be that the payment is made to those who, in some sense, "own" her sexuality. The clauses that follow (of which more in a moment) may provide some support for this speculation.

Thirty shillings is a substantial amount when compared with the other numbers. It is slightly less than a third of the wergeld for a free man (100 shillings), more than a half of the king's *mundbyrd* (50 shillings), and the equivalent of the payment owed for a substantial physical injury (30 shillings for a "grievous wound" [c. 63.1] or permanent injury to the shoulder [c. 37]).[17]

There are so many ambiguities in c. 72 that it invites speculation. What follows is, indeed, speculative, and undercuts much of what I have just said: When the king and his buddies start drinking, the sensible thing for the women in the house to do is to lock themselves up. That protects them against *leswæs*/*lyswæs*. The younger women may not know this, or they may be tempted not to protect themselves. It is the responsibility of an older woman to see to it that it happens. If she does not do so, she is responsible for the *leswæs*/*lyswæs* and owes compensation to the women who become victims of the

---

[16] See the previous note. Liebermann's examples to the contrary are not convincing. Clauses 61.1 and 62 both describe types of wounds, where it is obvious that the wound is not paying but the wounder.

[17] One of the arguments that Liebermann uses to support the proposition that the *friwif* is not a married woman is that this amount is not high enough for a compensation payment for adultery; see *Gesetze*, III:13. But the only other provision in the laws about adultery by a completely free woman (c. 31) does not say anything about whether she owes anything for the adultery, much less what. As discussed below, c. 31 deals entirely with the husband and the adulterous man.

leswæs/lyswæs, and/or to their kin. This woman might be called the *locbore*.[18] The advantage of this proposed interpretation is that it makes use of Fell's suggested meaning for *loc* (and avoids the messy, and perhaps fruitless, inquiry into hair styles) while at the same time preserving our more probable guess that *leswæs/lyswæs* has something to do with sex. It also avoids having to assume that someone other than the *friwif* "owned" her sexuality. The disadvantage of this interpretation—and it may be fatal—is that it assumes that the makers of the document understood the concept of vicarious liability, because under the scenario just outlined the *friwif* has not committed the *leswæs/lyswæs*, but has allowed it happen.[19]

Similar problems of interpretation arise in c. 73: *Mægþbot sy swa friges mannes*. The word *mægþ* occurs four times in the document, all by itself in c. 76, here compounded with *bot*, and in cc. 16 and 77 compounded with *man*: *mægdenman* (c. 16) and *mægþman* (c. 77). The three compounds are *hapax legomena* in the Old English Corpus. The word *mægþ* or *mægden* in various forms and with various spellings is very common. It means a girl or young unmarried woman. The emphasis that we find on virginity in Middle (and, to some extent, Modern) English "maid" is not particularly noticeable in the Old English usages.[20] Why the compilers of the document thought it appropriate to add the suffix *man* in cc. 16 and 77, but not in cc. 73 and 76, I do not know. The meaning seems to be the same in all four instances except that in c. 73 the word is compounded with *bot*. The literal meaning of c. 73 would seem to be "let young-woman-compensation be like [that] of a free man."

The phrase is cryptic, and we must be careful not to make assumptions about the status of these young women and then interpret the clause in the light of those assumptions. Bosworth, for example, in the 1838 edition of the *Dictionary*, assumed that *mægþbot* was compensation for an attack on the chastity of the young woman.[21] That seems highly unlikely unless we are to imagine that there was a special compensation payment for an attack on the chastity of a free man. The best that we can do with this

---

[18] The editors find this paragraph "unconvincing." I may too. They do, however, point out that the author of *Beowulf* knows of a *brydbur* ("women's quarters," "women's apartment") separate from the hall, which might be a place where the women could lock themselves up for protection. See *Klaeber's Beowulf and the Fight at Finnsburg*, ed. R. D. Fulk, Robert E. Bjork, John D. Niles (Toronto: UP, 2008): line 921; cf. lines 138-40, which seem to deal with the same place.

[19] The concept of accessory liability seems to be present in c. 23, where the person who provided the weapons is held liable if they are later used to commit an offense. The amount to be paid is not the same as that for the offense, but neither is it in c. 72. Assuming that we are right (the laws never quite say this) that the kin-group was responsible for paying at least the larger compensation payments in Æthelberht's time, then, of course, the concept of vicarious liability goes all the way back. Cf. c. 24.2.

[20] See *OED*, s.vv. "maid" and "maiden."

[21] Bosworth, *Dictionary* (1838), s.v. "mægð."

clause is to say that it sets up an equivalence. Compensation payments "to," "by," "for" (it does not say which) a young woman shall be like those "to," "by," "for" (it does not say which) a free man. There is no reason not to interpret the clause generally. For example, it would seem to mean that if someone strikes off a young woman's middle finger, she or her kin-group should be paid 4 shillings as would be the case if this were the middle finger of a free man (cf. c. 56).

As Oliver has shown in another book, these compensation payments for physical injuries were quite carefully designed around male activities.[22] It is not clear that they would, in all cases, have fit what young women were doing. The equivalence, then, may be a rough approximation. *Swa*, after all, means "like" not "the same as."

The major question, however, is why is this provision here at all, and why is it confined to the *mægþ*? What about women of other statuses, the *cwyn*, the *widuwe*, or just the *wif* generally? The document does not say, and it may be dangerous to speculate when it does not. The fact, however, that it was thought necessary to specify the *mægþbot*, but not the *wifbot*, may indicate that the provision about the *mægþbot* was an innovation or, at least, a provision about something that was uncertain. If that is right, it may be that prior to the provision it was generally understood that the *mægþ* was not entitled to the full compensation to which a man, or a more mature woman, was entitled.

Turning to clause 74:

> [74.] Mund þare betstan widuwan eorlcundre, L scillinga gebete.
> [74.1] Đare oþre, XX scħ.
> [74.2] Đare þriddan, XII scħ.
> [74.3] Þare feorðan, VI scħ.

That the *widuwe* of this clause is a woman who was married but whose husband is now deceased seems obvious. What her *mund* might be requires more comment.[23]

Mund makes its first appearance in c. 14: *Cyninges mundbyrd, L scillinga*. It occurs again in c. 20: *Ceorles mundbyrd, VI scillingas*. In between are two provisions regarding *eorlas* that do not use the word, but seem to involve the same concept: c. 18: *Gif on eorles tune man mannan ofslæhþ, XII scilł gebete*; c. 19: *Gif wið eorles birele man geligeþ, XII scilł gebete*.

---

[22] Oliver, *Body Legal*.

[23] What follows disagrees somewhat with E. G. Stanley, "Words for the *Dictionary of Old English*," in *The Dictionary of Old English: Retrospects and Prospects*, ed. M. J. Toswell, Old English Newsletter, Subsidia, 26 (Kalamazoo: Medieval Institute, 1996), 39-47. I share Stanley's reluctance to use etymology alone to determine the meaning of a word. I agree with him that in this case, it helps. I am willing to go further than he seems to have been in using the parallels in other languages to explain what is otherwise ambiguous in Æthelberht's laws.

Mund is derived from an Indo-European root that means "hand." Hence, the word is cognate with Latin *manus*.[24] In the Roman law of the Republic, and even occasionally in the early Empire, a married woman could pass into the *manus* of her husband. This meant that she became "like a daughter" to him.[25] If he died intestate, she would inherit from him and not from her father. The hand is a symbol both of power and protection in many cultures. In the Hebrew Bible the hand of the Lord not only creates, not only strikes those who have offended him, it also protects those whom he takes in his hand.[26] The word *mund* (*mundium* in Latin), occurs in many Germanic dialects as a technical legal term, and in all cases it seems to refer to power or protection, over or of other people, frequently, though not always, women.[27]

The etymology of the *byrd* part of "mundbyrd" is uncertain.[28] If, however, we examine the offenses listed from c. 8 to c. 20 that require the payment of the *mundbyrd bot*, both people and places seem to be within someone's *mund*." What *byrd* seems to be adding to the concept of "mund" is a concept of "area." If someone commits an offense against someone within this area, the offender owes compensation to the person within whose personal or geographical area of protection it was, as well as to the person offended.

The syntax of c. 74 is unusual. It does not begin with *gif* as do almost all the other main clauses in the document.[29] Rather, we are told "*mund* of the best widow, of the *eorl* class." What follows is "let him make a compensation payment of 50 shillings." The relationship of this phrase to what precedes it is unspecified.

The temptation to interpret the clause, as does Oliver, as meaning "[for violation of] protection of the foremost widow of noble rank, let him [presumably the one who did the violating] pay 50 shillings" is strong. It is particularly strong because the makers of the document do not seem to have a word to express the concept of "violating." They had the concept of *mund* and a price, but they do not generalize about what a later age

---

24 Julius Pokorny, *Indogermanisches etymologisches Wörterbuch* (Bern: Francke, 1959), 2:740-1.

25 Gaius, *Institutiones*, ed. Francis de Zulueta (Oxford: Clarendon Press, 1946), 1.108-115b, esp. 115b: *filiae loco, filiae iura.*

26 E.g., Amos 9:2, Ezra 8:31, Job 12:10, Ps. 31:15, Ps. 144:7-8, Ps. 139:10.

27 See *Lexikon des Mittelalters* (Stuttgart: Metzler, [1977]-1999), s.v. "Munt," with references.

28 The *OED*, s.v. "mund" suggests that it may be derived from *byrd* ("burden") It fails to explain how it came to mean what it clearly seems to mean in cc. 8-20. The meaning that is suggested in the text might suggest an etymology connected with modern English "border," but the etymology of that word is complicated (see *OED* s.v.), and I will leave it to the linguists to decide whether there is any plausibility to this suggestion.

29 The notable exception is cc. 1-7, but there are those who have doubted, quite rightly in my view, whether these clauses were part of the original document.

would call *mundbri(y)che.*[30] Rather than generalizing they specify, and leave it to the reader to make the generalization.

Perhaps, however, we should not move so quickly. The king has a *mund*; the *eorl* has a *mund*; the ordinary *ceorl* has a *mund*, but nowhere is it suggested that a woman has a *mund*, in the sense of an area of protection or persons whom she protects. Thus, if we are correct, that *bot* and *gebetan* always mean a compensation payment or to make a compensation payment, the verb in our clause is describing a payment made to someone other than the widow. Also, there is little suggestion in the language that we have that anyone has done anything wrong. There is a *mund* and an unspecified "he" is to compensate for it, with regard to it, on behalf of it (it does not say which).

Some help in interpreting these clauses may be found in the next one: *Gif man widuwan unagne genimeþ, II gelde seo mund sy.* Oliver's translation of the protasis is probably as close as we can get in modern English: "If a person takes a widow who does not belong to him."[31] *Unagne* is a property word, indeed a denial of property. "Does not belong" captures it quite nicely, so long as we keep in mind that property concepts are likely to be culturally quite specific and hence not to correspond to our own. *Genimeþ* is, indeed, "takes," but nothing is said about how the taking is accomplished (contrast c. 77: *nede genimeþ*).

Oliver's translation of the apodosis is more problematic: "the [payment for violation of] protection shall be two[-fold] as compensation." What it says literally is "Let the *mund* be two by payment" or "Two by payment the *mund* shall be." That the payment is a compensation payment is certainly possible, but the noun is not *bot* nor is the verb *gebete*. "Violation" is no place to be found in these words unless we are to imagine that it is encompassed in the word *mund*, but that is not what *mund* means elsewhere in document (unless that is what it means in c. 74), nor is it what it usually means in later uses of the word in Old English or in the parallel uses in other Germanic dialects. It usually means the protection, not the violation of it.

There are, of course, many things about widows that do not differentiate them from other mature women or, indeed, from the population generally. One of the things, however, that does differentiate them is their capacity to remarry. That such a remarriage would involve the transfer of the *mund* over the widow, in the sense of both the duty to protect her and the right to receive compensation payments if she were harmed is not quite said in these texts, but that something of the sort happened is certainly

---

[30] The word first appears in Edmund's laws (939-946), and becomes quite common in laws and charters of the late tenth and eleventh centuries. See the Old English Corpus.

[31] Oliver is quite right that *man* in Old English, like *man* in modern German (as opposed to *Mann*), is indefinite as to gender. If we find "a person" a bit precious or too politically correct, we can substitute "anyone," while keeping in mind that this particular act is unlikely to be done by a female.

compatible with what the texts say. What c. 74, then, may be giving us is a schedule of payments that should be made by the future husband to acquire the *mund* over the widow whom he is marrying. If the man makes the payment, the widow becomes *agne*; she, as it were, belongs to him, and he may marry her, or, perhaps, he does marry her by acquiring the *mund*. If he reverses the order of the transaction, marries ("takes") the widow when she does not belong to him, he has to pay double of what he would have to pay if he had done it in the right order. We can regard the payment in c. 74 as compensation to the *mund*-holder for the loss of the *mund* over the widow and the extra payment in c. 75 as compensation for the man's having taken the widow without paying in advance for her *mund*, but that may be a precision beyond what the text is telling us.[32]

There are many things, of course, that we still do not know. The four-fold classification of widows in c. 74 does not correspond to any of the other classifications of persons in the text, except for the highest. Thus, we know of an *eorl* class, but there is nothing else in the text that would allow us to differentiate the class of the free *ceorl* into three separate classes.[33] To bring in the *læt* and the *esne*, which could give us four classes, is probably unwarranted.

Perhaps more to the point, we do not know who the *mund*-holder is. It could be the kin of the deceased husband; it could be the widow's natal kin. I am inclined to think that it is likely to be the kin of the deceased husband, but my warrant for this is a passage in the Burgundian laws that seems to be dealing with the same general problem. The parallel is there. If we are willing to accept the notion that we may be looking at a piece of the same puzzle, the pieces do fit together.[34] Clause 76.3 of Æthelberht's laws,

---

32 This result is briefly suggested in F. L. Attenborough, *The Laws of the Earliest English Kings* (Cambridge: Cambridge University Press, 1922), 178. He puzzles, however, at the use of *gebete*. Both *bot* and *gebete*, however, have a quite wide semantic range, quite nicely caught in the modern English "compensate." A "compensation" does not have to be for a wrong. It is what is necessary to make me whole: "If you want my pen, you will have to give me another as compensation."

33 I am departing here from Oliver, *Beginnings*, 111-12, but she is thinking in terms of a compensation payment for violation of the *mund*, whereas I think it is more likely that we are dealing here with the price for acquiring it.

34 "Liber constitutionum sive lex Gundobada," in *Leges Burgundionum*, c. 42.2, p. 73: "[S]i a tempore obitus prioris mariti intra annum [vidua] nubere voluerit, habeat liberam potestatem et tertiam substantiae partem, quam permissa fuerat possidere, dimittat. Ceterum si emenso anno vel biennio maritum accipere voluerit, omnia sicut dictum est, quae de priore marito habuit, derelinquat et pretium, quod de nuptiis eius inferendum est, accipiat <ab illo> cuius partibus defuncti parentis debetur hereditas." See Charles Donahue Jr. and Stuart McManus, "Philologia ancilla historiae: An Emendation to lex Burgundionum, 42,2," *Zeitschrift der Savigny-Stiftung für Rechtsgeschichte: Romanistische Abteilung* 113 (2014): 414-23. As Donahue and McManus interpret the passage, whether the widow remarries within a year or after a year, she loses her inheritance from her deceased husband, and her deceased husband's heir receives the *wittimon*

the most difficult passage in the whole document, may also be telling us something about the *mund* of the widow.

The discussion of *mund* in 76.3 is prefaced by a series of clauses concerning marriage negotiations:

> [76.] Gif man mægþ gebigeð ceapi, geceapod sy gif hit unfacne is.
>
> [76.1] Gif hit þonne facne is, ef[t] þær æt ham gebrenge, 7 him man his scæt agefe.

Gebigeð is an alternative form of the third-person singular of *bycgan*, the standard and very common Old English word for "to buy" or "to procure." *Ceap*, the noun, means a bargain, a sale, a price; *ceapian*, the verb, means to bargain or to sell. *Unfacne* is very rare. It occurs only here, in c. 30 (where Oliver translates is "unblemished" because it goes with *feo*), and in the laws of Hlothere and Eadric (where it is a requirement of witnesses).[35] But *facen* meaning "deceit," "fraud," "guile" is quite well attested, and there is no reason to doubt that *unfacne* here is its opposite. We cannot quite capture the double use of the *ceap* root in modern English, and our attitude toward what is happening here may depend on what modern English words we use to translate. "If a man buys a young unmarried woman for a price, let the sale go through if it is without deceit" sounds like the purchase of a slave. Students with even mild feminist tendencies will bristle. If we say: "If anyone procures a young unmarried woman by a bargain, let the bargain stand if there is no deceit," that, at least, sounds like something more complicated than the straight commercial sale. I can usually persuade the students that there is too much evidence of female agency in these provisions to think that we are dealing here with slavery. There is, however, nothing said about whether the young woman has to consent. Indeed, there is no such a provision in the secular Anglo-Saxon laws until the reign of Cnut (1016-1035).[36]

If, however, the young woman is not really being bought, what is being bought? If we have c. 74 right, where it seems a bit clearer, what is being bought is the *mund* over her. The parallel to the acquisition of *manus* by *coemptio* in Roman law seems striking,[37] and we need not get into the question of a possible common Indo-European origin of both customs in order to see the parallel.

("bride-price") from the new husband, but if the widow waits for more than a year to remarry, the heir is obliged to turn the *wittimon* over to her.

[35] Clause 11 in Oliver, *Beginnings*, 132.

[36] *II Cn.* 74, in Liebermann, *Gesetze*, I:360-1. The editors point out the parallels in the Icelandic Grágás, both as to the absence of any notion that the woman must consent and in that the bridegroom seems to buy the woman's *mund*. See Roberta Frank, "Marriage in Iceland," *Viator* 4 (1973): 474, 475-6, esp. n. 14: *er móðir hans er eigi munde keypt*, describing the conditions that must be satisfied in order to obtain an inheritance.

[37] Gaius, *Institutiones*, 1.110, 113-115b.

It is tempting to speculate about what the *facen/facne* might be. Some students are convinced that it means that the young woman is not a virgin, but the text does not display a heightened concern with female virginity (though there is some with female fidelity).[38] The story of Jacob and Laban (Gen. 29:14-30) shows that there can be deceit in marriage negotiations that has nothing to do with female virginity. The solution of that story, however, that Jacob marry both daughters or, more generally, that the victim of the fraud keep the first woman and get another, does not seem to have been available.

The solution proposed is what modern Anglo-American lawyers call rescission and restitution. The deceived man brings the woman back, and he gets his money or property (*scæt* can mean both; see c. 76.2). The middle phrase, *ef[t] þær æt ham gebrenge*, is a bit awkward, but there seems little doubt that it means as Oliver translates it: "let him bring [her to her] home."

Clause 76.2 states that a wife is entitled to a share of her husband's estate if he predeceases her and if she has borne a living child: *Gif hio cwic bearn gebyreþ, healfne scæt age gif ceorl ær swylteþ*. The clause seems quite straightforward, though there is much that it does not tell us. If the husband predeceases her, what happens to the *mund*? Comparative evidence suggests that it remains with the husband's family, but that is not specified here. Must the child or children survive to the death of the husband? Once more, comparative evidence would suggest that no child needs to survive.[39] Much later English law will state a similar requirement: that the couple have had a child who "cried to the four walls," but nothing like that is specified here. What is the *scæt*? It probably includes household goods and any money that the husband had. It may include the animals, but that is less certain. What about land? It does not say. For this period and for a much later period we are ill-informed as to whether the Anglo-Saxons thought in terms of individual ownership of land, ownership by the kin-group, or ownership by the king or a lord, and, of course, there could be various combinations of those possibilities.[40] The fact that we do not know whether *scæt* included the land means that we do not know if the widow had the wherewithal to support herself. Finally, if the widow gets half of the *scæt*, who gets the other half? Clause 76.4 suggests that the other half goes to the children, but what if there are no surviving children? The fact that we cannot answer this question shows us that we are not being given a complete view of the inheritance scheme but only that part of it that deals with the widow.

---

38 E.g., c. 31.

39 See Heinrich Brunner, "Die Geburt eines lebenden Kindes und das eheliche Vermögensrecht," *Zeitschrift der Savigny-Stiftung für Rechtsgeschichte: Germanistische Abteilung* 16 (1895): 63-108.

40 For an introduction to the complexities, see John Hudson, *The Oxford History of the Laws of England, 2: 871-1216* (Oxford: Oxford University Press, 2012), 93-148.

The issue comes to a head in clause 76.3: *Gif mid bearnum bugan wille, healfne scæt age*. Perhaps no clause in the document has generated as much speculation as this one. A few years ago Carole Hough published an article in which she criticized those who had interpreted the clause as dealing with divorce. Her argument was basically that a woman who had been sold to her husband was unlikely to have the authority to walk out on him and take the children with her.[41] The point is well-taken, but, as I have said before, we have to be careful not to assume the answers to the questions we are trying to ask.[42] Hough goes on to suggest that we can make more sense out of the passage if we assume that the condition that ends the previous clause is carried over.

For some time, I treated this suggestion with skepticism. This would be the only place in the document where a condition stated at the end of the preceding clause is carried over without saying so to the next clause. If we assume that the condition is carried over, c. 76.3 would, in essence, repeat what was said in c. 76.2. This document is extremely terse. It virtually never repeats.[43] The twelfth-century scribe grouped the clauses, indicating the grouping by placing the initial capital slightly into the margin. The initial "G" of c. 76.3 is in the margin.

On balance, however, none of these objections is particularly powerful. This would be the only instance in the document where a condition stated at the end of a clause is carried over without saying so into the next one. The fact is, however, that there is only one other place in the document where a condition is stated at the end of a clause. That is c. 76, right above it, and the final condition (*gif hit unfacne is*) is not carried over into the next clause there because the condition of next clause is its opposite: *Gif hit þonne facne is*. It is true that c. 76.3 basically repeats what is in 76.2 in the apodosis, but it adds an additional condition: *Gif mid bearnum bugan wille*. It is true that the scribe of the manuscript put the initial "G" of 76.3 in the margin, but there is also a page break at this point, so the position of the "G" is less of a guide to what the scribe thought ought to go together than it would be were it not at the head of a new page.

Hence, I am inclined to think that Hough is right about the general context of 76.3. It deals principally, though perhaps not exclusively, with the situation where the husband has died. As Hough sees it, the Kentish widow has a choice if her husband predeceases her (she concedes this much agency to her): she may stay with the children that she had with her deceased husband or she may take another husband (c.76.4). If she takes

---

[41] Carole A. Hough, "The Early Kentish 'Divorce Laws': A Reconsideration of *Æthelberht*, chs. 79 and 80," *Anglo-Saxon England* 23 (1994): 19-34.

[42] That divorce could be initiated by the woman in a society in which her *mund* was purchased at the beginning of the marriage is suggested by the evidence presented in Frank, "Marriage in Iceland," at 478.

[43] Clauses 61.1 and 61.2 do seem to repeat. Oliver treats the repetition as a scribal error. It is also possible that c. 61.2 should be treated, as I will argue that c. 76.3 should be, as saying: "Even if [condition], the compensation payment should be as in [61.1]."

the first option, she gets half the property; if she takes the second, she gets the same share as a child. How those shares are calculated is not stated, but assuming that they are equal, the widow would get a half only if there were one surviving child; otherwise, she would get less (a third if there were two children, etc.).

I am inclined to think that this interpretation of c. 76.4 is likely to be correct.[44] The question is what is the alternative to the widow's taking another husband. There is a logic to thinking that the alternative to taking another husband is staying put with the children, particularly if we imagine that the widow might have no place else to go. Hence, Oliver, following Hough, translates *bugan* as "dwell."

Bugan is a real problem. It is an alternative form of the verb *buan*, although the intervocalic "g" is normally attested only in weak forms, *bugian*. It means "to dwell" or "inhabit." It is also independently a strong verb in its own right, the base meaning of which seems to be "bow" (what you do when you bend at the waist), but it has a wide semantic range. Frequently (*pace* Hough) it means "to turn away" from a place, even "to flee." The form *bugan* of the first verb is not found in the Corpus, unless this is an example. The form *bugan* (or *bugon*) of the second verb occurs many times. When we couple these facts with the fact that *bugan* and *bugian* seem to be later forms of a verb that was originally *buan* or *buwian*, it seems more likely that that we are dealing here with a form of the second verb.[45]

If this is right, then what 76.3 and 76.4 say about the widow is incomplete. We know what she gets if she departs with the children; we know what she gets if she remarries. It does not expressly say what she gets if she stays put with the children. But 76.2 gives us a clue: *healfne scæt age gif ceorl ær swylteþ*. That is the basic provision qualified only by the condition that she must have borne a living child. Then we are told in 76.3: *Gif mid bearnum bugan wille, healfne scæt age*. It does not take much spelling out to make this compatible with, but different from, 76.2: "[Even] if she wants to depart with the children, she [still] gets half the property." The implication is: "And, of course, if she stays put with the children, she gets half the property." We can almost hear the makers of the document saying: "We just said that, you ninny."

On the other hand, clause 76.4 suggests that the half the property rule does not apply if the widow takes another husband: *Gif ceorl agan wile, swa an bearn*. What happens to the children in this situation is not stated. We may imagine, but only by negative

---

[44] This is, of course, to reject the suggestion that others have made that the *ceorl* referred to in c. 74 is the woman's previous husband, who is taking the children. He seems to be dead. Even if we do not assume that he is dead, we should not shift the subject unless we absolutely have to.

[45] For all of these points, see *Old English Dictionary* (*OED*, svv. "buan," and "bugan," though the Dictionary does accept Hough's suggestion, making c. 76.3 the only instance in the Corpus in which *bugan* has the meaning "dwell." I realize that I am disagreeing here with Oliver, *Beginnings*, 113, and only regret that we cannot discuss it.

inference, that in this situation she does not take the children with her and that they remain, unless special arrangements to the contrary are made, with the deceased husband's kin. We probably should also imagine in this situation that the payments that seem to be called for in c. 74 were made. If our guess about who held the *mund* at this point is right, they are made with the kin of the deceased husband. It certainly looks, however, as if the choice whether to remarry is the widow's: *Gif ceorl agan wile*. There is some financial penalty in the widow's making this choice, a reduction in the fraction that she can take with her if she leaves behind more than one child, but it is a reduction, not a total deprivation, as it is in some legal systems.

The mysterious option is that of 76.3, if we take *bugan*, as I think we must, to mean something like "depart." Where would the widow go? What happens to the *mund*, both that over the widow, and that over the children? An independent existence of a widow with children is hard to imagine in a society that seems to have been organized into kin groups and was very poor.[46] The only alternative would seem to be that she returns with the children to her father's kin-group. There is some support for this hypothesis in c. 76.5. It would involve, one has to admit, giving the widow what must have been for this society an extraordinary amount of discretion. She would, it would seem, have the power to undo the transaction that put her *mund* with her husband's kin and transfer it and, perhaps, that of her children to her father's kin. There are no comparative parallels. Perhaps, however, this is not quite so extraordinary as it seems at first. The husband's kin group has lost a member who may have been vital to its economic survival. It could be that that kin group could not support the widow and her children. If her father's kin group was better off, it might make sense for all concerned if it took on the responsibility.[47]

The problem of inheritance is complicated by clause 76.5: *Gif hio bearn ne gebyreþ, fæderingmagas fioh agan 7 morgengyfe*. The condition parallels that of 76.2: *Gif hio cwic bearn gebyreþ*. Whether it is also its opposite, i.e., that it does not apply to miscarriages or to children born dead, but does apply even if the children do not survive is not stated. Can we infer whether this is intended? Also, should we carry over the second condition of 76.2 (*gif ceorl ær swylteþ*) and apply it here too?

Certainty is not possible. What this provision is telling us is that under certain circumstances the woman's *fioh* and *morgengyfe* go to her father's kin.[48] *Fioh* is a very broad

---

[46] We should note, however, that c. 76.5 tells us that the woman might have property in her own right, and this might, in some situations, have been enough to support her and her children on her own. Such situations would probably, however, have been very rare.

[47] *Hl.* 4, also deals with the situation of the widow with children. It may or may not be compatible with what is said here. It is, moreover, later, and may represent a change, perhaps even a rejection, of Æthelberht's laws on this topic.

[48] The text does not say "her" *fioh*, but it seems highly unlikely that it is not to be implied.

word for "property," probably broader than *scæt*. If land were subject to individual ownership, it would almost certainly be included in *fioh*, whereas it might not be in *scæt*. *Morgengyfe* is a word attested in a number of the Germanic laws and practice documents.[49] It is, as the name seems to imply, a gift that the husband gives to his wife notionally the morning after they have had sexual intercourse for the first time. It, too, can include any kind of property and could, in a society that was wealthier than the Kentish, be quite large. The combination of the two in this clause seems to be tautology ("fruit and apples") unless we limit *fioh* so as not to include the *morgengyfe*. The most obvious way to do so is to say that *fioh* here means property that the woman has received from her father's side of the family, hence roughly corresponding to what we and the Romans called "dowry," but it may also include any inheritance that she has received, perhaps even what she has acquired by her own efforts.

The text deals with the situation in which the woman has not borne children. If we carry over the condition from c. 76.2, as we did in c. 76.3 and 76.4, the woman has also survived her husband. That possibility is certainly not excluded by 76.5. The text says that her father's kin get her property. It does not say when they get her property. It would seem harsh, perhaps even senseless, to deprive the living widow of her property at the moment when she has just lost her husband and presumably needs it the most. Perhaps the woman was seen as returning to her father's kin group at this point and was required to throw everything she had into the pot. I think it more likely, however, that the property did not return to the father's kin group until she died.[50]

Nothing else in the document deals with inheritance from women. It may, however, be possible to reconstruct what the possibilities were in the situation not covered, where the woman did have children. Clause 76.4 suggests that a man's property went to his surviving children, his wife also taking a share if she survived him. We do not know what happened if he left no surviving children, but it seems likely that his property went to his kin-group. What happened if his wife survived him but none of their children is not stated, because both 76.3 and 76.4 seem to deal with the situation where there are surviving children. If we go back, however, to 76.2, and take it as stating the general rule, it would seem that the widow who had borne children who did not survive would take half of the property classified as *scæt* and the husband's kin group the other half.

Clause 76.5 tells us that a married woman could have property in her own right. It is possible that the system of inheritance was different for women from what it was for men, but the possible recipients of the deceased married woman's property include,

---

49 See *Lexikon des Mittelalters*, s.v. "Morgengabe," with references.

50 In this scenario what happens if she remarries is simply not covered. In a later age, the fact that widows had property made them more attractive on the marriage market, but this woman's chances on that market are probably not good granted that she was married and did not have children.

and are probably limited to, her surviving children, her surviving husband, his kin-group, and her natal kin-group, or some combination of these. That combination could involve sharing or it could involve separating the property by types, for example, one scheme for the *fioh* and another for the *morgengyfe*. Whatever the scheme was it was probably well known and, as a general matter, uncontroversial, because it is not stated.

What does need to be stated, probably because the result was controversial, was what was to be done if a married woman who had never borne a child died. If we are willing to draw the always-dangerous negative inference from c. 76.5, what seems to be being suggested here is that this is different from the situation in which the woman has borne a child. In that situation, the property would go, presumably, to her children, if they survived, possibly to be shared with their father if he survived, possibly to be shared with the father's kin group if he did not. The system of shares may have been even more complicated, with the woman's natal kin-group getting some, but not all of the property. I find myself attracted, however, to the notion that the woman's natal kin group got the inheritance if and only if the woman had never borne a child.

In that situation, c. 76.5 tells us, her father's kin inherit her property, and not, presumably, her husband's kin. It says this even if we assume that *gif ceorl ær swylteþ* is carried over. Whether her father's kin get the woman's property, if and only if her husband dies first, the provision does not say. It is possible that it is to be presumed that they do not. If the woman is survived by her husband, she died in his *mund*. That may give him and his kin the right to inherit from her. If he predeceases her, it may be presumed that she will return to her natal kin. The situation would thus parallel what we imagined for the widow who *mid bearnum bugan wille*.

The clause may, however, also apply to the woman who dies before her husband, never having borne a child. Here, too, her father's kin inherit from her, rather, presumably, than the husband. In order to make the provision apply to this situation, we cannot carry over the condition *gif ceorl ær swylteþ*. The text provides some support for not doing so. *Gif ceorl ær swylteþ* is governed by the condition *gif hio cwic bearn gebyreþ*, but we are now out of that condition: *gif hio bearn ne gebyreþ*. Our speculation as to the result here may depend on the strength that we attribute to two potentially conflicting principles. If the notion that a couple is not completely married until the woman has borne a living child is strong, then the property of a deceased childless woman probably goes back to her natal kin whether she predeceases her husband or not. If the husband, but not his kin, was seen as related to his childless wife in such a way that he, but not they, could inherit from her, then the property of the woman who died in her husband's *mund* might remain with the husband. There is evidence of the first principle in the text, none of the second. Hence, it seems more likely that c. 76.5 also applies to the childless woman who predeceases her husband.

But what is to happen if the woman has borne children, but they do not survive until her death? The text does not cover that situation. I suspect that the inheritance rights of the husband and of his kin were stronger in that situation and hence that her natal kin would be excluded from the inheritance, but I certainly cannot prove it.

Before we turn to c. 77, let us ask whether there is anything in the laws that deals specifically with divorce. There is not, but c. 31 is relevant: *Gif friman wið fries mannes wif geligeþ, his wergilde abicge, 7 oðer wif his agenum scætte begete 7 ðæm oðrum æt þam gebrenge.* The ambiguities are substantial. That *abicge* is the same root as is found in c. 76 (*gebigeð*) seems clear; it is also clear the prefix should lead us in the direction of translating it as something like "buy off." Just who is being "bought off" is not specified. It seems more likely that it is the husband, because it is not clear that the woman has been offended. She may have consented; it probably would have said so if she had not.[51] As Oliver points out, whose wergeld is being used to measure the payment is also not clear. *His* can be either masculine or neuter; *friman* is masculine and *wif* is neuter. If the wergeld is the man's, it is a substantial sum, 100 shillings for a *ceorl* and 300 for an *eorl*.[52] If it is the woman's, our only clue as to what it was is c. 73. That would suggest, but by no means prove, that it was the same as her father's or, perhaps, her husband's. If that is right, then in the usual situation where the couple were of the same class, there would be no reason to specify whose wergeld is meant. Conceptually, a wergeld is something that you pay when you kill someone. That the man has metaphorically been killed seems extreme. That his wife is metaphorically dead to him seems more likely.[53]

What is clear is that the offender has to obtain another wife for the husband with the offender's *agenum scætte*. The emphasis on *agenum* may be to distinguish it from the husband's *scæt*, but the phrase may mean that the payment is not the responsibility of the offender's kin group.[54] That it also specifies that the offender is to bring the new wife to the offended husband's home may indicate that this *Heimatsführung* could cost money.

What the provision does not tell us is what happens to the offending woman. If we assume that the Kentish were monogamous, she is no longer married to her former husband. Whether she becomes the wife of the adulterer, the text does not say. The alternative would seem to be that she returns to her natal group. Nor does the text say anything about what happens to her property or her children if she has any. We should

---

[51] Cf. *Abt.* 77.

[52] Cf. *Hl.* 1.

[53] There is a parallel in the Burgundian laws where the woman's wergeld may be being used to measure a payment for an offense that might be considered adultery. "Liber constitutionum," c. 52. The case is so unusual, however, that I hesitate even to mention it.

[54] Compare c. 24.2.

not, of course, apply the provisions of cc. 76 through 76.5 directly, but we might look to them for possible arrangements.[55]

The final provision in the main set of provisions on women reads:

> [77.] Gif man mægþman nede genimeþ, ðam agende L scillinga, 7 eft æt þam agende sinne willan ætgebicge.
>
> [77.1] Gif hio oþrum mæn in sceat bewyddod sy, XX scillinga gebete.
>
> [77.2] Gif gængang geweorðeþ, XXXV scill, 7 cyninge XV scillingas.

This provision parallels c. 75 and deals, as does c. 75, with the situation where a man acquires a wife in the wrong way. Here, however, the wife is a *mægþman* rather than a *widuwe*, and additional complexities are introduced. The taking of the *mægþman* is *nede*. That means "by force," but like "force" in modern English, *nede* can cover a variety of situations. At one extreme we might imagine a violent abduction and a rape, in the modern sense, of the young woman. At the other extreme we might imagine a prearranged elopement in which the only force applied was enough to get the window open so that the young woman could get out. The degree and type of force does not seem to make any difference in this provision, nor do we know what would happen if no force at all were applied. (It is possible that anything that was not with the consent of the *agende* was regarded as *nede*.) It is hard to imagine that the degree and type of force and perhaps even the consent of the *mægþman* did not play some role in the actual negotiations that followed, but that is not mentioned.

The compensation payment is substantial, 50 shillings, equal to the king's *mundbyrd* or half the wergeld of a ceorl. If the *mægþman* is returned, the *agende* gets only 35 shillings but the offender still has to pay 50 because he then has to pay an additional 15 to the king, the only time in any of these provisions regarding women where a fine to the king is involved.[56] If the young woman is pledged (*bewyddod*) to another man, the offender owes an additional 20 shillings to the other man. The parallel to c. 75 lies in the fact that having paid the compensation (which is higher than that in the case of the widow, except for the *eorlcundre*) the offender then also has to pay what he would have had to pay to obtain the *mund* over the young woman if he wants to marry her. Unlike the situation with the widow, there is no fixed sum for the *mund*. The offender *æt þam agende sinne willan ætgebicge*.

[55] The relevance of c. 72 is is discussed (though not resolved) in note 17. Less relevant is the other provision concerning adultery, c. 78: *Gif man mid esnes cwynan geligeþ be cwicum ceorle, II gebete*. It does not help in interpreting the provision about those who were not *esnas* and raises the substantial, and perhaps unanswerable, question of who the *esnas* were.

[56] There are other possible interpretations of the *hapax gængang* and of c. 77.2. Oliver, *Beginnings*, 108-9, discusses them, and, in my view correctly, comes to the conclusion that the one suggested in the text is the most likely.

Conclusion

Has this painstaking—a better word might be "painful"—analysis revealed anything about the role and status of women in Æthelberht's society? Some things have become a bit clearer. The treatment of the inheritance system that seems to lie behind these laws is more detailed than any that I know of. A number of possibilities have emerged in other areas that require more thought. Assuming (an assumption that may be heroic) that the interpretations just developed are reliable, they can be used to construct some pieces of the puzzle that the document presents.

First, women, at least at certain stages in their lives, had property that they could control. It would make no sense in c. 72 to prescribe a "bot" that the *friwif* was to pay if she had no means to pay it. The widow gets a share of her deceased husband's property if she has borne children (c. 76.2-4). The widow, and probably the married woman who predeceases her husband, has property that passes to her natal kin-group if she never bore a child with her husband (c. 76.5).

Second, the *mægþ*, the unmarried young woman, was valued as much as a free man (c. 73). This may have been an innovation of Æthelberht's laws, and we do not know how the equivalence would have been worked out, but the equivalence is clear. It may also be reasonable to assume that compensation payments for women who were older than a *mægþ* were already equivalent to those for a free man.

Third, the widow had a choice as to whether she would remarry (c. 76.4). Her new husband had to make a fixed payment to her *mund*-holder (c. 74) if he wanted to avoid a substantial financial penalty (c. 75), but whether or not she would remarry seems to have been the widow's choice. The widow with children also seems to have had the capacity to transfer the *mund* over herself and that over her children back to her natal kin-group (c. 76.3). It is unknown, however, whether the *mægþ* had to consent to the transfer of her *mund* to her husband, or, to put it more broadly, whether she had anything to say about her marriage (c. 76, 76.1). The fact that the payment for the *mund* of the *mægþ* is not fixed gives the *mund*-holder more discretion and probably less to the *mægþ*. Clause 77 focuses exclusively on the man who takes the *mægþ nede* and says nothing about whether it made any difference that the *mægþ* consented.

Fourth, women do not seem to have held *mund*. Individual men, or the kin-group collectively, seem to have held it over them. This chapter has emphasized, quite traditionally, the importance of this institution in explaining the context of many of the provisions of the laws. How important this seeming fact was to women's lives we do not know. In a society most of whose members, both men and women, had to struggle hard just to get enough to eat, it may not have been that important.

Hence, this chapter ends where it began. It is unknown whether this document was ever used to resolve practical disputes or as a guide for practice, but there is reason to suspect that it was not. As one of my students once described it, it is "a written code for a people who could not read." Evidence survives of the kinds of compromises that were involved in the negotiations about disputes later in the Anglo-Saxon period, and similar kinds of compromises likely occurred in Æthelberht's time. It is hard to imagine, for example, that intention, accident, negligence of the injured person, or intervention of a third party did not play some role in the compensation that actually got paid when someone was injured. It may be similarly hard to imagine that the wishes even of a *mægþ*, or at least of the women in the family generally, might, at least at times, have been considered when the transfer of her *mund* was being considered. Similarly, the economic situation of a widow with or without children could vary greatly. It is hard to imagine that these differences were not taken into account when what actually was going to happen was worked out. Of such things, however, the laws do not speak, and for Æthelberht's society the laws, for all practical purposes, are all we have. They tell us something, but not nearly so much as we would like to know.[57]

[57] When I wrote this essay I was aware of only one of the essays reprinted in Carole Hough's *An Ald Recht: Essays on Anglo-Saxon Law* (Newcastle-upon-Tyne: Cambridge Scholars Publishing, 2014). Had I been aware of more of them, I would certainly have said more in the text about her interpretations of a number of the provisions with which I deal. Suffice it to say here that I learned much from her essays, but have not been lead, perhaps out of stubbornness, to change the conclusions that I reach here. The essays have, however, lead me to emphasize what I say in the context of c. 72 and 76.5: "certainty is not possible."

Royal Law in Wessex and Kent at the Close of the Seventh Century

Stefan Jurasinski

Little would be known of Ine, king of Wessex from 688 until his abdication and pilgrimage to Rome in 726, were it not for the lengthy compilation of laws attributed to him in the *domboc* issued by Alfred the Great (d. 899) at some point toward the end of the latter's reign. In its absence, we would have to rely on mere scraps of historical evidence: a few sentences in Bede's *Historia ecclesiastica,* charters (many of doubtful provenance), and references in the *Anglo-Saxon Chronicle,* whose earliest recension aimed at celebrating the fortunes of the house of Cerdic and thus may exaggerate Ine's successes.[1] Even these few windows into late seventh-century Wessex might not have ensured that Ine would overshadow the obscure kings of the earlier Anglo-Saxon period, whose struggles Milton outrageously characterized as no more worth recounting than "the Warrs of Kites, or Crows, flocking and fighting in the Air."[2]

---

[1] Ine is mentioned twice in the *Historia ecclesiastica,* and in neither instance does Bede appear to take a favorable view of him. See Bertram Colgrave and R.A.B. Mynors, eds., *Bede's Ecclesiastical History of the English People* [hereafter *HE*] (Oxford: Clarendon, 1969), 380-1 (iv.15), 472-3 (v.7); the latter is a compressed biography of Ine relating nothing of his accomplishments as king of the *Gewisse.* But Bede was "poorly informed about Wessex," a fact perhaps accounting for the few words devoted to the king: see Clare Stancliffe, "Kings who Opted Out," In *Ideal and Reality in Frankish and Anglo-Saxon Society,* ed. Patrick Wormald (Oxford: Blackwell, 1983), 154-76, at 154. Charters attributed to Ine are discussed in Heather Edwards, *The Charters of the Early West Saxon Kingdom,* British Series 198 (Oxford: B.A.R., 1988); see also Lesley Abrams, "A Single-Sheet Facsimile of a Diploma of King Ine for Glastonbury," in *The Archaeology and History of Glastonbury Abbey: Essays in Honour of the Ninetieth Birthday of C.A. Ralegh Radford,* ed. Lesley Abrams and James P. Carley (Woodbridge: Boydell, 1991), 97-134. Few details about Ine's reign are to be found in the version of the *Anglo-Saxon Chronicle* occurring in Cambridge, Corpus Christi College 173 (MS E): the entry for 688 is manifestly indebted to *HE* iv.15, and scarcely more is said between this entry and the one relating his pilgrimage to Rome in 726. See *The Anglo-Saxon Chronicle: A Collaborative Edition, vol. 7 (MS E),* ed. Susan Irvine (Woodbridge: D.S. Brewer, 2004), 34-6. On the Alfredian background of the Chronicle, see Audrey L. Meaney, "St. Neots, Æthelweard and the Compilation of the *Anglo-Saxon Chronicle:* A Survey," in *Studies in Earlier Old English Prose,* ed. Paul Szarmach (Albany: SUNY Press, 1986), 193-244.

[2] *The History of Britain, That Part especially now call'd England. From the first Traditional Beginning, Continu'd to the Norman Conquest* (London: "Printed by R.E. for R. Scot, R. Chiswell, R. Bentley, and G. Sawbridge," 1695), 216.

The survival of Ine's laws in Alfred's has made, of course, for a very different situation.[3] Yet their occurrence only in Alfred's *domboc* has long raised suspicions that Ine's laws were in some sense tampered with, either by Alfred's circle or earlier copyists. Seeming evidence for such meddling has been furnished by the laws of Ine's near-contemporary Wihtræd, whose much briefer code contains a number of clauses that appear to echo either the wording or sentiments of the former's laws and thus may offer some sense of what they looked like before being absorbed into the *domboc.* That Wihtræd's laws are an early witness to Ine's is a possibility acknowledged by all modern editors that nonetheless has yet to see much in the way of sustained consideration. Nor is the inventory of allegedly "shared" clauses consistent from one treatment of this problem to the next. This chapter aims to bring some order to this situation by discussing closely these presumptive instances of borrowing and other clauses that may be indicative of textual influence. It is hoped that untangling these strands may disclose something of the circumstances to which these two kings sought to respond in issuing written legislation. That Ine's and Wihtræd's laws may indeed illuminate more broadly historical questions is shown toward the close of this essay, which offers new observations concerning the legislation of both kings on the administration of baptism and the Eucharist. The relationship of these provisions to the religious situation of early Wessex and Kent has, it is argued, been somewhat misconstrued.

Background: The Historical Setting

No scholar has dealt with the relation of Wihtræd's laws to Ine's at greater length than Felix Liebermann, and much of what follows is bound to respond to his claims, many of which have received little scrutiny in the century or so since they first appeared in the pages of his great *Gesetze der Angelsachsen.* His remarks are worth quoting in full:[4]

> Wi[htræd] ist in England das früheste Denkmal, das nachweislich literarisch bereits geformte Gesetze benutzt. Er bringt c. 28 wörtlich z[um] T[eil] gleichlautend einen auch bei *Ine* 20 stehenden Satz und c. 9ff. einen Abschnitt ähnlichen Sinnes wie *Ine* 3. Zwar sagt er hier archaischer *dryhten,* wo bei *Ine hlaford* steht; letzteres könnte aber Ælfredsche Änderung im *Ine* sein. Jedenfalls stammt *Ine,* als etwas früher und wahrscheinlich vollständiger (s.u. 28), nicht von Wi[htræd]. Auch liegt nicht etwa Lateinischer Wortlaut beiden vor: dazu ist die Übereinstimmung sprachlich zu genau. Vielmehr hat Wi[htræd]

[3] The achievements of Ine are extolled in Edward A. Freeman in "King Ine (Part I)," *Proceedings of the Somerset Archaeological and Natural History Society* 18 (1872): 1-59, at 1; also F.M. Stenton, *Anglo-Saxon England,* 2nd edn. (Oxford: Clarendon, 1947), 70-1.
[4] Liebermann, *Gesetze,* III: 23-24.

den *Ine* benutzt, aber in archaischerem Texte als dem Ælfredschen, wozu ich auch vier Wörter, die er mehr bietet, zähle. Dies is auch in England das früheste Beispiel für Benutzung des Rechtes eines Nachbarstammes.

[The laws of] Wihtræd represent the earliest work of legislation in England demonstrably to have used prior written laws. In c. 28 [of his laws] he gives a clause nearly identical to what also occurs in *Ine* c. 20 and in cc. 9ff. a section of the same sense as *Ine* c. 3. It is true that [Wihtræd] uses here the more archaic *dryhten* where *Ine* gives *hlaford;* the latter may, however, represent an Alfredian revision to Ine's laws. At all events, [the laws of] Ine, as they are somewhat earlier and probably more complete (see c. 28), are not derived from Wihtræd's. Nor does any Latin wording underlie either text, as the agreement in language evident in the two codes is too close. Rather Wihtræd used Ine's laws, but in a more archaic text than that found in Alfred's laws [. . .]. This is, at any rate, the earliest example England furnishes of use of the laws of a neighboring people.

Liebermann goes on to detail other alleged borrowings in Wihtræd from earlier written laws. He notes that the preface echoes some language of Hlothhere and Eadric's laws and that the code proper makes use of a Latin formula of exculpation (*Wi.*19; *Beginnings Wi.* 15), borrows (*Wi.* 5; *Beginnings Wi.* 4) from the Synod of Hertford (673), and perhaps relies for its laws for fasts and against idolatry on earlier provisions issued by Eorcenberht (*HE* iii.8; the laws in question are lost).[5] On this basis it is fair to say that, of the three examples of royal legislation surviving from seventh-century Kent, Wihtræd's have the most conspicuous debt to written rather than oral sources.

The smaller-scale borrowings just enumerated suggest that Wihtræd's laws might be expected to have drawn upon Ine's as well in the event that they were available. That the latter made their way to Kent in time to see such use is, however, a possibility resting on the most slender thread of evidence. From Liebermann's lifetime to the present, Ine's claim, in the preface to his laws, to have been counseled in their preparation by bishop Eorcenwold of London has seemed adequate ground for a *terminus ad quem* antedating the promulgation of Wihtræd's laws, since Eorcenwold "died on 30 April, probably in 693 and certainly by 694."[6] As Wormald notes, the other evidence for the date of Ine's laws is furnished by alleged borrowings in Wihtræd's observed by Liebermann: "[T]he fact that at least one of his [Ine's] laws was echoed by Wihtræd confirms that his code (or part of it) dates to the first years of his reign."[7] The risk of circularity in this argument may account for reservations about Liebermann's view occasionally voiced over the past century. In his edition of 1922, whose commentary otherwise depends closely

[5] Reference is given to chapter divisions as given both in Liebermann's edition and in Oliver, *Beginnings.*
[6] Wormald, *Making,* 103 n. 358; also Liebermann, *Gesetze,* III: 65 c. 15. There is no discussion of this matter in the editions of Benjamin Thorpe (1840) and Rheinhold Schmid (1832 rev. 1858).
[7] Wormald, *Making,* 103.

on Liebermann's, Frederick Levi Attenborough retreats from the great editor's claims toward a more qualified assessment of the problem:[8]

> The laws [of Wihtræd] appear to have been issued in the autumn of 695, probably on September 6 (cf. Liebermann, III, p. 24). Peace was made with Ine, king of Wessex, in the preceding year, according to the Saxon Chronicle (ann. 694); and it is worth noting that one of Wihtræd's laws (28) is practically identical with one of Ine's (20)—which points to communication between the two courts.

Stenton's remark that similarities between Ine's laws and Wihtræd's show the latter to have been "legislating in the same spirit at the same time" may be taken to signal further backpedaling, as does, in our own era, Carole Hough's assertion that their commonalities show "a degree of co-operation between the kingdoms of Wessex and of Kent."[9]

While the date of Earconwold's death ostensibly places the laws of Wihtræd and Ine about a year apart, there are reasons to think that reservations expressed in the works just referenced are wholly warranted. Prior discussions have been insufficiently attentive to the differences between their respective prefaces, which are best observed when they are placed side-by-side:[10]

Ine: Ic Ine, mid Godes gife, Wesseaxna kyning, mid geðeahte 7 mid lare Cenredes mines fæder 7 Heddes mines biscepes 7 Eorcenwoldes mines biscepes, [7] mid eallum minum ealdormonnum 7 þæm ieldstan witum minre ðeode 7 eac micelre gesomnunge Godes ðeowa,

Wihtræd: Ðam mildestan cyninge Cantwara Wihtræde rixigendum þe fiftan wintra his rices, þy niguðan gebanne, sextan dæge Rugernes, in þære stowe þy hatte Berghamstyde, ðær wæs gesamnad eadigra geþeahtendlic ymcyme. Ðær wæs Birhtwald, Bretone heahbiscop, 7 se ær

[8] Frederick Levi Attenborough, *Laws of the Earliest English Kings* (Cambridge: Cambridge University Press, 1922), 3, where is also said the following: "It has been observed that cap. 20 of Ine's laws is practically identical with cap. 28 of Wihtræd's laws, which date from 695. This may be regarded as pointing to communication between the governing authorities of the two kingdoms, such as would naturally follow the restoration of friendly relations in 694." See also Attenborough, *Laws,* 34. In both cases, Attenborough's assessment seems much more cautious than Liebermann's.

[9] Stenton, *Anglo-Saxon England,* 71 n.2; Carole Hough, "Legal and Documentary Writings," in idem, *"An Ald Reht": Essays on Anglo-Saxon Law* (Newcastle-upon-Tyne: Cambridge Scholars, 2014), 2-25, at 9 (a repaginated and corrected repr. of "Legal and Documentary Writings," in *A Companion to Anglo-Saxon Literature,* eds. Phillip Pulsiano and Elaine Treharne [Oxford: Blackwell, 2001], 170-87); also Mary Richards, "The Laws of Alfred and Ine," in *A Companion to Alfred the Great,* ed. Nicole Guenther Discenza and Paul E. Szarmach (Leiden: Brill, 2014), 282-312 at 303.

[10] Translations from Ine's laws, in this and subsequent quoted passages, are drawn (unless otherwise indicated) from Oliver and Jurasinski, *From Ine to Alfred the Great: The Earliest Laws of the West-Saxon Kingdom* [in progress]); citations and translations of *Wihtræd* are cited by chapter, in this and all subsequent instances, from Oliver, *Beginnings.*

wæs smeagende be ðære hælo urra sawla 7 be ðam staþole ures rices, þætte ryht æw 7 ryhte cynedomas ðurh ure folc gefæstnode 7 getrymede wæron, þætte nænig ealdormonna ne us undergeðeodedra æfter þam wære awendende ðas ure dómas.

I, Ine, by God's gift king of the West Saxons, with the advice and instruction of Cenred my father and Hædde my bishop and Eorconwald my bishop, with all my *ealdormen* and the senior counsellors of my people and also a great gathering of God's servants, have been considering the well-being of our souls and the foundation of our kingdom, to the end that just law and just royal judgments should be established and made strong throughout our folk, so that after this time no *ealdorman* nor any other subject to us should depart from these our judgments.

nemnda cyning; eac þan Hrofesceastre bisceop (se ilca Gybmund wæs haten) andward wæs; 7 cwæð ælc had ciricean ðære mægðe anmodlice mid þy hersuman folcy. Ðær ða eadigan fundon mid ealra gemedum ðas domas 7 Cantwara rihtum þeawum æcton, swa hit hyr efter segeþ 7 cwyþ.

To the most gracious king of the Kentish people, Wihtræd, ruling in the fifth winter of his reign, in the ninth indiction, sixth day of Rugern, in that place which is called Berkhamstead, there was gathered a consiliary assembly of great men. There was Brihtwald, archbishop of Britain, and the afore-mentioned king; likewise the bishop of Rochester, which same was called Gebmund, was present; and each order of the church of that people spoke with a single mind to the loyal populace. There the great men devised, with the consent of all, these decrees, and added to the just customs of the Kentish people, as it hereafter says and declares.

It may well be a mistake to assume, as did Liebermann and most subsequent commentators, that Wihtræd's and Ine's prefaces are similarly motivated. Wihtræd's preface, it should be noted, is narrated in the third person; a gesture that cannot be taken as indicative of egotism, as the king is assigned such a minor role in the preparation of his laws that they may scarcely be called "his" at all. The preface notes merely that he was present at the assembly where they were agreed upon, with credit for devising them ultimately being shared among *ða eadigan,* which may be translated as "the important people."

Ine, however, claims for himself sole responsibility for the preparation of his laws (*Ic Ine* [. . .] *wæs smeagende*). The bishops, magnates and assembly (for which no date is supplied) are, in all likelihood, mentioned for no other reason than to lend the compilation something of their authority. Given the way in which the king's father and bishops are invoked—they are credited in the preface only with furnishing, over an indefinite period of time, the "advice and counsel" (*mid geðeahte 7 mid lare*) that enlarged Ine's own reflections—it seems fair to wonder whether it is essential for all of them to have been alive when the laws first appeared.

We have in addition the problem of not knowing as well as we might like what it meant to issue royal legislation in this period or how it assumed its final form. Was the first promulgation of Ine's laws necessarily the *only* one? The tremendous scope of Ine's laws and the length of his reign suggest otherwise. Whereas Wihtræd's laws take up 28 chapters in the standard editions, their length being well within the limits of what we might expect an assembly of bishops to agree on, Ine's have 76, leaving them one shy of Alfred's 77.[11] (Alfred's laws, it ought to be remembered, are the longest work of legislation to survive from the Anglo-Saxon period.) To say the least, it is difficult to imagine Ine, Cenred, and the assembled bishops legislating on minutiae of agricultural practice and other obscurities covered in the code's 76 chapters, and for them to have done so at a single sitting seems impossible.

The problems just enumerated with Liebermann's relative chronology are not trivial, nor are the doubts expressed here the first to have been put in writing. While Wormald was content to repeat much of what Liebermann said about the relative chronology of Ine's laws and Wihtræd's, he also voiced, without pursuing all of its ramifications, the most convincing counterargument to Liebermann's thesis. "It is hard," Wormald wrote, "to see how Ine's laws could appear in the order that they do, were the code in any way pre-planned. [. . .] The most plausible conclusion is that Ine's so-called code was not a code at all but a series of enactments added to an original core over years or decades."[12] In saying so, Wormald had in mind not so much the length of Ine's laws as their frequent repetitions. This defect, he maintained, is found as well in some recensions of continental laws, where provisions clearly devised after the laws' first issuance are numbered as if they formed one continuous whole.[13] If Ine's laws gather in one place a range of judgments issued at various times—a possibility that seemed all but certain to Wormald—then any supposed date suggested by the preface must be taken with a grain of salt.

Other salutary warnings about the standard relative chronology may be added to those just given. We should resist, for example, the temptation to project onto seventh-century Wessex the importance it would enjoy during the reign of Alfred and his successors. While the reign of Ine may have put Wessex on the road to becoming the most important of the English-speaking kingdoms in the late ninth and early tenth centuries, the late seventh afforded few signs of its eventual triumph. Prior to Ine's accession, Kent had enjoyed success in war against Wessex, beating back an invasion by Ine's predecessor Cædwalla during the latter's attempt to make Kent a subkingdom ruled by Cædwalla's brother Mul.[14] It did so while continuing to establish itself as the preeminent center of ecclesiastical learning, the achievements of this period enjoying fame into the eighth century.[15]

---

[11] Reference here is to the chapters assigned by Liebermann, not those given in MS E.

[12] Wormald, *Making,* 105.

[13] Wormald, *Making,* 105.

[14] See *The Anglo-Saxon Chronicle* vol. 7 [MS E], ed. Irvine, 33 (s.a. 686).

[15] Stenton, *Anglo-Saxon England,* 62.

The reigns of both Ine and Wihtræd coincide with the archiepiscopate of Theodore of Tarsus and of his successor Berhtwald, under whom, according to Nicholas Brooks, "the see of Canterbury exercised greater authority than it was ever to possess again."[16] Brooks had in mind Theodore's having "exercised metropolitan powers by deposing Chad from the see of York" not long after arriving in England. The prologue of Wihtræd's laws itself makes clear that Theodore's successor Berhtwald had every intention of retaining such authority, as he is here named "Birhtwald, archbishop of Britain" (*Birhtwald, Bretone heahbiscop*).[17] This was not a kingdom lacking in self-esteem.

The condition of Kent brings into stark relief the deficiencies of the West-Saxon kingdom at this time. Bede depicts Wessex on the eve of Ine's accession as barely furnished with adequate clergy and ruled by a rapacious near-pagan.[18] That Wihtræd served under such circumstances as the subordinate king, with influence in matters of legislation flowing only from west to east, seems hard to credit. Even the settlement for the burning of Mul extracted from the kingdom of Kent not long after Ine's accession seems more ambivalent than is sometimes implied. Ine's agreement to such terms may attest less to the strength of his position than to the perceived necessity of patching up relations marred by the hectic reign of Cædwalla. It surely was not lost on Ine that settling this inherited dispute would put him in close touch with England's preeminent see. Given Theodore's role in bringing about a similar settlement (*HE* iv.21) between the kings of Northumbria and Mercia, it is just possible that the peace negotiated between Wessex and Kent reflects the initiative of Theodore's successor, with the groundwork perhaps having been laid by Theodore himself. The view shared by some historians that this settlement was a manifestation of West-Saxon hegemony probably owes something to the way it is narrated in the *Chronicle*—by happenstance, our sole witness to the event—whose language may be read as implying that the men of Kent sued for peace.[19] I suspect that the origins of the *Chronicle* in the Alfredian revival of prose writing may account for any hints of triumphalism in this entry.[20]

The assumptions of Attenborough and Stenton seem, accordingly, a bit safer than Liebermann's. The reconciliation of Wessex and Kent in 694—incidentally, also the

---

[16] Nicholas Brooks, *The Early History of the Church of Canterbury* (Leicester: Leicester University Press, 1984), 72.

[17] Ed. and trans. Oliver, *Beginnings*, 152-3.

[18] See, e.g., *HE* iv.15.

[19] "Here the people of Kent entered into negotiations with Ine, and they gave him thirty thousand [?*sceatta*], because they had previously burnt Mul; 7 Wihtræd became king, and held the kingdom for twenty-three years" (*Her Cantwara geþingoden wiþ Ine, 7 him gesealdon .xxx. þusenda, forþan þe hi ær Mul forbærndon. 7 Wihtræd feng to Cantwara rice, 7 heold thre 7 twenti wintra*); ed. Irvine, *Anglo-Saxon Chronicle vol. 7 [MS E]*, 34 (*s.a.* 694).

[20] See Meaney, "St. Neots."

standard *terminus ad quem* assigned Ine's laws—may well have led to a series of exchanges between the two courts and their respective clergy, with Ine eager to claim the benefits of new ties to Canterbury.[21] At the very least, the foregoing shows the rather different circumstances under which Wihtræd and Ine issued legislation. Wihtræd inherited a kingdom that had been for nearly a century the seat of ecclesiastical power in England and that had just thwarted an assault by its neighbor to the west.[22] Ine's kingdom, on the other hand, had for seventy years held at best nominal ties with the see of Rome with little to show for it. It is easy to see how Ine's success would depend upon forging relations with powerful neighbors, and it will be well to bear this in mind as we turn to specific provisions of laws shared by *Wihtræd* and *Ine*.

Allegedly Borrowed Material in Wihtræd's Laws

Of all materials shared by *Wihtræd* and *Ine*, the most familiar is the following clause:

Ine 20: [Be feorran cumenum men butan wege gemetton.][23] Gif feorcund mon oððe fremde butan wege geond wudu gonge 7 ne hrieme ne horn blawe, for ðeof he bið to profianne, oððe to sleanne oððe to áliesanne.	*Wihtræd* 28: Gif feorran cumen man oþþe fræmde buton wege gange, 7 he þonne nawðer ne hrieme ne he horn ne blawe, for ðeof he bið to profianne: oþþe to sleanne oþþe to alysenne.
If [either] a person who has come from far off or a stranger travels off the road through the woods and does not shout out or blow a horn, he is to be taken for a thief: either to be slain or to be redeemed [by ransom].	If a man [who is] come from afar or a stranger should go off the track, and he then neither calls out nor does he blow a horn, he is to be regarded as a thief, either to be killed or to be redeemed.

That the material just quoted appears in either Ine's or Wihtræd's laws as a result of borrowing of some sort is beyond doubt. Yet the source of influence seems less certain than Liebermann implied. Lisi Oliver even suggested that "the two clauses [might] stem

[21] On the possible role of Ine's counselor Eorcenwold as a conduit for diplomatic exchanges between Wessex and neighboring kingdoms, see Patrick Wormald, *The Times of Bede,* ed. Stephen Baxter (Oxford: Blackwell, 2006), 144-5. (The piece reprinted here is his Jarrow lecture of 1984.)

[22] The kingdom of Kent would, however, be subsumed into Mercia not long after Wihtræd's death; see the chapter by Rabin in the present volume.

[23] The rubrics postdate the issuance of the *domboc* and thus tell us little about Ine's laws. It is significant, nonetheless, that the phrasing of the rubric seems closer to that of Wihtræd's laws than Ine's. Was the rubricator aware of Wihtræd's laws and their commonalities with Ine's?

from a common original" given that the practice described therein is common in stateless societies.[24]

Further ambiguities are suggested by the situation of this clause in Ine's and Wihtræd's laws. Again, the lengthiest comments are Liebermann's:[25]

> Der Satz lautet grossenteils wie *Ine* 20, wo Einzelnes erklärt wird [. . .] *Ine* 21 scheint, weil auch der Nordischen Parallele eigen und sachlich zugehörig, ursprünglich, also *Ines* form vollständiger (auch in den Worten *geond wudu*). Auch scheint der Satz in Wi[htræd], als am Schlusse stehend, ein blosses Anhängsel. Gegen die Annahme . . . daß die Kirche, etwa eine Synode, die Vermittlerin sowohl für Wi[htræd] wie für *Ine* gewesen sei, spricht die vulgarsprachliche Form wie der fremdenfeindliche Sinn, während die Kirche vielmehr den Verkehr zwischen den Kleinstaaten förderte.

> The clause [*Wihtræd* c. 28] reads largely like *Ine* c. 20, where some particulars are clarified [. . .] *Ine* c. 21 appears original, as it corresponds in its peculiarities and subject to the Norse parallel [suggested by Jakob Grimm], and *Ine*'s form of the law is therefore the more complete (as in the words *geond wudu*). Also the version of the clause occurring in Wihtræd's laws, because it appears at the end, seems a simple appendage. As counter-evidence to the supposition [. . .] that the Church, perhaps some synod, was the intermediary for both *Wihtræd* and *Ine*, we may consider the vernacular form as well as the xenophobic attitude of the law, as the church sought instead exchange between the smaller kingdoms.

Liebermann alludes here to a number of circumstances that would seem to argue in favor of borrowing from *Ine*. The version of the clause in Wihtræd's laws occurs at the very end of the code, making it perhaps "a simple appendage" (*ein blosses Anhängsel*). Further evidence of its being out of place seems furnished by its contradicting Wihtræd 26, where the punishment of a freeman caught in the act of stealing is left to the judgment of the king. Would a "man from afar"—a "foreigner," in Oliver's view—have necessarily been treated worse than a freeman?

That Ine's laws offer the more complete (*vollständiger*) version of this provision is, according to Liebermann, suggested by its rather different situation in this text. Here it is followed by another that expands upon its implications, explaining what is to happen in the event of the foreigner's death, should the man's kin arrive to claim his wergild. In this instance, his attacker shall be permitted to swear an oath that he killed the man assuming him to be a thief. If he has concealed the homicide, he thereby "clears the way to the oath [being sworn] for the dead man, so that his kinsmen may prove him innocent" (Ine 20.2). But is all of this necessarily evidence that the clause originates with *Ine*? To add corrective qualifications seems just what we might expect of a king

---

[24] Oliver, *Beginnings,* 179.

[25] Liebermann, *Gesetze* III: 30 n. 28.

were the material extraneous to his own laws. And the evidence that this clause sits as uncomfortably in Ine's laws as it does in Wihtræd's seems to me quite compelling. At clause 16, *Ine* had established that "He who kills a thief may declare on oath, that he killed him because he was [found] guilty [in the act]; this does not apply to his associates." After *Ine* 20 (= *Wi.* 28), which likewise permits the presumptive thief to be slain or held for ransom, the condition laid down in *Ine* 16 must be stated again (*Ine* 20.1); the clause immediately following states what is to be done if the bane of the alleged thief should have concealed this act. This clump of repetitions and qualifications may indicate that the clause was a late addition to Ine's laws. Certainly it seems an unlikely part of Wormald's "original core." *Ine* 20/*Wihtræd* 28 also seems to contradict *Ine* 28—as it does Wihtræd 26 (noted earlier)—both of which reserve to the king alone the power to fix the punishment of a captured thief. Given that it is an outlier in both Ine's and Wihtræd's laws, its derivation from some source common to both, the possibility suggested by Oliver, seems more probable than its transmission from *Ine* to *Wihtræd.* The hypothetical source need not have been clerical, as Liebermann supposed (only to dismiss the possibility).[26]

Other "echoed" clauses suggested by Wormald (Wi 9-11/*Ine* 3-3.2, *Ine* 12/*Wihtræd* 25) seem far less impressive as proof of borrowing.[27] How *Ine* 12 and *Wihtræd* 25 entered this list is unclear, as they seem contradictory and do not resemble one another in any other respect than shared subject matter. This leaves Wi 9-11/*Ine* 3-3.2. Both are concerned with violation of the strictures against working on Sunday by servants and other bound laborers:

Ine 3: Gif ðeowmon wyrce on Sunnandæg be his hlafordes hæse, sie he frioh, 7 se hlaford geselle XXX scill. to wite. [3.1] Gif þonne se ðeowa butan his gewitnesse wyrce, ðolie his hyde. [3.2] Gif þonne se frigea ðy dæge wyrce butan his hlafordes hæse, ðolie his freotes.

Wihtræd 9 [*Beginnings* 8]: Gif esne ofer dryhtnes hæse þeowweorc wyrce an sunnan æfen efter hire setlgange oþ monan æfenes setlgang, LXXX sceatta se dryhtne gebete. [10; *Beginnings* 8.1] Gif esne deþ his rade þæs dæges, VI se wið dryhten gebete oþþe sine hyd. [11; *Beginnings* 8.2] Gif friman þonne an ðane forbodenan timan, sio he healsfange scyldig; 7 se

---

[26] Liebermann, *Gesetze,* III: 30 (n. on *Wi. 28*). Aside from these "borrowed" clauses, the evidence most often adduced to imply that *Ine* exerted some sort of influence upon *Wihtræd* is the latter's use of *gesiðcund* "noble," a West-Saxon word commonly attested in the *domboc,* in place of *eorlcund* (the equivalent used in prior Kentish laws): see Attenborough, *Laws,* 180 n. 5.1 ("The word *gesiðcund,* which is used in the laws of Ine and Alfred, now takes the place of the antiquated word *eorlcund,* which is used in the earlier codes"); also Oliver, *Beginnings,* 155 n.a and 168. It is nowhere implied outright that use of the term indicates textual influence, nor does any such implication seem warranted, as this term may (as the most guarded assessments imply) merely appear in Wihtræd's laws as a loanword.

[27] Wormald, *Making,* 103 n. 358.

man se þæt arasie, he age healf þæt wite 7 þæt weorc.

If a slave works on Sunday at his lord's command, let him be free, and the lord must pay 30 shillings as fine. If, however, the slave works without his [lord's] knowledge, let [the slave] pay with his hide. If, however, a freeman works on that day without his lord's command, let him pay with his freedom.	If a servant according to his lord's order does slave-work after sunset on the eve of Sunday until sunset on the eve of Monday, let the lord pay 80 shillings [*?sceattas*]. If a servant performs [work] on his own counsel that day, let him pay 6 towards his lord or his hide. If, however, a freeman [works] in that forbidden time, let him be liable for healsfang, and the man who detects that, he shall own half the fine and/or that work.

It will be evident that no clear pattern of borrowing emerges from the clauses just quoted. Similarities of phrasing are absent, and it may not even be said that they refer to the same classes of laborers, as being an *esne* was rather different from being a *þeow.*[28] Wihtræd's *þeowweorc*—a close translation of *opus servile* [cf. Leviticus 23:7]—gives away the route by which these provisions entered his laws.[29] Reference to the prohibited *opera servilia* are characteristic of Frankish legislation against Sunday labor, much of which employed the biblical phrase translated in *Wihtræd*.[30] There are few reasons to suppose that these texts or the conciliar legislation underlying them were not familiar to Berhtwald and perhaps to Gefmund as well.

An unattractive conclusion emerges from all this. One senses something near to enchantment in the way in which Liebermann and other scholars imagined the possibility of happy relations between Kent and Wessex blossoming into the first work of legislation to encompass the laws of two previously disputing kingdoms. That amity was restored—perhaps as much at Ine's urging as Wihtræd's (more likely, Berhtwald's)—is beyond dispute. But the evidence for a subsequent exchange of legislative ideas seems rather weak.[31] The more likely possibility is that apparent similarities show evidence of

[28] See the discussion of Old English *esne* in David A.E. Pelteret, *Slavery in Early Mediaeval England* (Woodbridge: Boydell, 1995), 271-4.

[29] On the development of these laws, see L.L. McReavy, "The Sunday Repose from Labor," *Ephemerides Theologicae Lovanianses* 12 (1935): 291-323.

[30] See the excellent discussion in Dorothy Haines, *Sunday Observance and the Sunday Letter in Anglo-Saxon England* (Woodbridge: D.S. Brewer, 2010), 2-17.

[31] The situation is perhaps analogous to that of the laws of Hywel Dda, where loanwords from English have been taken as signs of bonhomie between the Welsh and West-Saxon courts. Such assumptions are challenged in D.P. Kirby, "Hywel Dda: Anglophil?" *Welsh History Review* 8 (1976): 1-13. (I am grateful to Andrew Rabin for this reference.)

influences that were exerted upon both texts by others now lost or otherwise unknown to us. That some humility is in order on this question is suggested by what Bede has to say on the reign of the Kentish king Eorcenberht (r. 640-664; *HE* iii.8), whose active program of legislation, described by Bede in no less detail than Æthelberht's, focused upon establishing punishments for those who persisted in practices incompatible with the teaching of the church, such as devotion to idols or neglect of the Lenten fast. Those royal laws that survive from the seventh century are unlikely to have been the only legislation known to Ine or Wihtræd.

Wihtræd and *Ine* on "Church and State"

Though they are often discussed in conjunction, the remaining clauses of Ine's and Wihtræd's laws to be considered have to my knowledge seen no discussion of their value as evidence for their relative chronology. Nonetheless, they are routinely held to shed some light, however unsatisfactory, on the progress of evangelization within these two kingdoms by the end of the seventh century. That the laws of both kings should share the concerns made evident in these clauses suggests that a similar environment must have obtained for each, though the evidence, given the scarcity of other materials for this period, should probably not be pressed too far.

The first set of clauses involves the administration of baptism. Somewhat contrary to expectation, both Ine's and Wihtræd's laws suggest that, as some have pointed out, infant baptism may not yet have been the norm:[32]

Ine 2: Cild binnan ðritegum nihta sie gefulwad; gif hit swa ne sie, XXX scill. gebete. [2.1] Gif hit ðonne sie dead butan fulwihte, gebete he hit mid eallum ðam ðe he age.

A child must be baptized within thirty nights; if it is not, let him pay 30 shillings. If it should die, however, without baptism, let him compensate for that with all that he owns.

Wihtræd 5 [*Beginnings* 6]: Gif priost læfe unrihthæmed, oþþe fulwih[t]e untrumes forsitte, oþþe to þon drunken sie þæt he ne mæge, sio he stille his þegnungæ oþ biscopes dom.

If a priest allows an unlawful union, or neglects the baptism of a sick person, or is so drunk that he is not able [to perform his duties], let him be inactive in his service pending the bishop's decree.

The clauses just quoted from Ine's laws arrive after the following statement (1): "First we command that God's servants hold their proper rule according to law. Next we

[32] See, e.g., Barbara Yorke, *Wessex in the Early Middle Ages* (Leicester: Leicester University Press, 1995), 173-4.

command that the law and judgments regarding all the folk be held as follows" (*Ærest we bebeodað, þætte Godes þeowas hiora rihtregol on ryht healdan. Æfter þam we bebeodað, þætte ealles folces æw 7 domas ðus sien gehealdene*).[33] It would seem, therefore, that the provision concerning baptism refers to members of the clergy. Though this was not the view of Liebermann, it seems to me adequately corroborated by a number of parallels that have yet to be considered in relation to this clause.[34] We have, for example, the witness of the *Pœnitentiale Theodori.* Though its provisions were assembled some years later than the period in question, it likely shows some debt to the prelate's activities, as seems particularly to be the case in this clause given the unusual statement of attribution with which it concludes:[35]

> Infans infirmus et paganus commendatus pręsbitero si moritur presbiter deponatur. [29] Si negligentia sit parentum I annum peniteant et si moritur infans III trium annorum sine baptismo III annos peniteant pater et mater. Hoc quodam tempore quo contingit ad eum delatum sic iudicavit.
>
> If an infant that is weak and is a pagan has been recommended to a presbyter [for baptism] and dies [unbaptized], the presbyter shall be deposed. If the neglect is on the part of the parents, *they shall do penance* for a year; and if a child of three years dies without baptism, the *father and the mother* shall do penance for three years. *He gave this decision at a certain time because it happened to be referred to him.* (My emphasis).

The demand that the responsible party "compensate with all that he owns" (Ine 2.1) seems to refer to laicization, as is made explicit in the Theodorean canon and hinted at in an Alfredian ordinance issued much later.[36] The absence of monetary penalties for parents, along with the relatively mild year-long penance imposed upon them, likewise

---

[33] Liebermann, *Gesetze,* I: 88.

[34] "Ob die Buße vom Vater des Kindes erhoben werden soll, oder von dem Priester, dem c. 1 das Einhalten der canonischen Satzungen eingeschärft wird, ist nicht ausdrücklich gesagt, doch nach dem Schlußsatz (gebête mid eallum þe he âge) das Erstere anzunehmen" (Schmid, *Gesetze,* 1858: 21); "Nicht aber 'Der Priester' ist gemeint: der Satz steht ja unter Geboten für Laien." Liebermann, *Gesetze,* III: 69.

[35] *Pœnitentiale Theodori* I.xiv.28-9, ed. Paul Willem Finsterwalder, *Die Canones Theodori Cantuariensis und ihre Überlieferungsformen* (Weimar: Hermann Böhlaus Nachfolger, 1929), 310. Transl. John T. McNeill and Helena Gamer, *Medieval Handbooks of Penance* (New York: Columbia University Press, 1938), 197-8.

[36] Cf. *Af.* 21: "If a priest slays another man, let [?him] and all the share of the monastic property which he has bought for himself be given up; and the bishop shall unfrock him when he is ejected from the monastery and given up, unless the lord [of the monastery] is willing to answer for the wergeld [of the slain man]" (*Gif preost oðerne mon ofslea, weorpe mon to handa 7 eall ðæt he him hames bohte, 7 hine biscep onhadige, þonne hine mon of ðam mynstre agife, buton se hlaford þone wer forðingian wille*) (Liebermann, *Gesetze,* I: 62 [MS E]; trans. partially indebted to Attenborough, *Laws*). The Tironian note was regarded by Thorpe as "subversive of the sense" and therefore omitted from his translation: see Thorpe, *Ancient Laws and Institutes of England* (London: Eyre and Spottiswoode, 1840), 34 n.a.

makes reference to anyone but a priest in Ine's ordinance appear unlikely. A similar impression is given by a late Old English homily attributed to Wulfstan (Napier XXIV) that inveighs against priests for neglecting the baptism of infants.[37] Though the homily requires kin who have delayed the baptism of a deceased child to forfeit all possessions and undergo exile or penance imposed by the bishop—the latter signals a debt to Wulfstan's thinking—it is safe to say that the offense is conventionally categorized as one of priests, not parents.[38]

Wihtræd's law placing at the mercy of bishops those priests who allow illegitimate unions or neglect the baptism of the sick perhaps does more than any of the evidence so far discussed to show what was at issue in Ine's ordinance. While the clause is not concerned with the baptism of infants *per se,* it attests to the same concerns about the shoddiness of pastoral care that probably, given its setting and context within the laws, underlie *Ine* 2. In any case, given that exhortations to baptize infants promptly figure as well in the legislation and homiletic prose of Wulfstan, it seems difficult to accept the view of Stenton and others that the matter necessarily surfaces in *Ine* due to the newness of Christianity within the West-Saxon kingdom. An explanation more reflective of what we know about the condition of Wessex, where Christianity in one form or another seems to have been present since before the *adventus Saxonum,* might hold that this clause reflects Ine's efforts to discipline the secular clergy and thereby aid the work of bishops.[39] Given that Bede often bemoaned the inadequacy of pastoral care in Wessex, these concerns seem anything but out of place.

---

[37] "[A]nd we biddað and beodað, þæt ælc cild sy binnan þrittigum nihtum gefullad; gif hit þonne dead weorðe butan fulluhte, and hit on preoste gelang sy, þonne ðolige he his hades and dædbete georne; gif hit þonne þurh maga gemeleaste gewyrðe, þonne þolig ese, ðe hit on gelang sy, ælcere eardwunungе on wræcnige of eared oððon on eared swiðe deope gebete, swa bisceop him tæce," "In addition, we entreat and enjoin that every child is to be baptized within thirty nights; if it then happens to die without being baptized, and if it is because of the priest, then he is to forfeit his order and repent fervently. If it is because of a neglectful relative, then the person responsible is to forfeit all his property and depart from the realm, or deeply repent within the realm as the bishop directs." For the Old English, see *Wulfstan: Sammlung der ihm zugeschriebenen Homilien nebst Untersuchungen über ihre Echtheit* (Berlin: Weidmannsche Buchhandlung, 1883), 120; trans. in Andrew Rabin, *The Political Writings of Archbishop Wulfstan of York* (Manchester: Manchester University Press, 2015), 169, where it is also noted (168) that the homily is conventionally assigned a date of around 1020.

[38] The severe penalty imposed upon the relative, which, as we have seen, has no counterpart in the *Poenitentiale Theodori,* seems paralleled in other Wulfstanian legislation imposing exile upon those guilty of apostasy (cf. *II Cn.* 4.1). The penalty thus probably reflects the circumstances of the early eleventh century, in which Wulfstan had to contend with an expanding pagan population of Norse descent. Wulfstan's interest in placing bishops in control of penance is argued for in Jurasinski, "Wulfstan, Episcopal Authority, and the *Handbook for the Use of a Confessor,*" in *Old English Philology: Studies in Honour of R.D. Fulk,* eds. Leonard Neidorf, Rafael J. Pascual, and Tom Shippey (Woodbridge: Boydell, 2016), 215-32.

[39] See n. 47.

Also held symptomatic of recent conversion are Ine's and Wihtræd's laws prescribing legal advantages for *huslgengum,* literally, "those who receive the Host." Here as well, doubts may be raised as to whether this is the best explanation; but first, the clauses themselves deserve a closer look. *Ine* 15 asserts that communicants accused of having taken part in a raiding party need summon only half as many compurgators as non-communicants.[40] Chapter 19 similarly prescribes that the *geneat* of a king with a wergild of 1200 shillings be permitted to swear for sixty hides—i.e., accompanied by men in possession of sixty hides—*gif he bið huslgengea.*[41] Once again, Wihtræd's laws offer a clause potentially revealing the underlying motives of Ine's. *Wihtræd* 23 lays down that, should an accusation be made against a slave, an oath by the slave's lord will suffice to clear him, provided that the lord is a communicant (*gif he huslgenga sie*); should he not be, his oath may not be made without an oath-helper.[42]

That the twelfth-century translation known as *Quadripartitus* struggled in vain to make sense of Ine's laws regarding the *huslgenga* was, to Liebermann, evidence that the latter articulates what was by the time of the Conquest a "long-vanished privilege" (*längst erstorbene Vorrecht*).[43] Having seen a happy analogue to *Ine*'s provisions in later Danish law prohibiting the oath to litigants who suffered under bad reputations, Liebermann doubted that the term should be received literally: "Perhaps the term *huslgenga* is not to be understood according to the meaning of its constituents, but instead means, as do *huslbearn* and *huslwer* [in *Guthlac A*], simply 'wholly devout, superb in piety.'"[44] The great editor's figurative interpretation of this term did not exactly catch fire in the years that followed. More representative of prevailing views is Stenton's assertion that

---

[40] "LVIIII. Se ðe hereteama betygen sie, he hine be his wergilde áliese oððe he his were geswicne. Se að sceal bion healf be huslgengum," "He who is accused of taking part in a raid by a troop [of thieves]: let him redeem himself with his *wergild* or clear himself by [an oath equal to] his *wergild.* The oath shall be half for a communicant." Liebermann, *Gesetze,* I: 96 [MS E]; transl. Oliver and Jurasinski.

[41] "LXIII. Cyninges geneat, gif his wer bið twelfhund scill., he mot swerian for syxtig hida, gif he bið huslgengea." The usage is perplexing here; the sense must be, as is maintained in Dorothy Whitelock, *EHD,* 366 n.1, that one is to produce oath-helpers possessing between them the amounts of property prescribed in this legislation.

[42] Oliver, *Beginnings,* 160.

[43] Liebermann, *Gesetze,* II, s.v. *abendmahlsfähige* (263).

[44] "Vielleicht ist der Ausdruck *huslgenga* nicht nach der wörtlichen Bed[eutung] seiner Komponenten zu verstehn, sondern heisst, wie *huslbearn, huslwer* [in *Guthlac* A], nur noch 'volkommen religiös, ausgezeichnet fromm'": see Liebermann, *Gesetze,* II: 263 s.v. *abendmahlsfähige.* Liebermann's views are given fully in "Die Eideshufen bei den Angelsachsen," in *Historische Aufsätze: Karl Zeumer zum sechzigsten Geburtstag als Festgabe dargebracht von Freunden und Schülern,* ed. Mario Krammer (Berlin: Hermann Böhlaus Nachfolger, 1910), 1-8, at 5. It should be noted that Liebermann's proposed gloss of *hūsulbearn* and *hūsulwer[as],* both *hapax legomena* occurring in *Guthlac A* at ll. 559 and 796, respectively, is not repeated in Jane Roberts, *The Guthlac Poems of the Exeter Book* (Oxford: Clarendon, 1979), where both are glossed "communicant." I am unable to see on what basis Liebermann arrived at his sense of these words.

Ine's "assignment of more than ordinary value to the oath of a communicant" reflects a "definite purpose of advancing Christianity" manifest in his laws.[45] And here matters have stood, with Thomas Pollock Oakley's suggestion that "special oath-privileges for communicants" might have something to do with penitential practice, a claim made without evidence or elaboration, never being accepted or rejected outright.[46]

A third alternative has yet to be considered.[47] Not too far removed in time from Ine's accession are the events related in Gregory of Tours's *Historia Francorum* concerning how one Count Eulalius released himself from a suspicion of matricide. We are told that once the accusation reached the ears of Cautinus, then bishop of Clermont (d. 571), he withheld the Host, provoking the following scene:[48]

> On the feast of Saint Julian, the blessed martyr, when his flock assembled before their Bishop, Eulalius threw himself at the feet of Cautinus and complained that he had been excluded from communion without a proper hearing (*quaerens se inauditum a communione remotum*). The bishop gave him permission to remain in the congregation and to attend the Mass. When the moment came for Eulalius to receive communion and he went up to the altar, Cautinus said to him: "It is common talk among the people that you killed your own mother. I do not know whether you really committed this crime. I therefore leave it to God and to the blessed martyr Julian to judge this matter (*in Dei hoc et beati martiris Iuliani statuo iudicium*). If you really are innocent, as you maintain, draw near, take your portion of the consecrated bread and place it in your mouth (*sume tibi eucharistiae particulum atque inpone in ore tuo*). God will be looking into the deepest confines of your heart." Eulalius took the consecrated bread, communicated and went his way.

Gregory says nothing more about the episode, which seems to have been regarded as furnishing sufficient proof of Eulalius's innocence and, from the way it is narrated, was not an extraordinary measure. Nor was it some archaism or peculiarity of the church in Gaul, as Regino of Prüm's chronicle narrates for the year 869 such an ordeal

---

45 Stenton, *Anglo-Saxon England*, 71. See also Whitelock, *EHD*, where the ordinances are held to "reveal an attempt to encourage men to become full members of the Church by allowing greater weight to the oath of a communicant" (362).

46 Thomas Pollock Oakley, *English Penitential Discipline and Anglo-Saxon Law in their Joint Influence* (New York: Columbia University Press, 1923), 145.

47 The difficulty of these proposals becomes clear when one considers the nature of the sacraments in question. While encouraging the baptism of infants seems what one might expect of a kingdom new to Christianity, no king or bishop would encourage laymen, particularly under the unsettled circumstances of conversion, to proceed to the sacrament of the altar for its own sake given the danger inherent in unworthy reception.

48 Bruno Krusch, and Wilhelm Levison, eds., *Gregorii episcopi Turonensis libri Historiarum X*, MGH SS rer. Merov. 1,1 (Hannover: Hahnsche Buchhandlung, 1951), 489 (X.8); transl. Lewis Thorpe, *The History of the Franks* (London: Penguin, 1974), 554. See also Henry Charles Lea, *Superstition and Force* (Philadelphia: H.C. Lea, 1878), 307.

administered by Pope Adrian II to Lothair and his entourage, this time to prove the king's abstention from marital irregularities.[49]

Among the first to draw attention to these episodes in connection with the oath was Henry Charles Lea, who notes that the form of proof attested in both "was usually, however, a sacerdotal form of purgation, as is shown by the Anglo-Saxon laws."[50] Lea makes no reference to the laws of Ine and Wihtræd in connection with the "Eucharistic ordeal," nor have subsequent commentators. But it is fair to say that the episode concerning Eulalius, and several others like it, might bring us closer to understanding *Ine*'s and *Wihtræd*'s provisions than further speculation about their being meant to draw a population freshly converted toward full participation in the sacraments. Such motives seem improbable for the kingdom of Kent given the presence within it of England's most formidable bishopric. They may be equally improbable for Wessex, as it has been understood for some time that the teaching of the church cannot have been all that new to the *Gewisse* given the presence within the kingdom of a British church much more vital than Bede was willing to acknowledge.[51] We may also err in assuming *huslgenga* to mean something along the lines of "(regular) communicant" given the probable infrequency of lay communion in this period. Could reference instead be made in these clauses to those who approach the altar burdened by an accusation publically made?

The internal logic of such provisions begins to emerge when they are set in context. The often-repeated claim that the laws of Ine and Wihtræd "give [...] special

[49] *Reginonis abbatis Prumiensis Chronicon cum continuatione Treverensi*, ed. F. Kurze, MGH SS rer. Germ. 50 (Hannover: Hahnsche Buchhandlung, 1890), 97.

[50] Lea, *Superstition and Force*, 307-8. See also Bartlett, *Trial By Fire and Water* (Oxford: Clarendon, 1986), 95; reference is presumably to clauses such as *IV Atr.* 22. It is worth noting that the Eucharistic ordeal emerges as a measure to be applied to clergy rather late in the history of pre-Conquest legislation. In Wihtræd's laws (*Wi.*18; *Beginnings Wi.* 14), we are told that "A priest should clear himself with his own truth in his holy vestments before the altar, thus saying: *Ueritatem dico in Christo, non mentior* [cf. Romans 9:1]. A deacon shall clear himself in a similar way" (Oliver, *Beginnings*, 29). (On the background and implications of this ordinance, see Jurasinski, "Safe Swearing: Augustine, Wilfrid, and the Priest's 'Oath' in the laws of Wihtræd," in *Making Sense of the Oath in Late Antiquity and the Earlier Middle Ages*, ed. Stefan Esders, Lukas Bothe, and Gerda Heydemann [in process]). For Wulfstan, Archbishop of York and principal author of most later Anglo-Saxon legislation, this alone would not do. Instead, (*VIII Atr.* 19) the priest "shall say mass, if he dares, and by his own asseveration clear himself by the Holy Communion" (Agnes Jane Robertson, *The Laws of the Kings of England from Edmund to Henry I* [Cambridge: Cambridge University Press, 1925], 123). For the "minister of the altar," the "ordeal of consecrated bread" was available as an alternative to "clear[ing] himself by the Holy Communion" (22) but was the exclusive mode of proof for a kinless man in holy orders (24). The logic of the "ordeal of consecrated bread" was presumably that it avoided potential profanation of the Mass. If the Eucharist was in Wulfstan's view misused as a mode of proof for a "minister of the altar," it is easy to see why such a practice among laypeople might no longer be countenanced.

[51] See Yorke, *Wessex in the Early Middle Ages*, 177.

oath-privileges to a communicant" in blanket fashion is no adequate assessment of the evidence.[52] Twenty-five chapters of Ine's laws—more than any other example of pre-Conquest royal legislation—are concerned with the oath. (Alfred's much longer compilation dedicates only five chapters to the subject, whereas Cnut's laws come second to Ine's with twelve such clauses, many of them derivative.) Yet oath-privileges for communicants are granted in only *two* of the twenty-five instances in which Ine's laws mention the oath. Why were these advantages assigned in some cases and not others? We have seen that, in Ine's laws, "oath-privileges" are limited to persons accused of engaging in raiding and to the *geneat[as]* of the king. They are denied to those proceeding to the oath to refute an accusation of theft (15.2, 46 ["stealing cattle"]), *burgbryce* (45), "making an illicit compact" (52), harboring a fugitive (30) or wishing to assert the lawful slaying of a thief (16, 35); likewise to those who find stolen meat (17) and to traders who possessed stolen property (25.1). A married woman might proceed to the oath herself against a charge of having "tasted ... stolen [meat]" (57), and the owner of a herd of swine might do the same—the oath being equivalent in value to the pigs—should they be found encroaching on another's pasture (49.1).[53] But nowhere is it said or implied that being a communicant would make any difference in how the oath proceeded.

What makes the circumstances of 15 and 19 of Ine's laws different from these? It is fair to say that the clauses just referred to, dealing primarily with theft and its ramifications, involved matters of concern to those at the lowest strata of the early West-Saxon social order: merchants, tenant farmers, and the like. The king's *geneat* was manifestly not a member of this group, both through his association with the king and his wergild of 1200 shillings; nor, I think, were those likely to be accused of involvement in a *here,* given that they (along with the king's *geneat*) are the only persons in this code whose oaths are assessed in units of land, with the implication that they have the capacity to summon as oath-helpers those also possessed of substantial holdings, i.e., their fellow *hlafordas.*[54] It is, therefore, significant that the advantages given to "communicants" are assigned only within the context of *compurgation*—not simply of "oaths."[55]

---

[52] Oakley, *English Penitential Discipline,* 145; also Whitelock, *EHD,* where it is held that Ine's laws "reveal an attempt to encourage men to become full members of the Church by allowing greater weight to the oath of a communicant" (331).

[53] Quotations are from Attenborough's paraphrases of the contents of these chapters in his index (240).

[54] As Yorke notes, members of the West-Saxon nobility "generally own[ed] land of five hides or more" (*Wessex in the Early Middle Ages,* 72).

[55] *Ine* 46, which allows an accused cattle thief to "deny [the charge of] theft by [an oath of] 60 hides" (trans. Attenborough), is only a seeming exception, as the text goes on to add that compurgation is to be allowed him only if he is "oath-worthy" (*aðwyrðe*). The condition of oath-worthiness cannot have been

Wihtræd's ordinance seems in keeping with this principle. Admittedly, the text is corrupt.[56] Yet there is no doubt that the privilege of clearing this person without summoning oath-helpers is granted to the *drihten* ("lord") if he is a communicant (*gif he huslgenga sie*). In both the Kentish and West-Saxon laws, the communicant may invoke his having approached the altar to claim additional advantages should he be, like Eulalius in Gregory's *Historia,* a member of the secular elite. Having received the Host in recent memory—an undertaking that might, as the episode from Gregory of Tours reminds us, assume the aspect of a public spectacle—and not suffered some visible affliction, he was able to invoke the Host as a witness already pledged on his behalf. That such thinking was at work is perhaps hinted at by the language of *Wihtræd*'s ordinance, which reads:[57]

> *Wihtræd* 18: Gif man gedes þeuwne esne in heora gemange tihte, his dryhten hine his ane aþe geclænsie, gif he huslgenga sie. [18.1] Gif he huslgenga nis, *hæbbe him in aþe oðirne æwdan godne*, oþþe gelde, oþþe selle to swinganne.
>
> If a person should bring a charge against an unfree servant of a fellowship(?) in their midst, let his lord clear him by this oath alone, if he [the lord] is a communicant. If he is not a communicant, *he should have for himself in the oath another good oath-helper* [Bosworth-Toller: "witness"], or he should pay recompense, or he should give [his servant] to be flogged. (My emphasis.)

The apparently Kentish term *æwda,* confined only to the laws that survive in *Textus Roffensis,* is here used in such a way as to imply that the Eucharist is itself a kind of "oath-helper" or "witness."[58] The phrase *oðirne æwdan godne* may well be read as "another good witness [in place of the Eucharist]," for were the reference only to the acquisition of an oath-helper in the case, presumably it would have sufficed to say "he will need an oath-helper," or something along those lines.

It is, perhaps, easy to forget that the Eucharist not only might take on the attributes of an ordeal but *was,* for all intents and purposes, an ordeal, its nature as such becoming more perceptible when a communicant received the Host under an accusation.[59]

---

synonymous with participation in the Eucharist given the clauses just quoted; more likely, it restates the condition stipulated in the passage just quoted, i.e., he must have supporters worth sixty hides of land.

[56] In her edition, Oliver glosses *gedes þeuwne esne* as "unfree servant of a fellowship(?)"; her commentary leads one to think that this is as close as one can get to narrowing down the identity of the accused party. Oliver, *Beginnings,* 160-1.

[57] Text and translation are from Oliver, *Beginnings,* 160-1.

[58] That the term is limited to Kentish documents is noted in Angus Cameron, Ashley Crandall Amos, Antonette diPaolo Healey *et al.*, eds., *Dictionary of Old English* (Toronto: Dictionary of Old English Project, 2007), s.v.; see also Joseph Bosworth and T. Northcote Toller, eds., *An Anglo-Saxon Dictionary* (Oxford: Clarendon, 1898).

[59] The most thorough assemblage of such instances is to be found in G.J.C. Snoek, *Medieval Piety from Relics to the Eucharist* (E.J. Brill: Leiden, 1995), ch. 3. It is not hard to see what the Eucharistic ordeal owes

As ordeals and oaths are functionally identical, such evidence cannot be overlooked when considering Ine's laws concerning *huslgengum.* The associations of the Eucharist with the ordeal perhaps explain why these laws would advantage specifically litigants whose alleged offenses could be cleared only by compurgation, as the ordeal was the conventional alternative to the oath.[60]

A few words may be said in conclusion. Of the two texts, Ine's represents the only example of authentically royal law as it would develop particularly during and after the reign of Alfred. Wihtraed's laws appear to represent little more than the proceedings of an episcopal council. Of the two, it would be Ine's that would point the way toward the persona assumed by Alfred in particular at the outset of his laws, claiming as it did the business of issuing laws as the special prerogative of the king. And it is the ambition of Ine's laws that makes them least resemble those of his neighbors to the east, however much these two early legal traditions, given their shared historical circumstances, may have sounded similar notes.

to St. Paul's prescriptions to the Corinthian church regarding the proper use of the sacrament: see I Corinthians 11:17-33. It should be said that clergy even in the earlier Middle Ages were perfectly capable of seeing the problems inherent in such a use of the Eucharist; see Snoek, *Medieval Piety,* 157.

[60] See, e.g., Bartlett, *Trial By Fire,* 27. It should be noted that Lisi Oliver's examination of *Ine*, customarily held to be the earliest English code to mention the ordeal, raised doubts about this view. Her thoughts will be found in the interpretive commentary of Ine's laws and are taken up also in ch. 3 of *From Ine to Alfred the Great.*

Northumbrian Law before the Vikings: A Preliminary Assessment of the Evidence

Kristen Carella

Introduction

When reconstructing the past from a fragmentary record, historians all too frequently underemphasize even the most obvious gaps. Naturally, we focus on positive evidence, those pieces of the puzzle immediately before us; and, over time, we tend to forget about what lies beyond our gaze. Although we usually acknowledge, when pressed, that lacunae exist, we build our models from the existing remains as best we can, often without a full or proper account for what we do not know. Such models, such conceptualizations of the past, once blessed by peer review and a generation or more of acceptance among specialists, acquire a hefty inertia. Over time, students of a given historical period tend to forget that any gaps exist at all; and attempts to fill them become increasingly few and far between. This methodological failing describes the current state of affairs in Anglo-Saxon legal studies, particularly concerning the early period, that is, before c. 900. While the surviving evidence has been mined in detail, there has been an endemic lack of consideration for what lies outside the established canon of written law from this period, as it is currently imagined.

Before c.900—the period I am concerned with in this study—only a handful of Anglo-Saxon law codes survive due, at least in part, to the destruction of archives resulting from the viking invasions that for centuries wreaked havoc throughout Anglo-Saxon England, but most disastrously in the North.[1] Specifically, three codes remain from Kent,[2] and two from Wessex.[3] Based on this scanty record (alongside an even smaller corpus of narrative evidence culled from writers such as Bede and Alcuin, and other types

---

[1] For the sake of this study, I am limiting myself to a consideration of law codes proper, not other kinds of legal materials such as charters, narrative sources, the (mostly fragmentary) synodal *acta*, etc., that also contribute to a fuller understanding of the historical record. Certainly, a fuller examination of the period would need to include these other kinds of documents as well.

[2] I.e., the laws of Æðelberht (r. 560-616), Hlothhhere and Eadric (r. 674/5-85), and Wihtræd (r. 691/2-725) respectively.

[3] I.e., King Alfred (r. 871-899) and his predecessor Ine (r. 688-726). The latter is preserved only as an appendix to King Alfred's laws.

of legal documents, such as charters), scholars have reconstructed the legal tradition of early Anglo-Saxon England, including a sense of its development over time. Painting in the broadest strokes, most specialists would agree that the following, very general statements describe the early English legal traditon: (1) Anglo-Saxon law emerged as a written phenomenon in Kent sometime in the late fifth or early sixth century. (2) Unsurprisingly, these early documents bear a remarkable degree of similarity, even to the extent of cognate legal vocabulary, to the codes of other, closely related Germanic-speaking cultures on the European Continent, above all those (somewhat later) laws which emanated from Frisia. (3) Unlike their Continental analogues during the same time period, the Anglo-Saxons recorded their laws in the vernacular, a quality they shared, among the contemporary cultures of European Christendom, with no-one save the Irish. Elsewhere during this period in the early medieval Northwest, others recorded their laws in Latin. (4) Despite some notable ecclesiastical content—most apparent in the Laws of Wihtræd and the Prologue to the Laws of Alfred, where it predominates—these laws tend to focus on secular concerns, and (5) they appear to have been promulgated primarily by kings to whose name they are attached, and upon whose authority they seem to depend, at least in part. This is merely a thumbnail sketch of the early Anglo-Saxon legal tradition. I do not intend this description to be definitive; only to describe the current historical understanding of Anglo-Saxon law before c.900 very generally.

Let us now consider the gaps in the evidence for this roughly three-hundred-year period of legal activity to which the abovementioned five witnesses bear testimony, and with which historians have built the current model of early Anglo-Saxon law. We have no codes to provide a textual record of jurisprudence during most of the eighth and ninth centuries, that is, at least from the death of Wihtræd (d. 726) and Ine (d. 725) to the beginning of King Alfred's reign (871). What is more, all of these documents emanate solely from two kingdoms south of the Humber—Kent and Wessex—the one Jutish, the other Saxon. No Anglian laws survive; nor for that matter, do we possess any legal documents that originated in the North of England. Thus, what we have can, at best, be described as patchwork coverage of this period, with a gaping hole of more than a hundred and forty-five undocumented years situated squarely in the middle. It would be an understatement to characterize this record as incomplete. Now, to be sure, there is evidence to suggest that more legislation existed; possibly a great deal more. A few examples will suffice. Among the early Kentish kings, for example, Bede mentioned some kind of legislation, possibly a written law code, attributed to Earconberht (r. 640-664)[4] that does not survive. Likewise, in the prologue to his own laws, King Alfred mentioned a code attributed to the Mercian King Offa (r. 757-796), among those

[4] Bertram Colgrave and R.A.B. Mynors, eds., *Bede's Ecclesiastical History of the English People* (Oxford: Oxford University Press, 1969), III.8.

which had influenced him and from which he drew content.[5] Also, in his *Carmina I*, Alcuin described the Northumbrian King Oswiu (r. 642-670) as one renowned for just laws, though no trace of them remains, if indeed they were ever set to vellum. This short list includes references to jurisprudence in Mercia and Northumbria, Anglian kingdoms from which no currently identified Anglo-Saxon law codes survive during this period.

Given this understanding of early Anglo-Saxon law and the sparse record that bears witness to it, questions necessarily arise; among them: how similar were Offa's and Oswiu's laws to those we know from Wessex and Kent? Were they written down? If so, should we understand them as part of the same legal tradition that began with Æðelberht's code? To what degree? Or, more generally, did all (or most) Anglo-Saxon kings issue laws, or only especially prominent kings? Could other kinds of magnates—ecclesiastical figures for example—issue laws as well? Are the five codes that survive typical or exceptional? Were there mutual influences between laws issued by various kings across the whole of Anglo-Saxon England? What foreign influences, if any, are detectable? More sweepingly, how and to what extent would these lost pieces of the puzzle affect our understanding of early Anglo-Saxon legal history were even a tiny subset of such evidence to emerge? In other words, do the surviving witnesses provide a fairly representative sense of what Anglo-Saxon law was like throughout its various regions, or did it differ (to a greater or lesser extent) from kingdom to kingdom? These are just a few of the questions one might ask. I raise them here not with the intent of answering them all (or any them, for that matter), but rather only to point out just how poorly attested Anglo-Saxon lawgiving is before 900, how little we know about it, and how significant the identified "unknowns" are that obscure our current understanding of this period. At the very least, our limited knowledge of early Anglo-Saxon jurisprudence renders it as likely as not that our conceptualization of it is profoundly incomplete, skewed to emphasize southern material, and based on exceptional—rather than typical—witnesses. In sum, there is a good chance that the model we have of early Anglo-Saxon law would require substantial revision if we had access to more evidence, even a very small amount of it, especially if it bore witness to the laws of a different region of Anglo-Saxon England than those two from which witnesses survive.

---

[5] Section 49, 9 of the Prologue to the Laws of King Alfred Felix, in Liebermann, *Gesetze*, I: 46-7. Working from King Alfred's reference, Patrick Wormald went so far as to identify the *Legatine Capitulary* as King Offa's lost law code: "In Search of King Offa's Lost 'Law Code,'" *People and Places in Northern Europe, 500-600: Essays in Honour of Peter Sawyer*, ed. Neils Lund and Ian Wood (Woodbridge: Boydell, 1991), 25-45; revised in Patrick Wormald, *Legal Culture in the Early Medieval West* (London: Hambledon, 1999), 201-23. While Wormald's discussion moves the discussion of this text forward in important ways, I do not believe this identification to be correct. See, for example, my arguments in "Alcuin and the Legatine Capitulary of 786: The Evidence of Scriptural Citations," *Journal of Medieval Latin* 22 (2012): 221-56, and "The Earliest Legal Expression for Outlawry in Anglo-Saxon Law," *Traditio* 70 (2015), 111-44.

Given these concerns, it seems necessary to ask whether it is possible to fill any of these gaps in our knowledge of early Anglo-Saxon law? The answer, I would argue, is yes, at least in the case of early Northumbria; not by the discovery of new documents (though that would be welcome indeed), but rather by reconsidering the significance of two witnesses to the historical record, namely, the *Dialogue of Ecgberht* and the *Legatine Capitulary of 786*—the importance of which, I propose, has not been fully appreciated. As such, then, my purpose is not to introduce new evidence, but rather to propose that we reconsider existing evidence in a new light.

Little work has been done on these texts, especially when compared with the relatively large body of scholarship on the five abovementioned codes. Neither has been translated in full recently,[6] nor are they typically included in collections of Anglo-Saxon law.[7] As a result, these documents have receded into an undeserved obscurity. Yet, despite their predominantly ecclesiastical character, each one deals to a significant degree with matters of secular law, both directly and indirectly. Indeed, their intersections with worldly affairs suggest that it may be possible to distill a sense of what early Northumbrian law was like by conducting a close study of these two documents. While that task cannot be fully carried out in the present article, in what follows, I aim to demonstrate their value as a means to recover, to a degree at least, both the nature and some of the details of early Northumbrian law.

Historical Background

Despite their value as evidence of legal practices distinct from those of Kent and Wessex, neither the *Dialogue of Ecgberht* nor the *Legatine Capitulary* have benefited from

[6] Both the *Dialogue of Ecgberht* and the *Legatine Capitulary of 786* have been translated in their (virtual) entirety by John Johnson in his mid-eighteenth-century *Collection of the Laws and Canons of the Church of England from its First Foundations to the Conquest* (Oxford: J. H. Parker, 1720), 159-80 and 266-85, though Johnson standardized his translations of the many non-standard scriptural passages cited in the *Legatine Capitulary*, which can be quite misleading. Selections from the *Dialogue of Ecgberht* have also been translated in John T. McNeill and Helena Gamer, *Medieval Handbooks of Penance* (New York: Columbia University Press, 1938), 239-42, and several short excerpts from the *Legatine Capitulary* appear in Whitelock, *EHD*, no. 191, 836-40.

[7] Where the *Dialogue of Ecgbert* and the *Legatine Capitulary of 786* are anthologized, they are invariably categorized as ecclesiastical documents; not as "law" more generally. Thus, while a law code dealing predominantly with matters of ecclesiastical concerns, such as the Law of Wihtræd, is anthologized in major collections and translations of Anglo-Saxon Law, notably Liebermann, *Gesetze*, I: 9-14 and F. L. Attenborough, ed. and trans., *The Laws of the Earliest English Kings* (Cambridge: Cambridge University Press, 1922), 24-31, both the *Dialogue of Ecgberht* and the *Legatine Capitulary of 786* are excluded, despite their treatment of secular affairs.

the same degree of scholarly interest as their southern counterparts. As a result, they remain largely unfamiliar even to those historians who specialize in early English legal culture. The *Dialogue of Ecgberht*,[8] known more fully by its title in the sole surviving, complete version of the text, *Succinctus dialogus ecclesiasticae institutionis* (which will be referred to for convenience hereafter as the *Dialogus*) is a relatively short treatise presented in question-and-answer format. It consists of sixteen sections that address legal matters pertinent chiefly to members of the clergy and certain secular elements of society with whom they interacted. It is the only authentic document of several otherwise spurious works attributed to Ecgberht, Archbishop of York (d. 766), including a penitential, a pontifical, and a series of excerpts from canon law. Ecgberht likely composed the *Dialogus* sometime after the middle of his reign as Archbishop, probably after 747, though no more reliably than "the middle of the eight century." [9] Martin J. Ryan, who conducted the most recent study of the text (upon which I have relied substantially in the present article),[10] rightly emphasized the importance of the *Dialogus* for Northumbrian—and Anglo-Saxon—society during this period. He points out that the *Dialogus*

> [...] is precious evidence for the Northumbrian church—and, indeed, for Northumbrian society as a whole—in the eighth century. Moreover, the *Dialogus* sheds significant light on aspects of the relationship between the church and the secular world that are not dealt with by other texts from elsewhere in Anglo-Saxon England in this period. In comparison with texts produced by the south-Humbrian church in the eighth and early ninth century the specific subject matter of the *Dialogus* is in many ways distinctive.[11]

Similarly, Barbara Yorke noted the significance of this text for Northern history, especially given the loss of evidence due to the destruction of monastic archives during the Viking invasions:

> The high cultural profile of the early Northumbrian church means that Northumbria has the fullest range of ecclesiastical sources surviving of any early Anglo-Saxon kingdom. Such sources include hagiographies, histories of individual monastic communities and works of ecclesiastical legislation such as the Penitential and *Dialogus Ecclesiasticae Institutionis* of Archbishop Egbert of York (734-66). Many of these sources survive because,

[8] The standard edition, which I use here, is *Councils and Ecclesiastical Documents Relating to Great Britain and Ireland*, ed. Arthur West Haddan and William Stubbs, 3 vols. (Oxford: Clarendon Press, 1869-78) III, 403-13. This is edition is based on the only complete copy, preserved in London, British Library, Cotton Vitellius A. xii. Fragments also occur in Cambridge, Corpus Christi College 265 and Oxford, Bodleian Library, Barlow 37. A new edition is sorely needed, and I am working on one presently.
[9] Martin J. Ryan, "Archbishop Ecgberht and his *Dialogus*," *Leaders of the Anglo-Saxon Church, From Bede to Stigand*, ed. Alexander R. Rumble (Woodbridge: Boydell and Brewer, 2012), 57. See also 44-6.
[10] For a full account of the scant scholarship on Archbishop Ecgberht and the *Dialogus*, see Ryan.
[11] Ryan, 53.

> thanks to the work of Northumbrian missionaries, they found a safe haven in Continental religious houses; for the Viking raids and subsequent settlements have meant the loss of most of the monastic archives of the pre-Viking Northumbrian church.[12]

Here, Yorke describes the *Dialogus* as a work of "ecclesiastical legislation," albeit with little fanfare, and without indicating that, as such, it is the only thing of its kind from this place and time. Indeed, Ecgberht's *Dialogus* is a document rarely studied—or read, or written about, for that matter—by Anglo-Saxonists (or anyone else). Not only has the *Dialogus* been underappreciated, I would argue, but—even where it has attracted notice—its significance has not been fully recognized. Not only does this text warrant more attention, but we must also grant it a more prominent place within Anglo-Saxon legal history than it has enjoyed so far.

The *Legatine Capitulary of 786* is similarly unknown.[13] The *Legatine Capitulary*, as its name suggests, is a collection of twenty *capitula* produced by a legation dispatched by pope Hadrian for the purpose of correcting various abuses of law and morality within Anglo-Saxon society, both lay and ecclesiastical. It survives in a single manuscript witness and an early modern edition.[14] Like the *Dialogus*, it is generally regarded as authentic. The legation proper consisted of three individuals, namely, Bishop George of Ostia, its leader; Theophylact of Todi, a former head of the papal library and an experienced diplomat like George; and a Frankish abbot named Wigbod. Significantly, the *Legatine Capitulary* does not address those matters which the Pope sent the legation to root out; no list of these abuses, nor their remedies, has been preserved. On the

---

12 Barbara Yorke, *Kings and Kingdoms of Anglo-Saxon England* (London: Routledge, 1990), 73-4.

13 *Alcuini Epistolae*, ed. Ernst Dummler, MGH Epp. IV (Berlin, 1895), 1-493. The Legatine Capitulary is included as epistle 3, 19-29.

14 See especially Cubitt, *Anglo-Saxon Church Councils*, 270-1, and Joanna Story, *Carolingian Connections: Anglo-Saxon England and Carolingian Francia, c. 750-870* (Farnham: Ashgate, 2009), 58, n. 12. Wolfenbüttel, Herzog August Bibliothek, Cod. Guelf. 454, Helmst., fols. 113v-27v preserves the Legatine Capitulary in two fragments, the first part from the beginning to the middle of *capitulum* VI, and the second from the middle of *capitulum* XX to the end. I have examined the manuscript *in situ*, and can determine no convincing reason why the middle portion of the text was cut out. The entire text, however, was reproduced in full by the Magdeburg Centuriators in *Ecclesiastica Historica*, 13 vols. (Basel,1561-1574), at centuries 8-9, 575-81. D.A. Bullough, citing an unpublished lecture of H.J. Schuffels, pointed out that the manuscript came from Hildesheim, dating from about 1000: "Albinus deliciosus Caroli Regis," in *Institutionen, Kultur und Gesellschaft im Mittelalter: Festschrift fur Josef Fleckenstein zu seinem 65. Geburtstag*, ed. Lutz Fenske, Werner Rosener, and Thomas Zotz (Sigmaringen, 1984), 73-92, at 80, note 24. The standard edition of the text is Ernst Dümmler's (based on the manuscript fragments and the edition by the Magdeburg Centuriators), included among Alcuin's letters as Epistola 3 (MGH Epp. IV, Alcuini ep. 3, 19-29). As Wormald, *Legal Culture*, 205, note 11, pointed out, the text edited by Haddan and Stubbs in *Councils and Ecclesiastical Documents* vol. 3, 447-61, was reprinted solely from the text of the Magdeburg Centuriators despite Hermann Wasserschleben's discovery of the Wolfenbüttel manuscript, and is therefore inferior to Dummler's text.

contrary, these *capitula* address matters brought to the legation's attention after they split up and spread out over Britain, specifically when one leg of it arrived in Northumbria. There, as the epistolary introduction to the *capitula* relates, the legation was made aware of certain sinful practices requiring their attention, above and beyond those they had been sent to correct. So, it is explained in the text, they wrote a capitulary legislating against these vices. At the same juncture in Northumbria, two individuals—Alcuin and another Anglo-Saxon named Pyttel—joined the mission in a role described as *lectores*. It is not clear whether their arrival was an official, planned part of the mission, or a spontaneous event decided as a matter of expedience. Whatever the case, these *capitula* were read aloud in Latin and the vernacular, before a council of Northumbrian magnates both lay and ecclesiastical, all of whom signed and promised to obey. A second such council was convened in Mercia soon after, attended by King Offa and Archbishop Iænberht of Canterbury, which followed the same procedure. The resulting document, which survives only in Latin, is the so-called *Legatine Capitulary of 786*.

Alcuin's role in drafting the *Legatine Capitulary* has been a matter of some dispute.[15] To what extent, if any, did he exert influence on the content of these *capitula*? He was, after all, a native Northumbrian, who frequently expressed concern for his native people throughout his life. Did he author them? Did he work closely with other members of the legation? Was the *Legatine Capitulary* based on a draft originally composed by Alcuin? These questions, I posit, have been settled in a recent article I wrote demonstrating that the copious scriptural quotations in the *Legatine Capitulary* correspond closely and, at times, distinctively in form, grammar, and vocabulary to parallel quotations of the same verses found elsewhere in the corpus of Alcuin's writings. The evidence suggests that Alcuin either authored the document himself, or worked closely with whomever did, in a manner that substantially influenced the content of the text.

The significance of this conclusion goes beyond merely identifying the text's author when it is considered in light of Joanna Story's observations about the formal characteristics of the document. In particular, Story noted the *Legatine Capitulary*'s apparent adherence to protocol typical of Anglo-Saxon charters, and thus, of indigenous Anglo-Saxon legal procedures:

> The combined evidence of the ritual process of confirmation (the signing of the crosses, the oral pronouncement of the decrees, the oral agreement of the assembled counsellors to uphold the decrees, the *Regnante* invocation, and the list of attestations at the end of the letter) all support the suggestion that the Mercian and Northumbrian noblemen would have identified the written document which they were being asked to attest with a charter-style legal document [...] The legate's report is not a charter in the sense of a record of land transfer or a grant of privilege, and its charter-like affinities are closest to

---

[15] For a full discussion of this question, see my "Alcuin and the Legatine Capitulary of 786."

> Mercian charters of Offa's reign, yet this was a document originally composed in Northumbria and, as it stands, the closest surviving thing to a formal, secular legal document from pre-Viking Northumbria.[16]

Story, however, made this claim while skeptical of Alcuin's influence on the document. Given my later evidence that Alcuin, at the very least, collaborated formatively in drafting these *capitula*—if indeed he did not author them outright—it is possible to go a great deal farther. Once we acknowledge that the *Legatine Capitulary* not only exhibits the formal characteristics of other contemporary Anglo-Saxon legal documents, but also was composed by a native Northumbrian intimately familiar with indigenous procedure and legislating for his own people, we can reasonably posit that it is, for all intents and purposes, Northumbrian law.

These observations have important implications for our understanding of Anglo-Saxon legal history. Both the *Dialogus* and the *Legatine Capitulary* should most properly be regarded as eighth-century witnesses to Northumbrian law. Taken as such, these documents provide evidence from a region (Northumbria) and subculture (Anglian) heretofore unattested in the English legal tradition, and thereby allows for some coverage of the aforementioned gap in the legal record, that is, from the end of the first quarter of the eighth century to the last third of the ninth.

THE VALUE OF THE *DIALOGUS* AND THE *LEGATINE CAPITULARY* AS EVIDENCE OF NORTHUMBRIAN LEGAL HISTORY

It remains to assess the value of these two documents as witnesses to Northumbrian legal history. Given the constraints of space and word count, however, the discussion must necessarily be limited to only one example from each document, starting with the *Dialogus*. By all appearances, this document preserves minute details of Northumbrian legal practices which, given the technical nature of the legal issues it addresses and the high level of detail perceptible in the discussion, would seem to have been firmly grounded in Northumbrian legal thought. One example will suffice. Consider *interrogatio* XII, for instance:

> XII. Interrogatio
> Quod si quis ex laicis clericum vel monachum occiderit, utrum precium sanguinis, secundum legem natalium parentum, propinquis eius reddendum sit, an ampliori pecunia senioribus suis satisfaciendum sit, Vestra Unanimitas sanciat?[17]

---

[16] Story, *Carolingian Connections*, 77 and n. 65

[17] The text is from Haddan and West, *Councils and Ecclesiastical Documents*, vol. 3, 408-9. The translation is my own.

Responsio
Quicunque vero ex laicis occiderit Episcopum, presiterum, vel diaconum, aut monachum, agat poenitentiam secundum gradus poenitentiae constitutos, et reddat pecuniam aecclesiae suae; pro Episcopo secundum universalis consilii, pro presbitero octingentos siclos, pro diacono sexingentos, pro monacho vero quadrigentos argenteos; nisi aut dignitas natalium, vel nobilitas generis majus reposcat precium. Non enim justum est, ut servitium sanctae professionis in meliori gradu perdat quod exterior vita sub laico habitu habuisse jure parentum dinoscitur. Cui vero non est substantia, ut redimat se a perpetranto homicido, regi dimittendus est ad puniendum, ne interfectores servorum Dei se putent impune posse peccare. Haec vero vindicta, quam de homicidiis presbiterorum percensuimus, maneat erga abbates, qui sunt sine ordine; nisi aliquem ex his sinodale collegium altiori consilio aut superiorem aut inferiorem judicaverit.

XII. Question
If someone from the laity has killed a cleric or a monk, should blood money [= wergild], according to the law of his birth parents, be paid to his relatives, or should [the crime] be satisfied with a greater amount of money [paid to] his [ecclesiastical] superiors: What does your Unity sanction?

Answer
Let whoever from the laity who has killed a bishop, priest, deacon, or a monk perform penance according to the established grade of penance, and let him pay a fine to his church; for a bishop, [let him pay a fine] according to the ecumenical council, for a priest 800 shekels, for a deacon 600 shekels, for a monk 400 shekels; [that is], unless either the dignity of [his] birth or the nobility of [his] descent should demand a greater price. For it is not just that the service of a holy profession in a better [ecclesiastical] dignity should erase what he held on the outside in a lay habit, determined by right of parentage. But for the one who does not have the wealth that he should redeem himself from perpetrating homicide: he is to be conveyed to the king for punishment, lest murderers of God's servants should imagine that they are able to commit [such] sins with impunity. Truly, this punishment, which we have discussed concerning homicide, let it pertain to abbots who are without religious orders; unless a synodal college, by most lofty resolution, has pronounced such a one of these men [i.e., abbots who are outside religious order] as either [a cleric of] a superior order or of an inferior order.

Here, one senses an underlying system of jurisprudence that is already well-established. In this example, a certain point of law—the requirement that those who kill clerics must pay a wergild fine determined by the rank of the victim—is put under scrutiny, given special circumstances. In particular, the questioner requests clarification about how the rank of a cleric should be assessed for the purpose of calculating the proper amount of his wergild. That is, should the payment be calculated according to the victim's ecclesiastical rank, or his secular rank? Significantly, neither the questioner nor Ecgberht's answer breaks new legal ground: the questioner only seeks instructions about how to implement the law as it stands, given an ambiguous case. *Prima facie*, this is not the kind of query one would expect from inexperienced jurists wrestling with an inchoate system of jurisprudence. Quite the contrary, this is the kind of clarity-seeking one expects from skillful, informed jurists working with in-depth knowledge of a well-established legal system. Above all, this query implies a preexisting system of law, underlying this particular question about an exceptional case.[18]

Let me turn now to a different kind of example. In *capitulum* XVIIII, the *Legatine Capitulary* describes certain behaviors which the legislator treats not as crimes to be punished explicitly by sanction of any named authority, but instead as sins that he urges the subject to discontinue. I cite *capitulum* XVIIII below:

> XVIIII. Decimun nonum caput. Anneximus, ut unusquisque fidelis christianus a catholicis viris exemplum accipiat; et si quid ex ritu paganorum remansit, avellatur, contemnatur, abiciatur. Deus enim formavit hominem pulchrum in decore et specie; pagani vero diabolico instinctu cicatrices teterrimas superinduxerunt, dicente Prudentio: "Tinxit et innocuam maculis sordentibus humum." Domino enim videtur facere iniuriam, qui creaturam suam foedat et deturpat. Certe si pro Deo aliquis hanc tincturae iniuriam sustineret, magnam inde remuneration acciperet. Sed quisquis ex superstitione gentilium id agit, non ei proficit ad salute; sicut nec Iudaeis circumcisio corporis sine credulitate cordis. Vestimenta etiam vestra non gentilium, quos Deo opitulante patres vestry de orbe armis expulerunt, induitis. Miranda res et nimis stupenda, ut, quorum vitam semper odistis, exempla imitemini. Equos etiam vestros turpi consuetudine detruncatis, nares finditis, aures copulates verum etiam et surdas redditis, caudas amputates; et quia illos inlaesos habere potestis, hoc nolentes, cunctis odibiles redditis. Audivimus etiam, quod, dum inter vos litigium versatur, sortes more gentilium mittitis. Quod omnino sacrilegum istis temporibus reputatur. Equos etiam plerique in vobis comedunt, quod nullus christianorum in orientalibus facit. Quod etiam evitate. Contendite, ut omnia vestra honeste et secundum Dominum fiant.[19]

> XVIIII. The nineteenth chapter: We enjoined that every faithful Christian take an example from catholic men; and if anything remains of pagan customs, let it be plucked out, condemned and rejected. For God created man beautiful in grace and comeliness; but pagans cover themselves all over with shameful scars, on account of diabolical instinct, as Prudentius says: "He moistened the innocent earth with vile stains" [*Diptychon*, I.3]. For it is thought that he insults God, he who sullies and defiles his creation. Certainly, if anyone should undergo this offense of tattooing for God, he would receive a great reward from it. But anyone who does it on account of superstition as do the Gentiles, does not attain salvation for himself, anymore than the Jews do by the circumcision of the body without a believing heart. Also, you wear clothing according to the custom of the Gentiles

[18] Note also Ryan's discussion of question twelve, 55-60.

[19] The text is from MGH *Epistolae* IV, Alcuini ep. 3, pp. 26-7. The translation is my own.

> whom your fathers, with God's help, expelled by force of arms from the world. How wondrous and remarkable indeed that you should imitate the mannerisms of those you have always hated. Also, by shameful custom, you mutilate your horses, you slit their nostrils, you fasten their ears together—and, indeed, you render them deaf—and you cut off their tails. Since you have the ability to keep them unharmed, but do not wish to do so, you render yourselves entirely detestable. We have heard also that when you are engaged in a matter of controversy among yourselves, you cast lots according to the custom of the gentiles, which is entirely considered to be a sacrilege in these times. And many among you also eat horseflesh, which is not done by Christians in the East. Shun that also. Strive, in any case, "*that all your affairs be done decently and according to the Lord*" [I Cor 14.40].

A great deal might be said about this passage. For my purpose here, I wish only to point out how this *capitulum* addresses detailed matters of cultural practice which would appear to come from firsthand observation—tattooing, casting lots, mutilating horses, and eating their flesh—that, at least in the view of the legislator, violate the norms of Christian society, even if they do not in all cases violate Christian law outright. The legislator makes his case by citing patristic authority (Prudentius) and scripture, in a hortatory tone that verges on the homiletic. Neither of these features of the text, the reliance on such authorities nor the homiletic nature of this passage, are common elsewhere in earlier Anglo-Saxon legal tradition. Rather, they find their closest analogues in Insular canon law, such as *Collectio canonum Hibernensis* and in certain, slightly later examples of the Carolingian capitulary tradition, such as the *Admonitio Generalis of 789*. While I cannot discuss these analogues and compare them to the *Legatine Capitulary* within the confines of the current article, suffice it to say that contemporary legislation of this sort occurs in the geographic and cultural vicinity of eighth-century Northumbria, though is not common elsewhere in the Anglo-Saxon legal tradition. While far from securing the case, this observation raises the possibility that Northumbrian legal practices may have been influenced, for example, by Hiberno-Latin and/or emergent Carolingian law and legal methods.

Conclusion

My purpose in the present article has not been to describe Northumbrian law fully. That I plan to attempt in a future, book-length project. Here, far less ambitiously, my goal has been to argue that (1) some of the features—certain general characteristics and, in some cases, specific details—of early Northumbrian secular law are recoverable from ecclesiastical witnesses, and (2) to demonstrate, at least in preliminary fashion, the potential significance of two textual witnesses—the *Dialogue of Ecgberht* and the *Legatine*

Capitulary of 786—for this purpose. Clearly, there is a great deal more work to be done mining these two documents for what they can tell us about Northumbrian law, both in terms of the details of Northumbrian legal practices that can be observed in the documents themselves, as well as those practices which are implied by the texts. So, given what new evidence or, more accurately, what new perspective on old evidence I have discussed here, is it possible at this point to draw any preliminary conclusions about the character of Northurmbrian law?

First of all, given what evidence we have, it may well be that, north of the Humber, law codes could be written in Latin, a phenomenon not witnessed in the South during this period, as suggested by the fact that the *Legatine Capitulary* was read aloud, as we are told in the text, *tam latine quam theodisçe* ("in both Latin and the vernacular [...]").[20] It is worth noting in this vein as well that the two witnesses we have were both composed in Latin. Second, both witnesses suggest that, in the north, law codes could be promulgated by ecclesiastical, as opposed to solely regnal prerogative. That this was not always the case, that is, that kings could also promulgate law, is suggested by Alcuin's laudatory statement about King Oswiu (quoted below). Still, the fact that laws could be attached to the names of clerics (and implemented by ecclesiastical authority) represents a notable distinction from their contemporary southern analogues. Third, although I chose not to make much of this point in my discussion here, the authorities cited in the northern codes—a variety of canon law in the case of the *Dialogus* and the writings of the Church Fathers alongside a copious amount of scripture in the case of the *Legatine Capitulary*—differ from the southern laws and may indicate foreign affinities, possibly from Hiberno-Latin or Carolingian legal methods.

It is important to acknowledge that, while the northern witnesses I have described here—the *Dialogus* and the *Legatine Capitulary*—both bear direct witness to Northumbrian law, they are both also exceptional texts. In the case of the *Dialogus*, one gets the impression that its main purpose is to address exceptions to another, more fundamental expression of law. Generally speaking, it addresses questions regarding how certain, basic concepts of secular law should be applied in an ecclesiastical milieu (as the example discussed above shows), or when there is contact of legal consequence between clerics and seculars. Likewise, although the *Legatine Capitulary* would appear to have been written by a Northumbrian legislating for Northumbrians—the occasion of its composition (the visit of a papal legation) was unique. This fact must inform any analysis of it as a positive witness to Northumbrian law. Finally, we must remember that the two witnesses described here likely existed alongside a more traditional, royally-promulgated corpus of legislation (most likely akin to what we find in the south of

[20] MGH *Epistolae* IV, Alcuini ep. 3, p. 28, ll. 15-16. For a discussion and history of scholarship on this phrase, see Carella, "Alcuin and the Legatine Capitulary," 224 n 13.

England), as is suggested is by narrative sources, such as Alcuin's accolade of King Oswiu in *Versus de patribus, regibus, et sanctis Eboracensis ecclesiae*, which praises Oswiu for his role as a legislator, presumably because Alcuin regarded that particular feature as an especially prominent and important aspect of his royal character:

Legibus ille etiam fuerat iustissimus aequis,
Invictus bellis nec non in pace fidelis,
Donorum largus miseris, pius, omnibus aequus.[21]

He was also very just, with fair laws,
unconquered in war, and also trustworthy in peace,
Forthcoming with gifts to the poor; [He was] benevolent, fair to all.

Unfortunately, none of Oswiu's laws survive to for us to examine. What evidence does remain, as I have begun to discuss in this article, suggests that Northumbrian law —while distinctively Anglo-Saxon, sharing much in common with the southern codes— differed in significant ways, as well. Likely, the foreign intellectual contacts that made York famous as an early center of European learning, emanating both from the Continent and Ireland, played some role in the development of law there. On this point, however, I have moved toward speculation. The next step in unearthing early Northumbrian law and legal practices will be to mine these texts for what details can be deduced and reconstructed from these sources.

[21] Alcuinus, *Carmina*, Monumenta Germaniae Historica, Poetae I, Carmina I, p.182, verse 570, ll. 570-2. The translation is my own.

Crime and Sin in the Laws of Alfred

Nicole Marafioti

This essay begins with a question: how closely were criminal offenses against earthly authorities equated with sinful violations against God, in the laws of Alfred the Great? At first glance, the connection between crime and sin in Alfred's *domboc* appears substantial.[1] The lawcode's lengthy prologue adapts Old Testament regulations for an Anglo-Saxon audience, framing its Old English rendition of biblical law as God's commands to Moses.[2] The decrees that follow, which Alfred claims to have compiled from the codes of his predecessors, include some of the earliest prescriptions for religious confession and penance in Anglo-Saxon legislation.[3] These elements have led scholars to understand Alfred's *domboc* as a vital first step toward the integration of secular and spiritual priorities, which would become a distinguishing feature of royal law in later generations.[4]

Of course, the *domboc* was not the first English law-code to integrate religious regulations with earthly ones, or to govern ecclesiastical matters. Alfred's West Saxon

---

1 I use "crime" and "criminal" in this essay in reference to earthly offences committed in violation of royal law. The appropriateness of these terms in pre-Conquest history has been debated: for an overview, see T.B. Lambert, "Theft, Homicide and Crime in Late Anglo-Saxon Law," *Past and Present* 214 (2012): 3-43.

2 Unless otherwise noted, laws are cited from Liebermann, *Gesetze*. Translations are my own, but I have consulted Dorothy Whitelock, *EHD*; F.L. Attenborough, *Laws of the Earliest English Kings* (Cambridge: Cambridge University Press, 1922). For the prologue, see especially Wormald, *Making*, 418-30; Stefan Jurasinski, "Violence, Penance, and Secular Law in Alfred's Mosaic Prologue," *Haskins Society Journal* 22 (2010): 25-42; B. Carella, "Evidence for Hiberno-Latin Thought in the Prologue to the Laws of Alfred," *Studies in Philology* 108.1 (2011): 1-26; B. Carella, "The Source of the Prologue to the Laws of Alfred," *Peritia* 19 (2005): 91-118; Michael Treschow, "The Prologue to Alfred's Law Code: Instruction in the Spirit of Mercy," *Florilegium* 13 (1994): 79-110.

3 *Af.* Prol.49.9. For penance in the *domboc*, see Allen Frantzen, *Literature of Penance in Anglo-Saxon England* (New Brunswick, NJ: Rutgers University Press, 1983), 124-7; Carole Hough, "Penitential Literature and Secular Law in Anglo-Saxon England," *Anglo-Saxon Studies in Archaeology and History* 11 (2000): 133-41; Catherine Cubitt, "Bishops and Councils in Late Saxon England: The Intersection of Secular and Ecclesiastical Law," in *Recht und Gericht in Kirche und Welt um 900*, ed. Wilfried Hartmann and Annette Grabowsky (Munich: Oldenbourg, 2007), 151-67, at 157-8; but compare below, nn. 6-7. Alfred's adaptation of earlier law has been questioned: Stefan Jurasinski, "Sanctuary, House-Peace, and the Traditionalism of Alfred's Laws," *Journal of Legal History* 31.2 (2010): 129-47, at 130-2; David Pratt, *The Political Thought of King Alfred the Great* (Cambridge: Cambridge University Press, 2007), 218-22.

4 Especially Wormald, *Making*, 429.

predecessor Ine legislated special protections for the Church and clergy, as did earlier kings of Kent.[5] Notably, King Wihtræd's seventh-century lawcode expressed particular interest in Christian principles: sinners were to "take up a righteous life with repentance for their sins" or else suffer material punishment and exclusion from the Church.[6] Lisi Oliver has suggested that such mandates deliberately aligned secular regulation and ecclesiastical priorities, with Wihtræd's laws complementing penitential practices overseen by religious authorities. In her words, "royal and ecclesiastical law operate in concord, the former regulating the fine and the latter the penance. The non-observer is liable for both."[7] The probable motivation for such alignment, as Oliver implied, was to promote Christian principles during a period of religious conversion.[8] Requiring material punishment for violations against God, the Church, and the clergy would pressure all levels of society to conform to Christian standards of behavior.

Two centuries after Wihtræd, Alfred legislated in a different context. His laws do not reflect the problems of a converting populace but concerns faced by a Christian kingdom. The evocation of Old Testament law and the prominence of ecclesiastical matters take for granted that the code's audience was familiar with Christian practice. Notwithstanding these religious elements, however, the *domboc*'s treatment of sin and its remedies is surprisingly muted. When compared with *Wihtræd*'s moralizing prescriptions for personal conduct or later legislators' explicit condemnations of un-Christian behavior, Alfred's laws keep a tight focus on earthly offenses, conflict, and conduct. Accordingly, the present essay will consider how sin operates in the *domboc*. In this analysis, "sin" will be defined as actions, behaviors, or intentions believed to contravene God's will and—if not recognized, atoned for, and redeemed through penance—injure their perpetrator's soul. The following pages consider Alfred's regulation of religious observance, procedures, institutions, and personnel in order to evaluate how individual clauses address the spiritual dimensions of the activities they govern. In so doing, they seek to shed light on how the *domboc* articulated the impact of law-breaking, not just on the wellbeing of the kingdom, but also on the fate of the offender's soul.

---

[5] Wormald, *Making*, 103-6, 278-81.

[6] This is *Wi.* 3, on sexual impropriety: the text is edited in Oliver, *Beginnings*, 154-5, 167-8; and see Lisi Oliver, "Royal and Ecclesiastical Law in Seventh-century Kent," in *Early Medieval Studies in Memory of Patrick Wormald*, ed. Stephen Baxter et al. (Farnham: Ashgate, 2009), 97-112.

[7] Oliver, "Royal and Ecclesiastical," 110, on overlap between *Wihtræd* and the Penitential of Theodore. See also Stefan Jurasinski, *The Old English Penitentials and Anglo-Saxon Law* (Cambridge: Cambridge University Press, 2015), 26-35; Thomas Oakley, *English Penitential Discipline and Anglo-Saxon Law in Their Joint Influence* (New York: Columbia University, 1923), 141-9; Hough, "Penitential Literature," 133-4; Cubitt, "Bishops and Councils," 154-6.

[8] Oliver, *Beginnings*, 167.

Religious Offenses and Remedies in the *Domboc* Proper

In the *domboc* proper, I have identified twenty-one clauses which govern or punish behavior that could be construed as sinful. These clauses fall into two categories: offenses to be compensated with physical or monetary punishment; and offenses which merit spiritual action—confession, penance, or excommunication—as well as secular punishment. The first category is comprised of violations involving the earthly Church: ecclesiastical communities and individual members of the clergy are entitled to compensation for injury, just like their lay counterparts, and they also bear legal responsibility for secular offenses they commit. The second category is comprised of clauses which address a perpetrator's spiritual state alongside his actions: in these cases, ecclesiastical procedures complement secular reconciliation.

Material Compensation

Fourteen *domboc* clauses are concerned with offenses against the earthly Church, to be remedied with material compensation. Three of these involve misbehavior during holidays or Lent. First, a double penalty is required for theft committed on holy days:

> [5.5] Whoever steals on Sunday or Christmas or Easter or Holy Thursday during Rogation Days: we want these each to be compensated double (*twybote*), as during the Lenten fast.

In this clause, it seems that a known principle—double compensation (*twybote*) during Lent—is being applied to other major holidays. This is consistent with ecclesiastical approaches: the penitential attributed to Archbishop Theodore, for instance, prescribes extended penance for violating ecclesiastical rules during Lent.[9] Yet while the penitential prescribes excommunication for repeat offenders, the *domboc* requires no spiritual atonement or punishment for violations during holidays.[10] Despite its concern with religious observance, this clause mandates only material compensation for the material offense of theft. The focus on Lent reappears later in the *domboc*, in regulations on forcible entry (*burgbryce*). After establishing monetary penalties for breaching the property of various social ranks, it is decreed that:

> [40.1] If any of this happens when the army is out, or during the Lenten fast, let it be compensated double (*twybote*).[11]

---

[9] Penitential of Theodore, in Arthur Haddan and William Stubbs, *Councils and Ecclesiastical Documents Relating to Great Britain and Ireland*, vol. III (Oxford: Clarendon Press, 1871, repr. 1964), 186 at I.xi.4 [hereafter *CED*].

[10] Penitential of Theodore, in *CED*, 186 at I.xi.5. See also R.D. Fulk and Stefan Jurasinski, *The Old English Canons of Theodore*, EETS s.s. 25 (Oxford: Oxford University Press, 2012), 3 at A6.

[11] Compare *Af.* 40, below.

Here, the two conditions for double compensation (*twybot*) suggest that the offense has both ecclesiastical and secular implications. The provision on Lent applies the same logic as clause 5.5, with forcible entry added to a series of violations that are punished doubly on holy days. By contrast, the first condition—"when the army is out"—pertains to a variable set of circumstances, not a specific time of year; this might discourage law-breaking in periods of military uncertainty or protect the property of fighters who are away from home. Read in its entirety, though, this clause extends ordinary punishment at moments when forcible entry can do the most harm—whether to individual victims, the kingdom at large, or the perpetrator's own soul. Nevertheless, the spiritual dangers of house-breaking during Lent are not explicitly addressed here and no ecclesiastical reconciliation is prescribed. Instead, the *twybot* is a monetary fine to be rendered to human individuals whose earthly property has been violated. Another secular response to spiritual violation appears in the following clause:

> [40.2] If anyone publicly lays aside holy law (*halig ryht*) in Lent without permission (*butan leaf*), let him compensate with 120 shillings.

This provision seems to replicate the impulse behind *Wihtræd*'s religious regulations: to enforce Christian behavior among a reluctant populace. Yet this clause refers to no specific behaviors that would be problematic during Lent, nor does it threaten spiritual consequences or mandate penance.[12] Instead, the problem is a public refusal to adhere to established religious rules, thereby undermining the authority of the Church. This clause does not mention the state of individual souls; it is concerned only with proper obedience to the precepts of an earthly institution. Although it is likely that the requisite compensation would be paid to clergymen, since it would presumably be their permission that was neglected in violations of holy law, this is clearly a monetary fine to be paid in shillings, not a prescription for atonement.[13] Like clauses requiring double compensation during holidays, where the timing of an offense compounds ordinary punishments, this clause establishes Lent as a period with unique status under royal law.

Violations of clerical protection merit four clauses. Early in the *domboc*, fines are set for violating the surety or protection of high-ranking clergymen:

> [3] If anyone violates the king's surety, let him compensate for the charge as the law directs him, and for the breach of surety with five pounds of pure pennies. The breach of the archbishop's surety (*borges*) or his protection (*mundbyrd*) is to be compensated with three pounds. The breach of the surety or protection of another bishop or ealdorman is to be compensated with two pounds.

---

[12] Above, nn.9-10. Compare for example the 747 Council of Clovesho: *CED*, 367-8, at canons 14, 18.

[13] Monetary commutations of penance are identified as a later phenomenon by Fulk and Jurasinski, *Canons*, xxxviii-xxxix; but compare Oakley, *Penitential Discipline*, 169-74.

Penalties are assigned according to each victim's earthly standing, with the status of archbishops and bishops established in relation to those of kings and ealdormen. Fines determined by rank appear again in two subsequent clauses:

> [15] If anyone fights or draws a weapon in the presence of an archbishop, let him compensate (*gebete*) with 150 shillings; if this happens in the presence of another bishop or an ealdorman, let him compensate (*gebete*) with 100 shillings.[14]
>
> [38.2] If any of this [i.e. fighting or drawing a weapon] should happen in the presence of a representative of the king's ealdorman or in the presence of the king's priest, it is thirty shillings as punishment (*to wite*).[15]

Finally, penalties for forcible entry are established according to the victim's earthly status, with monetary payments due to clergymen interspersed among those for the laity:

> [40] Forcible entry into the king's dwelling (*burgbryce*) shall be 120 shillings; into an archbishop's, ninety shillings; into another bishop's or an ealdorman's, sixty shillings; into that of a man with a twelve-hundred wergild, thirty shillings [...]

Collectively, these clauses confirm the clergy's earthly authority: churchmen enjoy legal rights comparable to those of high-ranking laymen, their property is granted the same protections as that of their secular counterparts, and peace is required in their presence. However, despite their ecclesiastical status, priests and bishops are treated no differently here than laymen. Where penitentials often list offenses against clergy as a separate category of sin, assigning different penances than when the offense is committed against laymen, the *domboc* regulations determine punishments by the victim's comparative rank in earthly society—not by the spiritual prestige of his office.[16] There is no mention of sin or penitential consequences for offenses against the clergy; violations are compensated simply according to their victim's temporal standing.

Violations of *ciricfrið*—legal protections granted to individual churches—also require material compensation. Two clauses concern individuals who flee to churches to escape pursuit.[17] The first explains the consequences if an asylum-seeker is harmed by his pursuers during a three-day period of sanctuary:

> [2.1] If during that time he is afflicted with slaying or binding or wounding, let each of the perpetrators compensate (*bete*) according to just law, both with wergild (*were*) and a

[14] Compare *Af.* 7.

[15] *Af.* 38-38.1 award fines to ealdormen if anyone fights or draws weapons in their presence.

[16] For example, the Old English *Scriftboc* (canons 17.01.01, 17.02.01, 17.04.01,17.07.01, 17.08.01, 17.09.01) and Old English Penitential (canon 44.02.01), edited by Allen Frantzen, *Anglo-Saxon Penitentials: A Cultural Database* (2016), www.anglo-saxon.net/penance/.

[17] *Af.* 2 delineates sanctuary guidelines; below, n.19. See also Jurasinski, "Sanctuary, House-Peace"; Karl Shoemaker, *Sanctuary and Crime in the Middle Ages* (New York: Fordham University Press, 2011), 37-92.

fine (*wite*), and pay the community 120 shillings as compensation (*bote*) for breaking the church-peace, and forfeit his own claim [against the asylum-seeker].

In this scenario, the pursuers' breach of *ciricfrið* invalidates their original case against the asylum-seeker: not only do they forfeit any claim against him, but they must also make restitution for the physical injury they committed and compensate the religious community for violating their protected space. A second clause establishes penalties for anyone who removes an asylum-seeker from a church:

> [5] [...] Let no man drag him out for seven nights if he can live despite hunger, unless he himself fights his way out. If anyone does so, then he is liable for breaking the king's protection (*mundbyrde*) and the church's peace (*cirican friðes*)—more, if he seizes more from there.[18]

Compensation is again required for the breach of *ciricfrið*, but the perpetrator is subject to an additional fine for violating the king's protection. Both *ciricfrið* offenses are construed as violations of earthly privileges that must be compensated with material payments to wronged parties, much like the clauses establishing protections for individual clergymen. Moreover, both clauses present the breach of *ciricfrið* as part of a larger conflict, with one party pursuing another with an intent to cause harm; sanctuary protections were likely designed to give fugitives time to protect themselves or settle with their pursuers, without being apprehended or injured.[19] Although there may have been an expectation that fugitives who fled to churches would confess and repent their sins while in residence, these clauses make no explicit mention of any ecclesiastical process.[20] Instead, they regulate the behavior of the pursuants, rather than the actions of the asylum-seeker himself, prohibiting certain actions within the physical space protected by *ciricfrið*. The prescribed penalties follow a similar logic as the clauses on holidays: just as punishments are compounded when offenses are committed at certain times of the year, penalties for committing injury or violating royal protection are enhanced when these actions occur in certain privileged locations.[21] Yet unlike the holiday clauses, the *ciricfrið* prescriptions identify religious communities as injured parties who deserve compensation. Churches and their clergy may be drawn into private conflicts through

---

18 Additional logistics appear in *Af.* 5.1-2; and see Wormald, *Making*, 272.

19 *Af.* 2; Shoemaker, *Sanctuary*, 80-2.

20 This expectation is discussed by Rob Meens, "Sanctuary, Penance, and Dispute Settlement under Charlemagne: The Conflict Between Alcuin and Theodulf of Orléans over a Sinful Cleric," *Speculum* 82 (2007): 277-300, especially 296-8; Trisha Olson, "Sanctuary and Penitential Rebirth in the Central Middle Ages," in *Boundaries of the Law*, ed. Anthony Musson (Aldershot: Ashgate, 2005), 38-52. Compare also the *Collectio Canonum Hibernensis*: Herrmann Wasserschleben, *Die Irische Kanonensammlung*, 2nd edition (Leipzig: Tauchnitz, 1885), 94-8.

21 *Af.* 5.5 and 40.1, above.

claims of asylum, but the injuries that require compensation according to the *domboc* relate to the violation of protected physical space. As with offenses against individual clergymen, punishments are depicted as recompense to earthly entities for material harm, without mentioning spiritual consequences.[22]

Material penalties also apply in cases where churches are victimized directly. In the *domboc*, stealing from a church is punished more dramatically than ordinary theft:

> [6] If anyone steals anything in a church, let him render onefold payment (*angylde*), and the fine (*wite*) appropriate to that payment, and let the hand with which he did it be chopped off.
>
> [6.1] If he wishes to redeem (*lesan*) the hand, and that is permitted, let him pay according to his wergild.

Once again, the logistics of the offense determine the compounded sentence. This theft is exceptional because it violates ecclesiastical space and protections. Elsewhere in the *domboc*, the fine for stealing is set at 120 shillings; it is only theft from churches that requires amputation.[23] Such severity suggests that this penalty was intended as a deterrent, with the threat of corporal punishment designed to discourage thieves from pursuing ecclesiastical targets. Yet even as it awards churches unique protections under the law, this clause focuses exclusively on their material wellbeing.[24] Legal action is catalyzed by the theft of property, and resolution is achieved by restoring the property and rendering compensation. This is a rather different approach than an ecclesiastical authority might advocate, for penitentials tend to prescribe penalties in both spheres: theft from churches required material compensation—sometimes at multiple times the stolen goods' value—but penance was also prescribed.[25] The *domboc*, by contrast, is concerned only with the mundane aspects of violating sacred space. A separate process of penance may have been expected, but the *domboc* does nothing more than assign material compensation to an injured party.

Procedures are rather different when individual members of the clergy are directly involved in wrongdoing. Clause 21 concerns homicidal priests:

> [21] If a priest kills another man, let him be handed over, and all the possessions that he bought for himself; and let the bishop depose (*onhadige*) him, when he is surrendered out of the minster, unless the lord (*hlaford*) wishes to settle the wergild.

---

22 *Af.* 3, 15, 38.2, and 40, above; and compare *Af.* 42.2.

23 *Af.* 9.9, 16.

24 Compare *Abt.* 1, which requires theft from churches to be compensated twelve-fold.

25 Penitential of Theodore in *CED*, 179-80 at I.iii.2, I.iii.5; Fulk and Jurasinski, *Canons*, 6 and 9, at A35, A69. Compare the Old English Penitential, which considers the thief's status: Frantzen, *Database*, 42.25.01-2, 44.20.01. Compare Pope Gregory's advice on Church theft: Bede, *Ecclesiastical History of the English People*, ed. Bertram Colgrave and R.A.B. Mynors (Oxford: Clarendon Press, 1969), 82-3, at I.27.

Certainly, demotion from the priesthood touches on the man's spiritual status; this very instruction is included in penitential guidelines for homicidal clergy.[26] Yet the *domboc* presents deposition as part of a broader legal process that involves compensation payment and, possibly, additional punishment. Two scenarios are envisioned. In one, the priest's lord pays the compensation on his behalf, thereby resolving the conflict under the law. In the other scenario, the priest and his property are surrendered, presumably to judicial authorities or his victim's kin; if his property is insufficient compensation, the priest might suffer further punishment.[27] The requirement that the offender be stripped of holy orders, however, suggests that priests normally enjoyed a protected status that needed to be reversed, if such punishment was to be legitimate. Demotion is thus a prerequisite for further judicial penalties, not a spiritual punishment in itself.[28] Although there would surely be separate penitential consequences for a homicidal priest, the *domboc* focuses only on resolving temporal conflict.

Abducting a nun merits a similarly secular response:

> [8] If anyone brings a nun out of a nunnery without the king's permission (*lefnesse*) or the bishop's, let him pay 120 shillings: half to the king; half to the bishop and the lord of the church (*cirican hlaforde*) which has the nun.

Even though the abductor evidently leads the nun to break her monastic rule and abandon her spiritual office, this clause treats the offense as a violation of earthly authorities' permission rather than an affront against God.[29] This is generally not the case in penitentials, which may prescribe excommunication for abductors and extensive penance for fornicating nuns.[30] In the *domboc*, the abductor must pay fines to the bishop and king for defying their will, as well as to the patron of the nun's community. No penance or punishment is established for the nun in the immediate aftermath of

---

[26] Penitential of Theodore in *CED*, 184-5 at I.ix.1, I.ix.8; Old English Penitential in Frantzen, *Database*, 42.01.05, 44.01.01-44.01.05; Roger Fowler, "A Late Old English Handbook for the Use of a Confessor," *Anglia* 83.1 (1965): 1-34, at 21.

[27] Compare *Af.* Prol.13, below; Jurasinski, "Sanctuary, House-Peace," 142-4; *EHD*, 412n3. Similar phrasing appears in *Af.* 24.

[28] Deposition does not automatically mean excommunication or damnation: Penitential of Theodore in *CED*, 184, at I.ix.1; Fulk and Jurasinski, *Canons*, 12 and 57, at A105-06.

[29] For abducted and married nuns, see Barbara Yorke, *Nunneries and the Anglo-Saxon Royal Houses* (London: Continuum, 2003), 154-9; and compare *Ine* 1.

[30] Fulk and Jurasinski, *Canons*, 11 at A99; Penitential of Theodore in *CED*, 184, at I.viii.6; *Scriftboc* in Frantzen, *Database*, 01.02.02. Marrying nuns is prohibited in canon law, including a 721 Roman synod appended to the Old English Canons of Theodore: Frantzen, *Database*, 61.01.01-61.03.01; Fulk and Jurasinski, *Canons*, xxiii. See also the 786 Legatine Capitulary: E. Dümmler, *Epistolae Karolini Aevi* II, MGH Epistolae 4 (Berlin: 1895), 25 at ch.15; Patrick Wormald, "In Search of King Offa's 'Law-Code,'" in idem, *Legal Culture in the Early Medieval West* (London: Hambledon, 1999), 201-23, at 215-7.

her abduction. However, the subsequent clauses—which assume that the abduction would lead to a long-term union, with the possibility of children—limits the woman's inheritance rights and wergild privileges:

> [8.1] If she lives longer than the one who led her out [of the nunnery], she shall inherit nothing of his property.
> [8.2] If she has a child, let him have no more of that inheritance than his mother.
> [8.3] If her child is slain, let the share [of wergild] due to the mother's kin be paid to the king; let the share due to the father's kin be given to them.

The various moral transgressions encompassed in the abduction—breaking monastic vows, disobeying a bishop, initiating a sexual relationship—are never addressed directly; instead, these clauses focus exclusively on material consequences. It is noteworthy that these consequences differ for the male and female offenders, as well as for their families. Once compensation is paid, the abductor and his family retain their property rights, without any obligation to surrender an inheritance to the former nun or her child; nevertheless, they may claim a compensatory wergild payment should the child be killed. For the man, the abduction can be redeemed like any other offense and—after the initial fine and compensation have been rendered—not cause his family further financial harm.[31] The nun and her family, by contrast, are deprived of inheritance and wergild rights: neither she nor her child will receive any inheritance from the abductor or his family, and she and her family are not entitled to compensation should the child be killed.[32] The nun is thus subject to a more enduring earthly penalty, even though she is not liable at the time she leaves her nunnery. Perhaps the breach of monastic vows was deemed a long-term violation more serious than an abduction, justifying the nun's forfeiture of key legal privileges. Alternatively, the provisions of this clause may have been adapted from canon law.[33] In either case, no religious justification is articulated in the *domboc*. These clauses focus on financial rights and obligations, not spiritual transgression.

A secular bent is likewise apparent in a prohibition against harassing a nun:

> [18] If anyone lustfully grabs a nun either on her garment or her breast without her permission (*leafe*), let it be compensated double (*twybete*) what we earlier established for a layperson.[34]

---

[31] The union remained illegitimate vis-à-vis inheritance, even though the father's family could claim wergild: below, n.32.
[32] Compare *Ine* 27; 786 Legatine Capitulary in Dümmler, *Epistolae* II, 25, at ch. 16.
[33] Wormald, "Offa's 'Law-Code'"; Wormald, *Making*, 106-7, 280-1; Pratt, *Political Thought*, 220-1; Treschow, "Prologue," 105-6; and above, n. 30.
[34] Compare *Af.* 11; Fulk and Jurasinski, *Canons*, 7, at A43.

Here, the nun is unambiguously identified as the injured party, whose permission was violated. As in clauses governing clerical protection, her ecclesiastical status merits her relatively high compensation under the law, compared to her lay counterparts. This clause also echoes the holiday regulations, with double compensation compounding the ordinary penalty for grabbing an unwilling woman. It is presumably the nun's religious vocation which merits this weightier response; violating her will and person would violate the protection attached to ecclesiastical personnel. It is unclear, though, who would receive the compensation payment.[35] The clause does not specify whether the sum should be given to the nun herself, or—as with other breaches of ecclesiastical protection—to her community, bishop, or secular patron.[36] There is no indication that the double compensation should be understood as a penitential offering to offset the sin of harming a nun. Although this clause protects an ecclesiastical institution and its members, it is framed like any other *domboc* regulation on bodily injury, listing the offense and monetary penalty without any spiritual rationale.

Finally, there is a clause which governs monks who lose someone else's property:

> [20] If someone entrusts property to another man's monk without the permission of the monk's lord (*munuces hlafordes lefnesse*) and it is lost to him, the one who owned it before shall bear its loss.[37]

The fate of the property is unclear; it may be lost by its monastic custodian or stolen while in the monk's possession.[38] In either scenario, this clause is concerned with responsibility for the loss. The owner's liability hinges on the fact that property was entrusted without the permission of the monk's lord. This caveat implies that the monk's lord would ordinarily compensate the owner's loss in a case like this, but he is not responsible in this instance because he was never involved in the transaction. However, the monk is not liable for the loss either. Unlike the clause on homicidal priests, where the priest is himself subject to penalties if his lord does not settle on his behalf, the careless monk evidently bears no legal responsibility. Presumably, it is the monk's religious status that exempts him from the normal processes of restitution—perhaps because the loss was considered a relatively minor or accidental offense, or perhaps because monks were not supposed to be custodians of material property in the first place.[39] If such action violated a monastic rule, the monk might be subject to a separate

[35] This differs from the clause on laywomen, where compensation is rendered to the victim: above, n.34.
[36] Compare *Af.* 2.1, 8.
[37] I follow Whitelock's translation: *EHD*, 377.
[38] This clause does not treat the monk as a thief: compare *Af.* Prol.28.
[39] Compare *Af.* Prol.28; Treschow, "Prologue," 96-7; Wormald, *Making*, 420-1.

earthly punishment under a law of Ine.[40] Certainly, he could be subject to penitential discipline if he acted without permission or engaged in a transaction inappropriate to his office, but this clause is not concerned with any spiritual consequences, only with material liability.[41]

As a group, the *domboc* clauses concerning the earthly Church and its personnel focus overwhelmingly on material harm and compensation. Offenders must pay fines and compensation to injured parties, just as they would for transgressions against laypeople and mundane institutions. When beneficiaries are explicitly named—as in clauses on clerical protection, *ciricfrið*, church theft, and offending clergy—they are particular clergy, communities, or patrons. Payments are not directed in vague terms toward "the Church" but toward those members which suffered direct injury. By contrast, clauses which name no specific beneficiary—that is, those which governed offenses during holidays and violations against nuns—assume a special peace or protection, to be established by the earthly Church but enforced in the mundane sphere like any peace or protection set by secular authorities. Certainly, the *domboc* does not exclude the possibility that ecclesiastical remedies could—or should—be levied for violations against the earthly Church. Yet it does not prescribe penance or impose spiritual consequences like excommunication for this category of offense. Rather, individual clergy, churches, and communities are treated like any other earthly party, entitled to appropriate judicial profits, compensation payments, or secular penalties. These clauses confirm and delineate the legal rights of the Church in the world.

Ecclesiastical Processes

The *domboc* occasionally prescribes spiritual remedies: seven clauses involve confession, penance, and excommunication. The bulk of these concern oath- and pledge-breaking.[42] After establishing the only conditions under which an oath may be broken—that is, when a person has sworn to undertake treasonous or unjust activities—the *domboc* sets consequences for breaking legitimate pledges:

> [1.2] If someone pledges (*weddige*) something that is lawful and leaves it undone, he shall humbly give his weapons and possessions to his friends to keep, and spend forty nights in prison on the king's estate (*tune*); let him endure there the penance the bishop prescribes for him, and let his family feed him, if he has no food.

---

40 *Ine* 1.

41 Compare Old English Penitential in Frantzen, *Database*, 43.11.01.

42 *Af.* 1-1.8. Wormald, *Making*, 283-4; Pratt, *Political Thought*, 233-4; Matthias Ammon, "'Ge Mid Wedde Ge Mid Aðe': The Functions of Oath and Pledge in Anglo-Saxon Legal Culture," *Historical Research* 86.233 (2013): 515-35, at 518-20.

This clause diverges from those involving the earthly Church, in two significant ways. First, it explicitly requires offenders to undertake penance and provides logistical guidelines for doing so. Second, this clause does not identify an injured party or require any compensation or fine. The perpetrator must temporarily surrender himself, but it is clear that pledge-breaking is more than a violation against earthly parties; it is also a sin that required religious reconciliation. Despite the need for spiritual atonement, subsequent clauses indicate that the perpetrator might resist both parts of his sentence:

> [1.4] If it is necessary to force him and he will not go unless he is bound, he shall forfeit his weapons and property.
> [1.5] If he is slain, he shall lie without compensation.
> [1.6] If he runs away before that period is complete, and he is captured, he shall stay forty nights in prison, as he should have before.

These clauses require the perpetrator to complete a full course of imprisonment and penance, regardless of whether he is willing; it is not just the broken pledge being punished here, but the pledge-breaker's refusal to submit to justice and atone for his sin. Fundamentally, though, this sequence seems to require a sinner to be brought to penance through potentially deadly force—an impulse at odds with the *domboc*'s guiding principle of Christian mercy.[43] While a pledge-breaker might be disinclined to undertake a forty-day penance or accept the humiliation of imprisonment, the expectation of violence suggests that there was more at stake than a short-term prison sentence. The focus on physical custody implies that additional parties were invested in the broken pledge and might seek to bring the perpetrator to justice. If this reckoning involved physical retaliation, imprisonment on royal property could function like other sanctuary protections and save the offender from retributive violence.[44] Alternatively, the wronged party might seek to initiate formal judicial proceedings. This process would presumably be governed by subsequent *domboc* instructions:

> [33] If anyone accuses another about a pledge made before God (*godborges*), and wishes to accuse that he did not fulfill any of those pledges that he gave him, let the accuser give the preliminary oath (*foreað*) in four churches, and let the other one, if he wants to clear himself, do so in twelve churches.

When read alongside this clause, the earlier directions for imprisonment and penance may be understood as preliminaries to the exonerating oath, or as the procedure to be followed if the accused's judicial defense failed. Although clause 33 is concerned specifically with the breach of pledges made before God, which justifies the ecclesiastical

---

[43] See below.

[44] For feud, see Paul Hyams, *Rancor and Reconciliation in Medieval England* (Ithaca: Cornell University Press, 2003), 80.

setting for exoneration, the presence of a human accuser confirms that such commitments had real-world consequences, requiring remedy in the earthly sphere as well as the spiritual.

In this context, there seem to be two priorities driving the *domboc*'s opening clauses on pledge-breaking. One is the physical containment of the pledge-breaker for an extended period of time. Clause 1.2 is the first prescription for imprisonment in Anglo-Saxon royal law, and it likely had a purpose comparable to the three- or seven-day respite granted to sanctuary-seekers.[45] A forty-day "time out" would allow a settlement to be negotiated with the injured party; during this period, the offender would be protected by whatever fortification the king's prison provided, as well as the legal immunities extended by the king's protection on his estate.[46] Royal privileges and resources would thus be deployed to keep a potentially violent conflict from escalating or to facilitate a lawful resolution. The second priority is spiritual. The forty-day sentence mirrors the span of Lent, suggesting that the offender would undertake his legally-required penance during his imprisonment.[47] The requirement that pledge-breaking accusations be pronounced and refuted in churches likewise indicates that this offense had religious implications.

Strikingly, however, both sets of instructions focus more on procedure than salvation. Clause 1.2 delegates penance entirely to the bishop, and 33 requires oaths of compurgation in various churches, presumably under the supervision of their resident communities. There is no discussion of spiritual consequences; although the *domboc* requires ecclesiastical processes, it leaves the clergy to facilitate those processes themselves. Nevertheless, the outright requirement for penance—and the expectation that religious authorities participate in the prescribed procedures—establishes pledge-breaking as a violation where spiritual and secular priorities intersect. Broken pledges offend God and disrupt mundane society, and they therefore require both spiritual and secular reconciliation. This duality continues in instructions for any pledge-breaker who escapes prison:

> [1.7] If he escapes, let him be outlawed (*afliemed*) and be excommunicated (*amænsumod*) from all of Christ's churches.
> [1.8] If there is other human surety for him, however, he shall compensate (*bete*) for the breach of surety (*borgbryce*) as the law (*ryht*) instructs him, and for the breach of pledge (*wedbryce*) as his confessor (*scrift*) prescribes for him.

---

45 Daniel Thomas, "Incarceration as Judicial Punishment in Anglo-Saxon England," in *Capital and Corporal Punishment in Anglo-Saxon England*, ed. Jay Paul Gates and Nicole Marafioti (Woodbridge: Boydell and Brewer, 2014), 92-112.

46 Hyams, *Rancor*, 92-5; Thomas, "Incarceration," 97-9.

47 Thomas, "Incarceration," 104-9.

The double sentence of exile and excommunication in 1.7 construes the pledge-breaker's escape as a two-fold violation: he offends God by shirking his penance, and he offends the king by denying his authority to imprison. Unlike clauses 1.4-5, which prescribe only secular punishments for resisting arrest, clause 1.7 treats escape as both a crime and a sin, meriting maximum penalties in both spheres. Still, like the preceding clauses, 1.7 does not prescribe punishment for the original broken pledge but for the perpetrator's refusal to submit to mundane and ecclesiastical authorities. This rationale is reinforced in 1.8, where earthly justice and the priestly confessor are presented as comparable authorities, empowered to facilitate reconciliation in the secular and ecclesiastical spheres.[48] Yet this clause clearly differentiates these two modes of compensation. Pledge-breaking (*wedbryce*) is to be remedied by penance alone; earthly justice is concerned only with violations of the legal compact of surety (*borgbryce*). Although secular and ecclesiastical penalties are conflated in clause 1.2, subsequent clauses carefully distinguish the spiritual offense and remedies from the temporal.

As formulated in the *domboc*, pledge-breaking is a hierarchical offense. One violation is perpetrated against God, requiring spiritual compensation mediated by the clergy; another is committed against the earthly party betrayed by the broken pledge, requiring material compensation arbitrated among earthly authorities; and a third may be committed by flaunting the power of those authorities, including the king and clergy, requiring further acts of reconciliation. Yet these clauses suggest that the offender might not recognize the significance of this hierarchy. The opening instructions assume that the pledge-breaker's immediate concern would be the human parties he had wronged: the intimation that the perpetrator could suffer violence, that he would require protection, and that he might flee custody indicate that spiritual reconciliation was not necessarily his top priority. A period of respite under the king's protection would keep the offender out of physical danger and provide an opportunity to settle the conflict with those he betrayed, but it would also enable him to complete his spiritual atonement —which ought to be his primary consideration—in peace. Nevertheless, the *domboc* directives should not be understood as regulating sin in its own right, but as a means to compel individuals to submit to appropriate authorities and processes, in both the spiritual and secular spheres.

The two remaining *domboc* clauses which mention ecclesiastical processes focus on confession. One is concerned with sanctuary:

> [5.4] If anyone seeks a church because of any wrong (*gylta*) which has never been discovered, and there confesses (*geandette*) himself in God's name, it is to be half forgiven (*forgifen*).

[48] Hough, "Penitential Literature," 134.

This clause is rather different than those examined so far. Here, confession is not part of a dual penalty to be administered alongside secular punishment, like penance in the pledge-breaking clauses. Instead, 5.4 provides an incentive for individuals to expose their own misdeeds: wrongdoers who reveal secret offenses will avoid the severest earthly punishment. This clause turns on the word *gylt*, which could encompass spiritual and criminal wrongdoing alike.[49] In this construction, the distinction between crime and sin is left ambiguous. Still, a royal decree could not mitigate or pardon a sin against God, and it is improbable that this clause was intended to regulate penitential sentences issued by clergy. Although religious confession might be a first step toward counteracting the spiritual consequences of any type of offense, the point of this clause is to temper mundane responses to wrongdoing. On the one hand, recourse to a church would provide safety for the perpetrator of a serious offense, since *ciricfrið* protections might discourage or forestall retaliatory violence. By confessing an earthly violation directly to a clergyman, an offender could simultaneously take responsibility for his actions and secure himself a period of safety to negotiate with the injured party, much like the forty-day imprisonment prescribed for pledge-breakers or the respite allowed to asylum-seekers.[50] On the other hand, this policy made ecclesiastical confession a vehicle for revealing—and ultimately punishing—offenses governed by secular law. This is not to deny that religious reconciliation was also expected.[51] However, this clause gives wrongdoers a clear incentive to admit their guilt: whether or not they were concerned for their souls, confession to a clergyman ensured a reduced punishment in the secular sphere. From a royal perspective, this clause seems designed to facilitate peace between parties in conflict and to ensure that earthly justice is implemented—and appropriate fines exacted. The key objective of this procedure is not spiritual contrition but the exposure and resolution of mundane offenses.

The *domboc*'s final reference to confession concerns disabled offenders:

> [14] If someone is born mute or deaf, so that he cannot deny sins or confess them (*synna onsecggan ne geandettan*), let his father compensate (*bete*) for his misdeeds (*misdæda*).

The language of this clause is ambiguous. *Misdæda* could refer to either mundane or spiritual offenses, while the command to *bete* applies to both penance and material compensation.[52] The opposition of *onsecggan*, which is attested in judicial contexts, and

---

[49] Angus Cameron, Ashley Crandell Amos, Antonette diPaolo Healy, *et al.*, *Dictionary of Old English: A to I Online* (Toronto: Dictionary of Old English Project, 2018) [hereafter *DOE*], s.v. *gylt*.

[50] Confession may have been expected while the asylum-seeker was staying in a church: above, n.20.

[51] As Carole Hough notes, only confession—not penance—is prescribed: "Penitential Literature," 134.

[52] *Af.* Prol.49.7-8 uses *misdæda* of secular offenses; it is not used of sins in Anglo-Saxon legislation until the eleventh century. Antonette diPaolo Healy *et al.*, *Dictionary of Old English Web Corpus* (Toronto: Dictionary of Old English Project, 2009). On this clause, see also Andrew Rabin, "'Sharper Than a Serpent's Tooth':

geandettan, which is primarily used of religious confession, could also indicate that both categories of remedy were encompassed here.[53] By contrast, the only other occurrence of *syn* in the *domboc* denotes a spiritual offense, and its use here—alongside *geandettan*—places a rhetorical emphasis on religious atonement.[54] Yet while it is not impossible that fathers were expected to undertake penance on behalf of disabled sons, no other clause in the *domboc* establishes such precise guidelines for penitential practice, and it is improbable that spiritual culpability is being determined here by royal decree. Instead, the ability to confess sins serves as a threshold for legal responsibility. It is reasonable for a king to legislate the appropriate secular procedure in a complicated scenario like this, by establishing who would be liable for the actions of a disabled wrongdoer.[55] According to the logic of this clause, an offender's incomprehension would not negate the injured party's right to compensation under the law.

Collectively, clauses involving ecclesiastical processes take confession and penance for granted. The *domboc* assumes that an infrastructure for spiritual reconciliation is already in place, with clergy able to help resolve wrongdoing. Alfred seems to appropriate this system, by deputizing the clergy in the process of secular law-enforcement.[56] A confessor might be called upon to arbitrate questions about an individual's legal competence; he could persuade a law-breaker to come forward; or he could confirm that a repentant offender had confessed.[57] A similar role in secular procedure may have been envisioned for bishops who assigned penance to imprisoned pledge-breakers and the confessors who reconciled escapees.[58] Such activity may be understood as an element of pastoral care, for in each of these cases, the *domboc* grants clergy complete discretion in reconciling sinners. The law never prescribes specific penances or sets requirements for confessors; it simply mandates that ecclesiastical processes occur, in cases where secular violations were also deemed sinful. Alfred surely understood confession and penance as spiritual requirements, but this necessity was exactly what made religious processes useful judicial tools. Although prescriptions for confession, penance, and excommunication acknowledge certain behaviors as spiritually detrimental, the *domboc*'s rules and

Parent-Child Litigation in Anglo-Saxon England," in *Childhood and Adolescence in Anglo-Saxon Literary Culture*, eds. Susan Irvine and Winfried Rudolf (Toronto: University of Toronto Press, 2018), 278-9.

[53] *DOE* s.v. *geandettan*; T. Northcote Toller, *An Anglo-Saxon Dictionary Based on the Manuscript Collections of the Late Joseph Bosworth* (Oxford: Oxford University Press, 1989), accessed online at http://bosworth.ff.cuni.cz/, s.v. *onsecgan* (II); but see below, n.54.

[54] *Af.* Prol.49.7 and n.53, above. These definitions remain flexible: compare *Af.* 29, 35.

[55] Wormald, *Making*, 282; Hough, "Penitential Literature," 134.

[56] For similar approaches in Alfred's secular administration, see George Molyneaux, *Formation of the English Kingdom in the Tenth Century* (Oxford: Oxford University Press, 2015).

[57] *Af.* 14, 5.4.

[58] *Af.* 1.2, 1.8.

procedures prioritize secular resolution and punishment. Ecclesiastical remedies are only prescribed within broader processes of punishment or reconciliation, never on their own.

THE MOSAIC PROLOGUE

Unlike the *domboc* proper, the Mosaic prologue's recapitulation of biblical law seems to have a direct interest in sin. Though drawn predominantly from the Book of Exodus, the prologue's immediate source was likely the *Liber ex lege Moysi*, a Hiberno-Latin encapsulation of the Pentateuch.[59] The Old English adapts this material, rather than providing a verse-by-verse rendering; biblical clauses may be omitted, rearranged, or changed, and these divergences illuminate the priorities of the Anglo-Saxon translator.[60] Nevertheless, the prologue is presented as a reiteration of divine law: "The lord spoke these words to Moses."[61] This frames the subsequent instructions as requirements for moral behavior, with violations construed as transgressions against God. Yet the bulk of the prologue's directives are concerned with offenses which require only temporal resolution. The Old Testament adaptations never mention repentance or salvation. Instead, they provide instructions concerning slaves (11-12), injuries and homicides (13-20), conflicts involving livestock (21-4), problems surrounding theft and property (25-8, 35), sexual offenses (29, 31), underprivileged and untrustworthy individuals (33-4, 36, 40-2), and the administration of justice (43-7). Only twelve clauses explicitly mention God or religious practice. Of these, three are conditional constructions which outline punishments for violations ("if... then...") and nine are exhortations to particular behaviors ("you shall...").[62] The following analysis considers how these clauses represent religious wrongdoing and its impact on human souls.

---

59 The *Liber ex lege Moysi* [hereafter *Liber*] is edited in Sven Meeder, "The *Liber ex lege Moysi*: Notes and Text," *Journal of Medieval Latin* 19 (2009): 173-218; also worth consulting is the edition in B. Carella, "Alcuin and Alfred: Two Anglo-Saxon Legal Reformers" (Ph.D. Diss., University of North Carolina at Chapel Hill, 2006), 120-7. Further discussions are found in Carella, "Source of the Prologue"; Treschow, "Prologue," 83.

60 Jurasinski, "Violence"; Jurasinski, *Penitentials*, 55-62; Wormald, *Making*, 418-29; Carella, "Source of the Prologue"; Treschow, "Prologue," 90-102. For Roman, Continental, and Irish analogues, see Wormald, *Making*, 423-6; Pratt, *Political Thought*, 215-6; Carella, "Hiberno-Latin"; Carella, "Source of the Prologue," 115-7. Alternative Old English translations appear in Samuel Crawford, *The Old English Version of the Heptateuch*, EETS o.s. 160 (London: Oxford University Press, 1922, repr. 1969), 262-9.

61 *Af.* Prol.Int.

62 Conditional clauses are Prol.13, 32, 34; exhortative clauses are Prol.1, 2, 3, 4, 10, 36, 37, 38, 48. See also Wormald, *Making*, 271.

The first conditional punishment for a religious offense appears among other prescriptions for homicide. Prol.13 establishes death sentences for deliberate killings and compensation payments for those who seek sanctuary (*friðstowe*) after killing without malice.[63] The discussion then turns to intentional homicide:

> [Prol.13] [...] If anyone deliberately and intentionally kills his neighbor through treachery, separate (*aluc*) him from my altar, so that he may suffer death (*to þam þæt he deaðe swelte*).

The Old English may be read somewhat differently than its biblical source: where the Latin *euelles* indicates that the offender be dragged away, the vernacular *aluc* allows for a more formal exclusion from the altar.[64] Two interpretations are possible. On the one hand, the Old English rendering may anticipate that perpetrators would be extracted from churches by force. In this case, the *ciricfrið* protections of the *domboc* proper—as well as those extended to asylum-seekers earlier in Prol.13—would seem not to apply in cases of malicious homicide.[65] On the other hand, this clause could require excommunication before the death sentence. In this scenario, exclusion is presented in the same way as prescriptions for penance and excommunication in the *domboc* proper: it is part of a broader procedure that encompasses both earthly and spiritual consequences. Yet within the full scope of this clause, exclusion serves to compound a standard punishment. Where other types of killing were to be remedied simply with compensation or death, malice required a further spiritual penalty; it was the perpetrator's evil intention, in conjunction with the act of killing, that merited his exclusion. For Christian Anglo-Saxon readers, this clause would seem to impose spiritual consequences: if the offender could not reconcile his sins before death, he would likely pay for them in the afterlife.[66] In this context, the final causal phrase —"so that he may suffer death"—evokes the eternal death of the soul, as well as the immediate death of the body. However, as in the Bible, the punishment prescribed in the Old English is to be implemented entirely in the mundane sphere. Whatever the spiritual consequences, human agents must physically separate the offender from an earthly altar and subject him to bodily death.

---

[63] *Af.* Prol.13; compare Exodus 21:12-13 and the *Liber*, in Meeder, "The *Liber ex lege Moysi*," 193-4; "Carella, "Alcuin," 123. See also Jurasinski, *Penitentials*, 57-8; Jurasinski, "Violence," 29-31; Treschow, "Prologue," 91-2.

[64] The *Liber*, following Exodus 21:14, reads: "...ab altari meo euelles eum, ut moriatur"; Meeder, "The *Liber ex lege Moysi*," 194; Carella, "Alcuin," 123. *DOE* s.v. *a-lucan*; R.E. Latham *et al.*, *DMLBS* s.v. *evellere*.

[65] Jurasinski, "Violence," 38-9 evaluates discrepancies between the prologue and *domboc* proper.

[66] Nicole Marafioti, "Punishing Bodies and Saving Souls: Capital and Corporal Punishment in Late Anglo-Saxon England," *Haskins Society Journal* 20 (2008): 39-57.

Another spiritual concern in the prologue is the worship of false gods. Three clauses offer exhortations on this topic: it is prohibited to worship foreign gods (1), create gods of gold or silver (10), and swear by heathen gods (48). A fourth clause, with conditional structure, prescribes punishment for such activity:

> [Prol.32] He who sacrifices to idols above (*ofer*) God alone, let him suffer death (*swelte se deaðe*).

This clause immediately follows a prescription against bestiality, with the same structure:

> [Prol.31] Whoever has intercourse with an animal, let him suffer death (*swelte he deaðe*).

The similarity of their concluding phrases creates a rhetorical connection between these commands that does not appear in the Bible.[67] As in cases of malicious homicide, there is an expectation that earthly authorities will punish the offender's physical body. However, Prol.31 and 32 govern violations of a different nature. Unlike homicide, bestiality and the worship of false gods cause no immediate harm to human victims, and the implication is that these actions offended God alone. In Prol.31, this rationale goes unstated: there is no mention of God or spiritual consequences. By contrast, Prol.32 unambiguously places the offender—and the idols he worships—in opposition to God. The Old English, in fact, goes a step further than the Latin in assuming that the offender has subverted the natural order by placing false idols above the true God.[68] Still, this affront does not elicit an explicit spiritual penalty. Certainly, a Christian audience might understand damnation as all but guaranteed for anyone who refused to renounce false gods, even under threat of death. However, the clause prescribes an entirely secular response, with a religious offense remedied with a physical penalty.

In contrast to the punishments for homicide and worshipping false gods, which are entrusted to human agents, divine action is promised in two clauses. First, a conditional clause on widows and orphans states:

> [Prol.34] Do not harm widows and orphans, and do not injure them anywhere. If you do otherwise, they will call to me (*cleopiað to me*), and I will hear them, and I will then slay you with my sword, and I will act so that your wife will be a widow and your children will be orphans.

[67] Compare Exodus 22:19-20 in Meeder, "The *Liber ex lege Moysi,*" 198; Carella, "Alcuin," 126.

[68] The Latin implies that the true God, the only deity to whom humans could legitimately sacrifice, was an exception to a general rule: "qui immolat diis, occidatur, preter soli d[e]o": Meeder, "The *Liber ex lege Moysi,*" 198; Carella, "Alcuin," 126.

This eye-for-an-eye brand of justice is prescribed elsewhere in the prologue, but here it is deployed directly by God, in response to the victims' clamor.[69] A comparable scenario is envisioned in a subsequent exhortative clause:

> [Prol.36] If someone possesses only a single cloak with which to wrap himself and to wear, and he gives it as a pledge (*wedde*), it shall be given back before the sun sets. If you do not do this, then he will call to me (*cleopað he to me*), and I will hear him, because I am very mild-hearted.

The procedure imagined for the poor man is the same as for widows and orphans: justice will be done on behalf of victims of wrongdoing, if those victims call to God. In both clauses, divine power is deployed on behalf of the poor and desolate, either to help a victim or to punish an oppressor. Yet the Old English adapts the biblical text to present divine assistance in a judicial light. Prol.34 omits a reference to God's anger (*indignabitur furor meus*), depicting this exchange as a dispassionate exercise of divine justice instead of action spurred by fury.[70] Prol.36 truncates the description of the pauper's vulnerability—the Bible emphasizes that the pledged garment is the only one he possesses, to cover himself and sleep in—and thereby downplays the pathos of the Latin, concentrating instead on logistical matters of procedure and timing.[71] Additionally, Prol.36 presents the pledge as a more balanced exchange than the Bible does: while the Latin focuses exclusively on the recipient's actions, the Old English presents the poor man actively giving his cloak away and the recipient actively obliged to return it, in a mutually agreed-upon transaction. For the pauper, just as for widows and orphans, God is not commanding that the vulnerable be given charity but that they be granted justice when human procedures fall short. A poor man who gives his only cloak as a pledge (*wedd*) would risk bodily harm through exposure to the elements; God's command and promise of protection are meant to mitigate the dangers of participating in a standard legal procedure. Widows and orphans injured by more powerful individuals have no secular recourse or protection; God serves as their only defender. In both clauses, God operates like any earthly advocate, protecting his clients from harm and compelling oppressors to act justly.[72] There is no mention of spiritual punishment or reward, simply the promise of intervention to ensure the physical wellbeing of the indigent.

---

69 *Af.* Prol.19.

70 Exodus 21:12-13 and the *Liber*, in Meeder, "The *Liber ex lege Moysi*," 197-8; Carella, "Alcuin," 123. See also Treschow, "Prologue," 98.

71 Exodus 22:26-27 and the *Liber*, in Meeder, "The *Liber ex lege Moysi*," 199; Carella, "Alcuin," 126. See also Treschow, "Prologue," 99.

72 Andrew Rabin, "Old English *Forespeca* and the Role of the Advocate in Anglo-Saxon Law," *Mediaeval Studies* 69 (2007): 223-54.

The threat of divine action recurs in a prohibition against blasphemy:

> [Prol.2] Do not invoke my name in idleness, because you will not be guiltless against me (*unscyldig wið me*), if you invoke my name in idleness.

This rendition includes two significant departures from the Latin.[73] First, the vernacular commandment is articulated in the first person, not the Bible's third person. This change confirms that human actions can offend God personally and incur his displeasure, foreshadowing the divine interventions promised in Prol.34 and 36. Second, the context of the blasphemer's guilt is altered in the Old English. In the Latin, God assesses the offender's action and deems him guilty: "for the Lord will not hold (*habebit*) him guiltless." In the Old English, culpability is not a point of judgment but of fact: "you will not be guiltless," and violation is understood to offend God himself (*wið me*). This phrasing anticipates declarations of liability in the *domboc* proper, and this legalistic diction suggests that God is entitled to exact compensation for an offense against his person, like any earthly magnate.[74]

A more ambiguous exhortative clause may also touch on blasphemy:

> [Prol.37] Do not reproach your lord, do not curse the lord of the people. (*Ne tæle ðu ðinne dryhten, ne ðone hlaford þæs folces ne werge þu.*)

This may be understood in various ways. The biblical command prohibits any reproach of the gods (*diis*) or one's earthly lord (*principem populi*), and the Old English translator obviates the hint of polytheism by replacing *diis* with *dryhten*, "lord."[75] *Dryhten* is consistently used of God in the *domboc*, and Anglo-Saxon readers likely understood Prol.37 to encompass divine and mundane authority in sequence, like its Latin source.[76] However, *dryhten* could also signify an earthly lord, and it is conceivable that the Old English was meant to distinguish one's personal lord (*ðinne dryhten*) from the leader of the nation (*hlaford þæs folces*), sidestepping the problem of multiple gods by applying this clause entirely to earthly entities. This type of conflation appears in another Old English rendering of this commandment, and in the context of the *domboc*, such a proclamation

---

[73] Exodus 20:7 and the *Liber*, in Meeder, "The *Liber ex lege Moysi*," 191; Carella, "Alcuin," 122.

[74] *Af.* 4.2; also *I Ew.* 2.1, *II Em.* 1.2.

[75] The *Liber*, following Exodus 22:28, reads: "Diis non detrahes. Principem populi tui non maledices"; Meeder, "The *Liber ex lege Moysi*," 199; Carella, "Alcuin," 126. Reference to "the gods" in Exodus may be a biblical idiom for earthly judges and authorities: cf. Psalm 82:1.

[76] *Dryhten* never occurs in the *domboc* but appears six times in the prologue (Preface, 3, 4, 37, 49, 49.3), all in reference to God. *Hlaford* appears eleven times in the *domboc* (1.1, 4.2, 8, 20-21, 37, 42.5-6) and thirteen times in the prologue (11, 21, 23, 37, 49.7), all in reference to earthly lords. Compare *Wi.* 4, 8-8.1, 18-19 in Oliver, *Beginnings*, 154-7, 160-1. See also Anne Scheller, *Bezeichnungen für die christliche Gottheit im Altenglischen* (Hamburg: Kovač 2010).

would anticipate Alfred's opening command to eschew lord-betrayal (*hlafordsearwe*).[77] Although a ninth-century reader would most likely interpret the first phrase as referring to God, it is noteworthy that *diis* is rendered as *dryhten,* rather than (for instance) Old English *god.* By introducing ambiguity with this choice of vocabulary, the translator softens the boundary between mundane and divine authority. The association of temporal with heavenly lordship appears in other Alfredian texts, notably the *Pastoral Care,* which asserts: "when we offend against lords (*hlafordas*), we offend against God who created lordship."[78] By this logic, the violations in Prol.37—whether perpetrated against a divine or human lord—are offensive to God.

Finally, three exhortative clauses govern human obligations to God. One concerns tithing:

> [Prol.38] Give to God (*agif þu Gode*) your tithe-money (*teoðan sceattas*) and your first fruits of moving and growing things.

The Old English changes the Latin's first-person voice (*dabis mihi*) to the third person (*agif þu Gode*), as well as omitting the requirement that first sons be given alongside other first fruits; the subsequent biblical verse, which provides logistics for rendering oxen and sheep, is also omitted.[79] Taken together, these adaptations bring Old Testament sacrifices conceptually closer to Christian-era tithing and earlier regulations in Ine's laws.[80] Yet unlike *Ine*'s prescriptions and the biblical verse, Prol.38 is not framed as a prohibition but as an exhortation to good behavior, without any punishment for noncompliance. Like clauses concerning the earthly Church in the *domboc* proper, the focus rests on money and property; these are overtly material offerings to God. A mundane focus is also present in Sabbath guidelines:

> [Prol.3] Remember that you should sanctify (*gehalgige*) the day of rest; work six days and on the seventh, rest (*restað*). Because in six days, Christ wrought the heavens and the earth, the seas and all creatures that are on it, and he rested (*gereste*) on the seventh day, and therefore the Lord sanctified it (*gehalgode*).[81]

Like its biblical source, this clause contextualizes the Sabbath within the story of creation. The diction emphasizes humans' obligation to recognize and emulate divine action: they are to rest as Christ did (*restað / gereste*) and sanctify the Sabbath as the

---

77 *Af.* 1-1.1. Compare the Old English Heptateuch, "Do not reproach nor curse the leader of your people" (*Ne tæl ðu, ne wirig ðu þines folces ealdor*); Crawford, *Heptateuch*, 269.

78 Henry Sweet, *King Alfred's West Saxon Version of Gregory's Pastoral Care*, EETS o.s. 45 and 50 (London: Oxford University Press, 1871), 198-200.

79 Exodus 22:29-30; Meeder, "The *Liber ex lege Moysi,*" 199; Carella, "Alcuin," 126.

80 *Agifan* (give) and *sceat* (dues) appear in *Ine* 4 and 61.

81 Exodus 20:9, 20:11; Meeder, "The *Liber ex lege Moysi,*" 191-2; Carella, "Alcuin," 122.

Lord did (*gehalgige / gehalgode*). However, the clause is less concerned with human activity, omitting the Old Testament's list of individuals who must not labor.[82] Instead, the Old English focuses on Christ's own labor—the creation of the earth and its inhabitants—for which reciprocity is expected. The earthly benefits that God granted require acknowledgment in the temporal sphere, through human action. This also applies in an injunction to honor one's parents:

> [Prol.4] Honor your father and your mother, whom the Lord gave you (*ða þe Dryhten sealde*), so that you shall thereby live long on earth.

The Old English diverges from the Bible, in which God's gift is the land, not the parents.[83] These variations present rather different messages. The Latin offers a conditional exchange: by honoring one's parents, an individual will earn longevity on the land God has granted. The Old English is less straightforward in its reciprocal logic: God has already provided a gift of parents; honoring them will secure a longer earthly lifetime. In both formulations, God gives earthly rewards to the obedient and, by implication, withholds them from the disobedient. Still, God does not promise eternal benefits, only extended life on earth.

Like *domboc* clauses concerning the earthly Church, prologue clauses that touch overtly on religious affairs frame their instructions in mundane terms. While the Old English translations rarely diverge dramatically from their biblical sources, adaptations of the Latin accentuate the material and legal obligations of God's human creations. Even though they are presented as God's own commands and would therefore be understood by Alfred's subjects within a Christian framework, spiritual consequences of violation are never explicit. In the *domboc*, God legislates in the same mode as a human lawmaker: he ensures justice, incentivizes obedience, and assigns punishments for lawbreakers—all within the earthly sphere.

The caveat, of course, is that penitential practice—as well as Christian conceptions of eternal punishment and reward—would be anachronistic to the prologue's Old Testament perspective. This dissonance is explicated in the clauses that bridge the prologue and *domboc* proper, where the Old Law is distinguished from the New.[84] Nevertheless, the preceding clauses are predominantly concerned with the administration of earthly justice. There is only one instance in the prologue where an ecclesiastical process is directly required—exclusion from God's altar, in Prol.13, for premeditated homicide—

[82] Exodus 20:10; Meeder, "The *Liber ex lege Moysi*," 191-2; Carella, "Alcuin," 122.

[83] The *Liber*, following Exodus 20:12, reads: "Honora patrem tuum et matrem tuam ut sis longeus super terram, qua *[quam* in Carella] dominus deus tuus dabit"; Meeder, "The *Liber ex lege Moysi*," 192; Carella, "Alcuin," 122. Of the four extant *Liber* manuscripts, two have *qua* and two have *quam*; it appears that *quam* is intended here, which would refer to the land being given by God (not the parents).

[84] See below.

but this spiritual punishment serves to enhance a death sentence, not to remedy the offender's sin. This clause, like the others considered above, governs human action and the resolution of mundane conflict. Despite their biblical origins, these are earthly rules to be mediated and enforced by earthly authorities.

Conclusions

The lynchpin between the prologue and the *domboc* proper is a discourse on Christian mercy.[85] The Golden Rule is cited as the highest guiding principle for judges, implying that justice should be ruled by careful deliberation rather than unthinking adherence to written rules.[86] The subsequent clauses demonstrate empathetic deliberation through historical example:

> [Prol.49.7] [...] Because of the mercy that Christ taught, the holy bishops and other distinguished counselors then established that for the greatest misdeeds (*misdæda*), earthly lords could—with their faith, without sin (*synne*)—at the first offense (*gylte*) accept monetary compensation. [...]
> [Prol.49.8] Then, in many synods, they established compensation (*bote*) for many human misdeeds (*misdæda*), and they wrote in many synod-books—here one judgment, here another.

These clauses qualify the Old Testament laws adapted in the prologue, modifying the demands of Exodus for the day-to-day exercise of Christian-era justice. As framed in the prologue, earthly law was shaped over time by divine and human power, with Alfred's own innovations building on much longer traditions.[87] Nevertheless, neither the *domboc* nor its prologue define the limits of Christian faith and practice among Alfred's subjects. Although the laws are informed by religious principles and concerned with the wellbeing of the earthly Church, there is no indication that violation would automatically harm the soul. Instead, the focus is on earthly conflict and its resolution, predominantly through compensation to injured parties and punishments for offenders. Although sin and its remedies are referenced throughout the *domboc*, these are subordinate to decrees on proper behavior and secular responses to transgression—that is, rules to be enforced through temporal power.

---

[85] *Af.* Prol.49-49.10. Liebermann edited Prol.49-49.10 as part of the *domboc*'s prologue, but Carella has more helpfully designated these clauses as an "explanatory bridge" between the prologue and *domboc*: "Hiberno-Latin," 2; "Source of the Prologue," 92. See also Treschow, "Prologue," 86-7.
[86] *Af.* Prol.49.5-6. Compare Matthew 7:12, Luke 6:31; and see Treschow, "Prologue," 86-8; Rabin, "*Forespeca*," 228-36.
[87] Wormald, *Making*, 423-7; Wormald, "Offa's 'Law-Code,'" 214-5; Carella, "Hiberno-Latin," 5-6; Treschow, "Prologue," 102.

This is not to suggest that spiritual priorities were not valued in Alfred's regime, or that the Church was subverted to secular interests. The king's reliance on ecclesiastical councilors and his patronage of religious institutions are well attested, and his promulgation of vernacular translations of texts "most necessary for all men to know" ostensibly deepened his subjects' knowledge of Christian thought. [88] The *domboc*, by contrast, keeps its focus on the earthly sphere. When clergy and religious institutions are cited, it is to establish their status or role in the resolution of earthly conflicts, not to regulate their spiritual activities. When religious observance is mandated, it is to ensure that Christian customs are observed correctly by the populace, not to impose royal will upon the Church or its members. When biblical laws are offered as guidelines for religious practice, they are adapted to present God as a judicial authority, who follows the same logic as an earthly judge, advocate, or lawmaker. The only unambiguous discussion of sin in the *domboc* applies not to perpetrators but to judges—earthly lords who should temper written law through deliberation, "with their faith, without sin."[89] The articulated concern is not for the souls of miscreants or their victims. Rather, executors of secular justice are assured that fair and merciful judgments are consistent with their Christian faith.[90] Clauses on religious matters oblige earthly authorities to protect the earthly Church and create conditions for Christianity to flourish, but this responsibility does not include the secular regulation of sin or its remedies. Instead, the *domboc* gives members of the clergy complete discretion in their dealings with lawbreakers, confirming that clergy and laymen had distinct roles in facilitating and keeping peace. Nevertheless, the ideal relationship between these groups was one of mutual support. This, I propose, is the goal of the *domboc*'s ecclesiastical regulations: to establish a mutually beneficial relationship, in which the Church and its personnel are protected by secular power and, in turn, cultivate the spiritual health of the kingdom—in part by intervening in mundane conflicts.

To return to my opening question: how closely did Alfred's laws equate criminal offenses against earthly authorities with sinful violations against God? I would conclude that the text of the *domboc* barely equates these at all. There is only one offense—pledge-breaking—which is prescribed a penitential remedy. Yet this violation is more than a simple affront against God: if left unresolved, a broken pledge could inspire violence

---

[88] Sweet, *Pastoral Care*, 6-7; William Stevenson, *Asser's Life of King Alfred* (Oxford: Clarendon Press, 1904), 79-89; Wormald, *Making*, 118-25. Alfred's grants to churches, monasteries, and bishops include S 343, S 346, S 349, S 352, S 353, and S 357: P.H. Sawyer, *Anglo-Saxon Charters: An Annotated List and Bibliography* (London: Royal Historical Society, 1968). Compare Robin Fleming, "Monastic Lands and England's Defense in the Viking Age," *EHR* 100.395 (1985): 247-65.

[89] *Af.* Prol.49.7, above.

[90] Nicole Marafioti, "Earthly Justice and Spiritual Consequences: Judging and Punishing in the Old English *Consolation of Philosophy*," in *Capital and Corporal Punishment*, ed. Gates and Marafioti, 113-30.

or undermine royal authority. Penance, as prescribed in the *domboc*, could help defuse conflict before it escalated; it is just one element in a broader process of reconciliation. Although this is the only offense construed as both a crime and a sin, however, other *domboc* clauses imply that law-breakers required penitential atonement. The incentive to confess undiscovered wrongdoing to a clergyman and the use of confession to determine legal responsibility assume that systems of temporal and spiritual reconciliation would operate in parallel.[91] This may indicate that Alfred expected his laws to be buttressed by a robust ecclesiastical apparatus, capable of overseeing formal penitential activity. The *domboc*'s parallels with penitential literature and canon law suggest that Alfred and his advisors drew upon an existing corpus of spiritual regulation.[92] Alternatively, the infrastructure for pastoral care may have weakened during a century of Viking incursions, causing penitential practice to decline across the kingdom.[93] In either scenario, Alfred's laws established the necessary conditions for ecclesiastical institutions and personnel to flourish. It was the *domboc*'s legal protections of the earthly Church—not its prescriptions for individual sinners—that ensured the proper care of souls.

[91] Oliver, "Royal and Ecclesiastical"; Cubitt, "Bishops and Councils"; Carella, "Hiberno-Latin," 9-10; Jurasinski, *Penitentials*, 48-51; Oakley, *Penitential Discipline*, 136-96.
[92] Pratt, *Political Thought*, 223-28; Hough, "Penitential Literature"; Stefan Jurasinski, "'Sick-Maintenance' and Earlier English Law," in *Capital and Corporal Punishment*, ed. Gates and Marafioti, 74-91.
[93] Frantzen, *Literature*, 124-7.

II. Comparative and Theoretical Approaches to Early Law

Women and Migrations in the Early Middle Ages: Insights from the Kentish Laws

Daniela Fruscione

Evidence for the experiences of early medieval women amid migrations and other upheavals is often furnished, not by their own writings (which are, as might be expected, few and far between), but by those addressed to them by men. One such example comes from the correspondence of Magnus Felix Ennodius, a Gallic aristocrat, probably from Arles.[1] Between 514 and 521 AD he was bishop of Ticinum, the area around Milan. The principal source about his life is his own writing. He wrote many letters, seven of them to his sister Euprepia.[2] Euprepia had a son, Lupicinus, whose education in Milan was supervised by his uncle Ennodius. For a while Euprepia lived in Milan near her son and brother. Then she left Italy and returned to Gaul. Some of Ennodius' letters to his sister report the progress of his beloved nephew Lupicinus, but most of them are expressions of grief about Euprepia returning alone to Gaul, not answering her brother's letters and leaving her son and her brother to fret about her new situation.[3] Ennodius warns Euprepia: "We do not flee our sins by a change of location." We do not know why Euprepia moved or what the sins mentioned by Ennodius might be.

The letters involving Euprepia offer an excellent vantage point from which to observe Ennodius's concern about her change of attitude, a change that he considers a consequence of her leaving Italy. Ennodius thinks that by forgetting her maternal and familial tasks, Euprepia had assumed a provincial and barbarian attitude:[4]

> Suscepisti mentem provincialium, quos adisti. Mutasti regionem et propositum pietatis abdicasti. Nam abiurans Italiae communionem non solum circa amicos, sed etiam

[1] J.R. Martindale, *The Prosopography of the Later Roman Empire* [henceforth PLRE], *vol. 2: A.D. 395-527* (Cambridge: Cambridge University Press, 1980), 393; Maria Cesa, "Integrazioni prosopografiche tardoimperiali," *Atheneum* 64 (1986): 236-40. Also Stéphane Gioanni, *Ennode de Pavie*, Livre I-IV (Paris: Belles Lettres, 2006-2010).

[2] On the precise nature of Euprepia's relationship to Ennodius, see J.M. Ferrante, "Licet longinquis regionibus corpore separati": Letters as a Link in and to the Middle Ages," *Speculum* 76 (2001): 877-95, esp. 893-5.

[3] Ferrante, "Letters as a Link," 893-5.

[4] Magnus Felix Ennodius, Epistolae II, 15, MGH AA VII, 69. On the subjects of passion, gender, and family, see L. Jégou, S. Joye, T. Lienhard, J. Schneider, *Splendor Reginae. Passions, genre et famille. Mélanges en l'honneur de Régine le Jan* (Turnhout: Brepols, 2015).

circa interna pignora reppulisti. Postremo animae tibi mutatio accessit cum mutatione telluris.

You adopted the mentality of the place where you went. You changed region and abdicated your compassion. By abjuring your communion with Italy you rejected not only the obligations with your friends but also with your family. Finally, by changing land you have changed yourself.

Ennodius' letters show that, in the 6th century, the idea that one might be transformed as a consequence of migration was a familiar and plausible part of the mental landscape of the early Middle Ages, and that such transformations were seen as possible even for women and mothers.

This impressive story with its existential aspects can be regarded as a literary introduction to the subject of women's migration in the early Middle Ages.[5] Some of its features will be central to the points made subsequently in this chapter: Eutropia is a woman, she migrates, she does not follow in a passive way the destiny and lives of her kin. Possibly her lifestyle changes as a consequence of her migration. These patterns may help us to understand the migrations of other socially prominent women (about whom a bit more is known) in the early history of the British Isles. As we will see in what follows, evidence for women's experiences must be sifted from the extant sources. Materials of potential use encompass not only correspondence among members of the same family, but also documents of a more official nature as well as historical narratives and even clauses of legislation.

During the same period, little more than one thousand kilometres north of Milan, another migration was taking place. It was not the personal migration of a woman but a migration of men and women from the northern continental shoreline to Britain. It was a migration that had begun in the fourth century when the first groups of men from Germanic cultures (Saxons, Angles, Frisians), mercenaries and then warrior bands with or without a lord, arrived in the South of England. These men-in-arms were followed in the fifth century by family groups from the Continent.[6] We can only piece together the history from later and at times questionable sources, such as Gildas's *De excidio Britanniae* and Bede's *Historia ecclesiastica*.

According to the sources in the early Middle Ages, Kent was the scene of two stories of migration of women from royal families: Bertha, daughter of King Charibert, moved in 590 from the Court in Paris to the Court in Canterbury with a following which

[5] Cited by Cristina La Rocca, "La migrazione delle donne nell" alto medioevo tra testi scritti e fonti materiali: primi spunti di ricerca," *Archeologia e storia delle migrazioni. Europa, Italia, Mediterraneo fra tarda età romana e alto medioevo*. Atti del convegno internazionale di studi (Cimitile- Santa Maria Capua Vetere, 17-18 giugno 2010) a cura di Carlo Ebanista e Marcello Rotili (Cimitile: Tavolario, 2011), 65-83.

[6] Steven Bassett, *The Origins of Anglo-Saxon Kingdoms* (Leicester: Leicester University Press, 1989), 5.

included various prelates. She was to marry Æthelberht of Kent as part of a Frankish strategy to bring Kent into the Frankish orbit.[7] Pope Gregory I wrote to Bertha on 22 June 601, comparing her to St. Helena who introduced Christianity in the Roman Empire; he declared that God deigned to reserve for her the reward of converting the *gens Anglorum:* "You must, with assiduous exhortations, strengthen your illustrious husband's mind with love for the Christian faith" (*Itaque mentem gloriosi coniugis vestri in dilectione christianae fidei adhortatione adsidua roborate*).[8] Thus historical sources confer on Bertha the role of queen and converter of the king; her active role is stressed by the words of Pope Gregory. The fact that the main narrator of Anglo-Saxon history, Bede, omitted in his *Historia Ecclesiastica* to report Gregory's letter to Bertha shows that Bede wanted to play down Bertha's importance in order to exalt the missionary role of Augustine and his Roman companions.[9]

Later sources tell us about the deeds of another royal daughter. Referring to the legendary time of the arrival of the Saxons in Britain, Nennius in his *Historia Brittonum* (IX sec.) writes about the unnamed daughter (Rowena in Geoffrey of Monmouth's *Historia Regum Britanniae* VI, 12) of the Saxon King Hengist who won for her people the Kingdom of Kent by seducing the British King Vortigern: enamored with her beauty, the king gave her father the province of Kent in return for allowing the marriage.[10] This story shows thus another active king's daughter functioning in her father's politics, and confirms that at the very beginning of Kentish history there was a merger of British and Germanic peoples and influences.[11]

The cases of Bertha and the mysterious Rowena are, however, exceptions. Very little is told about the migration of women belonging to lower social classes. Female migration to the British Isles was rather a silent and invisible migration in the historical narrative sources.[12] That such narratives are invariably authored by male clerics makes

---

[7] Janet L. Nelson, "Queens as Converters of Kings in the Earlier Middle Ages," in *Agire da donna. Modelli e pratiche di rappresentazione (sec. VI-X)*, ed. Cristina La Rocca. Atti del convegno (Padova 18-19 febbraio 2005) (Turnhout: Brepols, 2007), 95-107.

[8] Gregory the Great, *Registrum Epistolarum*, XI,35, MGH Epist. II, 304. Cit. in: Janet Nelson, "Queens as Converters of Kings," 101.

[9] So Janet Nelson, "Queens as Converters of Kings," 101. A discussion of Bede's account in Stephanie Hollis, *Anglo-Saxon Women and the Church* (Woodbridge: Boydell, 1992), esp. 208-42.

[10] Nennius, *British History and the Welsh Annals*, ed. and trans. John Morris (London: Phillimore, 1980), 33.

[11] The same politics can be observed in the Visigothic kingdom. See M. R. Valverde-Castro, "La monarquía visigoda i su política matrimoniale. De Alarico I al fin del reino visigodo de Tolosa," in *Aquitania* XVI (1999): 295-315; M. R. Valverde-Castro, "La monarquía visigoda i su política matrimonial: el reino visigodo de Toledo," in *Studia Historica. Historia Antigua* (2000): 331-55.

[12] On invisible presences see: Nicoletta Giovè, "Donne che non lasciano traccia. Presenze e mani femminili nel documento altomedievale," in *Agire da donna*, ed. La Rocca, 189-209.

it difficult to substantiate female migration both from a quantitative and a qualitative point of view.[13]

With the exception of the archeological data[14]—whose significance is not always easy to evaluate[15]—it is very difficult to document the circumstances surrounding women's migration to Britain. In general, there has been little concerted effort to incorporate gender into the various theories of the migration period (*Völkerwanderungszeit*).[16] Yet understanding gender is critical in the migration context. Using the data with due caution, something can be learnt even from the theoretical works referring to contemporary migration: migrations affect men and women differently, as, for instance, the concentration of men and women in each migratory flow changes according to the different push and pull factors.[17]

Law and migration: Methodological questions

For the investigation of female agency and movements in early England, it can be useful to turn our attention to the first laws released in England after the migration from the Continent. An investigation into the traces of migration of women in Anglo-Saxon legislation involves some unavoidable simplifications and presents us with several

---

[13] As Nelson warns (2007, 99), the historian of women and of gender must be aware of the source-critical problems presented by the available sources in these fields: in other words, of the constructedness of all the sources we have to use, and the presence of gendered stereotypes.

[14] Bonnie Effros, "Dressing Conservatively: Women's Brooches as Markers of Ethnic Identity," *Gender in the Early Medieval World: East and West, 300-900*, ed. Leslie Brubaker and Julia M. H. Smith (Cambridge: Cambridge University Press, 2004), 165-84; Irene Barbiera, *Changing Land in Changing Memory* (Firenze: Firenze University Press, 2005).

[15] Cristina La Rocca, "Figlie e sorelle *peregrinae*. Le migrazioni delle donne nell" alto medioevo," *Storia delle donne* 9 (2013): 71-95; Hubert Fehr, *Germanen und Romanen im Merowingerreich* (Berlin: De Gruyter, 2010).

[16] Peter Heather, *Empires and Barbarians: Migration, Development and the Birth of Europe* (Oxford: Oxford University Press, 2009); Heinrich Härke, "Anglo-Saxon Immigration and Ethnogenesis," *Medieval Archeology* 55 (2011): 1-28.

[17] Insights from recent studies of gender and migrations in K. Donato, D. Gabaccia, J. Holdaway, M. Manalansan, P. Pessar, "A Glass Half Full? Gender in Migration Studies," *The International Migration Review* 40, 1 (2006): 3-26. The field of gender migration studies as a whole has remained marginalized because of the lack of sources. Like gender studies, migration studies have also tried to understand and avoid the creation and defense of disciplinary boundaries. Research on gender and migration in contemporary times takes a broad approach towards the gender dynamics of both international and internal migration and the interconnections between the two. It explores the reasons why women migrate and the role that gender plays in the decision making process. It also explores the implications of gender for the ability of women to access protection, to be employed within differential labour markets and to secure family reunion and other rights.

methodological questions. Some are connected to the particular subject matter of migration and some are inherent in the laws themselves.[18]

Literature about women in Anglo-Saxon legislation is abundant, but not always recent.[19] Comparisons within the Anglo-Saxon laws have been used to trace the transformations in the position of women over time[20] and, also, to consider the relative emancipation of women compared to men.[21] In this, opinions are totally discordant, and a new perspective might reconcile specialists' divergent views. On the basis of the clauses about women in the first set of Anglo-Saxon laws, i.e., those of Kent, especially in the legislation of Æthelberht, issued in the first years of the seventh century, questions about acculturation as a consequence of migration can become particularly relevant.[22]

Further methodological questions arise in regard to the relationship between law and migration. During the migration phase the institutionalization of law was quite impossible. Migration was a fracture of traditions without legal continuity. The customary law related to house and land was not applicable due to the absence of fixed residences. The end of migration and the beginning of a settled life favored the formation of hierarchically structured societies that needed regulation by legal norms. These norms were based partly on customary practice before migration and also took into view new settlement conditions and power structures. Migration and the process of becoming settled in a new surrounding explain the tradition of mixed structures of legal norms represented by Æthelberht's laws. The dominant legal tradition comprised customs known to the people, with local features probably different in different areas, passed along only in oral form.

---

[18] As Mary P. Richards and B. Jane Stanfield, "Concepts of Anglo-Saxon Woman in the Laws," in *New Readings on Women in Old English Literature*, ed. Helen Damico and Alexandra Hennessey Olsen (Bloomington: Indiana University Press, 1989), 89-99, well explain, laws regarding women are not necessarily a body of information on the subject of women's lives, but they are important sources if examined for the underlying ideas they convey about the status of women and the position held in regards to the rest of the community. Moreover, in the early Middle Ages any expression of law was incomplete and not comprehensive. The written laws represent only a fraction of the laws affecting women which may have applied in a restricted geographical area at a specific point in time. The material we have is written text conforming to a specific tradition established and maintained by the ecclesiastical foundation where they were copied and composed.

[19] Use of laws to understand the status of women in the Anglo-Saxon period is found for instance in Christine Fell with Cecily Clark and Elizabeth Williams, *Women in Anglo-Saxon England and the Impact of 1066* (Bloomington: Indiana University Press, 1984). See also Marc A. Mayer, "Land Charters and the Legal Position of Anglo-Saxon Women," in Barbara Kenner, ed., *The Women in England. From Anglo-Saxon Times to the Present*, (London: Shoe String Press, 1979), 57-82.

[20] The English historian Eileen Power speaks of the difficulty in determining what it is that constitutes the position of women in Anglo-Saxon society. Eileen Power, "The Position of Women," in *The Legacy of the Middle Ages*, eds C.G. Crump and E.F. Jacob (Oxford: Clarendon Press, 1926), 401-33.

[21] Anne L. Klinck, "Anglo-Saxon Women and the Law," *Journal of Medieval History 8*, (1982): 107-21.

[22] Daniela Fruscione, "Gender, Social and Marital Status in the 7th Century: the Legal Framework," *Medioevo Europeo* 1 (2017): 55-66.

ÆTHELBERHT'S LEGISLATION AND WOMEN

Several hints about the circulation of women can be found in the clauses of the legislation of Æthelberht issued in the first years of the seventh century.[23] These comprise a very remarkable set of decrees: together with those of Alfred, Ine and Cnut, the laws of Æthelberht contain the greatest number of references to women; moreover, the influence of Christianization on matters regarding women, marriage and family seems minimal.[24]

A first peculiarity of the laws of Æthelberht is that, in comparison to men, women are rarely mentioned, as might be expected of an environment in which the pursuit of vengeance or litigation was the province of men. The position of the decrees regarding women within Æthelberht's laws also suggest something about their place within the social hierarchy of early Kent. Excluding the first provisions, which concern the church and public assembly, the laws of Æthelberht deal first with the king, then move to his household, his nobles, and finally turn to the freeman of the land.[25] Following these provisions are personal injury laws, and, finally, laws regarding those, whose status differs from that of freeman: women, servants and slaves.

Clauses 72 to 77.2 of the Kentish legislation of Æthelberht regard women. In the Kentish laws, women are regarded within four categories: maidens (*mægþ*), wives (*wif*), mothers (*medder*)[26] and widows (*widuwe*). Laws concerning women address mainly family matters, marriage and sexual crimes; in general they consider women from the point of view of their marital status.[27] This peculiarity of the earliest English legislation does not apply to men. Rather, in Kentish laws the male's legal position focuses on

---

[23] Here I follow the numbering of clauses of Oliver, *Beginnings*, but I have not always followed her translation. On the Kentish legislation see also Patrizia Lendinara, "The Kentish Laws," in John Hines, ed., *The Anglo-Saxons from the Migration Period to the Eighth Century: An Ethnographic Perspective*, (Woodbridge: Boydell, 1997), 211-43 and, about the position of women in Æthelberht's laws, see now the essays in Carole Hough, *"An Ald Reht": Essays on Anglo-Saxon Law* (Newcastle-upon-Tyne: Cambridge Scholars Press, 2014).

[24] In terms of language and structure, but also content, Æthelberht's code seems more like traditional Kentish custom presented in a written rather than oral medium. See Lisi Oliver, *The Language of the Early English Laws* (Ph.D. diss. Harvard, 1995); *The Beginnings of English Law*; Patrick Wormald, "Inter cetera bona ... genti suae. Law-making and Peace-Keeping in the Earliest English Kingdoms," in *La giustizia nel Medioevo, sec. V-VIII* (Settimane di studio del centro Italiano di studi sull" Alto Medioevo XLIV, t. 2) (Spoleto 1995): 963-93.

[25] Dirk Korte, *Untersuchungen zu Inhalt, Stil und Technik angelsächsischer Gesetze und Rechtsbücher des 6. bis 12. Jahrhunderts* (Meisenheim am Glan: Archiv für vergleichende Kulturwissenschaft, 1974), esp. 72-7.

[26] *Hl.* 4, see Oliver, *Beginnings*, 128-9.

[27] Oliver, *Beginnings*, 105-14; Fruscione, "Gender, Social and Marital Status in the Seventh Century: The Legal Framework" (in print).

power and authority as defined by rank-oriented stipulations.[28] Social status, not marital, is thus relevant in the provisions regarding men and the classification of males is structured primarily on a top to bottom social order:[29] a man is king (*cyning*), noble (*eorl*), freeman (*frigman, ceorl*), or freedman (*læt*). Both fines for different kinds of offences and the system of compensatory payments due for killing or injuring a person are determined primarily by the social status of the victim.[30]

Laws regarding women are seldom classified by their social status. There are two exceptions: female servants belonging to someone's household, and widows. When it comes to social rank, a woman's worth and legal status is dependent upon those of a male.

In the laws of Æthelberht (chs. 74-74.3)[31] widows are divided into four social ranks. Fell assumes that rank is determined by whose protection the widow is under.[32] A man who removes a widow from the protection of her kin without an appropriate contract is required to pay an appropriate compensation, according to her status.

Clauses relating to female servants are also included in the list of offences structured according to a male social status. Those women belonging to households—such as the cupbearer (*birele*)—are classified according to their task and to the status of their owners. This feature of Æthelberht's laws is particularly evident from the following set of clauses:[33]

[19] Gif wið eorles birele man geligeþ, XII scill gebete [...]
[21] Gif wið ceorles birelan man geligeþ, VI scillingum gebete.

---

[28] Nicholas Brooks, "Arms, Status and Warfare in Late-Saxon England," in David Hill, ed., *Ethelred the Unready: Papers from the Millenary Conference*, BAR, BS 59, (Oxford 1978), 81-103 (see p. 86); Thomas Charles-Edwards, "Early Medieval Kingship in the British Isles," in Steven Basset, ed., *The Origins of Anglo-Saxon Kingdoms*, (Leicester: Leicester University Press, 1989), 28-39 (here esp. 30-1).

[29] Wormald, "Inter cetera bona," 969: "Two perhaps especially helpful indicators in the early English case are style and system. A set of clauses on the church make way for similar blocks on the king, earls, ceorls, enclosure, injury, women, serfs and slaves. System might seem to presuppose a body of material to be organized. In newly Christian Kent that pre-existing body of material would have been oral custom." See also Oliver, *The Language of the Early English Laws*, 37-8.

[30] Daniela Fruscione, "Beginnings and Legitimation of Punishment in Early Anglo-Saxon Legislation (VII-VIII century)," in Jay Gates and Nicole Marafioti, eds. *Corporal and Capital Punishment* (Woodbridge: Boydell, 2014), 35-47.

[31] "For the protection of the foremost widow of noble rank, let him pay 50 shillings. For a widow of the second rank, 20 shillings. For a widow of the third rank, 12 shillings. For a widow of the fourth rank, 6 shillings" (*Mund þare betstan widuwan eorlkunde L scillinga gebete. Ðare oðre XX scll,' ðare þriddan XII scll,' ðare feorðan VI scll'*), in: Oliver, *Beginnings*, 76-7.

[32] Christine Fell, *Women in Anglo-Saxon England*, 61; also: Theodore John Rivers, "Widows' Rights in Anglo-Saxon Law," *The American Journal of Legal History* 19 (1975): 208-15. A different interpretation in: Carole Hough, "The Widow's Mund in Æthelberth 75 and 76," *JEGP* 98 (1999): 1-16.

[33] Oliver, *Beginnings*, 66-7.

[21.1] Æt þære oþere ðeowan, L scætta.
[21.2] Æt þære þriddan ðeowan, XXX scætta.

[19] If a person lies with a nobleman's cupbearer, let him pay 12 shillings [...]
[21] If a person lies with a freeman's cupbearer, let him pay with 6 shillings.
[21.1] For the second rank of female slave, 50 sceattas.
[21.2] For the third rank of female slave, 30 sceattas.

Moreover the names that refer to a woman in servitude rarely occur as the subject of a sentence; more often they are linked with the preposition *wið* (with): "wið cyninges mægdenman/wif, wið eorles/ceorles birele." Thus, the subject of the sentence is the male offender. These clauses suggest just how embedded in the conventions of early Kentish legislative prose was the notion of women's legal agency as something inseparable from the responsibilities of men in positions of oversight.

Women in movement: marriage, separation and rape

From laws affecting an unmarried virgin to rules about widows, the legislation of Æthelberht gives us an idea of how law may have affected a woman over the course of her lifetime. The laws regard women far more diachronically than they do men. Movement and transformation characterize especially those sentences regarding marriage. The personal circulation of noble or royal women from the paternal home to the husband's is well documented in historical sources, but only the legal sources document the internal migration of free women, who, as a consequence of marriage, are regarded as subjects imported from another familial background. Two clauses show us the strong patrilocality of the Kentish society; in *Æthelberht* 76-76.1[34] one reads:

> Gif mon mægþ gebigeð ceapi, geceapod sy gif hit unfacne is. Gif hit þonne facne is, ef þær æt ham gebrenge, 7 him man his scæt agefe.
>
> If a person buys a maiden with a price, let the bargain be valid if there is no deception. If there is deception, afterwards let him bring her to her home, and let him be given his money.

In the law referring to the marriage contract, we are told that if a person takes a maiden for a (bride) price,[35] the bargain is valid only if there is no deception: this refers to the

---

[34] Oliver, *Beginnings*, 78-9.

[35] Regarding Kentish betrothal and marriage, discussion has begun about whether the laws refer to marriage by purchase or not. See Richards and Stanfield, "Concepts of Anglo-Saxon Woman in the Laws," 94; Angela M. Lucas, *Women in the Middle Ages* (New York: St. Martin's Press, 1983), esp. 64; James A. Brundage, *Law, Sex, und Christian Society* (Chicago: University of Chicago Press, 1987), 147 n. 94. Even

virginity of the bride.[36] Virginity was important to establish the legitimacy of the line of succession and to ensure that the children a man raised were his own. If the intended wife was not a virgin she could be returned (*æt ham gebrenge*) and the bride-price refunded. This rule thus maintains a form of patrilocality that causes the emergence of a dowry, the price for a bride that compensates the loss of her worth in the feminine labor force, something of major economic significance in handicraft and agriculture.[37] Moreover, this amount of money could secure the woman's survival in case of separation or death of the husband.[38]

Another clause that confirms patrilocality can be found in *Hlothere and Eadric* 4: "If a freeman should die with a living wife and child, it is right that the child should follow its mother" (*Gif ceorl acwyle be libbendum wife J bearne, riht is þæt hit, þæt bearn, medder folgige*). Here it is prescribed that the child of a deceased father should follow its mother if she decides to go back to her own kin group.[39] But it was not only the death of the husband that might require the return of the woman to the paternal kin. The laws of Æthelberht deal with married women mostly in their connection to separation.[40] Separation was allowed and both men and women could initiate it.[41] *Æthelberht* 76.5 states that at the end of a childless marriage, both the property that the wife brought into the marriage and the morning gift returned to the woman's family:[42]

> Gif hio bearn ne gebyreþ, fæderingmagas fioh agan 7 morgengife.
>
> If she does not bear a child, her paternal kin should obtain property and the morning-gift.[43]

---

if the vocabulary has a strong economic bias (*facn, ceapi*), the discussion has tended to go awry due to insufficient attention to the likely historical setting; certainly the evolutionistic nuance of this discussion is misplaced. If we consider that marriage contracts, *Eheverträge* and *contratti di nozze* are a very modern institution, it is inappropriate to state that in the early Middle Ages "die Frau im grunde nur eine Sache ist" (fundamentally, a women is only a thing), so Siegfrid Rietschel, "Ehe," *RGA* 1, 499-502, here 501; see also Hough, *"An Ald Reht,"* 125-6 n. 70.

36 Fell, *Women in Anglo-Saxon England*, 59.

37 P. Middleton, *Weaving Destiny: Changes in the Significance of Textile Production to the Economy of Anglo-Saxon England and Its Impact on Female Labour and Status*, 1995 (unpubl. M.A. thesis, University of Reading). Archeological data confirm that: "The exclusive association of textile tools with female burials is strongly suggestive of textile production having been (or been presented as being) in the hands of women." So Heinrich Härke, "Early Anglo-Saxon Social Structure," in Hines, ed., *The Anglo-Saxons from the Migration Period to the Eighth Century*, 125-170, here 136.

38 Uwe Wesel, *Geschichte des Rechts* (Munich: C.H. Beck, 1997), esp. 38.

39 Oliver, *Beginnings*, 112.

40 A different interpretation of the "divorce laws" in Hough, *"An Ald Reht"*, 130-49.

41 Reiner Schulze, "Ehebruch," RGA 6 (1986): 479-80.

42 J. Goody, *Die Entwicklung von Ehe und Familie in Europa* (Berlin: Surhkamp, 1986), 31.

43 Oliver, *Beginnings*, 78-9.

Although the woman seems to have played a passive role here, other clauses in the marriage laws support the premise that women also had a voice in the marriage transaction.[44] They could leave if they wished, so *Æthelberht* 76.3: [45]

> Gif mid bearnum bugan wille, healfne scæt age.
>
> If she should wish to leave with the children, let her obtain half the goods.

The wife's share of the property under these circumstances depended upon whether she took the children with her or left them with the husband (76.4):

> Gif ceorl agan wile, swa an bearn.
>
> If the husband wants to have them, provision as for one child.[46]

Another aspect connected to the spatial movement of women in Æthelbert's laws is the rape of a virgin. Provisions against rape play a major role in early medieval legislation and also in *Æthelberht* 77-77.2:

> [77] Gif man mægþmon nede genimeþ, ðam agende L scillinga ond eft æt þa agende sinne willan æt gebicge.
> [77.1] Gif hio oþrum mæn in sceat bewyddod sy, XX scillinga gebete.
> [77.2] Gif gængang geweorðeþ, XXXV scill(inga) ond cyninge XV scillingas.
>
> [77] If a person takes a maiden by force: to the owner of her protection 50 shillings, and afterwards let him buy from the owner his consent.
> [77.1] If she should be betrothed to another man by goods, let him pay 20 shillings to that man as well.
> [77.2] If return occurs, 35 shillings and 15 shillings to the king.[47]

One who abducts or rapes a maiden must pay the owner of her protection 50 shillings; he must then negotiate a bride-price with the owner of the maiden's protection. If a marriage contract with another man has already been made, the abductor must pay another 20 shillings.[48] These stipulations suggest a world in which wrongs and even acts of violence against women were conceived of primarily as wrongs against the men under whose supervision women would spend the duration of their lives.

---

[44] Reiner Schulze, "Ehebruch," *RGA* 6 (1986): 479-80.
[45] Oliver, *Beginnings*, 78-9.
[46] Oliver, *Beginnings*, 78-9.
[47] Oliver, *Beginnings*, 78-9.
[48] On this Oliver, *Beginnings*, 108-9, and Hough, *"An Ald Reht,"*, 150-7.

MIGRATION: INFLUENCES AND ACCULTURATION

The possibility given a woman to leave her husband is an exception in the Germanic early medieval continental laws and also in later Anglo-Saxon legislation, but not altogether unique in the British landscape of the same period. Irish and Welsh women also had this freedom. In the Irish *Cáin lánamna* (an early Irish legal tract on marriage, c. eighth century), *imscarad* ("divorce") is permitted for many reasons. In the following cases, the woman may retain her *coibche*, bride price:

1. If the man leaves her for another woman.
2. If the man is impotent or homosexual.
3. If he is so fat as to be incapable of intercourse.
4. If the man relates secrets of the marriage bed in the alehouse.[49]

British separation customs thus influenced the Germanic female population of Kent. A merging of cultures as a result of prolonged contact is natural and intermarriages must have occurred rather often. They were vehicles of acculturation. We have even seen an acknowledgement of them in the Geoffrey of Monmouth's (presumably fictional) account of the marriage between the daughter of the Saxon Hengist and the British Vortigern.

Cultural modification of the Germanic groups in Britain, through adapting to or borrowing traits from the local British culture—a somewhat neglected field of research—is partly at the basis of legislation regarding women. Thus, one question suggested by the laws of Kent is whether the right of Kentish women to separate is a sign of their relative emancipation. When we consider the Kentish regulations about women in their context, we realize that the principle of emancipation or equality gives little insight into the legal status of Kentish women. Instead, other principles appear to have a key role in an interpretation of the position of women in the Kentish laws: reproductive compulsion and inheritance strategy, for instance. The right to separation which is given to women has to do with the importance of procreation: the woman might leave if the marriage was no longer fruitful. This was convenient for the entire kin group and in the interests of the small ethnic groups in the South of England: the number of settlers in the new foreign environment, both as warriors and as farmers, was of great importance. Æthelberht's separation law can thus be regarded as an innovation, a result

[49] Christopher McAll, "The Normal Paradigms of a Woman's Life in the Irish and Welsh Law Texts," in Dafydd Jenkins and Morfydd E. Owen, eds. *The Welsh Law of Women* (Cardiff: University of Wales Press, 1980), 7-22; David M. Walker, *A Legal History of Scotland* (Edinburgh: Edinburgh University Press, 1988); Robin Chapman Stacey, "Divorce, Medieval Welsh Style," *Speculum* 77 (2002): 1108-27; Stefan Christian Saar, *Ehe-Scheidung-Wiederheirat: Zur Geschichte der Ehe und des Ehescheidungsrechts im Frühmittelalter (6.-10. Jh.)* (Münster: LIT Verlag, 2002), 323-7.

of the acculturation between the migrant female population in Kent and the native customs they found there.

Connected to the new social order created by the migration is, according to new research, the frequent emergence of rape and the consequent legislation. In a recent work, the French historian Sylvie Joye has shown that rape is not a form of marriage in early Germanic culture as maintained by earlier research.[50] The concept of rape was neither, in an evolutionistic interpretation, a first step toward marriage nor even a part of the brutal or emotional nature of "barbaric" kidnappers.[51] Rape in the early Middle Ages was, rather, a strategy of marital union without the consent of the father-protector.[52] It was the result of a migration that breaks prior social arrangements and, thus, creates a tension among different and new groups in a social ascent. As a consequence of rape, which we can consider a change in the marital status of the woman, there is a change in the social status of a man. Raping the proper virgin can be seen as a means for a man to change his material, and perhaps social, condition.

Conclusions

From the Kentish sources I have analyzed, the following traces of female migration emerge. With regard to humbler people from crowded settlements on the North Sea, where deteriorating climatic conditions made life untenable, few traces survive in the narrative sources. Yet the circulation of women in the early Middle Ages in Kent is well documented and perhaps should be considered a kind of migration in itself.[53] Migrations accompany marriage, widowhood and separation. Migration is a corollary to every change of marital status. From the movement from the paternal home to the husband's, or from one land to the other, the medieval woman lived her life as an outsider, as a subject imported from other states and from other familial backgrounds. As Janet Nelson writes: "In most of the cases the king's wife was a married-in outsider. Royal marriages, in other words, like marriages in general and more locally, meant locational stability for the bridegroom, spatial movement for the bride."[54]

---

50 Sylvie Joye, *La femme ravie* (Turnhout: Brepols, 2012).

51 Stephanie Jamison, "Penelope and the Pigs: Indic Perspectives on the Odyssey," *Classical Antiquity* 18 (1999): 227-72; Werner Boes, *Frauenraub und Raubehe bei den westgermanischen Stämmen des Merowingerreiches*, unpubl. Ph.D. diss. (Bonn 1956); Lothar von Dargun, *Mutterrecht und Raubehe und ihre Reste im germanischen Recht und Leben* (Breslau: W. Koebner, 1883).

52 Joye, *La femme ravie*, 306.

53 So for instance La Rocca, "Figlie e sorelle *peregrinae*", 83.

54 Nelson "Queens as Converters of Kings," 97.

Historians and archaeologists have highlighted the active role of these married-in wives as converters and as cultural transfers. Janet Nelson[55] and Cristina La Rocca[56] have demonstrated that the foreign royal wives were active players within their new territories, not only as bearers of new ethnic identities for their children, but also in proposing new models. Charting the Germanic migrations, Bonnie Effros comes to the conclusion that women are not the passive reflection of the ethnic identity of their family group,[57] as postulated by those scholars who persist in the idea that migrating women wore the clothing of a single ethnic heritage from birth to death.[58] The assumed passivity of early medieval women is more an aprioristic element than a reality.[59]

The supposed resistance of women to external influences and to the new surrounding is partly contradicted by the legal data. The old point of view, that migrating women did not change their life-context, is not sustainable for Kent, where a new ethnic identity and culture were acquired. Here the names of the people coming from the North Sea—the Saxons, Frisians, and Angles—disappear at least for a while. *Cantwara cyningas* were the "kings of Kent" and *Cantwara rihtum þeawum* the "just legal customs of the Kentish people."

Some laws of the Kentish people suggest that women questioned indeed the hierarchical relationships within the domestic sphere, both with their father and their husband. Æthelberht's separation law reflects a picture of a woman as a vehicle for innovation. Daughters who wished to challenge the paternal desire were obliged to do so by changing their marital status. An aspect of the representation of women in Æthelberht's law is the rape of the virgin. As the vocabulary of rape shows (*neþe genimeþ* "take by force," *gængang* "go against, return") [60], this transgression is considered a migration to an unknown, dangerous territory.

That women's migration could be considered from the (male) observer as a transgression of marital or familial rules is also illustrated by the account of Bishop Ennodius' sister Euprepia, with which this chapter began. Euprepia's story indeed reflects some important aspects of (female) migration: Every migration history has two sides. We know something about Euprepia's life in Italy, her country of origin; we know what she left

[55] Nelson, "Gendering Courts in the Early Medieval West," 195-7.
[56] La Rocca, "La migrazione delle donne nell" alto medioevo tra testi scritti e fonti materiali: primi spunti di ricerca," 66-7.
[57] Effros, "Dressing Conservatively," 179-84.
[58] Max Martin, "Fibel und Fibeltracht: Späte Volkerwanderungszeit und Merowingerzeot auf dem Kontinent," *RGA* 8 (1994): 574-7.
[59] La Rocca, "Figlie e sorelle *peregrinae*," 78.
[60] On these expressions: Oliver, *Beginnings*, 108-9; Carole Hough, "A Reappraisal of *Æthelberht* 84," *Nottingham Medieval Studies* 37 (1993): 1-6. Christine Fell, "An Appendix to Carole Hough's Article: A Reappraisal of *Æthelberht* 84," *Nottingham Medieval Studies* 37 (1993): 8.

and how her dearest felt about her departure. Not many insights about her life in the country of destination are kept. According to her brother's letters she simply went off to the "provinces."

Euprepia, while migrating, did not simply transfer the dynamics of her place of origin to the place of arrival. The new context of her life was not conceived exclusively as a pure geographical transfer; her migration and new life questioned the hierarchical relationships within the domestic sphere with her brother Ennodius and even with her child Lupicinus. The bishop's letters to his sister contain explicit statements of their physical separation and her change of location (*regionum mutatione*). Moreover, the documents involving Euprepia offer an excellent point from which to observe the author's emotions and judgements about his sister's migration. [61]

Whatever the reason for her migration—possibly the desire to be a pilgrim—Euprepia had to confront her brother's intense feelings about family matters and his concerns and his complaints about her way of life. Ennodius wondered where her love as a mother and as a sister had been hiding: "By the dispensation of heaven's mystery, at the same time I was denied a sister's affection and Lupicinus a mother's fondness, and after a while our double family tie was entitled to receive your absent devotion" (*Caelestis dispensatione mysterii uno tempore mihi sororis, Lupicinus refusus est matris affectus, et geminae copula necessitudinis peregrinantem recipere meruit post intervalla pietatem*).[62] As in the laws of Kent, where such tensions are perhaps more fully documented, no one exists outside the demands of kinship and other forms of authority, and the intensity of these demands is supremely evident in the lives of women who move to places that make them inaccessible to such pressures.

[61] On emotions in the early Middle Ages, see: Barbara H. Rosenwein, "Identity and emotions in the early Middle Ages," in Walter Pohl, ed., *Die Suche nach den Ursprüngen* (Wien: Verlag der österreichischen Akademie der Wissenschaften, 2004), 129-37, here 133. On emotions also Barbara H. Rosenwein, "Writing and Emotions in Gregory of Tours," in Walter Pohl and Paul Herold, eds. *Vom Nutzen des Schreibens. Soziales Gedächtnis, Herrschaft und Besitz,* (Wien: Verlag der österreichischen Akademie der Wissenschaften, 2002), 23-32.

[62] Magnus Felix Ennodius, Epistolae II, 15, MGH AA VII, 68. Translation taken from S.A.H. Kennell, *Magnus Felix Ennodius: A Gentleman of the Church* (Ann Arbor: University of Michigan Press, 2000), 132.

The Body Legal in Frisian Law: Bridging the Gap Between the *Lex Frisionum* and the Old Frisian Compensation tariffs

Han Nijdam

Lisi Oliver's *The Body Legal in Barbarian Law* is a monumental work. By writing this monograph, Lisi did what should have been done more than a century ago, i.e. comparing the various early medieval *Leges Barbarorum* to a level of detail which yields hard, verifiable and comparable data.[1] Through her work we now know which early medieval law code addressed which body part, which type of wound, and how they valued these.

One thing her analysis clearly shows is the enormous variation in the various *Leges Barbarorum*. Yes, there are similarities and regional and interregional tendencies, which Lisi nicely illustrates by including a number of maps in the book, but variation prevails.[2] This seems to confirm what legal historian Patrick Wormald had already observed: "a tariff recognizable as one's own was perhaps itself an ethnic marker."[3] Hence, it is impossible to reconstruct a Proto-Germanic tariff even though there seems to be a set of legal terms pertaining to this field of injuries and body parts that can be found over almost the entire Germanic speaking area.[4]

If a tariff was indeed an ethnic marker, then the Frisians surely did their best to express their ethnicity. Not only is the compensation tariff in the *Lex Frisionum* the longest of all *Leges Barbarorum*, it is even supplemented by additonal material that can be found in the curious *Additiones Sapientum* or "additions of the wise men" which forms an appendix to the law code of the Frisians. Again, we can cite Patrick Wormald

[1] Han Nijdam, "Indigenous or Universal? A Comparative Perspective on Medieval (Frisian) Compensation Law," in *How Nordic are the Nordic Laws? Ten Years After: Proceedings of the Tenth Carlsberg Conference on Medieval Legal History 2013*, ed. Per Andersen, Kirsi Salonen, Helle Sigh, Helle Vogt (Copenhagen: DJOF Publishing, 2014), 177-80.

[2] Lisi Oliver, *Body Legal*, 227-37.

[3] Patrick Wormald, "The *Leges Barbarorum*: Law and Ethnicity in the Post-Roman West," in *Regna and Gentes: The Relationship between Late Antique and Early Medieval Peoples and Kingdoms in the Transformation of the Roman World*, ed. H.-W. Goetz, J. Jarnut and W. Pohl (Leiden: Brill, 2003), 41.

[4] Nijdam, "Indigenous Or Universal?", 180-1.

here: "not content with providing by far the longest and most elaborate tariff, [it] proceeds to expand and modify this with a series of *Additiones Sapientum*."[5]

Not many scholars know that this abundance of tariff material continued into the later Middle Ages. The Frisians, living along the coast of the North Sea on the European continent, upheld their own indigenous legal system as a consequence of their political autonomy. This meant that the early medieval material as witnessed in the *Lex Frisionum* developed in an organic manner in the course of the Middle Ages, only to be drastically changed by the end of the Middle Ages because of the big political revolutions that took place in that period. Before that, however, the tariff genre bloomed. Since medieval Frisia can be labelled as an "economy of honour," the tariffs were a useful tool to avert or help settle vengeance and blood feud in a society that had no central ruler.[6]

This contribution seeks to fill the gap between the tariffs presented in the *Lex Frisionum* and those found in the (earliest) vernacular Old Frisian tradition. Are there certain continuities between them? And can we date the beginnings of the Old Frisian written tradition? Is it possible to identify a few fingerprints of the Frisians as far as compensation tariffs are concerned?

The *Lex Frisionum* and Its Compensation Tariffs

The *Lex Frisionum* is one of the most curious of all *Leges Barbarorum*. No original manuscripts containing the text have survived. Scholars have to rely on the edition made by Johannes Herold in 1557. The extensive study of the *Lex Frisionum* by Harald Siems has shown that there is no reason to doubt the authenticity of the law code. First, a few early medieval sources refer to "the law of the Frisians." Second, we know of at least two medieval manuscripts containing the text.[7]

On the basis of the types of money mentioned, the text is thought to have been drawn up between 785 and 793/4.[8] The form in which it has come down to us most

5 Wormald, "The *Leges Barbarorum*," 53.

6 Han Nijdam, "Compensating Body and Honor: The Old Frisian Compensation Tariffs," in *Medicine and Law in the Middle Ages*, ed. Wendy J. Turner and Sara M. Butler (Leiden: Brill, 2014), 25-57.

7 Harald Siems, *Studien zur Lex Frisionum* (Ebelsbach: Verlag Rolf Gremer, 1980), 49-57; Han Nijdam, "A Comparison of the Injury Tariffs in the Early Kentish and the Frisian Law Codes," in *Frisians and their North Sea Neighbours: From the Fifth Century to the Viking Age*, ed. John Hines and Nelleke IJssennagger (Woodbridge: The Boydell Press, 2017), 223-42.

8 D.J. Henstra, *The Evolution of the Money Standard in Medieval Frisia: A Treatise on the History of the Systems of Money of Account in the Former Frisia (c. 600-c. 1500)* (Groningen: RUG, 2000), 70-1, 277-90; D.J. Henstra, "Het probleem van de geldbedragen in de *Lex Frisionum*." *Jaarboek voor Munt- en Penningkunde* 88 (2001): 1-32.

likely represents a text that was not yet finished.[9] This would explain the *Additiones sapientum* or "additions of the wise men." Two legal experts, Wlemar and Saxmund, added material to the main text. These wise men most likely came from the two areas adjacent to either side of the Frisian core region. In the *Lex Frisionum*, Frisia is divided into three parts: a western region between Sincfal and Vlie (i.e. from the Dutch-Belgian border along the coast to the IJsselmeer), a central region between Vlie and Lauwers (i.e. the present-day Dutch province of Friesland), and an eastern region between Lauwers and Weser (i.e. the present day Dutch province of Groningen and the province of Ostfriesland in Germany).

The last section in the main text of the *Lex Frisionum*, Title XXII, is devoted to wounds and their compensations. It contains 89 clauses. In all, the main text counts 191 clauses. Following this main text, the *Additiones Sapientum* contains a further 102 clauses. A paragraph of one of these wise men, Wlemar, has mistakenly moved into the text of the *Lex Thuringorum* in the edition by Herold. It is unclear whether Herold made this mistake or whether this reflects the situation in the manuscript he used for his edition. This mistake has long since been spotted and emended. This section contains a further 11 clauses on wounds. This means that the total sum of clauses in the *Additiones sapientum* is 113. Of these, 99 clauses deal with compensations for wounds (see table I in appendix). If we add this to the 89 clauses of the main text, we can conclude that 188 of the total of 308 clauses of the complete text of the *Lex Frisionum*—roughly two thirds—deal with wounds. Surely, this says something about the importance this material had in the eyes of the Frisians.

There has been a lot of discussion on the tariff material that can be found in the *Additiones Sapientum*.[10] The tariff in the main text is thought to stem from central Frisia. But where did Wlemar and Saxmund come from and how does the tariff material from the *Additiones* fit together? Here, we have no other option than to rely on the edition by Herold. If we do so, it would mean that Title II and Title III, 1-58 and 76-8, as well as the section from the *Lex Thuringorum* (Title VI, 14-24) can be ascribed to Wlemar. Only Title III, 59-75 are said to stem from Saxmund, i.e. no more than 16 clauses. These seem to be little more than an addition to an addition, whereas the tariff dictated by Wlemar counts 82 clauses, which comes close to the 89 clauses of Title XXII of the main text and thus can perhaps be considered to be a tariff on its own.

The conclusion would then be that we have two "complete" compensation tariffs in the *Lex Frisionum*, i.e. Title XXII and the tariff by Wlemar in the *Additiones Sapientum*. That Wlemar gave his own complete version of what he knew about injury compensation

---

[9] Siems, *Studien*, 350-3.

[10] Siems, *Studien*, 353-65.

and did not simply add to what had already been stated in Title XXII explains why over 40 clauses occur twice: once in Title XXII and once in the *Additiones* section. Some even appear three times, when the Saxmund section yields a third instance of the same clause (see table 3 in appendix). Never are these clauses exact copies of each other: they are always phrased a little differently. To cite just one example:

> XXII.83. Si quis alium iuxta aquam stantem impinxerit, et in aquam, ita ut submergatur, proiecerit, IIII solidos componat, et pro freda solidos II.
>
> 83. If someone pushes another person, who is standing next to water, and throws him into the water, so that the victim is submerged, he has to compensate with 4 solidi, and with 2 solidi for the general peace.
>
> AS III.41. Qui alium in aquam impinxerit, ita ut mergatur, ter IIII solidos componat. [Wlemar]
>
> 41. If someone throws another person into the water, so that the victim is submerged, he has to compensate with three times 4 solidi.
>
> AS III.66. Qui alium in flumine, vel in qualibet aqua, in profundum impinxerit, ut pedibus terram tangere non possit sed natare debeat, ter XII solidos componat. [Saxmund]
>
> 66. If someone throws another person into a river, or in any type of deep water, so that the victim can not touch the ground with his feet but has to swim, he has to compensate with three times 12 solidi.

One last problem to be addressed here is that of the structure of the tariffs. The latest editors, Eckhardt and Eckhardt, deemed it necessary to change both the order of the clauses in Title XXII as well as those in the *Additiones* section.[11] In the latter case, it is obvious that something went wrong there since a section ended up in the *Lex Thuringorum*. For this present analysis, however, it means that we are dealing with such an amount of uncertainty, that the structure of the texts cannot be compared to the structures of the Old Frisian tariffs.

The Old Frisian Vernacular Law Texts

After the *Lex Frisionum* had been written down—forming the capstone of the incorporation of Frisia into the Carolingian empire—no legal sources are attested for centuries. The first complete manuscripts with Old Frisian—i.e. vernacular—law texts stem from

[11] Karl August Eckhardt and Albrecht Eckhardt, eds. *Lex Frisionum*. Monumenta Germaniae Historica. Fontes iuris Germanici antiqui in usum scholarum separatim editi XII (Hannover: Hahnsche Buchhandlung, 1982), 74.

the end of the thirteenth century. It is clear, though, that these codices are copies of earlier exemplars. But when exactly did the Frisians begin to put their laws into writing?

Answering this question is seriously hampered by the fact that during the Protestant Reformation, around 1580, all Frisian monasteries were closed down. Their lands and goods fell to the central government and their archives and libraries were largely destroyed. Only a handful of antiquarians picked up the scattered pieces: all extant Old Frisian codices have been in the hands of such individuals since the sixteenth century.[12] There has thus been a gigantic loss of written sources stemming from medieval Frisia in general.

That leaves us with two distinct questions: when was the Old Frisian vernacular first written down and what is the date of the oldest Old Frisian law texts? Until recently, the oldest piece of written Old Frisian consisted of a parchment leaf dated to c. 1200, used as scrap material to stuff the binding of a book. It contained a fragment of the psalms in Latin, with interverbal glosses in Old Frisian.[13] In 2015, however, a new find came to light. This comprised two small parchment fragments of what also had been a psalter turned to new use. The fragments had been used as medieval variants of Post-Its. They had been glued to the sides of pages of a book in order to find a specific chapter or spot in that book. The fragments came up for auction at Sotheby's and their original context or provenance is unknown to researchers.[14] Although they comprise less than a single leaf, the fragments still yield a few lines of Latin psalm glossed with words in the Frisian vernacular. In total, the harvest is eight Old Frisian words—the oldest Old Frisian found to this day. With the help of his paleographical database, Leiden scholar Erik Kwakkel was able to date the psalms themselves to the end of the eleventh century. The Old Frisian interlinear glosses proved to be slightly younger: Kwakkel dated them to 1100-1125.[15]

These recently discovered psalm fragments make the date scholars of the past put on the oldest Old Frisian law texts—the eleventh century—more plausible. Among these

---

[12] Rolf H. Bremmer, Jr. *Hir is eskriven. Lezen en schrijven in de Friese landen rond 1300* (Hilversum: Verloren, 2004), 13-17; Han Nijdam and Jorieka Savelkouls, "The Manuscript Collection of the Frisian State Historian Simon Abbes Gabbema (1628-1688) from an Old Frisian Perspective," in *Frisian Through the Ages. Festschrift for Rolf H. Bremmer Jr.* Amsterdamer Beiträge zur älteren Germanistik 77, ed. Michiel de Vaan and Stephen Laker (Leiden: Brill, 2017), 303-32.

[13] Erika Langbroek, "*Condensa atque Tenebrosa*; die altfriesischen Psalmen: Neulesung und Rekonstruktion (UB Groningen Hs 404)," in *Aspects of Old Frisian Philology*, ed. Rolf H. Bremmer, Jr., Geart van der Meer, and Oebele Vries (Amsterdam: Rodopi, 1990), 255-284.

[14] This information was not disclosed by Sotheby's.

[15] Erika Langbroek, in collaboration with Francis Brands. "So viel geschrieben, so wenig geblieben. Eine neue Entdeckung: unbekannte altfriesische Psalmglossen." *Amsterdamer Beiträge zur älteren Germanistik* 74 (2015): 135-46.

texts, the so-called *Seventeen Statutes* is the most prominent and most discussed.[16] The main arguments for dating the *Seventeen Statutes* to the eleventh century were the following. First, raiding Vikings are still mentioned in some paragraphs (the last raid took place in 1010). Second, the town of Münster is called *Mimigerdaford*, a name which fell into abeyance after 1040.[17] Third, more recently, numismatic scholar Dirk Jan Henstra showed that the amount of *wergild* mentioned in one of the *statutes* can be dated to the first half of the eleventh century.[18] Note too that all three arguments point to roughly the same period, i.e. halfway the eleventh century.

This classic view was challenged by Rolf Bremmer in 2004, who argues that the Old Frisian sources could not have been written before 1200.[19] Bremmer asserts that a written culture could not have arisen in Frisia before 1200 because the area lacked the necessary infrastructure such as cities or royal courts where archives were kept and where writing activities took place.[20] Bremmer suggests that such an infrastructure only arose after the large-scale foundation of monastic houses that took place between 1150 and 1200. Although Bremmer provides a compelling account of the institutional circumstances that gave rise to Frisian literate culture, there is good reason to believe that literacy of this sort may have existed earlier in the churches and monasteries that had been established in Frisia after its Christianization in the eighth and ninth centuries.[21]

Moreover, Hans Mol and Gilles de Langen have recently argued that the infrastructure of the earliest parishes and mother churches which covered the entire Frisian region which fell under the diocese of Utrecht was rolled out rather rapidly in the period 950-1000.[22] After the year 1000, then, an infrastructure of churches and parishes was in place, thus enabling regular synodal law court sessions, and the bishop visited the region officially every four years. Furthermore, these churches were modest centres of learning and writing. To give one example: in 1148 the St. Vitus church of Leeuwarden housed four priests, a vicar and three clerics.[23]

---

[16] N.E. Algra, *Zeventien Keuren en Vierentwintig Landrechten* (Doorn: GRAAL, 1992); Jens Hoekstra, *Die gemeinfriesischen Siebzehn Küren* (Assen: Van Gorcum, 1940).

[17] Algra, *Zeventien Keuren*, 252-5.

[18] D.J. Henstra, "De eerste optekening van de algemeen-Friese keuren," *It Beaken* 64 (2002): 99-128.

[19] Bremmer, *Hir is eskriven*; A.T. Popkema, "Old Frisian: A Legal Language in Principle," in *Directions for Old Frisian Philology*, ed. Rolf H. Bremmer Jr., Stephen Laker and Oebele Vries (Amsterdam: Rodopi, 2014), 369-96.

[20] Bremmer, *Hir is eskriven*, 81-6.

[21] Henstra, "De eerste optekening"; J.A. Mol, and K. van Vliet. "De oudste oorkonde van het Sint-Odulphusklooster van Staveren." *Jaarboek voor Middeleeuwse Geschiedenis* 1 (1998): 73-134; G.J. De Langen, and J.A. Mol. "Church Foundation and Parish Formation in Frisia in the Tenth and Eleventh Centuries: A Planned Development?" *The Medieval Low Countries* vol. 4 (2017).

[22] De Langen and Mol, "Church Foundation and Parish Formation in Frisia."

[23] Bremmer, *Hir is eskriven*, 30.

In all, it seems the early development of vernacular written culture in Frisia needs to be re-examined. Not only do the Old Frisian texts give us reason to do this, the most recent find of Old Frisian writing just after 1100 confirms this. In spite of the doubts concerning the traditional dating of the oldest Old Frisian law texts, there does seem to be enough evidence to support the classic view that the oldest Old Frisian law texts are indeed very archaic and were first written down in the 11th century.

THE OLD FRISIAN COMPENSATION TARIFFS

In the field of Old Frisian studies, the compensation tariffs have traditionally received less attention from scholars than the two oldest law texts, the *Seventeen Statutes* and the slightly younger *Twenty-Four Land Laws*.[24] Yet it is precisely these tariffs which can be linked directly to the *Lex Frisionum*.

Within the Old Frisian tariff tradition, the text known as the *General Old East Frisian Compensation Tariff* or, shorter, *General Compensation Tariff* is the oldest. It appears in the oldest Old Frisian law manuscripts which have survived, which date to c. 1300. There are three Old Frisian versions, one Latin and one Low German version of the text within the Old Frisian manuscript corpus. Moreover, the divergence between the various redactions in these manuscripts is so extensive, that the prototext must date back a considerable length of time. Small wonder then that this text is also traditionally dated to the eleventh century.

The Latin version of the *General Compensation Tariff* forms part of a collection of texts in Latin that can be found in the so-called First and Second Hunsingo manuscripts; two related manuscripts from the Groningen area that are dated c. 1325-1350.[25] This Latin collection contains translations of the Old Frisian law texts the *Seventeen Statutes*, the *Twenty-Four Land Laws* and the *General Compensation Tariff*. It also harbours a few texts that were originally written in Latin: the so-called *Privilege of Charlemagne*, a fabricated charter according to which Charlemagne gave the Frisians their rights to autonomy, as well as a text called *Quoniam contra falsam assertionem*. This last text refers to a decree stemming from the Fourth Lateran Council that took place in

---

24 Rolf H. Bremmer, Jr. *A Bibliographical Guide to Old Frisian Studies* (Odense: Odense University Press, 1992), 194.

25 Jelle Hoekstra, ed. *De eerste en de tweede Hunsinger codex*. Oudfriese taal- en rechtsbronnen 6 (The Hague: Martinus Nijhoff, 1950); Wybren Jan Buma and Wilhelm Ebel, eds., *Das Hunsingoer Recht* (Göttingen: Vandenhoeck & Ruprecht, 1969); Annelies Roeleveld, "*Providentia et plicht*: The Old Frisian Words in the Latin Texts of the Hunsingo Manuscripts," in *Aspects of Old Frisian Philology*, ed. Bremmer, Van der Meer and Vries, 371-90.

1215.[26] The *Privilege of Charlemagne* has been tentatively dated to the end of the thirteenth century.[27] In all, there is still much we do not know about this collection of Latin texts.

The five versions of the *General Compensation Tariff* differ in size, as can be seen in table 2 in the appendix. Two subgroups can be discerned: on the one hand there are the Latin, Hunsingo and Emsingo versions, which differ in size between c. 130 and 145 clauses. On the other, there is the Riustring tradition, of which we have both an Old Frisian and a later, Low German version (which goes back to a lost Old Frisian version). These are considerably smaller: both c. 100 clauses. The difference in size between these two subgroups is caused by the fact that in the Riustring tradition the tariff has been reduced to a wound list and nothing more. The other subgroup contains clauses on damage to other elements of a person's embodied honour, such as objects or persons which fell under his guardianship (OFris. *mund* or *were*).[28]

Comparing the five versions, we can reconstruct a prototext of c. 120 paragraphs. As already mentioned, since the five extant versions (dating c. 1300) diverge so much the prototext must date back a considerable length of time. One piece of evidence brings us back to the second half of the twelfth century. It consists of a small text titled *Fon jelde* ("On wergild") describing nine different stages or periods over which the amount of wergild changed.[29] Numismatic scholar Dirk Jan Henstra analysed the amounts of money and the currency in this text. He dated the first stage, with a wergild of 12 marks, to c. 1000: "In order to be able to compensate all their crimes with money, the people set the first wergild at 12 marks. After that the relatives received six marks on top of that, to be divided amongst themselves" (*Therumbe hu ma alle firna mith fia machte beta, tha keren tha liude allererst thet forme jeld bi XII merkum. Therefter tha krungen tha frund sex merc therto, ther hia under himman delden*).[30] Stage four fixes the wergild at 40 marks, and it is this wergild we find in the *General Compensation Tariff*. Henstra dates this stage to c. 1160: "The injury tariff was determined on the basis of a

[26] Bremmer, *Hir is eskriven*, 65-6; Karl von Richthofen, *Untersuchungen über Friesische Rechtsgeschichte*. 3 vols. (Berlin: Wilhelm Herz, 1880-1886), I:62.

[27] Antheun Janse, "De waarheid van een falsum. Op zoek naar de politieke context van het Karelsprivilege." *De Vrije Fries* 71 (1991): 7-28.

[28] Han Nijdam, "Honour and Shame Embodied. The Case of Medieval Frisia," in *Shame between Punishment and Penance. The Social Usages of Shame in the Middle Ages and Early Modern Times / La honte entre peine et pénitence – les usages sociaux de la honte au Moyen Âge et aux débuts de lépoque moderne*, ed. Bénédicte Sère & Jörg Wettlaufer (Firenze: SISMEL, 2013), 65-88.

[29] Henstra, *The Evolution of the Money Standard*, 313-18; Han Nijdam *Lichaam, eer en recht in middeleeuws Friesland. Een studie naar de Oudfriese boeteregisters* (Hilversum: Verloren, 2008), 446-8.

[30] Wybren Buma and Wilhelm Ebel, eds., *Das Fivelgoer Recht* (Göttingen: Vandenhoeck & Ruprecht, 1971), 170-1.

wergild of forty marks, and this was before the Peace of God was proclaimed. A half wergild was set at 20 marks, a third wergild at 13 1/3 marks" (*By fortega merkum setma thene undscrifta, er ma thene godfrethe bigrep. Therbi setma thet halve jeld bi xx mercum, thet thrimen jeld bi xiiij thrimen merc*). The reference to the *wundskrifta* ("injury tariff, register of wounds/injuries") is a further confirmation that we are on the right track here.

In all, the following hypothesis seems to be justified. The Frisian law texts were first written down in the vernacular in the eleventh century. The *Seventeen Statutes* certainly was one of these. The *General Compensation Tariff* is another likely candidate, since compensating for injuries with money (and/or other forms of capital) was so central to Frisian legal practice. The text *On wergild* seems to confirm yet again that writing down law began in the eleventh century, since the earliest stage of wergild mentioned there was dated to c. 1000 by Henstra. The wergild mentioned in the *General Compensation Tariff* can be dated to c. 1160, according to Henstra, and I would like to interpret this as an update of the original tariff as a written text. The thirteenth century saw the foundation of several monasteries in the Frisian region, and with this, written culture grew considerably. The oldest law manuscripts stem from the end of this century, by which time the number of law texts that had been written down had grown considerably and the oldest law texts had evolved. In other words: there was a slow start in writing down the law in the eleventh century, and this accelerated considerably from the thirteenth century onwards.

Two tariff traditions need to be addressed before we can begin our analysis. First, the *General Compensation Tariff* was gradually replaced by various more regional texts in the eastern region (between the rivers Lauwers and Weser) in the course of the fourteenth century. We know of a Riustring, Brokmer, Emsingo, Hunsingo and Fivelgo Compensation Tariff, as well as a tariff called *Kampa Jeldric's Tariff*. In the youngest legal manuscripts from these regions, dating c. 1450, the *General Compensation Tariff* has disappeared, and the regional tariffs have grown considerably in size (c. 300 to 400 clauses).

Second, there are the tariffs from central Frisia (between rivers Vlie and Lauwers). The surviving manuscripts from this region all date from the fifteenth century, although it is clear these contain material that is much older, just as in the eastern region of Frisia. In previous research, I have been able to reconstruct four tariff traditions in this corpus, which can be ascribed to the most important administrative units in central Frisia in the thirteenth century (which in the fourteenth and fifteenth centuries were split up into smaller units).[31] I called them groups A to D, where A = Oostergo, B = Wymbritseradeel, C = Franekeradeel, D = Wonseradeel. The texts from groups A, B and D

[31] Nijdam, *Lichaam, eer en recht*, 88-92; 485-528.

are relatively small and seem relatively unchanged and archaic, all consisting of around 120 to 140 clauses. The texts from group C grew in size to c. 300 clauses. It is likely that this tariff tradition was developing into the general compensation tariff for central Frisia.[32] Its edited and restructured redaction found its way to the incunable Freeska Landriucht (c. 1485), the printed canon of central Frisian law.[33]

Before we start comparing the *Lex Frisionum* with the Old Frisian tariffs, it should be observed that the tariffs are not the best sources for trying to date textual evidence from the perspective of written texts, since they were the products of both an oral and a written culture which constantly interacted.[34] With this I mean that the legal tradition of compensating injuries remained alive during the entire Middle Ages in Frisia. This meant that the texts were always updated before they could fossilize to the extent that they became useless. Moreover, there was probably more knowledge on compensating injuries present the minds of the legal experts which demonstrably was used to update the tariffs every now and then.

Comparing the *Lex Frisionum* with the Old Frisian Tariffs

The goal of this comparison of the injury lists in the *Lex Frisionum* with the Old Frisian tariffs is to find the closest match between the two. As part of the research for my book *Lichaam, eer en recht in middeleeuws Friesland* (*Body, Honour and Law in Medieval Frisia*), I created a database of all types of wounds and all body parts attested in the Old Frisian material. Furthermore, I did a philological analysis of all individual tariff traditions, establishing the relationship between the various redactions of one tariff. It was this analysis which enabled me to shed more light on the central Frisian tariffs, which had not been studied in detail until then. The insight that they can be grouped into four groups which represent the thirteenth-century administrative situation was one of the results of this research.

For this contribution, I have plotted the tariffs in the *Lex Frisionum* in Title XXII and the *Additiones Sapientum* (tables 3-5 in appendix). As far as possible, I identified

---

32 Han Nijdam, "Het Oudwestfriese boeteregister *Bireknade Bota* (deel 1)." *Us Wurk* 49 (2000): 81-113; Han Nijdam, "The Old West Frisian Composition Tariff *Bireknade Bota* (Part 2)." *Us Wurk* 50 (2001): 27-64.

33 Thomas S.B. Johnston, "Old Frisian Law and the Frisian Freedom Ideology: Text and Manuscript Composition as a Marketing Device," in *Approaches to Old Frisian Philology*, eds. Rolf H. Bremmer, Jr., Thomas S.B. Johnston and Oebele Vries (Amsterdam: Rodopi, 1998), 206.

34 In general Old Frisian law retained many traces of orality: Rolf H Bremmer, Jr. "The Orality of Old Frisian Law Texts," in *Directions for Old Frisian Philology*, ed. Rolf H. Bremmer Jr., Stephen Laker and Oebele Vries (Amsterdam: Rodopi, 2014), 1-48.

the building blocks of the tariffs: clusters of clauses addressing related topics (column "contents"), indicating which Old Frisian term best describes or fits a clause in the *Lex*, and matching the clauses of the *Lex* with the *General Compensation Tariff* (column "BAg"), the Eastern tradition (column "East") or Central tradition (column "Central").

A Frisian tradition

The first thing to do is to ascertain that the injury tariffs in the *Lex Frisionum* truly reflect a Frisian legal tradition. This can be established in two ways. In the first place, a number of vernacular words appear in the *Lex Frisionum*, some of which are later also found in the Old Frisian tariffs, thus pointing to a continuity of the legal system and practice. Overall, some vernacular words in the *Lex Frisionum* can be found in the text, some in the titles to the paragraphs. It is now commonly thought that the words in the titles are for the most part Frankish, not reflecting Frisian law per se, and that the words in the text itself are mostly reflecting Frisian, although historical linguists have pointed out that there are some linguistic incongruities: the forms do not perfectly reflect what we might expect.[35]

First, *durslegi* (XXII,3) can be compared to Old Frisian *dudslek*, *dustslek*, *dusslek* ("a hard blow causing a bruise"). The puzzle of the first element (*dur-* versus *dus-*, *dust-* or *dud-*) has not been completely solved yet.[36] Second, the body part term *mithridri* (XXII,55) is one of the least problematic, since it neatly reflects Old Frisian *midhrether* ("diaphragm").[37] Third, *wlitivam* (AS III,16) can be compared to OFris. *wlitewemmelse* ("facial deformation as a consequence of injury"). Although it is a perfect match, it must be noted that this term can be found in some of the other *Leges Barbarorum*, so it does attest to the continuity looked for here, but it is not uniquely Frisian (an aspect discussed further below).[38] Fourth, *liduwagi* (XXII,35 / AS III,32) can be linked to OFris. *lithwei* ("synovial fluid [running from a wound])." I have discussed this term in more

[35] Horst Haider Munske, *Der germanische Rechtswortschatz im Bereich der Missetaten. Philologische und sprachgeografische Untersuchungen. I. Die Terminologie der älteren westgermanischen Rechtsquellen* (Berlin: De Gruyter, 1973), 106-7; A.P. Versloot, "Die "friesischen" Wörter in der *Lex Frisionum*." *Us Wurk* 64 (2015): 1-10.

[36] Dirk Boutkan, and Sjoerd Michiel Siebinga, *Old Frisian Etymological Dictionary*. Leiden Indo-European Etymological Dictionaries 1 (Leiden: Brill, 2005), 80; Horst Haider Munske, *Der germanische Rechtswortschatz*, 145; Annette Niederhellmann, *Arzt und Heilkunde in den frühmittelalterlichen Leges. Eine wort-und sachkundige Untersuchung* (Berlin: De Gruyter, 1983), 222-4.

[37] Dietrich Hofmann and Anne T. Popkema. *Altfriesisches Handwörterbuch* (Heidelberg: Winter, 2008), 328; Boutkan and Siebinga, *Old Frisian Etymological Dictionary*, 261.

[38] Oliver, *Body Legal*, 101-2.

detail elsewhere and will return to it below, when trying to find the closest match between the two tariffs in the *Lex Frisionum* and the Old Frisian traditions.[39] Fifth, *sipido* (AS III,34) matches with OFris. *inseptha* ("scar tissue that lies deeper than the surrounding skin").[40] Finally, *smelido* (AS III,35) corresponds to OFris. *smelinge* ("shrinking [of a limb as a consequence of an injury"]), albeit with a different suffix.[41]

A second way of establishing that the tariff material in the *Lex Frisionum* is Frisian is by pointing at striking continuities with the Old Frisian tariffs. The first example can be found in the *Aditiones* section (AS II.6): "Cutting off the palm of the hand is to be compensated with 4 solidi; if the falling hand that is cut off touches the ground, this is to be compensated with 4 solidi" (*Abscisio palmae IIII solidis componatur; si manus abscisa terram cadens tetigerit, ipse casus IIII solidis componatur*).[42] The subordinate clause *si manus abscisa terram cadens tetigerit* seems to reverberate a well-known term from the Old Frisian tariffs, i.e. *gersfal* (noun) / *gersfallich* (adjective), which literally means "a fall on the grass / falling on the grass," and was used to denote that a body part had been cut off completely.

Second, of all the *Leges Barbarorum*, only the *Lex Frisionum* has a clause concerning cutting the wrinkles in the forehead, and such a clause also appears in the Old Frisian tariffs. It appears to be one of the fingerprints of the Frisian tradition.[43] In the *Lex Frisionum*, the topic is addressed in three clauses in the main text (XXII, 11-13), describing how the upper, middle and lowest wrinkle can be cut, and the compensation that is to be paid (2-4-2 solidi) and in the *Additiones* section (AS III, 20-1) all three wrinkles are mentioned together and require a total of (three times)[44] 12 solidi. The following clause then states that each wrinkle is worth 4 solidi, which partly corresponds to what is said in Title XXII. The Old Frisian tariffs lump all three wrinkles together, just as the *Additiones*. Moreover, they state that no more than the cutting of three wrinkles is to be compensated. Finally, they offer an explanation for the use of *transversam* in XXII,11: "If someone cuts across the upper wrinkle in the forehead, he has to compensate with two solidi" (*Si summam rugam frontis quis ictu transversam inciderit, duobus solidis componat*), for in some of the Old Frisian tariffs we find: "If the wound follows the direction of the wrinkle and it is not cut across, then this wound requires no higher compensation than an ordinary cut wound to the skin (*Jef dat dulgh geet alinga*

---

[39] Nijdam, "Compensating Body and Honor," 45-6; Oliver, *Body Legal*, 131-3.

[40] Nijdam, *Lichaam, eer en recht*, 75; Boutkan and Siebinga, *Old Frisian Etymological Dictionary*, 336.

[41] Hofmann and Popkema, *Altfriesisches Handwörterbuch*, 451; Nijdam, *Lichaam, eer en recht*, 75.

[42] See also Oliver, *Body Legal*, 141.

[43] Nijdam, "A Comparison of the Injury Tariffs," 238-9.

[44] I will not go into the problem of the money and amounts of money in the *Lex Frisionum* here. For this see Henstra, "Het probleem van de geldbedragen."

der wirsena ende hio næt tokoren se, soe aegh hit næt meer to bote dan hit ielkirs oen da felle se).[45]

Third, in the *Additiones* section (AS III, 22) there is this clause: "If a man is hit on the head by another man in such a way, that he is unable to endure either cold or heat because of the sensitivity of the wound, this has to be compensated with three times 4 solidi" (*Si homo ab alio ita in caput percussus fuerit, ut nec frigus nec calorem pro vulneris impatientia sufferre possit, ter IIII solidi componantur*). In the Old Frisian tariffs, we find the same clause, only described in such a terse way that it almost becomes incomprehensible: *hete and kelde* "heat and cold."[46] Now, matters are reversed, in that the *Lex Frisionum* gives an explanation for what is meant in the Old Frisian material. Luckily though, we also have the Low German translation of the *General Compensation Tariff*, which gives extra information: *Heeth vnd kolth nicht mogen vordragen* "Being unable to endure heat or cold."[47]

Fourth, a fine on piercing the nose can only be found in the Kentish laws and in the *Lex Frisionum* (XXII,16; AS III,11-13; AS III,63-4).[48] Within a Frisian context, this clause is continued in the Old Frisian tariffs.[49] An interesting detail is that only in the Frisian material (both *Lex Frisionum* and Old Frisian) are the various septa of the nose differentiated. The *Lex Frisionum* uses *paries* ("wall"), whereas Old Frisian has *wach* ("wall") so we find the same metaphor BODY = HOUSE here.[50]

Finally, Lisi Oliver's analysis of the *Leges Barbarorum* shows which body parts and types of injuries are uniquely treated by the *Lex Frisionum*. Dealing with the face, only the *Lex Frisionum* has clauses on the eyebrows, wrinkles in the forehead (already mentioned), the cheeks and tongue and the throat.[51] These body parts are also treated in the Old Frisian tariffs. Oliver also points to the fact that only the Frisians "show more than cursory interest in internal organs."[52] Although the Old Frisian tariffs do have several clauses on the intestines, there is some discontuity to be distinguished here as well. These instances will be treated below. Overall, the Old Frisian tariffs lose the degree of detail concerning this topic the *Lex Frisionum* shows.

---

45 *Bireknade Bota* (D XIV,57); Edition: Nijdam, *Lichaam, eer en recht*, 555-66; 557.

46 BAgHE, BKJ; Central Frisian groups A, C.

47 Nijdam, *Lichaam, eer en recht*, 77; edition of the text: 533-5; 533.

48 Wormald, "The *Leges Barbarorum*," 49; Oliver, *Beginnings*, 70-1; Horst Haider Munske, "Angelsächsisch-altfriesische Beziehungen in der Rechtsterminologie für Missetaten," in *Flecht op "e koai: stúdzjes oanbean oan prof. dr. Wybren Jan Buma ta syn sechstichste jierdei*, ed. Teake Hoekema et al. (Groningen: Wolters-Noordhoff, 1970), 40-52.

49 Nijdam, *Lichaam, eer en recht*, 76, 437, 460.

50 More on this metaphor complex in the Old Frisian tariffs: Nijdam, *Lichaam, eer en recht*, 248-250.

51 Oliver, *Body Legal*, 99-102.

52 Oliver, *Body Legal*, 133.

Adding up all the information, we can conclude that the *Lex Frisionum* indeed reflects a Frisian tradition of injury tariffs. There are some very strong instances of continuity, of which the unique clauses on cutting the wrinkles in the forehead may be seen as a fingerprint of the Frisian tradition. Not everything had stayed the same though, between the eighth century and the eleventh or twelfth century.

Discontinuity

Due to the very nature of the compensation tariffs, which were continually informed by the legal practice of compensating injuries, the texts were constantly in flux. It is not surprising then, that we find material in the *Lex Frisionum* which is absent in the later Old Frisian material.

I start with a few dossiers which include vernacular words in the *Lex Frisionum*. The term *cladolg* ("scratch wound") (AS III,44) disappears from the Old Frisian record.[53] Neither do we find *herthamon* (praecordium / pericardium) (XXII,48) in Old Frisian. Continuing with the dossier on the intestines, the *Lex Frisionum* is, as already mentioned, more complete than the Old Frisian material, where nothing can be found on guts spilling out and having to be pushed back. There is also a curious clause which describes how fat that protrudes from a wound is cut off as part of a medical treatment (XXII,56): "If the intestines appear out of the wound and are pushed back [...]; if something of the fat comes out so that it has to be cut off [...]" (*Si botellus de vulnere processerit, et iterum interius remittitur, [...]; si de adipe aliquid processerit ut praecidatur [...]*).[54] There is only one isolated Old Frisian clause which might resemble this: "If fat/pus is cut out of a man's wound: three shillings" (*Werth hir en mon ut sinre unde smere snithen: thre scillingar*).[55] OFris. *smere* is usually taken to mean "pus" here, instead of the literal meaning "fat, grease." So although these two clauses seem to resemble one another, they most probably cannot be viewed in terms of continuity. This should not surprise us, because medical treatment evolved quite a bit during the Middle Ages. Secondly, on the whole we see descriptions of medical treatment becoming very rare in the Old Frisian tariffs. This most probably is another way in which the genre evolved.[56]

Returning to a vernacular term, *smelo* (AS III,56) a technical term used as part of the procedure of measuring wounds (on which more below) disappears in Old Frisian. A rare Latin term is *grano* "mustache / whiskers" (XXII,17). Oliver explains that it is a

[53] Nijdam, *Lichaam, eer en recht*, 78.
[54] Oliver, *Body Legal*, 129, 133.
[55] E3 I,173 (BEm); Buma and Ebel, *Das Emsiger Recht*, 182-3.
[56] Nijdam, "Compensating Body and Honor," 44-51.

Latinized from of an older Germanic word.[57] The Old Frisian tariffs have no special clause on the mustache as such, but do have several clauses on injuring the beard (*berdbreke* / *berdis homelinge* ["mutilation of the beard"]; *berdfang* ["beard pulling"]; *berd eberned* ["beard burning"]). This discontinuity seems to be a case of change in hair fashion.

As we saw earlier, a clause on throwing someone into deep water can be found in three versions in the *Lex Frisionum*. This offense can also be found in almost all Old Frisian tariffs. There is an almost literal parallel in the Old Frisian tradition with the third version (AS III,66), especially with the subclause "so that his feet can not touch the ground but he has to swim" (*ut pedibus terram tangere non possit sed natare debeat*). In the tariffs, the description grew over time, because the schemas of eyes, hands and feet and of the five senses were implemented, so that we find:

> Thet is een riucht wapeldranch, ther werd worpen in een onwed wetter, ther hi ne moghe hor mith handem ner mith fothem thine grund reka ner mith aeghnum thine himel syaen ner mith ara thine ruft hera.[58]
>
> This is a legal case of submersion, if someone is thrown into deep water, so that he cannot touch the ground with his hands or feet, nor can see the sky with his eyes, nor can hear the calling (of the bystanders) with his ears.

What we do not find, however, in the Old Frisian tariffs, is the other side of the coin, so to speak: in the *Lex Frisionum*, a reward is to be paid to someone who saves a victim from drowning (XXII,87; AS III,67).

A peculiar discontinuity can be found in the way the teeth are valued (XXII,19-21; AS III,36-8). As can be seen from Oliver's overview of the treatment of the teeth in the *Leges Barbarorum*, Frisia deviates from most of the other laws in that it values the molars the highest.[59] Not all Old Frisian traditions show the same schema of the teeth (i.e. distinguish incisors, canines and molars), but those that do value either the incisors or the canines highest, because of their visibility and/or function (canines are the most important teeth from a functional perspective) and the molars lowest.[60]

Some of the discontinuities or discrepancies between the *Lex Frisionum* and the Old Frisian tradition are due to structural developments of the genre. The most poignant example is the elaborate way in which simple fleshwounds are measured in the *Lex*

---

[57] Oliver, *Body Legal*, 111.

[58] J XXIX,103 (Central Frisian group A); edition: Wybren Jan Buma, Wilhelm Ebel & Marina Tragter-Schubert, eds., *Westerlauwerssches Recht I. Jus Municipale Frisonum* (Göttingen: Vandenhoeck & Ruprecht, 1977), 550-1.

[59] Oliver, *Body Legal*, 102-7.

[60] Nijdam, *Lichaam, eer en recht*, 224-5.

Frisionum. Again, we find three different systems (XXII,66-70; AS III,50-8; AS III,58 [epilogue]). The first two systems work with the so-called hand span, of which various degrees are described. In the Old Frisian tariffs these systems were replaced by the *mete* ("measure") which was defined as the breadth of the upper joint of the thumb.[61] This system is already present in the *Lex Frisionum* as well, where it is described as the *uncia* ("inch") which should be used to measure wounds. It can be found in the epilogue to AS III,58: "Among the western Frisians between Vlie (Flehi) and Sincfal, as many inches a wound is long are to be compensated with just as many solidi" (*Apud occidentales Fresionea inter Flehi et Sincfalam quot unciarum fuerit longitudo vulneris, tot solidorum compositione persolvitur*).

In contrast to this modernisation however, the Old Frisian tariffs from central Frisia continue to state that bone splinters protruding from wounds should be thrown into a shield and only if they are heavy enough to give off a sound that can be heard over a certain distance are they to be compensated.[62] It must be said, though, that these clauses disappeared from the Eastern Frisian traditions, or rather, cannot be found there.

Concomitant with the disappearance of medical detail from the Frisian tradition seems to be the very factual description of "a sword touching" (*si gladium tetigerit*) a certain internal organ (XXII,6,48,55). This way of describing injuries makes way for a more generic, categorical approach in the Old Frisian tariffs.

This development probably also explains why we do not find exact parallels in the Old Frisian material for the clauses on the various instances where a weapon pierces the body of the victim (XXII,84-5; LT VI,14-19; AS III,61-2; 65). The exceptions are the clauses on piercing the nose, which we still find in the Old Frisian material (mentioned earlier).

A related development that can be observed in the Old Frisian tariffs with regard to the *Lex Frisionum* is a more frequent use of triads. There are already a number of threes present in the *Lex Frisionum* such as three wrinkles in the forehead and three bone splinters. In the Old Frisian tradition, triads abound. Three instances of a type of wound often become a maximum number to be compensated. Also, we find three degrees of severity of certain types of injuries: the lowest (OFris. *minnesta*), the middle (OFris. *midlesta*) and the most severe / highest (OFris. *hagesta*).

---

[61] Han Nijdam, "Measuring Wounds in the *Lex Frisionum* and the Old Frisian Registers of Fines," in *Philologia Frisica Anno 1999. Lêzingen fan it fyftjinde Frysk filologekongres 8, 9 en 10 desimber 1999*, ed. Piter Boersma et al. (Leeuwarden: Fryske Akademy, 2000), 180-203.

[62] Han Nijdam, "Klinkende munten en klinkende botsplinters in de Oudfriese rechtsteksten: continuïteit, discontinuïteit, intertekstualiteit." *De Vrije Fries* 89 (2009): 45-66; Nijdam, *Lichaam, eer en recht*, 77.

Finding the closest match

Finally, is it possible to find a close match between the tariffs in the *Lex Frisionum* and particular Old Frisian tariffs? And how do we go about it? Do we look at the oldest vernacular tradition, i.e. the *General Compensation Tariff*, or do we look at the region of origin of the texts, i.e. to central Frisia for Title XXII and to the eastern region for the *Additiones* section that can be ascribed to Wlemar?

As can be concluded from table 3, the tariffs in the *Lex Frisionum* overlap considerably. The same picture emerges from the Old Frisian tariffs. In other words, we have to look for a combination of unique clauses, terms, ways of structuring and ways of approaching a specific topic in order to find a match.

Matching the oldest Old Frisian tariff, the *General Compensation Tariff*, to the *Lex Frisionum* material does not yield the desired results. The *General Compensation Tariff* lacks clauses on the following body parts, which can be found in the other Old Frisian tariffs:

jaw (AS III,14).[63]
collarbone (XXII,22).[64]
rib (XXII,23).[65]
penis (XXII,57).[66]
testicles (XXII,58,59; AS III,60; LT VI,19).[67]
leg and foot (XXII,62; AS III,1).[68]

This mismatch is a sign that the *General Compensation Tariff* is not the ideal candidate, even though it is the oldest recorded Old Frisian tariff.

The most telling clue for a match between the *Lex Frisionum* and a particular Old Frisian tradition is, I think, the way injuries to the arm, hand and fingers are treated (XXII,24-44). Here we also see a difference between Title XXII (table 3 in appendix) and the tariff by Wlemar (table 4 in appendix). In Title XXII, the injury called *liduwagi* (OFris. *lithwei*) is described for the various knuckles of the fingers and the thumb and for the other joints along the entire arm (wrist, elbow, shoulder: XXII,35-44). In Wlemar's tariff, on the other hand, *liduwagi* is mentioned only once (AS III,32). Here, the injury is decribed in a generic way, i.e. if a joint (any joint) is hit and synovial fluid

63 BAgH, BKJ, BRu, BEm, Central Frisian groups: A, C.
64 BRu, BEm, BB; Central Frisian groups: A, C, D.
65 BAgH, BRu, BEm, BB; Central Frisian groups: A, B, C, D. Oliver, *Body Legal*, 128.
66 Central Frisian groups: A, C.
67 BEm, BHu; Central Frisian groups: A, C.
68 BAgH, BKJ, BEm, BHu, BB; Central Frisian groups: A,B,C,D.

occurs. Exactly the same difference in the treatment of this topic can be found for the central Frisian versus the Eastern Frisian traditions (including the *General Compensation Tariff*). Moreover, this section in Title XXII starts with a few instances of fractures of bone. This is called *benbreke* in Old Frisian, and in the central Frisian tariffs, we find combinations of *benbreke* and *lithwei* described for all parts of the arm, hand and fingers.

Adding everything up then, it would indeed seem that Title XXII does match the central Frisian tariffs best, even though these have only been recorded in the fifteenth century and textually cannot be traced further back than the thirteenth century. Matching the tariff by Wlemar to a specific area is more difficult. It does seem to match the tariffs from the Eastern regions slightly better than those from the central Frisian region, but there are no examples that jump out.

Conclusion

In conclusion, it is unmistakable that the tariffs in the *Lex Frisionum* represent earlier stages of the Old Frisian compensation tariff traditions. These traditions show continuity on the one hand and discontinuity and internal dynamics and evolution on the other. We have seen some of the mechanisms that explain certain developments between the *Lex Frisionum* and the Old Frisian stage. It also appears that the tariffs in the *Lex Frisionum* were largely the product of recording from an oral tradition.[69] In the Old Frisian tariffs we can see how this oral tradition had evolved three to four hundred years later. Also, we can see the influence of written culture beginning to make its influence felt.

It would seem that, as the rest of the text suggests, the tariff in Title XXII can indeed be matched to the tariff tradition of central Frisia and less convincingly, that the tariff by Wlemar stems from the Eastern region.

[69] I doubt whether the *Lex Frisionum* was indeed influenced by the *Lex Alamanorum*, as has been suggested by previous scholars. See e.g., Siems, *Studien*, 355-60.

Appendix

Table 1:
Overview of the number of paragraphs in the *Lex Frisionum*

Tit.	number	Add Sap Tit	number	
I	21	I	3	
II	10	II	10	
III	9	III	78	
IV	9	IIIb	1	
V	2	IV	1	
VI	2	V	1	
VII	2	VI	1	
VIII	2	VII	1	
IX	17	VIII	2	
X	1	IX	1	
XI	3	X	2	
XII	2	XI	1	
XIII	1	Lex Thur VI	11	
XIV	7			
XV	4			
XVI	1			
XVII	5			
XVIIII	2			
XIX	2			
XX	3			
XXI	1			
XXII	89			
TOTAL:	195		113	308

Table 2:

Overview of the various redactions of the *General Compensation Tariff*

BAg = General Compensation Tariff; H = Hunsingo redaction; E = Emsingo redaction; L = Latin redaction; R = Riustring redaction; NR = Low German Riustring redaction

Version	Clause Number	Unique Clause
BAgH	145	27
BAgE	134	21
BAgL	131	16
BAgR	99	1
BAgNR	101	4

Table 3:

Concordance of Title XXII and the *Additiones Sapientum* and correspondences between Title XXII and the Old Frisian tariffs.

XXII	AS II	AS III	LT VI	Contents	Old Frisian	BAg	East	Central
1		8		Head	daveddusinge	X	X	X
2		8		Head	wonspreke?	X	X	X
3				Head	dustslek	X	X	X
4				Head				
5				Head	breinponne			
6		23		Head	thruchkeme	X		
7				Head	helebrede	X	X	
8				Head	helebrede	X	X	
9		9		Head	are of	X	X	X
10		10		Head	nose of	X	X	X
11		20, 21		Head	leseka	X	X	X
12		20, 21		Head	leseka	X	X	X
13		20, 21		Head	leseka	X	X	X
14		15		Head	breskredene	X	X	X
15		19		Head	aghlid	X		X
16		13.63		Head	nose thruch	X	X	

17		17		Head	berdbreke?	X	X	X
18		14, 65		Head	ziake		X	X
19		36		Teeth	toth a farahaved	X	X	
20		37		Teeth	slektoth	X	X	
21		38		Teeth	inre toth / kese	X	X	
22				collarbone	wideben		X	X
23		29		rib	rib		X	X
24				Arm and hand				X
25				Arm and hand				X
26				Arm and hand				X
27	1			Arm and hand				X
28	5			Arm and hand		X		X
29	2			Arm and hand				X
30	3			Arm and hand				X
31	4			Arm and hand				X
32	4			Arm and hand				X
33				Arm and hand				X
34	6			Arm and hand				X
35		32		Arm and hand	lithwei			X
36		32		Arm and hand	lithwei			X
37		32		Arm and hand	lithwei			X
38		32		Arm and hand	lithwei			X
39		32		Arm and hand	lithwei			X
40		32		Arm and hand	lithwei			X
41		32		Arm and hand	lithwei			X
42		32		Arm and hand	lithwei			X
43		32		Arm and hand	lithwei			X
44		32		Arm and hand	lithwei			X
45		48		Eye	blind	X	X	X
46		47, 59		Eye	age ut	X	X	X
47				Torso	briast			
48				Torso				

49				Torso				
50				Torso	midhrether		X	
51				Torso	midhrether		X	
52				Torso	bukwunde	X	X	X
53		31		Torso	nittaskredene	X	X	
54				Torso	mage		X	
55		31		Torso				
56				Torso				
57				Torso	pint			X
58		60		Torso	pralling		X	X
59				Torso				
60				Leg and foot				
61				Leg and foot				
62		1		Leg and foot	fot of		X	X
63		2, 3, 4		Leg and foot				
64		32		Leg and foot	lithwei		X	X
65		40		Hair pulling	faxfang	X	X	X
66				measuring wounds				
67				measuring wounds				
68				measuring wounds				
69				measuring wounds				
70				measuring wounds				
71		24		bone splinters	benis utgong			X
72		24		bone splinters	benis utgong			X
73		24		bone splinters	benis utgong			X
74				bone splinters	benis utgong			X
75		49		on procedure				
76		46		on procedure				
77				on procedure				
78	10	46		on procedure				
79				on procedure				
80				lung through wound	lungenskedene	X		X

81				lung through wound	omma utgong	X	X	X
82				tying someone up	bende	X	X	X
83		41.66		throwing someone into water	wapeldepene	X	X	X
84		61		piercing wounds				
85				piercing wounds				
86			18.19	piercing wounds				
87		67		saving someone from drowning				
88				touching woman indecently	unriucht onfeng		X	
89				touching woman indecently	basefeng	X	X	

Table 4:
Correspondences between the tariff by Wlemar and the Old Frisian tariffs

Wlemar	AS II	AS III	LT VI	Content	Old Frisian	BAg	East	Central
1	1			Hand and fingers				
2	2			Hand and fingers				
3	3			Hand and fingers				
4	4			Hand and fingers				
5	5			Hand and fingers				
6	6			Hand and fingers	gersfal			
7	7			Hand and fingers				
8	8			Hand and fingers				
9	9			Hand and fingers				
10	10			Hand and fingers				
11		1		Leg and foot	fot of		X	X
12		2		Leg and foot				
13		3		Leg and foot				
14		4		Leg and foot				
15		5		Leg and foot				

16		6		Leg and foot				
17		7		Leg and foot				
18		8		Head	davedusinge / wonspreke?	X	X	X
19		9		Head	are of	X	X	X
20		10		Head	nose of	X	X	X
21		11		Head	wagar		X	
22		12		Head	wagar		X	
23		13		Head	wagar		X	
24		14		Head	ziake		X	X
25		15		Head	breskredene	X	X	X
26		16		Head	wlitewemmelse	X	X	X
27		17		Head	berdbreke?	X	X	X
28		18		Head	muthbreud? / agbreud?		X	
29		19		Head	aghlid	X	X	X
30		20		Head	leseka	X	X	X
31		21		Head	leseka	X	X	X
32		22		Head	hete and kelde	X	X	X
33		23		Head	breinponne	X	X	X
34		24		bone splinters				X
35		25		cutting bone	benes biti		X	
36		26		cutting bone				
37		27		cutting bone				
38		28		rib	rib			
39		29		rib	rib			
40		30		rib	rib			
41		31		piercing wounds				
42		32			lithwei	X	X	X
43		33			merchrene		X	X
44		34		sipido	inseptha	X	X	X
45		35		smelido	lithsmelinge	X	X	
46		36		Teeth	toth a farahaved	X	X	
47		37		Teeth	slektoth	X	X	

48		38		Teeth	inre toth / kese	X	X	
49		39		Hair	top heres?	X	X	
50		40		Hair	faxfang	X	X	X
51		41			wapeldepene	X	X	X
52		42			stefslek	X	X	
53		43			stefslek			
54		44		cladolg				
55		45			lungensiama		X	
56		46		on procedure	lom lith			
57		47		Eye	age ut	X	X	X
58		48		Eye	blind	X	X	X
59		49		measuring wounds				
60		50		measuring wounds				
61		51		measuring wounds				
62		52		measuring wounds				
63		53		measuring wounds				
64		54		measuring wounds				
65		55		measuring wounds				
66		56		measuring wounds				
67		57		measuring wounds				
68		58		measuring wounds	metedolch	X	X	X
69		76		stealing a wife				
70		77		illegal marriage				
71		78		illegal marriage				
72			14	piercing wounds				
73			15	piercing wounds				
74			16	piercing wounds				
75			17	piercing wounds				
76			18	piercing wounds				
77			19	piercing wounds				
78		18	20	Face	muthbreud? / agbreud?		X	
79			21	smelido	lithsmelinge	X	X	

80			22	smelido	lithsmelinge			
81			23	hand harpist/goldsmith				
82			24	hand weaving woman				

Table 5:
Correspondences between the tariff by Saxmund and the Old Frisian tariffs

Saxmund	AS III	Content	Old Frisian	BAg	East	Central
1	59	eye	age ut	X	X	X
2	60	testicles	pralling		X	X
3	61	piercing wounds				
4	62	piercing wounds				
5	63	piercing wounds	nose thruch	X	X	
6	64	piercing wounds	wagar		X	
7	65	piercing wounds	ziake		X	X
8	66	throwing someone into water	wapeldepene	X	X	X
9	67	saving someone from drowning				
10	68	injuring cattle			X	X
11	69	unintentional injuries	urbek dede		X	X
12	70	unintentional injuries	urbek dede		X	X
13	71	compensation free man				
14	72	compensation nobleman				
15	73	compensation unfree man				
16	74	tongue	tunge	X	X	X
17	75	grave robbing	likraf / hreraf		X	X

Servitude in Anglo-Saxon England: Searching for the Serfs*

Paul Hyams

When the Blickling homilist wrote hopefully of the *freodom unaræfnedlican þeowdomes* ("freedom from intolerable servitude"), he was comparing the spiritual slavery of humankind to the Devil before the Incarnation with the inferior human brand of servitude.[1] This paper aims to set the horrors that some humans inflict on those whom they dominate into its full context. It is time that this includes serfdom, which unlike slavery, a major theme of most accounts, appears if at all as an aside.[2]

Modern discussion of servitude in early medieval Europe has always been shaped around a posthumous paper of Marc Bloch's, whose question was "Why and how did the slavery of Antiquity come to an end?"[3] He thus implied that slavery from Late Antiquity on was an institution moving towards a definite end, from a starting point

---

* I have benefited from many helpful critical comments about this, more than I can thank here. I am grateful to them all, and trust that they know who they are. Mark Atherton, Stephen Baxter, and the late Lisi Oliver herself, deserve to be singled out for special thanks. I much regret having lacked the books of Tom Lambert, *Law & Order in Anglo-Saxon England* (Oxford: Oxford University Press, 2017) and Alice Rio, *Slavery after Rome, 500-1100* (Oxford: Oxford University Press, 2017) until it was too late for more than a few minor changes. The excellent current authority on legal history in the period is John Hudson, *The Oxford History of the Laws of England*, vol. II (Oxford University Press: Oxford, 2012), whose chapter 8 can be consulted for a different view than here.

[1] I quote from David A.E. Pelteret, *Slavery in Early Medieval England* (Woodbridge: Boydell, 1995), 277. This book, by far the most comprehensive, scholarly, and judicious treatment of the subject, has been my guide throughout. Though I keep citations to a minimum, I am proud to have unwittingly played a very minor role in its development, ibid., xi. He was kind enough to read a late draft. I have taken careful note too of David Wyatt, *Slaves and Warriors in Medieval Britain and Ireland, 800-1200* (Leiden & Boston MA: Brill, 2009).

[2] I confess to an additional motive for this inquiry, as a preparation for a book on the series of serf manumissions over the "long" thirteenth century. Since this overlapped with an earlier series of "slave" manumissions in the 1130s and 1140s, I needed to consider what measure of social change actually took place in Norman England. I have sketched my project most recently in "A Three-cornered Dynamic of Redemption in the 'Long' Thirteenth Century: Villein Manumissions and the Theology of the Incarnation," *Anglo-Norman Studies* 26 (2013), 1-16.

[3] "Comment et pourquoi finit l'esclavage antique" [1947], in his *Mélanges historiques*, ed. C-E. Perrin (S.E.V.P.E.N.: Paris, 1963), 261-85.

in imperial Rome with its highly developed systems of law and slavery, towards this new kind of servitude we call "serfdom." Bloch's approach has remained very influential, and the idea of slavery and serfdom as distinct institutions remains a premise of much early medieval social history.[4] Treatments of Anglo-Saxon society generally place slavery almost alone on center-stage.[5] Another consequence of starting the narrative with the particular Roman brand of slavery is a fixation on finding a clear legal line between freedom and unfreedom, resembling that which became in thirteenth-century England the main concern of the common law of villeinage.[6] We depict a high proportion of the English population before 1066 as slaves, so that any freed slave must indeed have crossed a line to freedom.

One would certainly like to know how common slaves were, and whether we should term Anglo-Saxon England a slave society, in the sense that slavery was a significant determinant of its overall culture. The sources make such knowledge impossible. The first opportunity to estimate how many slaves there were in the country and in which direction the numbers might have been moving does not come until after the Old English kingdom had already ended. Scholars have counted the *servi* recorded in Domesday Book and compared the totals in the time of King Edward with that of William, to argue for a substantial decrease in the two decades between 1066 and 1086. Many then portray this as the end of a process of numerical decline from much higher numbers in the distant past. Though quite unprovable, this view has survived the discrediting of the abolitionist assumptions that once underpinned it.[7]

Another central assumption to receive attention below is the belief that Latin *servus* and its various Old English equivalents denote something close to our modern "ideal type" of slave. The literature takes them to be terms with a relatively precise, "legal" meaning. I would suggest that, before the legal revolution of the eleventh and twelfth centuries with its revival of law schools and a learned law tradition, English law functioned rather less precisely than this. One pointer in this direction is the absence of some of the familiar distinctions of modern Western law derived ultimately from

---

[4] The literature has advanced a long way since Bloch, without quite losing the institutional premise. I have gained much from the sophisticated preliminary studies of Alice Rio toward her *Slavery after Rome*.

[5] One important exception is R. Faith, *The English Peasantry and the Growth of Lordship* (London: Leicester University Press, 1997).

[6] My own account of this is *King, Lords and Peasants in Medieval England* (Oxford: Oxford University Press, 1980).

[7] An older generation of scholars wanted to believe that the Church disapproved of slavery and worked against it. More recently, scholars like Wyatt, *Slaves and* Warriors,1-2, 10-2, 17-18, 29-31, 58-60, and S. Jurasinski, *The Old English Penitentials and Anglo-Saxon Law* (New York: Cambridge University Press, 2015), 86-95 have effectively critiqued such views.

Rome.[8] I therefore examine both the nature and location of any line between free and unfree, and the extent to which our modern conceptual differentiation of slavery and serfdom might apply to tenth- and eleventh-century England.

While the Old English laws make fairly frequent use of an opposition between free and unfree when expounding differential punishments for "criminal" offenses and failure to meet various social obligations, there is no general statement that everyone was either one or the other in the way Gaius famously provided for Roman law.[9] The English valued their freedom as much as any other people, but seem not to have thought of it as any protective legal fence. It appears, then, that they envisioned it rather as a kind of continuum along which men and women were located by relation to their local reference groups.

One cannot easily argue this from the contemporary names by which they were known, for we know relatively little about the terms in which people conversed in their villages. Many "in-between" groups complicated matters, their status seldom specified, but neither obviously slave nor noble. Kings never addressed the whole mass of the non-noble as a single entity in the laws written for them or elsewhere. But a few elite churchmen did include them in an imagined collective, under the name of *laboratores* or *weorcmen*, those who worked the land to feed and clothe everyone else. It may help if we consider what effect these elite efforts at social taxonomy might have had in the "real" world. My hope here is, that we may thereby return to the Anglo-Saxon serf and his womenfolk their rightful place in the sallow English sun.

This study comes in three sections. I first sketch some of the ways in which clever churchmen divided up their society in order to locate it within the reforming Christian visions they sought to promote, with particular attention to the most famous of these, the Three Orders. In so doing, I argue that this theory's implications come close to defining the conceptual shape of Anglo-Saxon servitude. A central section then proposes a model of slavery as it appears in late Anglo-Saxon society and culture. Key in my opinion is the quantum of *control* over slave lives exercised by their master or lord. I suggest we call the residue serfs, numerically significant, considered unfree, but enjoying a certain level of independence over themselves and their lives. A third section then contends that much contemporary material conventionally read as evidence for slavery is better understood as a kind of servitude that shades off from the unbearably harsh if

---

8 I have made some preliminary suggestions in my "Property Talk: Did Anglo-Saxon England know the Concept of Seisin?" in *Texts and Contexts in Legal History: Essays in Honor of Charles Donahue*, ed. J. Witte, S. McDougall, and A. di Robilant (Berkeley: Robbins Collection, 2016), chapter 3.

9 Gaius, *Institutiones*, III. 9: " Et quidem summa diuisio de iure personarum haec est quod omnes homines aut liberi sunt aut serui." I consider some of the evidence for the complications behind this simplicity below, [144-5].

sometimes quite short-lasting at one end of the spectrum, to a milder subordination at the other. Various conceptions of freedom coexisted within English society. Where it is visualized as bounded by a line, this serves to mark off the nobility from their dependents, those who pray and fight from all who labor to support the really free men (and their womanfolk) who lived off estates considered their own. All lesser folk risked being represented as in some sense unfree and so compelled to stay where they were and work at their lord's will.

Social Taxonomy in Anglo-Saxon England

Slaves can be categorized, separated from the rest, and labeled as such, only by others —lords, masters, or owners with an interest in profiting from them.[10] But some atypical individuals, a thinking few, sometimes felt the need to separate the sheep from the goats, and construct consciously stylized descriptions of their society. Giles Constable has warned that in the Middle Ages it was only "churchmen and writers" who responded to this urge, and that "the medieval schemas bear little relation to the realities of how people live and interact [...] but [...] reflect a profound need to understand and impose order upon their society." [11] The writings, motivated by their felt need to tame a frightening, tumultuous, sinful world, tend to be cerebral and spiritual. They tell us most about the fears and hopes of a few elite clerics worrying about future salvation and current threats to their way of life. They show little interest in that lived by peasants or, for that matter, women, townsmen, artisans, and merchants. Not so long as food reached the refectory tables and peace reigned within the enclosure. One may well wonder what their writings can contribute to the present study.

For all their unworldly character, these writings have much to teach us. Their authors tended to start from a binary distinction, such as that already mentioned one of these, Gaius's mantra of "aut liber, aut servus." But the most famous exemplars of the genre are Trinitarian, organized into three groups. The famous Three Orders of those who

---

[10] I should make it clear that I use the word "lord" throughout for anyone who enjoys lordship over dependents, including possible slaves. I explain why, below, 142

[11] Giles Constable, *Three Studies in Medieval Religious & Social Thought* (Cambridge: Cambridge University Press, 1995), chap. 3 "The Orders of Society," 251, 294-5. I have also used Thomas E. Powell, "The 'Three Orders' of Society in Anglo-Saxon England," *Anglo-Saxon England*, 23 (1994): 103-32 and M. Arnoux, "Between Paradise & Revolt: *Laboratores* in the Society of the Three Orders," in *Normandy and its Neighbours, 900-1250: Essays for David Bates*, ed. David Crouch and K. Thompson (Turnhout: Brepols, 2011), 201-14, and now I. Moilanen, "The Concept of the Three Orders of Society and Social Mobility in Eleventh-Century England", *EHR* 131 (2016): 1331-52.

pray, fight, and work allots a place to a lower laity, the *laboratores*. Its writers, perturbed by the threats from sin and from pagans, divided their society by function, by the contribution each order made to the wellbeing of Christendom.

Some unknown had sensed the need to divide the laity functionally and distinguish the fighters from those who fed them. To do so, he converted *laboratores,* a rather rare Latin term to denote a workers' collective, and his Old English adaptor strengthened the point by translating Latin "ordo" as *geferscipe*, fellowship, connoting significantly more than a random collection of individuals. The *laboratores* were to owe the same loyalty as the rest.[12] Each *ordo* should serve the whole willingly. Why should the *laboratores* or *weorcmen* respond favorably to this new duty? They were already bound to do the onerous support work required to feed and support their betters. There is no sign that they ever protested, and none of the elite is likely to have done so. But Ælfric seems at least once to have noticed that unfreedom could make a relatively valued plowman unhappy. Perhaps this is why he welcomed his *weorcmen* as a *geferscipe*, and termed them *yrþlingas*, farmers. Perhaps some churchman felt a need to reassure the subaltern masses that they too belonged to the Christian nation.[13] Notably, none of these texts ever mentions the question of freedom.

When one views the Three Orders in this perspective, it is tempting to link it to the frequently made opposition of *pauper* and *potens*, which highlighted at much this time the exploitation of the disempowered by the great. Since kings expected to counter this and protect God's *pauperes* were increasingly defaulting under pressure of invasion, churchmen came to recognize the need to substitute protection from God and his saints for this secular default, and in due course provided an alternative of their own in the so-called Peace of God.[14] In this manner, an exercise in social taxonomy helped pave the way for a significant religious initiative into politics.

Taxonomic schemas of this kind always imply some degree of comparative assessment between groups or individuals. There is a certain natural compulsion for people to situate themselves socially by measuring themselves against those they consider closest

---

[12] Powell, "The Three Orders in England," 104 (for *geferscipe*), 112, 116-17, 129. Pelteret, *Slavery*, 96, quotes some pertinent words of Abbo of St. Germain.

[13] *Ælfric, "Laboratores* sind yrþlingas and æhtemen, tó ðam ánum betæhte, ðe hig ús bigleofan tiliaþ," *The Old English Version of the Heptateuch*, ed. Crawford (London: EETS 160, 1922, reprd. 1969), l. 1208. Wulfstan, *Sermo Lupi ad Anglos*, ed. D. Whitelock (London: Methuen: 3rd edn., 1963), ll. 46, 102 sq. (= pp. 52, 58-60). Cf. also *Ine* 11.

[14] K. Bösl, "*Potens* und *pauper*. Begriffsgeschichtliche Studien zur gesellschaftlichen Differenzierung im frühen Mittelalter" (1963): in his *Frühformen der Gesellschaft im mittelalterlichen Europa* (Munich and Vienna, 1964), 106-34; G. Koziol, *The Peace of God* (ARC Humanities Press: New edn., Kalamazoo MI, 2018). I return to the question of power and *potestas* below.

to their own condition.[15] We do this ourselves, and expect rulers and employers to separate us from our inferiors by maintaining correct differentials. Relations with near neighbors are of more everyday importance than dreams of nobility. Servitude is not exempt from this. Instead of asking the too simple question: who was to be free and who unfree, lords and others might ask *how* free, *how* dependent on their lordly will, was this group or that? Were they free enough to leave the lordship, alienate their land and dispose of it at will, or not so free that they could marry off their daughters as they wished? Lords might *claim* absolute power, but prudent ones and their estate managers monitored local standards to check how they measured up with neighboring landlords.[16] In political cultures with legal discourses less focused on the sharpness of conceptual definition, we might expect status to be assigned largely without recourse to courts or law, by force majeure or, at best, negotiation along lines determined by power and established habit. I can locate just enough evidence to argue for such an hypothesis.[17]

Modeling the Slave from Anglo-Saxon Sources

No single model of the slave will ever win universal approval. The term has been applied to almost every known type of servitude. Popular candidates for a common feature, like "exclusion," loss of identity and "social death," seem to be more characteristic of a few extreme variants rather than functions of an institution.[18] Since there seems little point in seeking some essentialist model of Anglo-Saxon "real" or "ideal" slavery, I start from lords' power, a power to control and profit from a dependent's time, strength and capacities. Of course, some kinds of labor are much freer than others, much less painful or unpleasant. Much turns on the nature of the obligations and how far they are specified in advance. Money rent is preferable to physical work, predictable weekwork to work at someone else's arbitrary whim, and—some might say—tasks requiring special skills like plowing as against muck spreading. Practical men seldom thought in terms of the kind of high-falutin" schemas discussed in the last section. They made or followed rough judgments, made at some past time to institute and maintain differentials between socially contiguous groups, mostly ones inherited from predecessors or imitated

---

[15] My thinking started from W.G. Runciman, *Relative Deprivation and Social Justice* (Berkeley: University of California Press, 1966). But I might have taken my cue from https://en.wikipedia.org/wiki/Keeping_up_with_the_Joneses. And see further below, 145.

[16] Something of this kind is abundantly documented in ante-bellum America. Slaves knew which masters were the best for them, and feared being sold "down the river," as in Mark Twain's *Huckleberry Finn*.

[17] I argue this case and supply some supporting evidence below, 145-6.

[18] I found A. Testart, "L'esclavage comme institution," *L'Homme*, 38 (1998): 31-69, a very useful starting-point for my own thinking. See esp. 31, 41: "L'esclave est un joker que chaque société utilise selon son logique propre," and 36-8 for "exclusion."

from neighboring lordships and estates. Even when using widely known terms like "servi," they were primarily making decisions for their own estate, understood in their own individual way.[19] So here I simply rehearse in my own way some of the criteria that indicated those we might term slaves, serfs, or free enough to be neither.

There is first a false trail to close. Not all the men and women who were transferred at others' initiative should be considered unfree, let alone slaves. It is true that in societies that have laws about ownership,[20] public disposals of men are good ways for the acquirer to demonstrate control. But non-slaves, too, were on occasion bought and sold in the early Middle Ages. Serfs were certainly being sold long after the final disappearance of "slavery." When Wulfstan complained of the rash of human sales at a time of crisis in his *Sermo Lupi*, he called the practice *mannsilen*, using the neutral and gender neutral term for (hu)man, avoiding the more ominously servile language he employed elsewhere.[21] Dependents at almost any social level might sometimes find themselves transferred to new lords without the opportunity to refuse. A similarly wide range of people could be stolen, for man-theft was seldom qualified with the "slave" vocabulary.[22] The best known of all English slave market stories, Bede's account of Gregory the Great's inspirational discovery of Angle angels at Rome refers only to *pueri* offered for sale.[23] And again, leases and wills transfer livestock (human and animal) with the lands they worked by means of the bland phrase, "mid mete & mannum."[24] Humiliatingly thing-like though the language may be, it does not prove that the humans involved had lived like classic slaves beforehand, or had to do so afterwards.

All men and women find their freedom diminished when they are transferred at the will of others. The very fact that this happened demonstrates lost independence.

---

19 Ruth Mazo Karras, *Slavery and Society in Medieval Scandinavia* (New Haven: Yale University Press, 1988), 39, accepts Gurevic to the effect that "estate indices [...] determine the individual's social position."

20 Which, I have argued in my "Property Talk," England did not at this date. But Pelteret, *Slavery*, 287 s.v. "freosceatt" offers a little evidence to suggest the contrary.

21 Pelteret, *Slavery*, 300.

22 *Abt.* 89; *Hl.* 5; *Af.* 9. 2; *VI As.* 6. 3; *Ine.* 11, 53; charter S 1447 ("ænne wimman"). And cf. Pelteret, *Slavery*, 73-4, 87; *Af. El* 15 (Ex., xxi. 16); also *Af.* 11-11.5, which eschews the free/unfree binary. Distinguish *DOE* "forstalian"; Bosworth-Toller, 308 meaning "steal away," i.e. escape, from "forstelan," to steal something. An anecdote told by Lantfred, c. 20 had a trader sell back to a former owner a *servula* whom he had never considered to be to be unfree. I have consulted the lexicons online at *http://doe.utoronto.ca/pages/index.html* and at *http://www.bosworthtoller.com/*. Although the University of Toronto's Dictionary of Old English has only reached the letter "H" to date, its text base is accessible at *http://tapor.library.utoronto.ca/doecorpus/*.

23 Bede, *Historia Ecclesiastica*, ii. 1: "pueros uenales positos"; cf. Pelteret, *Slavery*, 266, s.v. *ceapcniht* for Ælfric's homily on the incident. The Lewes Domesday entry, below n. 46, calls its merchandise *homines*. But Latin dictionaries do offer "slave" as a possible meaning for *puer*.

24 Pelteret, *Slavery*, 127, 167 gives some examples. But *VI As.* 6. 1-4; *I Eg.* 2. 1 do not confuse human runaways with *ceapgild* due for stray or stolen animals.

It inevitably associates them with trade in and rustling of livestock which they saw around them.[25] But thinking humans understand their plight in ways far beyond the capacity of animals. So the *style* of transfer mattered and was visible to onlookers, who could bear witness if required to difference between the shackles and beatings of slaves, and the erect posture of an honorable free farming neighbor summoned to the scene to acknowledge his new lord.[26] A transfer might either lead to no obvious change of condition or have serious and lasting consequences.[27] The issue was one of human will and control.[28] I now turn, therefore, to the central issues of coercion, consent, and the nature of the control which some humans exercised over others.

Housing is a key determinant. A lord who houses his dependents, in barracks or his own household, can maintain the tightest surveillance, but at a cost. To permit them to build their own shacks on their own plot is cheaper and more convenient. Plantation-type slavery is unknown in northern Europe after the Romans, so the English alternative is mostly residence in or around the hall, too close perhaps for the comfort of their superiors.[29] One must not exaggerate the difference. *Servi casati* did not suddenly become free, but they did experience a somewhat freer, more nearly independent life with more scope for fathering a lasting family together with the responsibility for their upkeep and survival.[30]

The massive imbalance in the numbers of male and female "slaves" (*servi* and *ancillae*) recorded in Domesday Book[31] may seriously distort our picture of servitude. There

---

[25] In the twelfth century Orderic Vitalis, *Ecclesiastical History*, vol. 6, ed. Margery Chibnall (Oxford: Oxford University Press, 1978), 58, reports the demeaning transfer of a Norman count like some animal, without suggesting that he lost his land.

[26] Common lawyers in the thirteenth century referred to public transfer ceremonies of assent by free tenants to sales of the land on which they resided as "attornments," and distinguished them from sales of villeins. I suggested in my "Property Talk," 54, that something similar may also have happened before 1066; perhaps Domesday Book, ii. 174b (Norfolk, 9. 23) might be an example.

[27] Another such temporal moment, flight and pursuit, I consider below, 139-40.

[28] Where Karras, *Slavery and Society*, 6 talks of "power," I prefer "control," to bring out the fact that the power is exercised *over* human animals with wills of their own, and represents a dominating relationship between the two parties. Kyle Harper, *Slavery in the Late Roman World, AD 275-425* (Cambridge: Cambridge University Press, 2011), chapter 8, uses "mastery" to construct a seductive model by the selective use of words like *dominatio*.

[29] Though barracks are not quite inconceivable (see below, 136) domestic service is the more likely option, and perhaps explains some of those Domesday manors with just one or two *servi*. Hagiography shows servants in town houses but, notably, never mentions field work.

[30] Twelfth-century references to food handouts suggest a phased transition toward fuller independence.

[31] Faith, *English Peasantry*, 66; J.S Moore, "Domesday Slavery," *Anglo-Norman Studies* 11 (1988): 191-220. Michael Lapidge, *The Cult of St. Swithun* (Oxford: Clarendon Press, 2003), 289, 302 (= Lantfred, cc. 6, 20) are stories about an *ancillula* and a *servula* respectively. There must be others.

must have been significant undercounting of women in 1086.[32] The way that raids and warfare are said to have followed the biblical pattern that killed male enemies and took over their women and children would lead one to expect there to have been initially more women slaves than men.[33] If we know anything about men and women, it is that most experience sexual desire, which frequently results in offspring who need nurturing through a longer period of non-productive vulnerability than other livestock. Historians should ponder the circumstances in which *servi* could find women of their own kind with whom to mate without their lords' losing the fruits of the unions. All in all, it seems to have been in the lords' interest to put slaves onto plots of land from which they might be permitted to raise families and compelled to rely more on their "own" resources for food and shelter.

For heavier field work, men were presumably preferable and thus perhaps have a stronger claim to reside beyond the hall complex, whereas women were more needed in-house for service on demand, sometimes surely of a sexual nature.[34] All children would belong to the lord, if, as seems likely, the "worse blood prevails" rule was the norm. There was therefore no economic reason for lords to police their dependents' morals; fornication boosted the workforce.[35] Some unions will have been lasting, and treated as legitimate marriage, others not. And, despite the Church's long memory for the Roman incomplete recognition of slave unions as full marriages, churchmen with any strong concern for the salvation of souls must surely have striven to Christianize village unions.[36] Old English wills and stand-alone manumission documents commonly

---

32 Pelteret, *Slavery*, 202-3, suggests that only women in "positions of responsibility" were recorded, and scents under-recording elsewhere too. See further below, 136.

33 J. Gillingham, "Christian Warriors and the Enslavement of Fellow Christians," in M. Aurell and C. Girbea, eds., *Chevalerie et christianisme aux XIIe et XIIIe siècles* (Rennes: Presses universitaires de Rennes, 2011), 242-7; Pelteret, "Slave Raiding and Slave Trading in Early England," *Anglo-Saxon England* 9 (1980): 111. Num., xxxi. 7-9 documents a model worth pursuing into Old English bible adaptations and commentary.

34 Most scholars now recognize sexual exploitation as a constant possibility in social systems that give men open access and authority over the unfree. On the lord's possible sexual demands, see Stefan Jurasinski, *The Old English Penitentials and Anglo-Saxon Law* (Cambridge: Cambridge University Press, 2015), 139-45, and note that the value of a *theow* could be affected "be his wlites weorðe," his (or her) good looks, VI As 6. 3.

35 I noticed no scholarly discussion of slave breeding, though Karras, *Slavery*, 31 mentions the matter. Lords surely bred animals on their estates, e.g. R.H.C. Davis, *The Medieval Warhorse* (New York: Thames and Hudson, 1989), 44. I discussed later rules about the status of issue from mixed marriages in my *King, Lords, and Peasants*, 175-82.

36 J. Brundage, *Law, Sex, and Christian Society in Medieval Europe* (Chicago: University of Chicago Press, 1987), 31-2, 36, 71, 87, 196, 360-1; M.M. Sheehan, "Theory & Practice: Marriage of the Unfree & the Poor in Medieval Society," *Medieval Studies* 50 (1988): 474-8; Anders Winroth "Neither slave nor free," in *Medieval Church Law and the Origin of the Western Legal Tradition*, ed. W.P. Muller and M.E. Sommar (Washington DC: Catholic University Press, 2006),105-9; S. Jurasinski, *Old English Penitentials and Anglo-Saxon Law*, chap. 4.

specify whether or not a father's emancipation was to affect the status of his wife and children.[37]

When slaves start to live off their own resources, in family groups, they begin to look unlike chattel slaves. It would seem that even Domesday *servi* could be householders.[38] If so, estimates of their numbers should be increased by a multiplier comparable to that of their neighbors.[39] The shift to individual housing was not new in 1066. It becomes visible in the early twelfth century, from clusters of tiny inland holdings and a diminishing pattern of food handouts from the hall.[40] Homes of their own gave workers a buffer against the worst maltreatment that had been their lot; they recovered a modicum of independence. But lords invested less administrative and organizational effort in their labor force and lost little in so doing, which is why it happened.

The move to *servus casatus*, then, marks an important step on the road to serfdom, a serious diminution in seignorial control over workers' lives. Instead of living those lives "in servitude," as Dominique Barthélemy puts it, their condition became one in which they could make choices limited by known dues and duties.[41] Though still unfree, they no longer fit the classic slave model. At least some Domesday *servi* must have lived in this way. Manors listing larger numbers of a couple of dozen or so are candidates for *inland* (demesne) cottages and shacks. Only a real archaeological surprise is likely to make the case for seignorial housing on any scale, though place names point to places where some lord had initially settled servile groups by fiat.[42]

---

[37] David Pelteret and Oliver Padel are compiling a comprehensive edition of the manumissions. In the meantime, I use the list in Pelteret, *Slavery*, xiii-xvi. Manumissions often name live children but also use terms such as Old English *ofsprinc* (variously spelled), and Latin *posteritas* etc., eg Pelteret, nos. 1. 1; 3. 1, 3, 47; 5. 3, 16; 6.1; 8. 2, 11, 14. Pelteret, nos. 3. 25, 28, 47, 49; 10. 1 use the word *teám*, defined by BT, 972, sense 1, as a "line of descendants, offspring, progeny, family, children." This was the equivalent of the later Latin "sequela."

[38] Faith, *English Peasantry*, 60-4; Pelteret, *Slavery*, 174-6; Moore, "Domesday Slavery," 219. Scott Thompson Smith *Land and Book: Literature and Land Tenure in A-S England* (Toronto: U. Toronto Press, 2012), 126-34 shows how the process might apply to cottars. etc. The *sequela* clause, routinely included in transfers of later villeins and other humans (see previous note) implies that these included wife, children, and chattels. This surely encouraged scribes and others to record *servi* as something more than isolated individuals.

[39] Pelteret, *Slavery*, 216, suspected that *servi* had been under-recorded or even omitted in some Domesday shires. Hurstbourne Priors, Hants., could be a case to point, Domesday Book, i. 41b.

[40] Faith, *Growth of Lordship*, 59-77 and chap. 5. M. Postan, *The Famulus: The Estate Labourer in the XIIth and XIIIth centuries* (London: Economic History Society, 1954), 11-13 argued for this, and shrewdly noted the parallel with the way knights who left the household remained partially dependent on seignorial support.

[41] Dominique Barthélemy, *The Serf, the Knight, and the Historian* (Ithaca NY: Cornell, 2009), 64-5. This formulation is closely influenced by the way Roman law was read in the Middle Ages. Philippe de Beaumanoir, *Coutumes du Beauvaisis*, ed. A. Salmon (Picard: 2 vols., Paris, 1970), ii. 231-3 (s. 1452), uses in the 1280s the same French word (*sers*) for both states of servitude.

[42] Faith, *English Peasantry*, 60-1, 67-70; David Pelteret, "Slavery in the Danelaw," in *Social Approaches to Viking Studies*, ed. R. Samson (Glasgow: Cruithne, 1991), 184.

Residence, then, helped to determine the level of control and surveillance which lords exercised over their dependents.[43] Extremes of control occurred at particular moments. The worst, at the very beginning, might set the captives' pattern for life. Enslavement was one of the routine risks of early medieval warfare. Those who fell into enemy hands and were not killed invariably became disposable at somebody else's will.[44] The survivors and their women and children entered a human trade waged little less violently than the warfare that fed it. Everything conspired to rip people apart from the cultural roots by which they had been accustomed to live and exposed them to the will of their new lords and masters. This dehumanization gives life to the chroniclers' animal metaphors. Like other livestock the unfree could be beaten at will, perhaps even put to death, and could be secured in place, especially when publicly offered for sale, or as needed for punitive purposes.[45] At least some of the iron shackles found and preserved in museums belong to this period. Their use is confirmed by hagiographic accounts of the way saints could, when asked nicely, smash the shackles and free their devotees.[46] Much turned on the nature of that initial capture.

Thereafter, most slaves most of the time, then, stayed in the condition to which they were born. Misery there must have been, but over time conditions could change, in either direction. The most spectacular demonstrations of extreme subjection and humiliation come at the point of sale or transfer, and after punishment. Slaves are little use to their masters when shackled; we see no chain gangs in Anglo-Saxon England. The diverse factors that affect the degree of independence mostly fell far short of these extremes. Those with power were not all sadists, so that human relationships, even with their lord and lady, might conceivably soften their condition.[47] The administrative needs of lords and their manorial officials as well as the collective memory of the working

---

[43] Physical distance created difficulties for lords. For runaways, see below, 139-40; also below n.57 for the way that lords strove to retain control of their men off the lordship.

[44] Gillingham, "Christian Warriors & the Enslavement of Fellow Christians," 237-56.

[45] Evidence for public market sales is thin. Bede's retelling of the Gregory the Great's angels story comes from one end of the period, the Domesday reference to a toll on sales of men at Lewes and William of Malmesbury's notices from the other. Domesday Book, i. 26a; *The Vita Wulfstani of William of Malmesbury*, ed. R.R. Darlington (London: Royal Historical Society, 1928), 43. The sight of traders hawking round the country a string of shackled prisoners would broadcast the humiliation and horror of servitude quite as effectively.

[46] Lapidge, *Cult of St. Swithun*, cc. 6, 20, 39 (ibid., 289, 302, 332-3) with extant examples from Winchester duly noted, 289, n. 175. Pelteret, *Slavery*, 322, s.v. *wealsada*, removes any doubt that these were used on humans.

[47] The interest of penitential writers in noblemen and women having sex with their *servi* documents a limiting case. Less titillatingly, some wills that name dependents as recipients of personal bequests go on to make other grants and bequests that treat nameless others as mere ciphers, estate stock alongside the animals.

tenantry—custom as we might say—restrained the harshest behavior. This is not to whitewash the horror of servitude. Ælfric's plowman, whatever the precise nature of his status, was surely not alone in bemoaning his lack of freedom. But most of us English put up with the inequities of this world, much as we do our weather. And it was doubtless already true that some of the unfree were influenced by the message from Church and nobility that their job was to be patient and obey orders.[48]

Those who refused had two obvious options. They might resist in some way, yet there is strikingly little evidence of this reaches us. Resentment turned to resistance is more likely to start in non-violent fashion with a go-slow.[49] Another likely response is to vote with your feet. Every successful flight from an estate slightly shifts the balance of control within, by broadcasting the availability of an alternative. Landlords surely understood that land without workers lost its value. And there were still lots of places to go in the eleventh century, where land was free or could be opened up by those with initiative, sometimes with lords asking few questions. Thoughts of worker flight were never too far from the minds of prudent estate managers who strove to ensure that no workers left without permission. There is hardly a scrap of Anglo-Saxon evidence for court decisions about status or the right to leave.[50] There were indeed assertions in Domesday Book that this or that group of inhabitants were or were not entitled to leave and/or find a new lord. But this material now seems to have been intended to separate freer tenants from those less free (but still *liberi homines*) who held by "dependent tenures."[51]

---

[48] I remain very struck by what Marxists call "hegemony." J.D. Slack, "The Theory and Method of Articulation in Cultural Studies," in *Stuart Hall: Critical Dialogues in Cultural Studies*, ed. D. Morley & K. Chen (Routledge: London, 1996), 117, explains this as "a process by which a hegemonic class articulates (or co-ordinates) the interests of social groups, such that those groups actively consent to their subordinated status."

[49] I have always read in this way the materials gathered by R. Hilton, "Peasant Revolts in England Before 1381," *Economic History Review*, 2nd s. 2 (1949): 117-36. But I am arguing here from silence; James Campbell, "England, c. 991," in *The Battle of Maldon*, ed. Janet Cooper (London: Hambledon Press, 1993), 9, supplies one scrap of evidence.

[50] Twelfth-century suits about status and claims to lordship over the unfree in the twelfth century had to begin in the undocumented shire court. I cite two possible instances below, [n. 85]. It is not inconceivable that similar suits occurred before 1066. I shall suggest elsewhere that treatment of such cases within the lordship could be part of the origins of "private justice".

[51] Stephen Baxter, "The Making of Domesday Book and the Languages of Lordship in Conquered England" in *Conceptualizing Multilingualism in England, c.800-c.1250*, ed. E.M. Tyler (Turnhout: Brepols, 2011), 271-308, presents with admirable clarity arguments worked out in detail in his "Lordship & Justice in Late Anglo-Saxon England: The Judicial Functions of Soke & Commendation Revisited," in *Early Medieval Studies in Memory of Patrick Wormald*, ed. idem et al. (Burlingon VT: Ashgate, 2009), chapter 25. Cf. further below, 147 and Domesday Book, ii.59 (Essex 30.20).

The notion that dependents lay within the power and authority of their lords is indicated in contemporary Francia by the Latin word *potestas* or its French equivalent. They were sometimes described as "homines de potestate" ,"hommes de poesté," and usages of this kind occur also in Norman England.[52] There is nothing legalistic about this. It is neither about function nor free status, just power. It derives from a world where the individual *pauper* is defined by the fact that any *potens* might seek to press him into service by force or threat. In such circumstances, who would not conclude that hope lay on the road out of the village.

This can be conveniently illustrated from a series of post-Conquest royal writs that enable one to deduce what was perhaps a lord's normal reaction to worker flight: bring them back! All surviving exemplars of the writ of naifty (a writ by which a lord claimed someone as his serf) earlier than 1150 are special favors directed to churchmen with archives,[53] and so a special case of royal assistance, and initially meant what they said, no more than: "Get these runaways back to Saint Cuthbert (etc.) with their families and goods." The text demonstrates no interest in legal rights. The king commanded it; those addressed were to make it happen. From the 1130s, however, the drafting clerks make explicit the possibility of court argument. The first writ to incorporate a status label dates from 1155.[54] Earlier writs merely referred to anonymous *homines* along with such possessions as wives, children and *pecunia*. The few fugitives whom the writs actually named were presumably neither slaves nor obvious serfs. None is described in the language of slavery. And if anyone was being sued, it was some rival lord not the fugitives, for detention not flight.[55]

There must have been far more Norman manorial runaways than these writs document. A Durham monk's story of pursuit across the north-east ending in a miraculous escape on the sands of Lindisfarne sheds a glimmer of light on more routine occasions.[56] A Tees-side lord exploited his *pauper* tenants way beyond the rent that they owed as *coloni*, and is said to have picked particularly on one man somewhat better off than the

---

[52] Examples at Domesday Book, i. 32c, 36a, 137d, 163b; Reginald of Durham, *Libellus De admirandis Beati Cuthberti Virtutibus* (London: Surtees Society, vol. 1, 1835), 206: "homo dominio potestatis"; *The Anglo-Norman Dictionary*, s.v. poesté (at *http://www.anglo-norman.net/D/poesté*), and cf. Taylor, *Shape of the State*, 200-4.

[53] R.C. Van Caenegem, *Royal Writs in England from the Conquest to Glanville* (London: Selden Society, 77 for 1958-9), nos. 103-13 prints extant examples. Cf. my *King, Lords, and Peasants*, 223-39.

[54] Van Caenegem, *Royal Writs*, nos. 114-15, 120-1, allege that the fugitive was *nativus*, born into his status.

[55] The form of the action of naifty between two claimant lords survives into the time of Glanvill, *King, Lords, and Peasants*, 163, but by 1200 the issue was almost always the status of the alleged fugitive, and the flight often fictional. The general twelfth-century picture is confirmed by Scots material cited by Taylor, *Shape of the State*, 64, 138, 153, 167-8, 173, 300.

[56] Reginald of Durham, 234, previously summarized from a different viewpoint in *King, Lords, and Peasants*, 225-6.

rest. He, unwilling to bear this any longer, determined to move his family away. The decision was made after heart-searching and debate, for he had much to lose. He decided that Saint Cuthbert, to whom he was devoted, was calling him to his own shrine at Lindisfarne, just off the Northumbrian coast, where he would find peace under the saint's "hand of protection." One dark night, he hit the road with his wife, children, and herds. The lord and his men pursued them on horseback, got within earshot of the heavily burdened caravan on the sands, but then rode right past on, so close that fearful fugitives could recognize old acquaintances. And our hero, never wavering from his hopes of a better life with St. Cuthbert, made it safely to Lindisfarne.

Decisions to uproot oneself and one's family and follow the refugee option are always fraught with risk. Lords might peacefully license departure and tax the absentees; such an arrangement retained a modicum of control and might last for generations.[57] But most sought preemptively to restrict mobility, for example, by agreeing with their neighbors not to receive each other's fugitives.[58] All parties saw the ability to leave freely as critical. The knowledge of its availability reduced the lord's freedom to exploit and gave residents hope for relief, whatever their status label. This must have been as obvious before 1066 as in the better documented decades around 1100.[59] Old English laws sporadically refer to the reception of strangers. These enactments are usually, and rightly, treated as a law-and-order measure, the point being to ensure that lords would produce their tenants to answer all accusations.[60] But some doubtless felt empowered on occasion to muster a local posse, pursue their own interest, and recover runaways by potentially lethal force, as if they were thieves. London guildsmen certainly required their fellow members to ride with them on such occasions.[61] Successful flight was bad for business all round.

---

[57] They exacted annual status acknowledgements in the form of annual, small ritual payments. This was called head money, *chevage* in French. David Pelteret, "Two Old English Lists of Serfs," *Studies in Mediaeval Culture* 12 (1978): 472-513 and Faith, *English Peasantry*, 43-4, 81-4 give a little evidence. I very briefly sketch the links between these methods and those the Normans brought with them after 1066 in my Paul R. Hyams, "La joie de la liberté et le prix de la respectabilité: autour des chartres d'affranchissement anglaises et d'actes français analogues (1160-1307)," BEC 164 (2006): 371-89, at 383.

[58] Written non-reception agreements survive from twelfth-century France, G. Langmuir, "'Judei nostril' and the Beginning of Capetian Legislation," *Traditio* 16 (1960): 203-39.

[59] Baxter, "Lordship and Justice," 402-3. The existence of a runaway problem was already a matter of public concern in *Ine* 24, 39, and treated as capital self-theft by London guildsmen; read *VI As.* 3 alongside *IV As.* 6. 5.

[60] I refer to the sources and some literature in my *King, Lords, and Peasants*, 235 and n. 62, where *II As.* 27 is a mistake for *II As.* 22, and *AGu.* 4, 6 is also incorrect. Cf. now Lambert, *Law and Order*, 333-5 on the offense of harboring fugitives. The laws use the gender non-specific term, *mann*, meaning that they covered women, and probably children.

[61] *VI As.* 4-6. 4. *VI As.* 3 authorizes the hanging or even stoning of runaways.

This question of control is worth further thought. Although various circumstances might affect the freedom of the labor force to move out, there is little sign that it turned on the defining labels, and less still that legal status as later understood was determinative. Conversely, being tied to lord or land did not prove that anyone was unfree, still less a slave. Rather, those who wished or claimed freedom must plead a past of honorable independence. To understand how contemporaries thought and felt about this, a good starting-point is the commonplace analogy between slavery and captivity, in senses ranging from arbitrary seizures by evil men, war captures, and also the imprisonment of lawbreakers and others. Imprisonment, like slavery, is represented as a merciful alternative to death.[62] In practice it was often very brutal, since prisoners, were entirely at their captors' mercy.[63] This perhaps makes well- documented modern systems of incarceration a useful measure of harshness for the various levels of servitude too, a way to bypass reliance on contemporary labels.[64]

Terminology, evidence and problems[65]

Let us return to that poster-boy for Anglo-Saxon slavery, Ælfric's plowman. Scholars agree that plowmen with their special skills were a cut above most other estate workers, and so kept closely tied to the inland and its plow teams. Evidence from the decades around 1100 shows plowmen becoming *famuli* residing on their own small plots. So he, if anyone, ought to have been a slave c. 1000. But Ælfric's text says only that he is not free and greatly regrets this.[66] Ælfric could have used an Old English equivalent

[62] See generally Orlando Patterson, *Slavery and Social Death* (Cambridge, MA: Harvard University Press, 1982); cf. also F.M. Blecker, "The Civil Rights of the Monk in Roman & Canon Law: The Monk as Servus," *American Benedictine Review* 2 (1966): 185-98, and my own *King, Lords, and Peasants*, 126-7.

[63] The valuable study of Daniel Thomas, "Incarceration as Judicial Punishment on Anglo-Saxon England," in *Capital and Corporal Punishment in Anglo-Saxon England*, ed. Jay Gates and Nicole Marafioti (Woodbridge: Boydell, 2014), chap. 5, 92-112, notes that judicial imprisonment was rare and usually very temporary, and dedicated jails few. Even so, captivity itself must have been a familiar idea, constantly replenished by its biblical references. Jailers were well placed to extort concessions. The situation encouraged harsh treatment. There is scope for further work on the analogy, especially since Old English verbs like *alysan* and, more distantly, *freogan* occur in both contexts.

[64] The minute detail of Nikolaus Wachsmann, *KL: A History of the Nazi Concentration Camps* (London: Little, Brown, 2015) suggested to me that the point reached by 1942, before brutal incarceration became extermination, might serve as a measure of maximum control.

[65] This was the real starting-point for this study, the lexicography of servitude, on which I had originally hoped for guidance from Lisi.

[66] *Ælfric's Colloquy*, ed. G.N. Garmonsway ([1939] repr. U. of Exeter: Exeter Medieval Texts, 1978) ll. 34-5, 35: "labor est, quia non sum liber," which means "micel gedeorf (tribulation?) hit ys, for þam ic neom freoh."

to "slave" but did not. Many other writers similarly saw no reason in normal circumstances to attach to dependent groups the status labels we trust. This speaks to a mentality that is less legalistic than we have assumed.[67]

Analysis of the Old English slavery vocabulary is therefore less than conclusive.[68] No word usage can prove the actual social condition of those so labeled. Old English social taxonomy followed different lines than those of our own sociology, derived ultimately from the "new serfdoms" of the later Middle Ages and the institutionalized slavery systems of the modern age.[69] The language did not encourage contrasts between those we call slave and serf.[70] Neither Old English nor contemporary Latin distinguish between the master of slaves and the lord of other dependents. Where Romans like St. Jerome in his Vulgate bible had intended their term *dominus* to denote the master—as we should say—of slaves, early medieval Englishmen surely read it to denote the ring- and loaf-giving *hlaford* they knew, using the same word for lordship over slaves and thegns.[71] Here, therefore, I speak exclusively of lords, to avoid begging the question.[72] Thus liberated, we may envision a society in which all *laboratores* were at risk of being deemed unfree by their lord, because they *supplied* compulsory labor rather than benefited from it. Some of these unfree workers will have approximated to the slave

[67] Status labels remain rare in charters and estate surveys into the twelfth century. The inclusion of Alfric del Fen's land in an 1113/25 alms grant makes the point. The grantor, his lord, and his son each called Alfric something different, *rusticus*, *villanus*, and the generic *homo*, respectively, but Alfric was neither slave nor serf, *Eye Priory Cartulary & Charters*, ed. V. Brown (Rochester NY: Sussex Chs 12-13, Boydell, 1992, 1994), nos. 19, 346-7, & index s.v. "Fen" (c. 1113/25). The routinization of these labels in the course of the twelfth century lubricated the slide toward a new serfdom.

[68] In the next few paragraphs, I nevertheless gratefully draw on Pelteret's appendix "The Old English Terminology of Servitude and Freedom," *Slavery*, 261-330.

[69] In a preliminary draft she kindly let me see, Alice Rio portrayed the early medieval Latin vocabulary before 1100 as stable but capable of accommodating new functions and even additional status labels within a flexible set-up.

[70] The quest for a single legal term to denote the unfree serf in Angevin England led to the specialized use of Latin *villanus* and our word "villein," *King, Lords, and Peasants*, 250, n. 113. Cf. also ibid., 222, n. 22 for the first clear evidence that the English recognized that an African slave was different than a villein-serf.

[71] Peter Brown recently restated the standard classicists' view of God the slave master, *New York Review of Books*, 21 Oct 2017, http://www.nybooks.com/articles/2017/10/26/sarah-ruden-augustine-dialogue-god/.

[72] Consider Old English *dryhten*, for which *DOE*, s.v. has "lord, ruler, chief," and which denoted both the one Christian God and his pagan rivals. It can equally mean the lord of a thegn, but not it would seem lordship over the unfree. The standard Old English lord term is *hlaford*, which can refer to the master of a household or servants or disciples or "free or servile labourers" (ie *ðeowan*), BT, 540 and suppl., 549. Liebermann, *Gesetze*, II: 55-6, 115-6, drew somewhat different conclusions based on the legal evidence alone. We need an English study comparable to D.H. Green, *The Carolingian Lord* (Cambridge: Cambridge University Press, 1968). Certain other "slave" terms are apparently lacking in Old English; I see no equivalents to "overseer" or "slave driver" in the lexicons.

model, but since most were less closely subject to lordly control, we may choose to call those less closely subject to lordly control—very likely the majority—serfs.

As for freedom, there were at least four views.[73] There is first a negative sense, that the free man is free ***from*** his lord's control over his life and actions.[74] He escapes the worst burdens of lordship, most obviously work in the fields or household along with other servile handicaps.[75] A second sense—possibly the most common usage—is more positive, denoting the power ***to*** do something or exercise some right denied to the unfree.[76] And this shades into a third, long-established but poorly evidenced sense that freedom means the capacity to participate fully in public life, and a direct relationship with the king. The freeman was uniquely "worthy" to bear arms and fight with the *fyrd*, to speak his mind and to swear a valid oath at the moot.[77] Finally, *freo*, like its Latin equivalent *liber*, often goes beyond the mere absence of servitude to indicate nobility.[78] The *bellatores*, too, were proud to be free. As befits men who were expected to swear a personal loyalty oath to the king, there were far fewer of them, [79] There is little doubt that freedom, however conceived, was deeply felt, lamented when absent, and dearest to those who feared they might lose it.

[73] I leave aside here the relationship of personal freedom with the rhetoric of church liberty, so well covered by Julia Crick, "*Pristina Libertas*: Liberty & the Anglo-Saxons Revisited," *Transactions of the Royal Historical Society*, 14 (2004): esp. 58-66.

[74] The useful if philosophically crude distinction comes from Isaiah Berlin's *Two Concepts of Liberty* (Oxford: Clarendon Press, 1958). Cf. Pelteret, *Slavery*, 282, s.v. "freols."

[75] E.g. *DOE*, s.v. *freo*, *frig*: A.5. cites texts where this means free from tax, work, duties etc., cf. also ibid., A.8. I focus here on *freo* as adjective and noun, but one could of course devote a whole, heavy book to freedom words. BT, 333 and Suppl., 264-5 contains further material on *freo* not selected by DOE. The eleventh century view of work was not yet as deprecatory as it became later. A well-born saint who had voluntarily submitted to servitude could work in the fields without his efforts constituting a humiliating *opus servilis*, M.R. James, "Lives of St. Walstan," *Original Papers of...the Norfolk & Norwich Archaeological Society*, 19. 3 (1917): 244-9.

[76] eg. DOE, ibid., sense A. 5: especially where one is free to leave, or travel at will. For "full" freedom, see Pelteret, *Slavery*, 277-9. 283; F.E. Harmer, *Anglo-Saxon Writs* (Manchester: Manchester University Press: 1952), 494.

[77] This sense may be better documented from the Continent, so that Sarah Harvey, *Domesday: Book of Judgement* (Oxford: Oxford University Press, 2014), 186 takes it as a given. *Ine* 46, *I Ew.* 3, *II As.* 26, *II Cn.* 36. 1 emphasize the importance of oathworthiness, as also does *II Cn.* 20. 1 (below, n. 84). S. 1109, despite uncertain authenticity, might still be good evidence, Harmer, *Anglo-Saxon Writs*, 248, 274-5. For the association with the bearing of arms as an indication that the free were expected to bear the feud as well as fight in the fyrd, see Lambert, *Law and Order*, chap. 5, esp. 227-8.

[78] R.H. Hilton, "Freedom and Villeinage in England," *Past & Present* 31 (1965): 4, n. 2 cites continental instances where *liber* often indicated nobility, citing Continental instances. DOE, s.v. *freo*, A.10 so reads the application of the word to God. Cf. Bosworth-Toller, 333, and also Pelteret, *Slavery*, 278, s.v. *freo-dryhten* (= 'noble lord').

[79] No source hints that the freemen's oath to the king could be sworn through a proxy. This severely limits the number of full freemen (as in *II Cn.* 20, text at n. 84 below) there could have been.

Most manumissions purported to "free" somebody without explaining what that meant. They cannot have conveyed immediate full freedom, since freedman was a distinct status.[80] The Latin term *ingenuus* (meaning fully free) had once been restricted to those who had never experienced life in servitude.[81] Anglo-Saxon sources offer no definitions of freedom or any of the terms used for the free. The laws take the distinction between free and servile to be self-evident,[82] and wished status not to affect standards of proof in accusations of lawbreaking.[83] Wulfstan pressed a broader point in his laws. The king must protect the weak but give the free equal treatment. He makes his point well in his famous law on the duty of any freeman "who "wishes to have the right to purge himself of accusations by oath and be worthy of his *wer*" and other *freorihta*, to bring himself within the tithing system of collective surety. He must be available to answer any charges brought against him. Wulfstan wanted to ensure that free status was free from private manipulation of the kind practiced, he goes on to explain, by many *stræc* men who would represent their dependents as best suited their own interests, sometimes as free, sometimes unfree, *swa frigne swa for ðeowne*.[84] But there is no sign that any laws were much used in the courts, or that status cases were routinely fought there.[85] None of the many legal writings into the twelfth century ever advised litigants how to plead such matters. Nor, oddly, did they ever connect questions of free status with the wergild groups that are so central to the early laws.

One possible conclusion from this is that personal freedom was not considered a matter of general public concern. Perhaps people felt that decisions about freedom

---

[80] Pelteret, *Slavery*, 288-9, 297-8 considers *freotmann* and *lising* the terms used in the last two centuries before 1066. Lords retained some claims over the *freotmann*. *Lising* was a recent arrival from Old Norse. Cf. Pelteret, *Slavery*, 281 (*freo-læta*), 290-2 (*healf-freo*), 294-6,

[81] Only a few manumissions use Latin *ingenuus* meaning freeborn, as in *DMLBS*, ed. R.E. Latham et all. (London: Oxford University Press for the British Academy, 1975-2013), *Mediae Latinitatis Lexicon Minus*, ed. J.F. Niermeyer and C. van den Kieft (Leiden: Brill, 2002), and A. Berger, *Encyclopedic Dictionary of Roman Law* (Philadelphia: American Philosophical Society, 1953), s.vv. "ingenuus" and "ingratitudo." There were vernacular equivalents. Pelteret, *Slavery*, 285-6, 289 275-6, gives *freomann* and *freowif*, to denote the free-born, and adds that. *freobearn*, another possible equivalent, "strays close to nobly born"; cf. *DOE*, ad idem, and esp. entry c, for the gloss *æthelborene cild*, and note its different view of "freo-broþor," "freo-dohtor," "freo-wif."

[82] E.g. *EGu*. 7-8; *Rect.* 3. 4.

[83] *IV As*. 6.

[84] *VI Atr*. 52; *II Cn*. 20-20. 1; 68-68.1b. I understand *stræc* as denoting "a hard man," someone strict and unyielding in his efforts to have his own way, BT, 925. The twelfth-century Latin translations read *stræc* as meaning *potens*, surely in the sense mentioned above, 131. Wulfstan also speaks of the differing rights of the free and the *þeow* in the *Sermo Lupi*, ll. 47-8 (p. 52).

[85] Wormald. *Making*, 143, noted that "not a single legal decision...deferred to an extant decree, let alone quoted one." There are, however, two possible status pleas among Pelteret's "manumission documents," nos. 3. 50 (959/75), and 9. 8 (c. 1110).

should be decided on the estate. The servile goats were assigned to their social groups and separated from the freer sheep according to their standing in the local community by means which needed no formal court. [86] Anglo-Saxon lords desired no clear cut-off line for status.[87] They bargained from positions of power, and could justify their decisions to others if necessary by reference to local practice. Nor had they much reason to envision social divisions in terms of status absolutes which their vocabulary scarcely enabled them to state with clarity. The lay modes of thought employed are likely to have been less cerebral and more emotional, even pictorial, than those of clerical writers.

I propose that they might, instead, have envisioned freedom and servitude on a continuum between the harshest of the slave models and the greater freedoms of the nobles.[88] Individuals would not have been free or unfree in absolute terms but assignable to social groups that were freer and less free, more or less servile. Lords could grade their dependents the same way they talked about their own standing in the community, by measuring themselves against their peers. The pronouncements of distant kings and their over-educated clerical advisers could not be allowed to interfere with life on the manor. It is unlikely that the laws cited above cut much ice when lords were at odds with their "men" over who owed which harvest works or when to manure the lord's fields.[89] The *laboratores* operated under the shadow of their lord and those friends and neighbors who would, when push came to shove, ride with him.

This vision of the past, closer to the realities of the rural life but largely undocumented until the twelfth-century increase in records offers a glimpse of how late Saxon England might have been. Rodney Hilton long ago observed how little twelfth-century

---

[86] We might search for "oddities of language and organization which do not occur elsewhere in that county, and which must have been introduced at estate rather than at shire or circuit level," cf. John Blair, "Estate Memoranda of c. 1070 from the See of Dorchester-on-Thames," *EHR* 116 (2001): 121-2. John Mullan and Richard Britnell, *Land and Family: Trends and Local Variations in the Peasant Land Market on the Winchester Bishopric Estates, 1263-1415* (Hatfield: University of Hertfordshire Press, 2010): 42-6 treat a lordship which permitted customary variation between its different manors.

[87] While Hudson, *Oxford History*, 207-8 believes that "the essential contrast regarding personal freedom made in the Anglo-Saxon laws was between free and slave", the twelfth-century *Leges Henrici Primi*, ed. L.J. Downer (Oxford: Clarendon Press, 1972), 78. 2a may be the first text to approximate to Gaius' global binary.

[88] Given the differences between regions and localities what follows claims no more than plausibility. Though I refer anachronistically to manors for convenience, few estates fit the "classical" model and some areas totally lacked manorial structure.

[89] Much that Lambert, *Law and Order*, chap. 3, says, both about the lord's responsibility to produce men to answer accusations and on the estate management focus of his reeve's activities, implies that kings essentially left the details of private estate management to lords and their reeves. *Gerefa* 5-7 encourages reeves to use their lord's power (ie force?) mediated by good past custom against uppity workers when necessary.

estate surveys say about legal status, noting that those termed "free men" seemed "socially close" to gentry. He went on to cite evidence for "the relativity of peasant freedom." [90] The freedom a lord allowed his men could most accurately be indicated by Latin consecutive clauses, that is *ut* and the subjunctive following the "so" words *ita* or *sic*. Though these are uncommon in post-Conquest sources, we can supplement his examples from Domesday Book[91] and, more pertinently, from two Canterbury charters in Old English.[92]

A little direct pre-Conquest evidence exists to strengthen the case. Charter draftsmen normally applied status descriptions only to principals and witnesses. They never bother to specify whether workers were free. They did, however, use "swa...swa" clauses[93] to express comparisons between men and groups, as one can see from a unique letter written a decade before 1066. The Cumbrian Gospatric informed his *wassenas* that Thorfynn mac Thore was to

> be as free in all things that are mine in Allerdale as any man may be (*swa ænig mann beo*) [...] And it is my will that the men dwelling with Thorfynn [...] shall be as free, along with him *(swa freals myð hem swa)*, as Melmor and Thor and Sigulf were in the days of Eadred [...]

The seductive ring of the vernacular tempts me to hear in this the authentic voice of an Old English earl addressing his sworn men about freedom. His warning that no *mann* "be so bold [...] that [he] anywhere break the peace which Earl Siward and I have granted him as freely as to any man living under the sky," does not, of course, refer to those who worked these lands. He is, however, showing us how he and his like

---

[90] R.H. Hilton, "Freedom and Villeinage," 11-12. *Reading Abbey Cartularies*, ed. B.R. Kemp (Royal Hist. Soc: Camden 4th s., 2 vols., 31, 1986 & 33, 1987), ii. 835 (1173/86) is another random example.

[91] Domesday Book, i. 68a, 154d, 175a, 269d ("sicut" comparisons with obligations of contiguous groups); i. 35c, 40b and ii. 59a, 172a-b, 201a, 216b (ability to leave land and lord); i. 172a (shire custom on sake and soke); i. 180c (*milites* who were not thegns).

[92] W. Somner, *A Treatise of Gavelkind* (London, 1772), 206: "swa fela ðegenas swa ic heom to geleten hebbe..." As Harmer, *Anglo Saxon Writs*, 173 notes, this clause echoes charters from Cnut's reign such as S 985, S 1088. Forgers gave the "saw...swa" locution a healthy afterlife on into the twelfth century. More would have survived had draftsmen written more of the conditions of tenure. The major exception is grants in alms, which fairly often declare that their donation is to be as free and quiet as any alms grant can be or something similar, as in *Danelaw Charters*, ed. F.M. Stenton (London: British Academy, 1920), nos. 14, 317. Grants in alms constitute the first tenure to emerge in English law, as noted in my "Notes on the Transformation of the Fief into the Common Law Tenure in Fee" in *Laws, Lawyers, and Texts: Studies in Medieval Legal History in Honour of Paul Brand*, ed. Susanne Jenks, Jonathan Rose and Christopher Whittick, (Leiden: Brill, 2012).

[93] Mark Atherton instructs me that this construction, called "correlation," is fuctionally similar to the Latin consecutive clause.

sometimes thought and spoke of freedom.[94] Nor need this document have been unique; *swa* and *swa...swa* clauses are common enough in surviving texts.[95]

We need next to give the "free man" an eleventh-century context. I already mentioned the Domesday distinction between freemen who could change their lords and leave their land at will, and those who could not.[96] What this meant for lordship and the extent of their freedom has been much debated. Stephen Baxter suggests that it indicated the terms on which they held their lands, that is, whether their tenure was "dependent" or something grander[97] with both the power to transfer their interests to heirs (even strangers) and with, as an honorable tenant by bookright, responsibility to the king for such public duties as geld payment and fyrd service that entitled them to the elevated status of a tenant by bookright.[98] The less free group had at best impermanent life leases supposed to revert eventually to their lessors or—worse yet—the inferior title of one who paid a money rent or owed his lord actual field work.[99] Even without a Conquest, children of such "dependent" freemen might ended up demoted to join the rural labor force as serfs.[100]

---

[94] D.A. Woodman (ed.), *Charters of Northern Houses* (Oxford: Oxford University Press, 2012), no. 21, 370 is the most recent edition of S 1243 (1041/64), with full commentary, 371 sq.

[95] There are 2,800 citations for *swa* in DOE's Corpus of Old English. The 131 hits in the Electronic Sawyer show that it is common in charter boundary clauses, also used for the quality of a grantor's title and the extent of the freedom conferred upon the grantees, eg "swa full 7 swa forþ swa [name]." Cf. also S 1085 (1065/6), S 1088-1092 (from Christchurch, Canterbury), and S 1507 (Alfred's will, 873/88). The comparative mode statement in the "Rectitudines singularum personarum," c. 18 that the bedel should "for his wycan sy weorces *frigra* ðann oðer mann," receive a larger land allotment, Liebermann, *Gesetze*, I: 451.

[96] *III As.* 7. 1; *IV As.* 5; *V As.* 1. 1 emphasize that lords were not to hinder the departure (*hlafordsoknam*) of any free man with an untarnished reputation. Lambert, *Law and Order*, is one who allots the freeman a major role in Old English society; cf. esp. 55-6, 205, 227-30, 349-50, 357-60 etc.

[97] I am avoiding any "ownership" talk here; cf. my "Property Talk," 55-6. Holders of "dependent" *læns* could be men of real power and importance.

[98] Baxter, "Lordship and Justice," 394-5, 406 and n. 122, 410. He goes on to explain rather persuasively the relationship of commendation and soke. It is remarkable how seldom previous scholarship has considered the *liber homo* and bookland in the same context. But see now Lambert, *Law and Order*, 134, 304-5, n. 30, etc, and the work of Richard Purkiss there acknowledged.

[99] Baxter, "Lordship and Justice," 394. Robin Fleming, "The New Wealth, the New Rich, and the New Political Style in late Anglo-Saxon England," *Anglo-Norman Studies* 23 (2001): 21 and n. 142 cites Domesday evidence that Odda of Deerhurst had insisted that his *liberi homines* should do agricultural works "as they were ordered" or "as their lord needed."

[100] I am tempted to try to fit into the picture the thesis of Fleming, "The New Wealth," that the eleventh century saw the introduction of a new social fissure by which some thegns separated themselves from the *laboratores* by assembling large quantities of silver out of which they constructed a new, more luxurious lifestyle. It is possible that bookright proliferated at this time without leaving a trace.

I return now to the terminology of *un*freedom, but restrict myself to the few Old English words most confidently promoted along with Latin *servus* as denoting slavery. None of these denotes slave in all contexts. Writers struggled to describe the harshest servitude, by qualifying their nouns with adjectives, comparatives, etc. Good men are honored to be God's *servi*, and the pope himself is often called His servant, *servus servorum Dei*. Each of the two Old English words most frequently used in the laws to mark men off as unfree, *þeow* and *þræl*, obviously expressed a meaning which needed no translation, but which readers and those who merely heard them spoken aloud interpreted for themselves.[101] Although the term sometimes covered men who could be nothing but slaves[102], its verbs *þeowan*. and *(ge)-þeowian* are less clear, and many *þeow-* compounds imply "service" quite as much as "servitude.[103] The Old Norse loanword *þræl* may be slightly stronger, so that Wulfstan used it to distinguish the demonic followers of Anti-Christ and the Devil from God's *þeowan*.[104] Other words like *esne*, and *wealh*, sometimes taken as proof of slavery, are less probative.[105]

The beguilingly global view of the slavery question in Domesday, though Latin and post-Conquest, has influenced more than it should our readings of Anglo-Saxon servitude throughout the eleventh century.[106] The Domesday *servus* undeniably denotes denizens of the lowest social levels. Like other dependent workers, these are never said to hold of their lords, are numbered not named,[107] and grouped with plow teams and animals rather than other dependent workers. It has seemed logical to conclude that all *servi*, as human livestock without either public role or direct relationship to the king, must have been "real" slaves.

Outsiders have every reason to beware of Domesday, a desert proverbially strewn with the bones of once renowned scholars. Some of the book's many apparent anomalies

---

101 Pelteret, *Slavery*, 305; BT, 1053. They would read the words in accordance with their sense of lordship, as above 131.

102 E.g. *Af.* Prol.16.

103 Pelteret, *Slavery*, 305-9. An investigation of *þeow-* terms, starting from Pelteret, 305-15, could ascertain what proportion of the usage show a core sense of "service" or "servitude" as against "slavery."

104 BT, 1064: "a thrall, slave, servant"; cf. Pelteret, *Slavery*, 250, 307, 317, and "Slavery in the Danelaw," 183-4.

105 Pelteret, *Slavery*, 271-4, 319-22 may be compared with the citations and definitions of the lexicons.

106 Harvey, *Domesday Book*, an individual and learned survey, cites much of the vast literature on the subject, and her "Domesday England," in *The Agrarian History of England and Wales*, vol. 2, ed. J. Thirsk (Cambridge: Cambridge University Press, 1988), 45-136 has good sections on dependents and their condition. But J.S Moore, "Domesday Slavery," *Anglo-Norman Studies*, 11 (1988): 191-220 and H.B. Clarke, "Domesday Slavery (Adjusted for Slaves)," *Midland History* 1 (1972): 37-40 remain important.

107 The absence of "tene(n)t" and such subordination words as "sub" in relation to these worker groups is noteworthy.

relate to *servi*.[108] Three deserve mention. First, there is the assembly of information. On each circuit the commissioners had to decide what to record and how to present it. Much of this only reached them in the form of oral testimony and writings derived from powerful interested parties. Much of the raw information that reached the commissioners will have required considerable further treatment before it could be used, not least the demeaning details of local status groups and livestock.

All this suggests that we approach with care the account the survey produced of England a generation earlier.[109] We may never know how far the claimants of 1086 distorted their findings, especially on the all-important TRE *antecessores* and their holdings. Yet Domesday's *ex parte* accounts are often all the documentation we have for landholding and labor before 1066. How were the *servi* counted and listed? How and why were the commissioners supposed to distinguish them from other workers? Someone permitted to live on his own plot soon might be indistinguishable from his cottar or bordar neighbors. Domesday hundred courts never rule on men's freedom. How can the commissioners have known what they were counting? Their clerks probably contributed further errors. French speakers probably read their sources with minds developed across the Channel.[110] Despite the fact that Normandy is said to have been without recent direct experience of servitude,[111] for example, some surely understood Old French *sers* in ways that we should consider serfdom not slavery.[112]

Two other comments take up less space. First, we may need to rethink upwards slave numbers in 1066. Many of the most dependent rural workers were by then very likely married with families, and one cannot assume that the unmarried remained celibate.[113] If we were to apply the standard Domesday multiplier to *servi* families, the new count would make a real difference to the balance between *servi* and the rest.

---

[108] Pelteret, *Slavery*, 202-32, lists many of these. The apparently slaveless Danelaw is one example, for its placenames and the slave counts of neighboring shires persuaded Pelteret, "Slavery in the Danelaw," 181 that slaves had formerly lived there.

[109] I suggested this already in my "'No Register of Title'": The Domesday Inquest and Land Adjudication," *Anglo-Norman Studies* 9 (1987): 131-6.

[110] Whether or not individual scribes of Greater Domesday Book were French by birth, as some are thought to have been, is less important than their origin in French-dominated social circles. Theresa Webber has advised me on the evidence; see further her "Salisbury and the Exon Domesday" in *English Manuscript Studies, 1100-1700*, 1 (1989). Half of the hundred jurors were French, see C.P. Lewis, "The Domesday Jurors," *Haskins Society Journal*, 5 (1993): 17-43.

[111] L. Musset, "Réflexions autour du problème de l'esclavage et du servage en Normandie ducale (Xe-XIIe siècles," *Cahiers des annales de Normandie* 22 (1988): 5-24 conceded that there were still serfs near, and even within, the duchy's borders.

[112] As Beaumanoir still could in the thirteenth century, above n. 41.

[113] Above, 135-6.

The final issue is the real mare's nest: that of the purposes behind the whole Inquest. The king would surely never have initiated so major an enterprise without hopes of increasing his revenues. That was generally the point of a "descriptio,"[114] and it is no surprise that the nearest thing to a written statement of aims ends with the instruction to see "if any more may be had."[115] Private lords too hoped for more from their tenants and dependents. Domesday is full of hints of the aggressive methods (including straight land grabs) adopted by new lords anxious to exploit their new riches to the full. They watched their officials carefully for sticky fingers[116] and negligence in the maintenance and increase of livestock.[117] The *laboratores* paid the price. One might therefore wonder why the recorded numbers of *servi* fell. If *servi* were all slaves, whom lords could treat as they liked, why should their new lords not retain them, or even add to their number especially after a conquest? It is hard to believe that the *servi* of Domesday Book can have been homogenous enough to be seen as a single entity at any other time. The *servi* or *þeowan* of Anglo-Saxon England seem never to have seen themselves as a solidarity with a status and interests in common.[118] Those who choose to call them slaves, as they may, are themselves arguing from something close to silence.

Tentative Conclusions

This paper is self-evidently an exercise in ideas not social history. Its apparent claim to treat the whole of Old English society is, of course, unsustainable, even when limited to its final two centuries. The arguments cry out to be tested against the realities of England between Alfred and the Conquest. Conditions differed between

---

[114] J.O. Prestwich, "Mistranslations and Misinterpretations in Medieval English History," *Peritia* 10 (1996): 327 sq.

[115] The Ely questionnaire ends "et si potest plus haberi quam habeatur," William Stubbs, *Select Charters... of English Constitutional History* (Oxford: Clarendon Press, 9th edn., revd., 1921), 101 It contains three distinct understandings of freedom, plus other oddities that deserve further study. Cf. also, W.H. Stevenson, "A Contemporary Description of the Domesday Survey," *EHR* 22 (1907): 77.

[116] Harvey, *Domesday*, chap. 7, esp. 163-5; R.V. Lennard, *Rural England, 1066-1135* (Oxford: Clarendon Press, 1959), 207-12 assembles evidence for improving lords, mostly ecclesiastical, at the time of Domesday. The model lay landlord, pious yet ever alert to his own interests, has to be Ernulf of Hesdin counting the freshly harvested sheaves in his barn, ibid., 69, 210-2.

[117] Bringing in officials to account periodically for receipts was likely standard practice already on large estates, Harvey, *Domesday*, 170, and because procedure was still (even in the Exchequer) largely oral, there seems no reason why lesser landlords could not do the same.

[118] But there are no obvious solidarities of thegns and freemen either. The Old English term, *efen-þeow* is irrelevant here, Pelteret, *Slavery*, 269-70.

the various regions under West Saxon rule for every kind of reason, ranging from the heritages of older kingdoms and peoples to the quality of soil and climatic conditions, from the Danes of East Anglia to the Celts of the south-west. I have largely ignored the recent literature on the extraordinary expansion of wealth from an early central core under the West Saxon kings to cover the bulk of southern Britain ready to greet William in 1066.

To win acceptance, my picture of servitude, must accord with a current vision drawn from archaeology and landscape history as much as from written sources. I have not tried to cover atypical areas like East Anglia where many free landholders seem to have managed their estates largely without servile workers. I have perhaps also leant too far in the out-dated direction of a confrontation between lords with a peasant collectivity in something like the old "classical manor" model. Manorialization, in the sense of estate management radiating outwards from the intensive exploitation of "inland," was in 1066 still far from the norm. Free farmers—if that is what ceorls were—and town-dwellers need to be fitted into the picture. And even the theorists of the Three Orders in their deliberately simple vision of the world ignored those *laboratores* who were not directly in the business of feeding the other two orders. Many served house or hall, for instance, or were artisans, urban or not.[119]

Even so, a rough match may exist between the social caesura I argue for and preliminary findings from recent studies of material culture. It has been argued, for instance, that, some groups profited enough from the new wealth of the period surveyed here to separate themselves from their fellows, to use their barrels of silver pennies to fortify their homes, solidify their social position, and flaunt their superiority, their noble freeness, through conspicuous expenditure and "bling," eleventh-century style.[120] So maybe the clerical writers on the Three Orders were not too far off the mark with their *laboratores*, on the wrong side of a symbolic line between those substantial men who controlled labor in the fields (the free) and the unfree workers who contributed the blood and sweat.

Since my case is partly speculative, I close with a check list of what I should *like* to believe about servitude before 1066:

1. Anglo-Saxon England was no slave society in the tenth and eleventh centuries. Many of its inhabitants, neither noble nor slave within our understandings of slavery,

[119] I rely here almost exclusively on the summary of John Blair, *Building Anglo-Saxon England* (Princeton: Princeton University Press, 2018), chaps 8-9 (which I saw in draft) and on consultations with Rosamond Faith, author of *English Peasantry* and co-author with Debbie Banham of *Anglo-Saxon Farms and Farming* (Oxford: Oxford University Press, 2014). But the inspiration for the next paragraph was Fleming, "The New Wealth," 5-12, 18-19.

[120] Following Fleming, "The New Wealth," as above n. 99.

nevertheless lived lives much the worse for their being considered unfree. I am not denying the existence of slavery, just seeking examples to satisfy normal standards of proof.[121]

2. It might be best to seek slaves (and serfs) not by reference to tenth- and eleventh-century terms, but by measuring what we can know of their condition against modern definitions and models. One should approach these issues through the quantum of power and control lords actually exercised over individuals, to the extent that one can measure these. What we know of lordship better documented at higher social levels is a poor guide to the treatment of servile workers, empty of both honor and social clout and expected to do the dirty work or face the consequences.
3. It is unrealistic to imagine that kings would pay much attention to the ways that their men administered that kind of lordship. Pre-Conquest sources have none of the twelfth-century traces (in writs etc.) of royal interventions within private lordship.[122] It seems unlikely that kings under pressure to respond to appeals for aid against foreign invaders or over-mighty neighbors would be much troubled by men unable to control their own workers.
4. One can therefore understand why the *leges* never define freedom in legal terms and have relatively little to say on servitude. This was not a matter that normally came before "public" courts dominated by local landowners. It was hard in the early Middle Ages to restrain lordship by law.
5. And that is why, as in Vegas, the rule was that what happened on the manor generally stayed on the manor. The dependent tenants who supplied labor (most in person, a few through their own subordinates) must deal directly with their lord on his own turf. *Pauper* always bargained against *Potens* from a fragile position, where his best hope was to reason by analogy with services habitually performed by others from the same estate or nearby.
6. Thus, all *laboratores*, even the most substantial, ran the risk of being stigmatized as unfree, when in conflict with their lord or anyone else who wished to do them down.

I recognize now better than when I began this study how much of the position with which I have ended up runs counter to current opinion on royal power and law in the "late Old English state." I greatly respect and honor my two departed friends, the main creators of the view that I termed "maximalist," because they took more seriously than their predecessors the evidence for governmental power in the tenth and eleventh

[121] Which the *nydþeow* seems to do, *BT*, 717, sense VI; Pelteret, *Slavery*, 301.

[122] And royal servants might meet with straight refusals, like that expressed in *The Letters and Charters of Gilbert Foliot*, ed. C.N.L. Brooke and A. Morey (London: Cambridge University Press, 1967), esp. 196.

centuries.[123] While recent work has certainly strengthened the case, there still seems little hard evidence that kings (other than conquerors) really were likely to over-rule their nobles on their own turf. I remain a moderate minimalist, but then Lisi herself never much minded being in the minority.

[123] James Campbell gloried in the label, and called one of his best statements of his view "The Late Anglo-Saxon State: A Maximum View" *Proceedings of the British Academy*, 87 (1994): 39-65. Patrick Wormald disliked it, and, alas, left only hints of what would have doubtless been his master-work *The Making of English Law* in *Papers Preparatory to the Making of English Law: King Alfred to the Twelfth Century, Vol. II: From God's Law to Common Law*, ed. Stephen Baxter and John Hudson (University of London: Early English Laws, 2014), at *http://www.earlyenglishlaws.ac.uk/reference/wormald/*.

Raw Materials: The Role of Paleography in Medieval Studies*

Elaine Treharne

In *The Making of English Law*, Patrick Wormald reminds scholars of the importance of the physical record for the interpretation of the past. He comments at the opening of his chapter on "The Manuscripts of Legislation" that:

> The last of the contextual levels to stand between historians of early English law and their legislative raw material consists of the manuscripts which have fossilized the evidence since its days of active life and made it available for modern inspection. The geological metaphor is apt. What seem barriers to scholars intent on instant wealth of knowledge help others to explain what lies below and how it got there. Like his colleagues in nineteenth-century academia, Liebermann tended to see medieval scribes as obstacles rather than aids to the recovery of the past.[1]

Wormald's awareness and defense of the primary role of the manuscript and its scribes in determining contexts of composition, compilation and consumption is, typically of his work, reflective of contemporary trends in modern scholarship and contributory to them. The material turn of the last two decades or so in Medieval Studies has resulted in a new prominence for approaches exploring the production and reception of extant sources. These sources themselves have been made increasingly available; where once the manuscripts and diplomata that were published tended to be those that were already well known, published successively in edition, in facsimile, and in collections of plates, now the digitization of manuscripts is permitting the vast and rapid expansion of the investigable corpus. Thus, for example, all Anglo-Saxon manuscripts in London's British

* It is a heartfelt pleasure to offer this extended note to honor and commemorate Lisi Oliver, whose explicit appreciation of early medieval primary source materials and their skilled interpretation was widely stated, and absolutely apparent, throughout her work. In the Introduction to her excellent *Body Legal* at 3-4, as in the opening pages to Oliver, *Beginnings*, Lisi demonstrated her capacious gathering of resources to make informed conclusions from all available evidence; these conclusions, as she showed, could be seen—through imaginative connection—to have contemporary resonance. Perhaps more, though, in this following discussion of what constitutes particular forms of expertise, I am indebted to, and reminded of, Lisi's own intellectual generosity, her groundedness, and her kindness—desirable and much needed traits in the modern scholarly world.

[1] Wormald, *Making*, 162.

Library have been made available in Open Access browsable and downloadable files, opening up dozens of codices and fragments for new and universal examination.[2] Similarly, the Parker on the Web project, with its images hosted and served by Stanford University Libraries, from January 2018 has made freely available Matthew Parker's entire collection of manuscripts at Cambridge, Corpus Christi College, where previously that database had been an expensive purchase for institutions.[3] The field of Manuscript Studies, then, is newly served by the world's most significant repositories. It is now incumbent on scholars of paleography and codicology to make available their knowledge and expertise to provide interpretative frameworks for the exploration of the digital corpus, irrespective of the online host, whose metadata and modes of explanation vary significantly.

Given that paleography has rarely been taught in Higher Education institutions internationally, many scholars come to their manuscript work with skills they have acquired through painstaking practice. As such, tools like Digipal, directed by Dr. Peter Stokes, or online courses such as "Digging Deeper," led by a team of scholars, including myself, and Drs Benjamin Albritton, Orietta Da Rold, and Suzanne Paul, have a vital role to play in bringing expertise to wider audiences.[4] What has become very clear to those of us involved in the facture and provision of these freely available courses and websites is how little prior standardization of data or definitive explication of the discipline's core elements exists in print or digital format. Different schools of training (in the United Kingdom, these could anecdotally be broken down to the historic "London" school and the "Oxford" school) produced paleographers using distinctive descriptive methods to evaluate parts of letters.[5] Peter Stokes has consistently advocated for clarity

---

[2] See the information and the links at http://blogs.bl.uk/digitisedmanuscripts/2017/03/digitising-our-manuscripts-from-anglo-saxon-england.html.

[3] Parker on the Web is available at https://parker.stanford.edu/.

[4] Peter Stokes, with Stewart Brookes, et al, *DigiPal*: Digital Resource and Database of Palaeography, Manuscript Studies and Diplomatic www.digipal.eu; Elaine Treharne, Benjamin Albritton, Orietta Da Rold, Suzanne Paul, with Kenneth Lidga, Jonathan Quick and Colin Reeves-Fortney (2015), "Digging Deeper I and II," https://online.stanford.edu/course/digging-deeper-making-manuscripts and https://lagunita.stanford.edu/courses/English/diggingdeeper2/Spring2015/about

[5] A couple of examples will suffice: Julian Brown, "St Ninian's Isle Silver Hoard," in *A Palaeographer's View: Selected Writings of Julian Brown*, ed. Janet Bately, Michelle Brown and Jane Roberts (London, 1993), calls the rounded part of **a**, **p**, **b**, **d**—the "bow" (p. 247; in the case of **d**, the upward stroke is the *stem*; **e** and **t** have crossbars; **e** has a "head" (p. 205); **f** has "bars." For Malcolm Parkes in *Their Hands Before Our Eyes: A Closer Look at Scribes* (Aldershot: Ashgate, 2008) **b**, **d**, **p** and **q** have "lobes" (p. 150); **c** and **e** have "stems"; **h** has limbs; **m** and **n** have arches; **f**, **r**, and **t** have headstrokes and stems; **e** has a tongue (from p. 63 forward); but **d** and **q** have lobes and stems (p. 97, 98); **e** and **c** have stems (p. 97). For Bernard Bischoff, in his *Latin Palaeography: Antiquity and the Middle Ages*, trans. Daibhi O. Cróinin and David Ganz (Cambridge: Cambridge University Press, 2008), **a**, **r**, **u**, **r**, **p**, **m**, **n** have shafts; **m** and

in the terminology employed to describe letterforms, and this itself has given rise to debate about who decides such terminology. In an exchange on DigiPal's paleography blog a few years ago, the discussants focused on the ways in which early minuscule graphs might be described, particularly in relation to their electronic representation and the functionality of specific search terms.[6] This public discussion took an interesting turn when one of the participants commented to Dr Peter Stokes, the initiator of the blog: "Surely you need to be talking to *real* paleographers [...]?"

Setting aside the particulars of that conversation, which in themselves would form the focus of a separate discussion about connoisseurship, respect, and kindness within academia, a key question raised by this public correspondence concerns the issue of what constitutes a *real* paleographer in the present moment? Perhaps more significantly for scholars and engaged citizens is what might be said to constitute *real* paleography in a world where images and excerpts from manuscript folios are not only accessible through academic and institutional repositories, but also abundantly populate Pinterest pages, Twitter and Instagram accounts, and Facebook pages.

As the role of Social Media has taken on a new force in terms of cultural engagement in recent years, for academics working in an era of underfunding and over-accountability, defining subjects of interest and their relevance to the world at large has become an urgent task. Thanks to the digital era, so much of the Academy is suddenly and instantly public: increasing calls for Open Access, for statements measuring the impact and general merit of research, and for clarity about the value offered by government-funded educational institutions involve lengthy op-eds from columnists and commentators. The desire for defined and understood disciplines and areas of concentration seems greater than for previous scholarly generations, perhaps, since resources are scarce and competition fierce; the consequences include so-called "crises" in Humanities and much ink spilled on what it is that scholars do.[7] Since the "digital revolution" constitutes a key moment in the history of text technologies, it is worth bearing in mind that a good number of these social and intellectual trends—such as the fearful response about who might be a "real" expert, or who might be dilettantish; to parallel anxieties about control and authority, censorship, and "truth"—are discernible at all periods of transition

n have arcades; **d, h, p, v, y** and **p** have bows (pp. 128-30). The body imagery—lobes, arches, head, tongue, limb, shoulder—is quite fascinating.

6 http://www.digipal.eu/blogs/blog/describing-handwriting-part-v/. Participants include myself, Peter Stokes, Stewart Brookes, Paul Caton and David Ganz.

7 There is an immense bibliography on "crises" in Humanities and universities (see the recent article, "There is no case for the Humanities," by Justin Stover at https://americanaffairsjournal.org/2017/11/no-case-humanities/): on what constitutes "arts," research, valid publication strategies, and so forth. See also, for example, various posts at http://4humanities.org/; and multiple columns at http://chronicle.com/section/Home/5, including http://chronicle.com/article/The-Ideal-English-Major/140553/.

from one medium of communication to another. Major themes repeated through time are precisely these desires for definability, clarity, and authenticity, and a persistence in the rhetoric of scholarly writing and scholarly self-identification for expressions of "authenticity" and validation. Thus, when William Caxton introduced Chaucer's *Canterbury Tales* through the new technology of print, he was at pains to demonstrate the authority and accuracy of his endeavor by his printing of a second edition that explicitly sought to permanently remedy errors contained in the "certain [fewer] number" of the first print run;[8] in the late nineteenth and early twentieth centuries, as will be discussed further below, when photographic technology permitted the "exact" reproduction of pages from manuscripts, paleographers proclaimed that truth or a visible reality in illustrating script was, at last, possible. This enhanced paleography's justification to be called a Science—objective, measurable, and without the foibles of human interference.[9]

Printing brought with it significantly increased potential for the democratization of literacy; and photographic technologies yielded much greater access to previously inaccessible primary resources. One of the major differences in contemporary twenty-first century text technological transformation, though, is the sheer scale, size and speed of information provision. Such is the amount of data available in online or other digital media for those interested in manuscripts and early writing more broadly—such a proliferation of images, databases, transcription projects, catalogues, and e-editions—that a number of significant questions are raised by the concept of the "true" or the "real" at all, particularly with regard to paleographical research, or manuscript studies, more broadly.[10] At what point does sustained engagement with online manuscript materials by interested non-specialists result in their being "manuscript studies specialists"? What level of training in the seminar-room or online constitutes expertise in paleography? In relation specifically to the paleographical and the "real," questions include: Is paleography an Art or a Science and does it matter? What *now* constitutes the definition of

---

[8] William Caxton, *Prohemye* to the Second Edition of Geoffrey Chaucer's *Canterbury Tales* 1484, digitized at https://www.bl.uk/treasures/caxton/record.asp

[9] I have discussed this at length in "The Good, the Bad, the Ugly: Old English Manuscripts and Their Physical Description," in Matthew Hussey and John Niles, ed., *The Genesis of Books: Studies in the Scribal Culture of Medieval England in Honour of A. N. Doane*, Studies in the Early Middle Ages 9 (Turnhout: Brepols, 2012), 261-83. For Palaeography as a Science a century ago, see, *inter alia*, William Saunders, *Ancient Handwritings: An Introductory Manual for Intending Students of Palaeography and Diplomatic* (Walton-on-Thames: Bernau, 1909), 3; and H. Jenkinson, *Palaeography and the Practical Study of Court Hand* (Cambridge: CUP, 1915).

[10] The best starting points for evaluating what is available online for Manuscript Studies are Siân Echard's valuable finding aids at http://faculty.arts.ubc.ca/sechard/512digms.htm and Juliet O'Brien's site at http://metametamedieval.com/2012/03/11/manuscripts-manuscript-studies/ Notwithstanding the vast amount of material available online, Dr Benjamin Albritton at Stanford University advises me in a personal communication that only about 2% of the western medieval record is currently available digitally.

paleography? What constitutes the *real* in what is actually a very disparate academic area of study? What constitutes the "real" within a digital environment? How can scholarship best reflect upon new, and often virtual, paleographical realities? How can online materials assist the field?

In what follows, then, this essay will address what standard British sources indicate paleography might be, who fits the label of professional paleographer, and how the discipline is regarded externally, all questions central to its use for the study of early legal manuscripts. Its conclusion, then, will briefly consider how scholars might think about paleography's function, purpose, and methods with special reference to C.C.C.C. 173, the earliest manuscript of the Anglo-Saxon Chronicle and the laws of King Alfred.

Definitions

How can anyone know what a "real" paleographer might be, if, as practitioners in various disciplines, there is no clarity about what paleography is?[11] There is, of course, a common shared object of investigation: ancient script, and, increasingly, a text's physical support and context, together with the study of its socio-historical and intellectual moment of production. The *Oxford English Dictionary*'s definition—to go back to basics—is simultaneously precise and vague:

> 1a. Ancient writing; an ancient style or method of writing (first recorded in English in 1749).
> 1b. The study of ancient writing and inscriptions; the science or art of deciphering and interpreting historical manuscripts and writing systems (first recorded in English in 1806, A. Clarke *Bibliographical Misc.* ii. 202 (*table*): Literary, ancient, modern, Bibliography, Paleography).[12]

The precision of this definition comes in its clarity of the object of study—ancient writing—but its lack of clarity otherwise. Paleography is either a "science or art,"[13] and perhaps both. Paleographers engage in deciphering and interpreting manuscripts, but

[11] What follows will focus on British and American paleography and Manuscript Studies. As most will already know, Continental European practices and definitions of paleography differ from the Anglophone. See, most notably, the statements of the Comité international de paléographie latine at <http://www.palaeographia.org/cipl/cipl.htm>

[12] The *Oxford English Dictionary* at www.oed.com, *s.v.* "Palaeography." Adam Clarke's 1806 *Bibliographical Miscellany* is available, fully digitized, at <http://archive.org/details/bibliographical01clargoog>

[13] In 1908, the International Congress of Historical Science, meeting in Berlin, classified "Palaeography" as one of the "Sciences Subsidiary to History," alongside Archives, Libraries, Chronology, Diplomatic, Epigraphy, Genealogy, Historical Geography, Heraldry, Numismatics, and the Study of Seals (*London Times, The Times Digital Archive*, Thursday May 28, 1908, p. 12).

also entire writing systems in all media. Adam Clarke's *Bibliographical Miscellany* provides, in itself, for the *OED*, the most general definition: under a tabulated heading of "Suitable Knowledge" for "History," "Paleography" appears as a pertinent topic for studying (the sub-heading of) "Civilization" and (a sub-sub-heading of) the "Literary." Paleography is distinct from "Calligraphy" and "Inscriptions," which appear under "Archaeology," which in turn appears under "Positive" (that is, measurable? empirical?) branches of History. The *OED* provides this illustration as the term's first appearance in English, which, while it permits us a *terminus post quem* for this particular use of "Paleography," is not necessarily the clearest definition. Here, paleography properly pertains not to the "positive" historians or archaeologists, who instead focus on "calligraphy," but to the "literary" scholars.

By contrast, Julian Brown's definition is one of inclusion and capaciousness, but appears to focus specifically on handwriting in manuscripts, as opposed to including inscription and epigraphy:

> Palaeography means, in the strict sense, the study of ancient handwriting, and its basic objects are these: first, to read ancient texts with accuracy; secondly, to date and localise their handwriting [...P]alaeography in the wider sense [...] *studies all aspects of books produced by hand.*[14]

Moreover, for Brown, paleography encompasses what others would define separately as "codicology," the study of the physical make-up of the book. Codicology, according to the *OED,* is

> The study or science of manuscripts and their interrelationships. Used mainly by continental writers, when writing in English, as a *calque* on German *Handschriftenkunde.*
> 1953, D. C. C. Young in *Scriptorium* VII. 7: "If the suggestion that O [= MS. Vat. gr. 915] for Theognis is by Gregoras be accepted, much may follow for the codicology of the other texts in O."
> 1970, *Times Lit. Suppl.* 21 May 568/2: "The recent development of "codicology," which Greg would have subsumed under bibliography—the study of manuscripts as physical objects in order to identify the workshops that produced them."[15]

For Julian Brown, like W.W. Greg cited in the *OED* quotation immediately above, codicology is subsumed under "palaeography in its wider sense." This does away with—what for *some* is—the confusing and unhelpful separation of manuscript-interpretative skills to do with script (paleography) and those concerned with other elements of the book's physical production (codicology).

---

[14] *A Palaeographer's View: Selected Writings of Julian Brown*, ed. Janet Bately, Michelle Brown and Jane Roberts (London, 1993), 47. My emphasis.
[15] *OED*, *s.v.* "codicology."

Given how varied the definition of paleography can be, and given how many foundational manuscript scholars there have been in the last one hundred or so years (and earlier than this in the continental European history of paleography and diplomatics), it is interesting to discover how few paleographers are categorized as such in national sources. The contributors to the *Oxford Dictionary of National Biography*—the most fundamental of research tools[16]—only label five "palaeographers" as such: the Reverend John Gwenogvryn Evans (1852-1930), palaeographer; Elias Avery Lowe (1879-1969), palaeographer; Richard William Hunt (1908-1979), palaeographer; Neil Ripley Ker (1908-1982), palaeographer; and Malcolm Beckwith Parkes (1930-2013), palaeographer. Out of 60,000+ entries, there are about one hundred references to "palaeography" and "paleographer," but only these five men are labelled as just "palaeographers" by their biographers. In fact, of course, even with this small group of notable scholars, one could argue they were practitioners existing within a broader intellectual context, incorporating within their work the different disciplines of English, History, and Classics, as well as exemplifying their own professional activities of publisher, librarian and academic. Within the digital covers of the *ODNB*, other figures are labelled by their biographers as "palaeographers," in *addition* to another profession or activity: Thomas Allen (1862-1950), Greek scholar & palaeographer; Dorothy Coveney (1904-1979) historian & palaeographer (discoverable in her role as wife to W. Medlicott); Julius Gilson (1868-1929), librarian & palaeographer; James Harris (18852-1941), biblical scholar and palaeographer; John Hayter (1755-1818), Church of England clergyman & palaeographer; Sir Frederic Madden (1801-1873), palaeographer and librarian; Sir Ellis Hovell Minns (1874-1953), archaeologist and palaeographer; Theodore Skeat (1907-2003) (found *s.p.* "W. Skeat"), palaeographer and librarian; John Westwood (1805-1893), entomologist and palaeographer; Francis Wormald (1904-1972) palaeographer and art historian; and Humfrey Wanley (1672-1726), who under his own entry, appears as "Old English scholar and librarian," but who, under Nathaniel Wanley's entry, appears as "librarian and palaeographer."[17]

Exploring the *ODNB*, confined to Britain, incomplete and occasionally arbitrary as it may be, thus appears to confirm Julian Brown's comments that "full-time palaeographers will be rare birds." Brown comments further and with great relevance to the current discussion:

> What chiefly matters is that most of the best palaeographical writing—including Ludwig Traube"s—has come, and always will come, from scholars whose chief commitment has

[16] *Oxford Dictionary of National Biography:* http://www.oxforddnb.com (Oxford University Press, 2013-17). It need hardly be said that the lack of reference to female scholars requires urgent remedying. (Thus, for instance, Professor Tilly de la Mare does not appear at present in the *ODNB*; Celia Sisam's name appears in her father's profile only.)

[17] This expands on a similar point in Treharne, "The Good, the Bad, the Ugly," 271.

> been to some other discipline, but who found themselves, in the course of the work they were paid to do, attending to a palaeographical problem and finding a solution to it. When "amateurs" of this kind turn to palaeography, nobody who has taught them will regret that he saw too little of them to make them orthodox, since amateurs, to quote Kenneth Sisam, "are less likely to be over-influenced by [...] those simplifying assumptions and generalisations which, in an historical subject, are convenient enough for teaching but unfavourable to research."[18]

As such, then, if *almost* all—if not *all*—paleographers are "amateurs" in the non-demeaning sense that Brown discusses, there is, then, no such thing as a *real* paleographer: most are principally committed to "some other discipline."

Got No Discipline

That paleography exists extra-disciplinarily is one view, frequently articulated: its theory and practice function not in their own right, but in order to support the major disciplines in which one is truly skilled. Paul Oscar Kristeller commented in his punchy ACLS lecture some years ago: "My method, which tries to combine the philosophical interpretation of original texts with the pertinent skills of history and philology, and *of their auxiliary disciplines such as diplomatics and chronology, palaeography and bibliography*, is now considered hopelessly traditional and even antiquated, as I have been told more than once by foundation officials, administrators and colleagues, reviewers and critics."[19]

This view of paleography as "antiquated"—a view occasionally echoed by external academic bodies and university administrative chiefs—has by no means passed. The DigiPal website recorded *The Times Higher Education's* coverage of Digital Projects, where it labelled DigiPal "highly obscure,"[20] demonstrating thereby not just a lack of understanding, but a lack of accessible information about manuscript studies that should be easily discoverable for the journalist. Such a description as "highly obscure" demands to be challenged: desiderata for such a challenge would include a promotional effort to advertising effectively what paleographers do in order to build a better public profile; demonstrating the subject as the foundation upon which so many other disciplines

---

[18] *Selected Writings of Julian Brown*, 35-6.

[19] Italics are my emphasis. Paul Oskar Kristeller, "A Life of Learning," Charles Homer Haskins Lecture for 1990, ACLS Occasional Paper 12, p. 4. Available to download at http://www.acls.org/Publications/OP/Haskins/1990_PaulOskarKristeller.pdf

[20] http://www.digipal.eu/blogs/blog/digipal-highly-obscure-says-times-higher-education/, December 14 2011.

already necessarily, and increasingly will, rely; and providing incremental levels of training online and in other media to assist in the interpretation of primary sources, particularly as more and more digital information is deposited into an already immeasurable data cloudfill.

This need to manage the public image of paleography and to promote the field efficiently and positively was shown most critically, perhaps, by the mobilization of paleographers to defend the continuation of the Chair of Palaeography at King's College, London. The relabeled chair, now (perhaps tautologically) designated the Chair of Palaeography and Manuscript Studies, has been held by Julia Crick since 2012. Prior to her appointment, however, and to the dismay of many scholars, there had appeared to be the cessation of support for the subject from the administration of King's College, London. In the public statements from colleagues around the world calling for the Chair to be retained, various definitions of paleography emerged, illustrating how the field is viewed currently. For Dr Irving Finkel, assistant keeper in the department of the Middle East at the British Museum, "It is academic forensic science [...] A palaeographer can help determine which [historical text of a variety of contenders] is likely to be the most authentic." Here, in a Classical definition, the professional is a textual critic performing scientific method to authorize origins. For Kent Emery at Notre Dame University, paleography represents "the scientific credibility of historical investigation within the intellectual life of western Europe," a definition which again stresses the scientific nature of paleographers' roles and their interpretative facilitation.[21]

From these comments, and others like them from the nineteenth century onwards, the opinion that paleography is a science—that it is in some way a means of authentication, a provider of credibility—is intriguing. As I mentioned briefly earlier, this thinking is similar to the discussion well over a century ago of photography's many uses and properties, at a time of text technological transformation so akin to our own present when the potential for new truths through innovation was much heralded. Then, claims of a new and absolute credibility for paleography were made, tied to the proliferation of publishable images with their visible demonstration of script. Such developments were regarded as forecasting new opportunities for interpretative techniques, and the employment of scientific method by historians, librarians and scholars, who saw the emergence of cheap reproductive technologies as an opportunity to study the *truth* closely *with one's own eyes.*

---

[21] See John Crace, "Writing off the UK last palaeographer" in *The Guardian*, February 8th 2010, in which Crace calls palaeography an "esoteric" subject: http://www.theguardian.com/education/2010/feb/09/writing-off-last-palaeographer-university.

For Edward Maunde Thompson, the transformation in available technologies by 1906 meant that the field of paleography and manuscript studies could be widened very broadly, and its value confirmed institutionally and culturally:

> Palaeographical knowledge was formerly confined to a few, chiefly to the custodians or owners of collections of manuscripts; works of references on the subject were scarce and expensive; and facsimiles, with certain exceptions, were of no critical value. In these days, when photography has made accurate reproduction so simple a matter, the knowledge is within the reach of all who care to acquire it. The collection of facsimiles which have been issued during the last twenty years have brought into the private study materials which the student could formerly have gathered only by travel and personal research [...] There is no longer any lack of material for the ready attainment of palaeographical knowledge. [...] In our own country, where the development of such studies is usually left to private exertion and enterprise, Palaeography has received but little notice in the past. In the future, however, it will receive better recognition. In the Universities its value has at length been acknowledged as a factor in education. The mere faculty of reading an ancient manuscript may not count for much, but it is worth something. The faculty of assigning a date and locality to an undated codex; of deciding between the true and the false; in a word, of applying accurate knowledge to minute points—a faculty which is only to be acquired by long and careful training—is worth much, and will give a distinct advantage to the scholar who possesses it.[22]

Maunde Thompson's focus here is very emphatically on the access to the "truth" provided by paleographical training. "Accurate knowledge" gained by the expertly trained is verbally allied with the "knowledge" that emerges from "accurate reproduction" of manuscript folios. Both the "long and careful training" and the sureness that paleography would, in future, "receive better recognition" in a world where scholars could apply correct wisdom to "minute points" might ring hollow to Maunde Thompson now. For despite tremendous advances in our understanding of scripts, manuscript production, and scribal environments, there is a long way to go to fulfill the scientific promise of paleography, or for the promise of new technologies to reach their potential. Concomitantly, and perhaps most seriously, the more democratic knowledge seems in its digital immediacy, the less expertise there is to go around in universities and online.[23]

---

[22] Edward Maunde Thompson, *Handbook of Greek and Latin Palaeography* (London: K. Paul, Trench, Trübner & Company, 1906), viii-ix.

[23] Such indeed might have been Hilary Jenkinson's point in his lectures on *Palaeography and the Practical Study of Court Hand* (Cambridge: Cambridge University Press, 1915), which, while carefully defining the merits of palaeography as a "scientific" tool, is nevertheless quick to point out how much training is really required to read and understand medieval writings, and especially those issued as a consequence of centralized bureaucracy.

The early twentieth century—Maunde Thompson's day, marked by the modernist propensity for classification and professionalization—is an important parallel to the present day. We could usefully look back at the first decades of the twentieth century to learn from the parallels, one such being that as great a scholar as Maunde Thompson thought paleography would become much better served by tools and resources made available for its practice. Resources have flourished by way of the proliferation of facsimiles, digital images, databases, and scholarly project websites, but the numbers of paleography posts and training courses in institutions have not kept pace.[24] "Palaeographers are a highly endangered species," J. P. Gumbert remarks online, and must be protected "[o]therwise we must envisage a future where all manuscripts will have been digitized and made accessible on the Internet, but there will be no one left to understand or even read them, and so they will, for all practical purposes, have turned into dead matter."[25] Paleographers and codicologists are needed to train students and any other interested parties in how to read chirographic materials, but more especially in how to interpret the mass of digitized books, fragments and single-leaf documents, and in how to edit and preserve that information once gathered. Increased numbers of images online will not lead to an increase in skilled manuscript scholars, but the provision of paleographical training whether in person or through online courses will. Such provision must come with a sense of inclusiveness and warm welcome, not exclusiveness and dismissal. This is the moment to grasp a truth, then; that paleography has more to offer the scholarly and amateur world than it has ever before. Current practitioners cannot afford to be exclusive, protecting an idealized "real" paleography that belongs only to a few, since that has not had anywhere near the desired effect of maintaining the field and its contribution to classical, historical and literary studies.

Training Tools

The kinds of tools currently available make an important contribution to the delivery of multiple forms of online paleographical training. However, to an extent they replicate past efforts towards systematization, classification, and description (cataloguing). In relation to systematization, examples of projects include Denis Muzerelle's *Codicological*

[24] Courses like those put on by the Institute for Advanced Studies in London (https://www.ies.sas.ac.uk/study-training/study-weeks/london-international-palaeography-summer-school) and the Rare Book School in Virginia (http://rarebookschool.org/courses/manuscripts/m10/) attempt to address the need for training, but these are necessarily selective and limited. Other, broader efforts include the InScribe course, with a few modules complete, available here: https://www.history.ac.uk/research-training/courses/online-palaeography

[25] J. P. Gumbert, http://www.palaeographia.org/cipl/actu/paleoatkings.htm.

Terminology list (which recognizes the multiplicity of linguistic/national distinctions), or Peter Stokes' proposals to determine appropriate labels for letterforms that permit a universally understood method of description, or the efforts of CLaMM, including its work with words as units across manuscripts.[26]

With regard to cataloguing and description, there are large numbers of projects that seek to enhance the provision of (irreplaceable) hard-copy catalogues, such as the *Catalogues of Dated and Datable Manuscripts*, or those by scholars like Neil Ker.[27] Online catalogues include those that effectively digitize what also exists in hard copy form, or enhance hard copy publications, like the *Digital Index of Middle English Verse*, or *A Repertorium of Middle English Prose Sermons*.[28] Other catalogues provide database catalogues of manuscripts for particular purposes or chronologies or languages: these include *The Production and Use of English Manuscripts, 1060 to 1220*; *Manuscripts of the West Midlands*; and the ground-breaking *Parker on the Web*.[29] In essence, these catalogues, most employing best practice in terms of coding standards and in-built sustainability, do not in themselves act as training tools, or give particularly user-friendly insights into how to access medieval manuscripts, read them, or interpret them. The same can be said of virtually all repositories that host and display manuscript images; from the British Library's pioneering Digitized Manuscripts website to the Walters Art Gallery, The Morgan Library, or Cambridge, Trinity College, none of these major scholarly productions have yet been able to provide full explicatory resources, or comprehensive interpretative frameworks for their primary materials.[30] In the case of the

---

[26] Muzerelle is available at http://vocabulaire.irht.cnrs.fr/pages/vocab2.htm; Stokes' website accompanies the DigiPal Project at http://www.digipal.eu/; CLaMM, *Graphem*, and related projects, can be found at http://clamm.irht.cnrs.fr/

[27] A. G. Watson, *Catalogue of dated and datable manuscripts c. 700-1600 in the Department of Manuscripts, The British Library*, 2 vols. (London: British Library, 1979); idem, *Catalogue of Dated and Datable Manuscripts c. 435-1600 in Oxford Libraries*, 2 vols. (Oxford: Clarendon Press, 1984); P. R. Robinson, *Catalogue of Dated and Datable Manuscripts c. 737-1600 in Cambridge Libraries*, 2 vols (Cambridge: D.S. Brewer, 1988); idem, *Catalogue of dated and datable manuscripts c. 888-1600 in London libraries* (London: British Library, 2003); and N. R. Ker, *Catalogue of Manuscripts Containing Anglo-Saxon* (Oxford: Clarendon Press, 1957; repr. 1990, with Supplement).

[28] Linne Mooney, et al., http://www.cddc.vt.edu/host/imev/; Veronica O'Mara and Suzanne Paul, http://www.hull.ac.uk/middle_english_sermons/sample-sermons.php

[29] Orietta Da Rold, Takako Kato, Mary Swan, Elaine Treharne, *The Production and Use of English Manuscripts 1060 to 1220* (University of Leicester, 2010): http://www.le.ac.uk/ee/em1060to1220/; Wendy Scase, *Manuscripts of the West Midlands* (University of Birmingham, 2009): http://www.hrionline.ac.uk/mwm/; Stanford University and Corpus Christi College, Cambridge, *Parker on the Web* (Stanford, 2013; Parker on the Web 2.0, 2018): http://parkerweb.stanford.edu

[30] British Library, https://www.bl.uk/manuscripts/; Walters Art Gallery, http://www.thedigitalwalters.org/; Cambridge, Trinity College, http://trin-sites-pub.trin.cam.ac.uk/james/search.php; The Morgan Library and Museum, http://www.themorgan.org/collection/medieval-and-renaissance-manuscripts

British Library, very full manuscript descriptions accompany digitized images, but for the non-scholarly audience, these are too difficult to unravel; in the case of Cambridge, Trinity College, the original early twentieth-century *Catalogue* of M. R. James is provided alongside as the descriptive tool.[31] James was a great and prolific scholar, but his descriptions are eclectic, rather outdated, and often provide no folio numbers for components he decided were points of interest.

Other digital programs and packages seek to provide information for their audiences at some level; that is, to give assistance to the autodidact, the member of the scholarly or public audience who wants or needs to learn to work with ancient handwriting. Many well-known textbooks already seek to do this and among the best are Denholm-Young's *Handwriting in England and Wales*, Hector's *Handwriting of English Documents* and Roberts's *Guide to Scripts*.[32] The anticipated audience member of online or hard-copy resources could be any student in a university degree program working with an instructor; a doctoral student at an institution with little to no resource; it could be a person interested in their family history, who has reached far back in time and is now encountering terrifically difficult scripts; it could be an antiquarian book-dealer who has been brought a fragment of an unfamiliar manuscript. The audience of online materials, in particular, though, is unknown and unknowable, contextless for the producer of the training materials, and from that point of view, discoverability, intelligibility, and accessibility are all-important. Sites that currently exist include stand-alone videos produced by a variety of institutions and individuals, and those that programmatically (and over a course of units or sections) engage the viewer in reading and practicing for themselves.[33] These vary in terms of specificity from individual manuscripts to individual languages or individual repositories, and many are not easy to find, or present broken links when sought. What connects most of these sites is the overwhelming emphasis on

[31] M. R. James, *The Western Manuscripts in the Library of Trinity College, Cambridge: a Descriptive Catalogue*, 4 vols (1900-1904).

[32] Neil Denholm-Young, *Handwriting in England and Wales* (Cardiff: University of Wales Press, 1954); L. C. Hector's *The Handwriting of English Documents* (London: Arnold, 1966); Jane Roberts, *Guides to Scripts Used in English Writings up to 1500* (London: British Library, 2006; repr. Exeter Medieval Texts and Studies, Liverpool: Liverpool University Press, 2015). An excellent recent example of a wide-ranging textbook that focuses on multiple approaches to manuscripts is Ray Clemens and Timothy Graham, *An Introduction to Manuscript Studies* (Ithaca: Cornell University Press, 2007).

[33] See http://www.digipal.eu/blog/learning-and-teaching-online-i-inscribe/ for Peter Stokes' helpful list and some sample videos. See also Harvard University's online modules, run through EdX: http://online-learning.harvard.edu/series/history-book; and Dorothy Porter's weekly videos from the Schoenberg Institute for Manuscript Studies: https://repository.upenn.edu/sims_video/. Excellent courses that have been published for quite some time include Dave Postles's at http://paleo.anglo-norman.org/medfram.html; and Dianne Tillotson's at http://medievalwriting. 50megs.com/whyread/reading.htm

script: how to recognize letterforms and what categories of script letterforms might belong to; and on the possible dating attainable from classifying scripts (as opposed to hands). In many respects this is both a limited and a limiting methodology and one that could rarely *train* the audience in how to understand and transcribe a manuscript text, whether it is a book or a leaf or a diplomatic artifact.

Moreover, just as there is no broadly agreed definition of paleography (real or otherwise) beyond its focus on ancient script, and just as there is no agreed-upon set of classification systems for the systems of scripts, there is also no standard way of teaching paleography and/or codicology, other than through the rigors of practice. Since there is also no agreement about describing individual elements of historic graphs, any attempt at such description is subject to the individual's own observations about a specific graph's most notable features, and this is why it may be helpful to put into place universal best practice for describing letterforms and scribal practices. The implications of not addressing these concerns are that contemporary paleographical training risks emphasizing that which the scholar thinks they see and knows they and others value; that which project developers decide requires tagging and describing for their own project's main focus; and thus that which can be searched for and discovered. This is an already-existing problem witnessed in one of paleography's main and entirely *unscientific* characteristics; namely, a scholarly subjectivity, impelled by a frequently detectable, but utterly unspoken, aesthetic impetus derived from the art of calligraphy and collecting—a connoisseurship that is driven by value judgements not always helpful to describing medieval scribal practices and the work of individual hands.[34] Subjectivity itself is not the problem; the denial of it in pursuit of the "scientific" is.

Even with the work of Anglophone and European paleographical organizations and projects, at present, it seems unlikely that any one system of description will come to dominate the field. Precisely because we are dealing with an art, not a science, writing created by individuals will, at the most detailed level, resist rigid classification. Indeed, whereas it might seem that paleography is about similarities and the fit of letters to particular models, one of the key sets of components paleographers examine and extrapolate from is *difference*, idiosyncrasy, non-matching hands or elements of hands. This examination of difference inevitably results from and results in the individualization of the scribe, the traits that make the hand the result of human (fallible, inconsistent) endeavor. This imagining of the person behind the text's physical production correlates well with the larger work of the Humanities, at the present time. As Julian Brown presciently put it: "We are beginning to find that we can go behind the books to the

[34] See Treharne, *passim*, "The Good, the Bad, the Ugly." It is this connoisseurship that partly ensures paleography retains its esoteric reputation.

thoughts and behaviour of men [and women], while they were composing, copying, and decorating them; and the time has come to accept that kind of knowledge as a conscious aim."[35]

Space: the Final Decider

The claims of *science, measurability, classification* will always be tested and qualified by the quirks of the person holding the pen. The most expert scribes of all (Eadui Basan and Eadmer of Christ Church, Canterbury in the earlier eleventh and earlier twelfth centuries respectively, or the Leofric-circle of scribes at Exeter in the second half of the eleventh century[36]) could be remarkably consistent in their hand, but most scribes were not this expert. Even hands that are almost indistinguishable, however, cease to be so when a paleographer moves beyond the letterform alone to incorporate what *actually* constitutes the letter. This is not the subjective "aspect," nor the measurable "duct," but the letterform plus the space that demarcates that letter from adjacent graphs: it is letterform+space that forms the character of a hand. No matter how accurate the pen-stroke, without the precisely imitative proportional spacing, an emulative hand will not look like its exemplar.

It takes an artist to recognize this fully, rather than a science-focused analyst. In his work on "Notes on Movement involving Touch," Lloyd J. Reynolds reminds us of the phenomenology of writing: its reification, its uniqueness—that which defies literal or metaphorical boxing in—the method deployed by most handwriting analysis programs. Reynolds comments:

> We begin with the rectangle of paper. It is empty, a no-thing awaiting the pen. It is not even empty space, but only potential. But the moment the pen touches the paper and leaves even a slight trace of ink, the paper does become space, and the boundaries of the area are awakened and respond across the space to the tache of ink. It is as if a magnetic field were suddenly activated. Each subsequent stroke pours added energy into the field, modifying all previous relationships within its edges. Since this activation of tensions and directional movements occurs if only spatters of ink are dropped on the page, how vital

[35] *Selected Writings of Julian Brown*, 34.

[36] See, *inter alia*, T. A. Heslop, "The Production of *De Luxe* Manuscripts and the Patronage of King Cnut and Queen Emma," *Anglo-Saxon England* 19 (1990): 151-98; Teresa Webber, "Script and Manuscript Production at Christ Church, Canterbury after the Norman Conquest," in R. Eales and R. Sharpe, eds., *Canterbury and the Norman Conquest: Churches, Saints and Scholars* (London: Hambledon Press, 1995), 144-58; and Elaine Treharne, "The Bishop's Book: *Leofric's* Homiliary and Eleventh-Century Exeter," in Stephen Baxter, Catherine E. Karkov, Janet L. Nelson, and David Pelteret, eds., *Early Medieval Studies in Memory of Patrick Wormald*, Studies in Early Medieval Britain (Aldershot: Ashgate, 2009), 521-37.

> is the effect if the pen sweeps across the paper in an ordered sequence of rhythmical, dance-like movements, whether free or forming letters and words[...] The logic of the system of movements characterizing any particular alphabet is a dialectic relation of inked moved and designed letter counters and interspaces. Letter design, then, fuses an implicit meaning of its own with the explicit semantic meaning of the text which is inscribed [...][37]

This wonderful evocation of the writing process, with its emphasis on the space being filled by movement, and of the letters as connections of space, is a timely reminder of the human endeavor in writing. It is timely because, while measurable, quantitative research might still not record this process accurately. In other words, the scientific approach may simply not account for the "implicit meaning" of the act of the handwritten. Spaces around the graphs are as important as the letterforms; the whole spatial unit (akin to drawing a square around the letter plus its contiguous space) counts for assessing a hand's characteristics. If it were all down to individual letterforms extrapolated from context, which current lexical recognition software or digital tools offers as a method, the writing on a folio, such as 5r of London, British Library, Additional 47967, the Tollemache Orosius, would hardly be identified as that of a single scribe, yet it is. The list of Roman emperors' ascendancy evinces many different forms of individual graphs in the course of its twenty-five lines,[38] though it is a sequence written by the same hand. Looking at whole words, however—and especially a combination of words, as in folio 5r, lines 3 to 5, permits analysis of graph+space (and, in this case, interlexical space, too), demonstrating unequivocally such similitude that there can be no doubt.

Figure 1: London, British Library, Additional 47967, f.5r/3-5

To test this graph+space theory further, it is worth returning to a decades-old debate about other, related, early tenth-century scribes, probably from ecclesiastical circles

[37] In A. S. Osley, ed., *Calligraphy and Palaeography: Essays Presented to Alfred Fairbanks* (New York: October House, 1965), 197-206, at 198-9.

[38] Digitized on the British Library's website at http://www.bl.uk/manuscripts/Viewer.aspx?ref=add_ms_47967_fs001r (move through the folios to folio 5r).

associated with Winchester,[39] and specifically the second scribe of Cambridge, Corpus Christi College 173 (C.C.C.C. 173), the Parker manuscript of the the *Anglo-Saxon Chronicle* and the laws of King Alfred. This scribe wrote annals 892-920 of the manuscript having received the first quire containing annals up to 891.[40] This is the same scribe who is generally regarded as being responsible for the Old English *Orosius* (London, British Library, Additional 47967)[41] and possibly for parts of Oxford, Bodleian Library, Junius 27, the Junius Psalter.[42]

The particular focus of investigation, then, is the scribe or scribes copying folios 16v-25v of C.C.C.C. 173. Malcolm Parkes' analysis indicates two scribes copying here: Scribe 1, from folio 16v to folio 21r/21; Scribe 2 from folio 21r/22 to folio 25v. David Dumville regards this entire section of the *Chronicle* as belonging to one scribe's effort, but copied during three distinct stints, with the first folios (16v-17v) being copied last. Janet Bately detects a potential six scribes in all, four of whom are responsible for folios 21r/22 to 25v.[43] In one practical sense, the number of scribes matters, because scribal activity denotes resource and institutional investment: six scribes would suggest

---

39 A barely discernible cross is added above "Wilfriþ biscop" folio 8r of C.C.C.C. 173. Wilfrith was bishop of Worcester, who died in 928 or 929. Such sporadic interventions in the *Parker Chronicle* might confirm its function within an episcopal environment.

40 The manuscript is fully digitized at Parker on the Web: https://parker-stanford-edu.

41 Edited by Janet Bately, *The Old English Orosius*, EETS s.s., 6 (Oxford: Oxford University Press, 1980); and fully digitized here: http://www.bl.uk/manuscripts/FullDisplay.aspx?ref=Add_MS_47967

42 There are important ramifications of localizing this scribe's activities: the knock-on effect of a Winchester origin involves a host of manuscripts, as will be seen. These include Oxford, Bodleian Library, Tanner 10 (Bede's *Ecclesiastical History* in Old English), London, British Library, Royal 12. D. xvii, Bald's *Leechbook*, and, in Latin, Cambridge, Trinity College B.15.33. The digitization of most folios or the entirety of these manuscripts at their respective repository websites positively benefits research and more could be done now to build on the work of those scholars cited in surrounding footnotes here. To the corpus of known manuscripts from this period could be added a contemporary, but non-extant, version of Augustine's *Soliloquies*, which may have been the exemplar for the scribally imitative version in the twelfth-century manuscript, London, British Library, Cotton Vitellius, A. xv, Part I, the Southwick Codex. See, further, Elaine Treharne, "Invisible Things in London, British Library, Cotton Vitellius A. xv," in Maren Clegg-Hyer and Jill Frederick, eds., *Texts, Textiles and Intertexts in Honour of Gale Owen-Crocker* (Woodbridge: Boydell and Brewer, 2016), 225-37.

43 Malcolm Parkes, "The Palaeography of the Parker Manuscript of the *Chronicle*, Laws and Sedulius, and Historiography at Winchester in the Late Ninth and Tenth Centuries," in *idem, Scribes, Scripts and Reader: Studies in the Communication, Presentation and Dissemination of Medieval Texts* (London: Hambledon, 1991), 143-70; D. N. Dumville, *Wessex and England from Alfred to Edgar: Six Essays on Political, Cultural and Ecclesiastical Revival* (Woodbridge: Boydell, 1988), Chapter 3; J. M. Bately, ed., *The Anglo-Saxon Chronicle: A Collaborative Edition, iii: MS A* (Cambridge: D.S. Brewer, 1986). See also Ker, *Catalogue of Manuscripts containing Anglo*-Saxon, item 39, 57-9; and Patrick Wormald, *The Making of English Law*, 162-72, where he offers a full assessment of C.C.C.C.173, other related tenth-century manuscripts, and the scholarship upon them.

a sizeable effort to build a major writing office; two scribes working together are what might be regarded as the minimum requirement for forming a writing office (a scriptorium, perhaps); one scribe does not a writing office or scriptorium make.

Close analysis of these folios at the level of the graph suggests that multiple scribes might be at work. Thus, for example, forms of **e**, **g**, **f**, and **þ** differ from folio to folio:

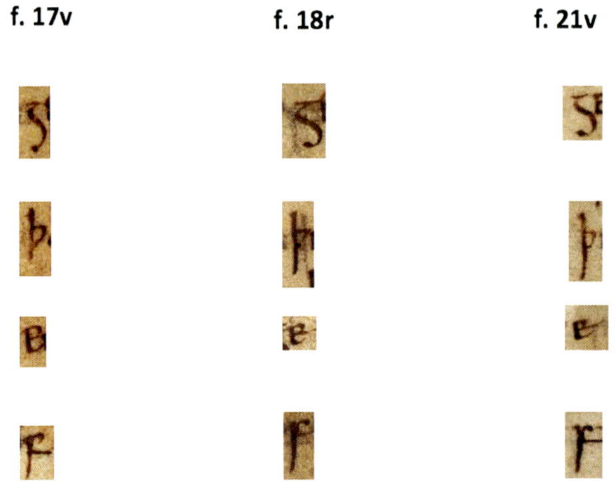

Characteristic of the changes seen in letterforms between the stint at folios 16v-21r/21 and the stint(s) that follow include considerable variation in the form of **y** from straight-limbed or left-leaning to almost exclusively **f**-shaped. Greater angularity in the bowls of wyn and thorn, together with an increasing propensity to split the shoulders of **r** and **s** mark individual stints; **st** ligatures and the use of ligatures including high -**e** vary notably; **g** changes from having a quite angular second stroke to a more rounded form; ascenders become noticeably more wedged as the folios advance. Moreover, the script becomes more laterally expansive by the later folios, with a concomitant reduction in the average number of words per line, and by folio 22r, a reduction from 26 lines per page to 25 lines, which affects, *prima facie*, the aspect of the hand.

One could continue on a graph-by-graph account of the many differences (or, indeed, similarities) in individual letterforms from folio to folio, and, on the occasions noted at the primary junctures in the hand(s) (at folio 21r/21, for example), one might be convinced that there are different scribes at work here. However, working beyond the level of the graph to the level of the graph+adjacent space, particularly as evinced through the lexical unit or syllabic unit (as defined by the scribe's own practice), it is possible to assert with as much certainty as one can within the art of paleography that there is only one scribe working on these folios.

This is a scribe, though, whose hand is quite variable, suggesting multiple stints over time, or the acquisition of a form of evolving writing through hands-on experience. The similarities between his hand[44] and multiple others during this first half of the tenth

[44] I am making an assumption that this scribe—and other writers in C.C.C.C.173—is male, but, given the foundation of Nunnaminster in Winchester, and associations between this entire group of scribes and a manuscript, such as London, British Library, Harley 2965, the Book of Nunnaminster (Ker, *Catalogue*, item 237, pp. 308-9), which has additional materials added to it contemporary with the group of books touched upon here, such assumptions might well be misplaced.

century do, ultimately, suggest one or more training programs—programs that Wormald and Dumville attribute tentatively to a peripatetic group of scribes closely connected with the royal court.[45]

Such a theory is attractive, because it might go some way to explaining the significant number of interrelated manuscripts and diplomata extant from this period, which are linked either by scribe or by contents or by comparable initials,[46] and, in some cases, by layout (the use of annal numbering in C.C.C.C. 173 compared with the table of contents in Cambridge, Trinity College B.15.33 and London, British Library, Royal D. xvii, among others), but which otherwise have potentially disparate places of origin. Scribal relationships exist between this extended group of manuscripts in fascinating ways, reminiscent of those in the extensive corpus of Latin and Old English books produced, I suggest, specifically for Bishop Leofric's use at Exeter in the 1050s, or so.[47] The link between C.C.C.C. 173 and the episcopacy is confirmed by the well-known marking with a cross of the name of Frithestan, bishop of Winchester from 909 to 931.[48] In addition, the link between this manuscript and the court—specfically of King Æthelstan—is confirmed by the scribe of annals 925-55. Ker describes this scribe as having "a handsome fluent hand of s. x med.";[49] and this scribal hand seems quite likely to be the same as the scribe of the dedication on folio 15v of London, British Library, Cotton Tiberius A. ii, the "Æthelstan Gospels."[50] Since the contemporary recipient of the Gospels was Christ Church, Canterbury, it may be that an early Christ Church provenance (in the 950s, to tally with the date of the annals entered by the scribe) is possible,[51] or this might be a scribe who was as closely connected to the court as to the

---

[45] For this, see the rather compelling arguments elucidated by Wormald, *The Making of English Law*, 169-72.

[46] Compare, for example, the initials of Cambridge, Trinity College, B. 15. 33—Isidore's *Etymology*—with those of the Parker *Chronicle* up to folio 25v. The *Chronicle* emulates, inexpertly, the minor decorative devices of Trinity B. 15. 33. These two manuscripts are, I would suggest, among the most closely related of the group in terms of anticipated audience.

[47] Elaine Treharne, "Producing a Library in Late Anglo-Saxon England: Exeter, 1050-72," *Review of English Studies* 54 (2003): 155-72.

[48] This cross appears at folio 20v in C.C.C.C. 173. Unusually shaped, the same cross mark appears in Trinity B. 15. 33, f. 20r. Wormald, *The Making of English Law,* discusses this at p. 168, fn 16. In this note, Wormald mentions a cross-mark at f.23r in the Trinity manuscript, where there is no such mark, however.

[49] Ker, *Catalogue*, item 39, p. 58, his Scribe 3.

[50] Digitized at the British Library website, http://www.bl.uk/manuscripts/FullDisplay.aspx?index=1&ref=Cotton_MS_Tiberius_A_II.

[51] According to Ker, *Catalogue*, 58, this scribe is also responsible for London, British Library, Royal 12 D. xvii (*Bald's Leechbook*), and London, British Library, Cotton Otho B. xi, both of which are assigned a localization of Winchester by Ker, *Catalogue,* 333 and 234, respectively.

church. As such, it can be no surprise to find a scribe—functioning among a small group of scribes—copying for senior clerical and courtly circles a dedication document, chronicles (both Anglo-Saxon and Bede's *Ecclesiastical History*) and essential medical materials.

It is within this context that the Old English Laws, written on two quires as the work of a single scribe, but intimately associated with the *Anglo-Saxon Chronicle* in C.C.C.C. 173, should be understood. The Laws were written sometime after about 930, and understood from the beginning as being part of the endeavor of the slightly earlier *Chronicle* scribes,[52] since the format is made to accord with the *Chronicle*, the lawcode numbers mirror the *Chronicle*'s annal numbers, and the initials are very similar in style.[53] The consequence of the efforts of this individual scribe, as with those individuals who copied the chronicle entries throughout C.C.C.C. 173, is the neat and utilitarian effect of the work. This is in contrast, of course, with the more expensive and time-consuming productions written by others in this team of scribes, in total over what was likely to be a couple of decades. Rather than seeing this as a "scruffy book" because of its plainness, as Wormald describes it,[54] it could be understood in its tenth-century context of production as an *essential* day-to-day compilation of historical and legal necessities that spanned court and ecclesiastical settings. In this, C.C.C.C. 173, perhaps (though an admittedly remote possibility) belonging to a bishop like Frithestan, but deployed at key moments of lay and clerical assembly, preempts the better documented setting for Wulfstan I's work, some eighty years later. The significance of *record* established by this select group of scribes is significant. Their manuscripts are the foundation of the English historical and literary traditions. And just as one can hope to fill in the space of time by close analysis of the extant corpus of manuscripts, so the art of paleography can be revisited through new methods to produce fresh perspectives, particularly as the raw materials of the scholar's trade are now so readily accessible through digital media.

---

52 Quire signatures, a to e, appear to have been added to the *Parker Chronicle* and the quires containing the lawcodes (at folios 33r to 52v), and these are discussed by Wormald, *The Making of English Law*, 166-7, and fn 9. I cannot see Wormald's "a" and "b," though there are certainly traces of ink on the appropriate folios. While it's impossible to be certain of scribal hand, based purely on one letter form, the "e" at folio 42r is closest to either Scribe 2 of the *Chronicle*, at folios 16v to 25v, or the scribe of the laws himself.

53 As they are to the initials of Trinity B. 15. 33 (though C.C.C.C. 173's are less elaborate).

54 Wormald, *The Making of English Law*, 170.

III. Genres of Law

'Qui brecht ungewaldes, betan gewaldes': Proverbs in the Anglo-Saxon Laws

Rolf H. Bremmer Jr.

The Anglo-Saxon laws have proved to be an attractive arena to generations of scholars for a wide range of reasons.[1] In 1568, they were published for the first time for reasons that had little to do with the purpose for which they were once composed. Rather than informing the people what rules they should live by, their *editor princeps*, William Lambarde, wanted to illustrate for his contemporary Englishmen how their ancestors had arranged their legal lives in order to inspire them to political action.[2] With the Romantic era came legal historians such as Friedrich von Savigny and Jacob Grimm who, as the nineteenth-century legal historian Frederick Maitland was well aware, made Anglo-Saxon law part of "die germanische Rechtsgeschichte."[3] Grimm, for one thing, was struck by the style of the early Germanic law codes in which he detected poetic features, such as the use of alliteration, a penchant for metaphors and the application of proverbial, i.e. popular, wisdom. The presence of such stylistic attributes in the early medieval legal discourse, according to Grimm in his scholarly manifesto "Von der Poesie im Recht," was because "both poetry and law have risen from one and the same bed."[4] Ever since Grimm and his contemporaries, the Germanic laws have continued to exercise their magnetism on scholars, not least for their stylistic ornaments. One of these scholars to be irresistibly drawn to Anglo-Saxon legal prose was Lisi Oliver, who in sundry places in her ground-breaking book *The Beginnings of English Law* devoted attention to this aspect in the Laws of Æthelbert, king of Kent.[5]

---

[1] My gratitude is due to Richard Harris and, especially, Susan Deskis for their constructive comments on a draft version of this paper. I am indebted to Paul Hyams for helpful advice.

[2] Rebecca Brackmann, *The Elizabethan Invention of Anglo-Saxon England: Laurence Nowell, William Lambarde, and the Study of Old English* (Cambridge: D. S. Brewer, 2012), esp. chap. 7, and literature quoted there.

[3] Stefan Berger, and Peter Lambert, "Intellectual Transfers and Mental Blockades: Anglo-German Dialogues in Historiography," in *Historiker Dialoge. Geschichte, Mythos und Gedächtnisim deutsch-britischen kulturellen Austausch 1750-2000*, ed. Peter Lambert, Stefan Berger and Peter Schumann (Göttingen: Vandenhoeck & Ruprecht, 2003), 21.

[4] Jacob Grimm, "Von der Poesie im Recht," *Zeitschrift für geschichtliche Rechtswissenschaft* 2 (1816), §2: "Dasz recht und poesie miteinander aus einem bette aufgestanden waren, hält nicht schwer zu glauben" (That both law and poetry have risen from one and the same bed is not difficult to believe).

[5] Oliver, *Beginnings,* 38-41.

Speculating about possibly oral elements in the personal injury section of Æthelbert's laws, Lisi dwelled on a selection of regulations that could be seen to contain traces of alliteration, for example:

> Gif man þeoh þurhstingþ, stice gehwilce .vi. scillingas.
>
> If a person stabs through a thigh, for each thrust 6 shillings. [*Abt.* 67]

By highlighting the alliterations in *þ* in bold print, Lisi made them visible to the reader. On the other hand, she left unmentioned a similar case of alliteration in the same line, viz. the initial sounds of *-stingþ* and *stice*. We can only guess at the reason why Lisi left the latter instances unmentioned. Perhaps, she overlooked them, or maybe more likely, there appears to be some arbitrariness in identifying alliterations in Æthelbert's legal discourse. In her comment on this and a few other examples of alliteration, Lisi remarked: "Conceivably what we are seeing here is a remnant of law couched, not in poetry, but in an elevated prose style employing the poetic device of alliteration."[6] Clearly, Lisi remained a little aloof and did not venture to claim that the laws had once upon a time been composed in poetic form, as had many decades ago been suggested in so many words by Dorothy Bethurum, whom Lisi extensively quotes in support of her argument.[7] Rounding off her section on the style of the laws, Lisi carefully concluded: "In summation, there are stylistic elements in the laws of Æthelbert that seem to hark back to a preliterate version."

There is a danger of logical fallacy lurking in such a conclusion. As is known, Old English poetry, and, indeed, all early Germanic poetry, heavily leans on alliteration, but this structural characteristic does not therefore make all instances of alliteration "a poetic device," as has often been claimed with respect to legal texts and was apparently also subscribed to by Lisi. Before becoming a structural element, together with a four-beat stress and a marked vocabulary, in the composition of verse-lines, alliteration arose as a technique operating outside verse to facilitate memorization, as is attested by its occurrence in other languages than Germanic.[8] At the same time, alliteration will very early have been used as a means to distinguish formal from informal speech, whether or not the formal speech was cast in verse. Often, concepts were expressed in alliterative conjoined word-pairs or collocations, quite a few of which date back to before the time of the Anglo-Saxon invasions as is evidenced by their occurrence in other Germanic

---

6 Oliver, *Beginnings*, 39.

7 Dorothy Bethurum, "Stylistic Features of the Old English Laws," *Modern Language Review* 27 (1932): 263-79.

8 See, e.g., the contributions by György Kara, Vilmos Voight, Frog and Eila Stepanova, and Martin Orwin on the function and use of alliteration in Mongol, Hungarian, (Balto-) Finnic and Somali, respectively, in Jonathan Roper, ed. *Alliteration in Culture* (Basingstoke: Palgrave MacMillan, 2011).

languages.[9] Thus, for example, the hapax collocation *banes bite* "a bite of bone," i.e., "a violent incision (with a sword) into the bone" in the Kentish laws (*Abt.* 35) finds a parallel in Old Frisian similarly hapax *benes biti*, likewise used in a list of compensations for injuries. The same applies to the alliterating compound *feaxfang* "seizing by the hair" (*Abt.* 33), another Old English hapax, which has its counterpart in the rather common Old Frisian legal term *faxfeng* in the same register of compensations.[10] Such parallels are more suggestive of a preliterate origin for the Kentish laws than the incidental alliterations.

Alliteration, though potentially indicative, is not enough to identify possible traces of an oral origin for the Kentish Laws, or indeed for any legal text. More is needed to arrive at such a conclusion. Fortunately, sufficient research has been carried out to find out what mnemonic techniques are needed to make thoughts, ideas, notions, rules, sayings, and the like, conveniently memorizable in a primary oral culture. In such a culture all information is stored in the memory and can be made available when necessary. Now in order to solve the problem of retaining and retrieving carefully articulated thought, according to Walter Ong, recourse must be taken to thinking in "mnemonic patterns, shaped for instant oral reproduction. Thought must come into being in heavily rhythmic, balanced patterns, in repetitions or antithesis, in alliterations and assonances, in rhyme, in epithetic and other formulaic expressions."[11] Proverbs also belong to these mnemonic aids, which are "constantly heard by everyone so that they come to mind readily and which themselves are patterned for retention and ready recall."[12] Just note the proverb quoted in the title of my paper: it contains both alliteration and rhyme; it has a balanced structure of verb and adverb, of condition and requirement. Proverbs, according to Walter Ong, have through their mnemonic form become a constituent part of common memory.[13] They are "storehouses of wisdom" and in themselves often resemble legal rules;[14] note the use of the imperative infinitive in the title

---

9 Rolf H. Bremmer, "Dealing Dooms: Alliteration in the Old Frisian Laws," in *Alliteration in Culture*, ed. Jonathan Roper (Basingstoke: Palgrave MacMillan, 2011), 86-8, but cf. E.G., Stanley. "On the Laws of King Alfred: the End of the Preface and the Beginning of the Laws," in *Alfred the Wise. Studies in Honour of Janet Bately on the Occasion of Her Sixty-fifth Birthday*, ed. Jane Roberts and Janet L. Nelson with Malcolm Godden (Cambridge: D. S. Brewer, 1997), 214-15, for a caveat against the value of alliterative word-pairs shared across more than one Germanic language.

10 "The Rüstring Register of Compensations," VI 7e and 1a, respectively, in Wybren Jan Buma and Wilhelm Ebel, ed. and trans. *Das Rüstringer Recht*. Altfriesische Rechtsquellen 1 (Göttingen: Musterschmidt, 1961), 68-71.

11 Walter Ong, *Orality and Literacy. The Technologizing of the Word*, 3rd edn. (London: Routledge, 2012), 34.

12 David Crowley, and Paul Heyer. *Communication in History: Technology, Culture, Society*, 6th edn. (Boston: Allyn & Bacon/Pearson, 2011), 52.

13 Ong, *Orality and Literacy*, 34.

14 Stefan Brink, "'*Verba volant, scripta manent?*' Aspects of the Oral Society in Scandinavia," in *Literacy in Medieval and Early Modern Scandinavian Culture*, ed. Pernille Hermann (Odense: Odense University Press, 2005), 96-7.

above "He who breaks unwillingly must compensate willingly." Proverbs also transmit communal norms and values to posterity; they give advice or warn, articulate desired behaviour or unwanted conduct.[15] Although the role and nature of proverbs in Anglo-Saxon England have been fairly well studied, their particular place in, but also absence from, the Anglo-Saxon laws has not yet received the attention they deserve.[16] To do so is the purpose of my paper in memory of Lisi.

But what is a proverb? As a matter of fact, providing a definition of a proverb has proven to be notoriously difficult.[17] One way of avoiding this difficulty is following the great American paroemiologist B. J. Whiting. In an article on the nature of the proverb he cheekily concluded: "Happily, no definition is really necessary, since all of us know what a proverb is."[18] Another twentieth-century giant in this field, Archer Taylor, was even more pessimistic when he professed: "The definition of a proverb is too difficult to repay the undertaking [...]. An incommunicable quality tells us this sentence is proverbial and that one is not." Taylor believed that "no definition will enable us to identify positively a sentence as proverbial."[19] Still, attempts can and indeed should be made and I here offer you two definitions. The first is provided by Susanne Schmarje: "The proverb is a brief, popular sentence or complex of sentences, grammatically complete and independent with respect to its thought, which teaches a lesson which on its own authority lays claim to absolute validity."[20] The focus in this definition is directed at the brevity and popularity as well as on the didactic and apodictic nature of proverbs. However, equally useful is the following definition presented by Wolfgang Mieder:

---

[15] Brink, "'*Verba volant, scripta manent?*'" 91; Claude Sumner. "The Proverb and Oral Society." *New Political Science* 21 (1999): 22.

[16] For a convenient and judicious survey to date, see Johanna Kramer. "The Study of Proverbs in Anglo-Saxon England: Recent Scholarship, Resources for Research, and the Future of the Field." *Literature Compass* 6.1 (2009): 71-96. A cursory consultation of Singer's *Lexikon der Sprichwörter des romanisch-germanischen Mittelalters* suggests that its editors seem to have ignored the Anglo-Saxon legal proverbs. See Samuel Singer, *et al. Lexikon der Sprichwörter des romanisch-germanischen Mittelalters*, 13 vols. Berlin: De Gruyter, 1995-2002.

[17] For a discussion of the problem with an extensive bibliography, see, most recently, Neal R. Norrick. "Subject Area, Terminology, Proverb Definitions, Proverb Features," in *Introduction to Paremiology: A Comprehensive Guide to Proverb Studies*, ed. Hrisztalina Hrisztova-Gotthardt and Melita Aleksa Varga, (Berlin: De Gruyter, 2014), 7-27.

[18] Bartlett J. Whiting, "Proverbs and Proverbial Sayings," in *The Frank C. Brown Collection of North Carolina Folklore*. Vol. 1 (Durham, NC: Duke University Press, 1952), 331.

[19] Archer Taylor, *The Proverb and An Index to The Proverb* (Hatboro, PA: Folklore Associates / Copenhagen: Rosenkilde and Bagger, 1962, repr. of 1931-1934), 3.

[20] Suzanne Schmarje, *Das sprichwortliche Material in den Essais von Montagne* (Berlin: De Gruyter, 1973), 39: "Das Sprichwort ist ein kurzer, volkstümlicher, grammatikalisch in sich geschlossener und sinngemaß unabhängiger Satz oder Satzcomplex, der eine Lehre ausspricht, welche aus sich heraus den Anspruch auf absolute Gültigkeit erhebt"; translation taken from Wendy Pfeffer, *Proverbs in Medieval Occitan Literature* (Gainesville: University Press of Florida, 1997), 2-3.

"A proverb is a short, generally known sentence of the folk which contains wisdom, truth, morals, and traditional views in a metaphorical, fixed, and memorizable form and which is handed down from generation to generation."[21] This definition has some advantages over that given by Schmarje, in that it makes the didactic element more explicit, gives credit to tradition and signals the metaphorical aspect of proverbs. Mieder also requires proverbs to belong to "the folk," with which word he links up with German *Volk* "people," a concept that was essential in the theories of Grimm and other Romantic scholars. They held that sententious sayings needed to be *volksläufig*, i.e., they had to circulate among the people in general, from high to low, in order to count as a proverb. It will be understood that this latter requirement is almost impossible to apply to Anglo-Saxon proverbs, because many are recorded only once.[22] Furthermore, the condition of a wide circulation throughout "the folk" excludes the use of Latin proverbs and proverb collections, such as the *Disticha Catonis*, which were highly appreciated and used by the small, literate part of the population, including authors of laws composed in Latin. Finally, as Ruth Schmidt-Wiegand points out, proverbs often contain a modal auxiliary, such as *shall, must, may, can*, expressing propriety, prescription, obligation or even force; alternatively, when combined with a negation, such modals express prohibition.[23]

With these preliminary aspects in mind I continue with a discussion, in chronological order of occurrence, of about half a dozen proverbs that have been identified by Felix Liebermann and others in the Anglo-Saxon laws. Pride of place for using the first proverb must go to King Ine of Wessex, who reigned from 688 to 725. The date of the composition of his legal code is generally set at c. 694, which makes them the oldest laws of Wessex in existence and at the same time in all likelihood the first laws outside of Kent to be committed to parchment. In other words, they were composed in a context of semi-primary oral culture. In his prologue, in which he foregrounds the divine nature of his office, Ine gratefully mentions by name three people who had helped him in composing his rules. First comes his father, immediately followed by two spiritual fathers. Ine furthermore acknowledges the advice and instruction of numerous wise men, both secular and ecclesiastical, in order to emphasize the broad communal support for his legislation:

> Ic Ine, mid Godes gife Wesseaxna kyning, mid geðeahte 7 mid lare Cenredes mines fæder 7 Heddes mines biscopes 7 Eorcenwoldes mines biscopes mid eallum minum ealdormannum 7 þæm ieldstan witum minre ðeode 7 eac micelre gesomnunge Godes ðeowa

[21] Wolfgang Mieder, *"Proverbs Speak Louder Than Words": Folk Wisdom in Art, Culture, Folklore, History, Literature, and Mass Media* (New York: Peter Lang, 2008), 11.

[22] But see Susan Deskis, "Proverbs and Structure in Maxims I.A." *Studies in Philology*. Vol. 110, no. 4 (2013): 667-89 who demonstrates that it is quite possible to recover the circulation of a number of proverbs, more than was hitherto thought.

[23] Ruth Schmidt-Wiegand, "Wissensvermittlung durch Rechtssprichwörter," in *Wissensliteratur im Mittelalter und in der Frühen Neuzeit*, ed. Horst Brunner and Norbert R. Wole (Wiesbaden: Reichert, 1993), 261.

wæs smeagende be ðære hælo urra sawla 7 be ðam staþole ures rices, þætte ryht æw 7 ryhte cynedomas ðurh ure folc gefæstnode 7 getrymede wæron, þætte nænig ealdormonna ne us undergeðeodedra æfter þam wære awendende ðas ure domas. *Ine* Prol.[24]

I, Ine, by the grace of God, king of the West-Saxons, with the advice and with the instruction of my father Cenred and of my bishop Hedde and of my bishop Erkenwald, along with all my ealdormen and the oldest (i.e., chief) councillors of my people and also a great assembly of the servants of God, have been inquiring about the salvation of our souls and about the security of our kingdom, that true law and true statutes might be established and strengthened throughout our people, so that none of the ealdormen or of our subjects might afterwards pervert these our decrees.[25]

There is a distinct rhythm to this prologue, brought about by balancing the short syntactic elements with which it is constructed, by employing pairs of near synonyms (*mid geðeahte 7 mid lare; ryht æw 7 ryhte cynedomas; gefæstnode 7 getrymede*), by repetition of words (*Heddes mines biscopes 7 Eorcenwoldes mines biscopes; ryht æw 7 ryhte cynedomas*) and by repetition of constructions (*be ðære hælo urra sawla 7 be ðam staþole ures rices*: PREP*be* + NPdat + NPgen). These aspects taken together would amount to sufficient evidence for claiming a veneer of orality for this passage. Yet, it is evident, perhaps if only because of the complex syntactic structure of this introductory sentence that the prologue was especially composed for the occasion. It would seem therefore that Ine (or whoever wrote these lines for him) was employing (and exploiting) features of oral discourse on purpose in order to lend this message a familiar ring and find a willing ear with the intended audience.

A different, perhaps more genuine aspect of orality seems to surface in *Ine* 43, which includes a cluster of regulations concerning behaviour in a forest:

Be wuda bærnette: Đonne mon beam on wuda forbærne, & weorðe yppe on þone ðe hit dyde, gielde he fulwite: geselle LX scill., **for þam þe** *fyr bið þeof.* Gif mon afelle on wuda wel monega treowa, & wyrð eft undierne, forgielde III treowu ælc mid XXX scill. Ne ðearf he hiora ma geldan, wære hiora swa fela swa hiora wære, **for ðon** *sio æsc bið melda*, nalles ðeof.

Concerning burning in a forest: When someone burns a tree in a forest, and it becomes manifest who did it, let him pay a full fine: 60 shillings, because fire is a thief. If someone fells a good many trees in a forest, and it becomes public afterwards, let him compensate three trees, each with 30 shillings. He need not compensate more for them, no matter how many there were, because the axe is a messenger, not at all a thief.

[24] All quotations from the laws, unless otherwise noted, are taken from Lieberman, *Gesetze*.

[25] Translation, with some modification, from Whitelock, *EHD,* 399.

The rule reveals unequal sanctions for burning a tree and chopping down one. The former deed is censured far more severely than the latter and the reason why is given in statements that to all intents and purposes look like proverbs, keeping the aforementioned definitions in mind: they are above all brief, metaphorical and easy to remember. What we cannot establish is their popularity, for this is the only place in the Anglo-Saxon corpus where they occur. However, as a quick browse of the Internet will attest, the notion of fire stereotypically to act like a thief is not uncommon. An advertisement for fire-proof storage furniture opens as follows: "Fire is a thief and in the blink of an eye, it can steal everything from you."[26] Or a newspaper, reporting a recent forest fire on the island of Madeira: "'The fire is a thief,' she says almost groaning, a woman of about 60 years, while looking powerlessly at the rise of the voracious flames in the direction of her house."[27] Finally, the metaphoric phrase also turns up in an anthology of Yiddish proverbs, published in 1941, however, without providing any further context.[28]

Grimm did not recognize *fyr bið þeof* to be a proverb, but already referred to *sio æsc bið melda* in his ground-breaking article "Von der Poesie im Recht," published in 1816. It was the only example in the Anglo-Saxon laws he had been able to find of a visual and sentential expression, which, as he saw it, was at the same time a poetic expression.[29] Grimm returned to this passage in Ine's laws in his *Deutsche Rechtsalterthümer*, when he discussed the use of proverbs in the laws. In order to underscore his claim that "The axe is an informer, not at all a thief" is really a proverb, Grimm adduced examples from Germany, such as *Mit der exe stelt men nicht* ("One does not steal with the axe") and *Wan einer hauet, ruft er* ("When someone is chopping, he is calling").[30] Grimm did not

[26] See the opening sentence at http://safeandvault.com/faq/154-quality-assurance-orders-directives/748-nfpa-232-requirements.

[27] http://madeiraislanddirect.com/blog/2009/07/uncontrolled-fire-in-gaula-homes-threatened/.

[28] Joseph A. Weingarten, *Yiddish Proverbs* (New York: n. p., 1941), 20.

[29] Grimm, "Von der Poesie im Recht," §7, p. 57; cf. E.G. Stanley, "Old English Documentary Discourse Faithfully Transmitted in Adorned Prose or, Unfaithfully Transmitted in Adorned Prose, or Even in Rhyming Verse." *NOWELE* 68.1 (2015): 34-5.

[30] Jacob Grimm, *Deutsche Rechtsalterthümer* (Göttingen: Dieterich, 1828), 68-9. On Grimm's authority both phrases ended up in nineteenth-century proverb-collections, such as Eduard Graf and Matthias Dietherr, *Deutsche Rechtssprichwörter, unter Mitwirkung der Professoren J. C. Bluntschli und K. Maurer gesammelt und erklärt* (Nördingen: Beck, 1864). Under number 468 (p. 365) we find "Das Feuer ist ein Dieb," with a reference to the Anglo-Saxon Laws 40. 43. From Graf and Dietherr's collection, both proverbs found their way to Karl F. W. Wander, *Deutsches Sprichwörter-Lexikon. Ein Hausschatz für das deutsche Volk in fünf Bändern* (Leipzig: Brockhaus, 1867-1880). Especially, "Das Feuer ist ein Dieb" became popular in proverb collections and was claimed to be "altgermanisch" on more than one occasion, e.g., Ralf Bernd Herde, *Roter Hahn und Rote Kreuz: Chronik der Geschichte des Feuerlösch- und Rettungswesen.* Diskussionspapiere der Hochschule für offentliche Verwaltung in Kehl 2004/2 (Norderstedt: BoD, 2005), 8. The

explain why he took this phrase in Ine's laws to be a proverb; apparently, like Whiting, he knew when he was dealing with one.

As it is, not everybody today is satisfied with such an intuitional approach. According to Paul Cavill, "fire is a thief" and "the axe is an informer" would rather be gnomes or maxims than proverbs.[31] Gnomes and maxims, in Cavill's view, are linguistic moulds into which observation, experience and thought can be poured in order to clarify, solidify and preserve them. Gnomes and maxims, thus Cavill, are structured forms of language which organize thought into conventional patterns. Sententious sayings, on the other hand, are only proverbs, according to Cavill, when they are actually marked in the text as such, that is, if they are announced with words such as "it is said" or "the old saying that says."[32]

However, the validity of Cavill's formal requirement of the presence of some kind of identification such as "as the proverb has it" seems questionable to me. In Old Frisian law, to give an example, we can find the same proverb being quoted both with and without such a marker. The sixteenth of the *Seventeen Statutes*, a major legal document dating back to the early thirteenth century, stipulates that all Frisians have the right to compensate their violent deeds with money. In no way should they be subjected to corporal punishments, let alone capital punishment, unless a man were caught red-handed in a deed of nightly arson or in any other heinous secret deed. Moreover, execution of a perpetrator is also permitted, if he has no money with which to compensate his deed. The statute justifies the exceptions to compensation as follows: *hwande morth mot ma mith morthe kela* ("for murder must be cooled with murder").[33] The same

proverb was given a new lease of life in the German-speaking world by its inclusion in Ruth Schmidt-Wiegand, *Deutsche Rechtsregeln und Rechtssprichwörter. Ein Lexikon* (Munich: Beck, 1996). However, Schmidt-Wiegand seems to have lost any idea of the context in which it was originally used. Forestry is no longer mentioned; instead she comments: "The proverb relates to arson, which like theft bears the mark of secrecy." (Das Sprichwort bezieht sich auf die Brandstiftung, die ebenso wie Diebstahl den Makel der Heimlichkeit trägt) (p. 105), a paraphrase of what Wander more wrote in his lexicon, s.v. *Feuer* 16 (vol. 1, col. 993), more than a century previously: "Mit Bezug auf Brandstiftung, weil in ihr wie beim Diebstahl der verabscheute Charakter der Heimlichkeit liegt." (With regard to arson, because in it, as with theft, lies the despicable mark of secrecy).

31 Paul Cavill, *Maxims in Old English Poetry* (Cambridge: D. S. Brewer, 1999), 11-12.

32 Cavill, *Maxims in Old English Poetry*, 63. Still another approach to these two sayings in Ine's laws is offered by Tiffany Beechy, *The Poetics of Old English* (Farnham: Ashgate, 2010), 83-4, who by, for me at least, a rather complicated way of arguing prefers to see them as riddles. She does not mention previous scholars, such as Lieberman, who referred to Grimm for their proverbial character, *Gesetze*, II, s.v. *Anzeiger*. Riddling does not seem very practical to me when it comes to laying down the rules for a society to live by. "Fire is a thief" is a metaphor that is quite unambiguous and still used in our times, see notes 25 and 26 above.

33 Buma and Ebel, *Das Rüstringer Recht*, III.16.

proverb is also used in the *Jurisprudentia Frisica*, a fifteenth-century systematically ordered handbook offering an amalgam of native, canon and Roman law, probably compiled for private usage, if in a completely different context. In chapter 59, entitled *De restitucione spoliatorum* ("On the restoration of robbed properties"), the following rule is given:

> Dat riucht spreckt aldus: Hweerso een man syn gued næt crygya mey myt riucht, so mey hy'tmyt oerleff dis riuchtis aldeer om strida jeffta tijeflick nyma. Hwant ma seyt to een byspilwird: "moerd schelma mey moeerd kela" ende "græt onriucht moetma mey macht kera" ende "hwaso dat riucht wrsmayt ende breckt, dam so aegh dat riucht næt to helpen"[34]

> The law speaks as follows: If a man cannot obtain his property rightfully, with the consent of the law he can fight for it or take it furtively. For they say with a proverb: "murder must be cooled with murder" and "great injustice must be averted with force" and "whoever despises the law and breaks it, the law need not help him."

The rule is clear: When the peaceful road to settling a dispute appears to be blocked, it is permitted to resort to violence in order to obtain redress. As we have seen before, it is quite appropriate for a generalizing proverb to follow a causal conjunction meaning "because" or "for." In this particular Frisian instance, however, the author showed to be conscious of this possibility and made it explicit by using a proverb to underpin his legal argument, first with the words *ma seyt* ("they say"; German *man sagt*). This or a similar phrase, is a frequently used marker in Icelandic sagas to announce a proverb, for example: *er þat ok satt, at sagt er, 'at úlfar eta annars ørendi'* ("It is true, as they say, 'when one wolf hunts for another, he may eat the prey'").[35] In saga conversations, such formulas intend to protect the speaker from the hearer's blame, but in the context of the legal regulation the phrase rather serves to appeal to commonly shared wisdom. The author of our text did not leave it at that, but added *to a byspilwird* ("as a proverb"), thus showing his awareness of what he was doing.[36] Finally, if taken literally, the saying "murder must be cooled with murder" makes no sense, because the rule does not deal with homicide. It is therefore evidently used proverbially here. If we follow Cavill, however, only the marked case would concern a proverb, while the same sententious phrase (*morth mot ma mith morthe kela*), when used without identifying markers such

---

[34] Montanus De Haan Hettema, ed. *Jurisprudentia Frisica of Friesche Regtkennis. Een handschrift uit de vijftiende eeuw*, 3 vols. (Leeuwarden: H. C. Schetsberg, 1834), Tit. 59.8.

[35] Einar Ól Sveinsson, ed. *Laxdœla saga*. Íslenzk fornrit V (Reykjavík: Hið íslenzka fornritafélag, 1934) V, 23.64. I owe this particular reference to Richard Harris. For an abundant list of such markers, see Hugo Gering, "Altnordische sprichwörter und sprichwörtliche redensarten," *Arkiv för Nordisk Filologi* 32 (1916): 1-6.

[36] Cf. Cavill, *Maxims*, 60-1.

as *ma seit*, would be a gnome, which does not stand to reason. Moreover, the fact that the *byspilwird* is followed by two further sayings that fulfil the same function as the first one, *viz.* backing up the legal rule with a generalizing sententious saying, makes clear that they must also be counted for proverbs. Returning to Ine's laws, the two sayings discussed above can be classified as proverbs not only because of their brevity, their grammatical completeness and their application of metaphors, but they also serve the same purpose: they conclude a rule with an appeal to communal wisdom as shaped in a proverb which by its very nature allows no contradiction. Their incontradictability is introduced by causal conjunctions: *for þam þe* and *for ðon* ("because"). The recurrence of this feature in analogous passages indicates its importance to the legal usage of proverbial phrases.

The next proverb-like statements occur in the Laws of King Æthelred, included in an appendix to the peace treaty he concluded with the Danes in 994. The context is a regulation concerning the vouching of warranty. This procedure entailed that someone had been accused of possessing certain movables that the plaintiff claimed to be his and which the defendant therefore held illegally. The defendant was summoned to court to give warranty of title either by producing the man from whom he had bought it (the "warrantor") or by bringing along someone who had been present at the transaction and was willing to confirm the defendant's possessing the piece of property rightfully. If the defendant was unable to prove his case, death by hanging was waiting for him. Things became complicated when the warrantor had meanwhile died and had no heir to give warranty. Then the warrantor was held guilty, unless there were friends who would clear him. If they did so successfully, the person in possession of the chattels would be held guilty: **forðam** *a bið andsæc swiðere ðonne onsagu* ("because denial is always stronger than accusation").[37] Are we dealing with a proverb here? Again, its popularity cannot be evidenced, since no parallels have been found to date. However, its construction with a comparative (compare: "better safe than sorry"), the consuetudinal connotation of the verb "to be," the generality with respect to time (*a* "always"), the alliterative linking of ***andsæc*** and ***onsagu*** and the economy of words make it a strong candidate. Finally, the use of the causal conjunction *forðam*, which we have already seen before, clinches the case. The provision in this appendix continues by indicating how the process of vouching to warranty could be stopped. This was simply when the defendant proved his ownership by witness, a point confirmed with a sententious argument: **forðam** *agnung bið ner ðam ðe hæfð ðonne ðam ðe æftersprecð* ("because ownership is closer to him who has than to him who claims").[38] This phrase, admittedly, lacks effective use

[37] *II Atr.* 9.3. On warranty in Anglo-Saxon England, see John Hudson, *The Oxford History of the Laws of England*, Vol. 2: *871-1216* (Oxford: Oxford University Press, 2012), 155-9.

[38] *II Atr.* 9.4. On the legal concept of "closer, near," see *Deutsches Rechtswörterbuch*, s.v. näher <https://www.rzuser.uni-heidelberg.de/~cd2/drw/e/na/naher.htm>. Accessed Spring 2016.

of alliteration; it is also less succinct and hence will have been less memorizable than when it had been phrased like "ownership is closer to the haver than to the claimer." Furthermore, the phrase displays grammatical balance and repetition and it features the consuetudinal use of "is." Most significant, however, is the by now familiar introduction by a causal conjunction that gives away its proverbial character.[39]

The next sentential phrase is found in the *Rectitudines*, a manual of estate management, dating to c. 1025. Its author is unknown but the tone is remarkably personal, knowledgeable and self-assured. He knows that legal customs vary according to place and should be respected and learned by the legal specialist, if he is to maintain a good reputation. This condition is, again, introduced by the causal conjunction *forðam*:

> **forðam** laga sceal on leode luflice leornian, lof se ðe on lande sylf nele leosan. [Rect 21.3]
>
> Because he must learn the law of the people with love, who himself does not wish to lose his good name in the country.

The passage has been praised for its use of alliteration and verse-like characteristics in the context of a law text,[40] but has not yet been connected to proverbiality, in so far as I can tell. Modern translators sometimes remove its claim to generality, so Swanton: "Wherefore one must learn the law of the district lovingly, if one does not want to lose good opinion on the estate."[41] Such a translation in my opinion obscures the statement's proverbial character. Indicative of the latter are the presence of the modal *sceal*, here expressing obligation, the presence of alliteration, and the introductory **forðam**. A counter-argument for the phrase being proverbial might be found in the complex syntax in which it is couched, which seems not conducive to memorization. Moreover, also pleading against this *sententia* being a traditional proverb is the addition of an adverb of manner, *luflice*, which seems rather redundant, as does the phrase *on lande*—in parallel to *on leode*. It should be noted, though, that both extrametrical verbal elements increase the alliterative ring of the phrase. It might very well be that in multiplying the alliterations the author wanted to add authority to his claim that legal customs vary according to place.

We return to safer ground with a proverb quoted in the laws attributed to Edward the Confessor. They were composed in Latin in the middle of the twelfth century but dated by the author to c. 1070, when allegedly they were related to William the

---

39 Neither phrase was recognized as a proverb by Lieberman, *Gesetze*.

40 E.g., Henry R. Loyn, *Anglo-Saxon England and the Norman Conquest*, 2nd edn. (London: Longman, 1991), 200; Kemp Malone and Albert C. Baugh, *The Middle Ages*, 2nd edn. A Literary History of England, vol. 1 (London: Routledge & Kegan Paul, 1967), 37.

41 Michael J. Swanton, *Anglo-Saxon Prose* (London: Dent, 1975), 28-30.

Conqueror by "English nobles who were wise men and learned in the law."[42] The claim of an English oral origin explains, perhaps, why the text occasionally slips into late Old English / early Middle English. This is the case in a passage that stipulates the fines to be paid to the king or the archbishop when one of their freemen has been killed. The wergild must be settled with the relatives. Should reconciliation fail to be achieved, revenge will be the inevitable outcome, a conclusion which is underscored *in expressis verbis* with a proverb:

> Manbote in Danelaga de uillano et sokeman xii ornas, de liberis hominibus xl solidi. Manbote in lege Anglorum regi et archiepiscopo xl solidi de liberis hominibus. Emendationem faciat parentibus uel guerram patiantur, unde Angli prouerbium habebant: "***Bugge** spere of side* ođđe ***bere***," quod est dicendum: "Lanceam eme de latere uel fer eam." [ECf 12.4-6][43]

> The fine in the Danelaw for a villager and tenant [is] 12 ore, for freemen 40 solidi. The fine in the law of the English for a king and an archbishop [is] 40 solidi for freemen. Let him (the perpetrator) either make amends with the relatives or suffer revenge. Hence the English had a proverb: "*Bugge spere of side ođđe bere*," that is to say "Buy the spear from their side or carry it."

Compensation, whether in cash or in kind, will make the relatives of the victim put down their spears; if not, you must be prepared to use yours. Note the imperative mood and the presence of alliteration that are indicative of the phrase's proverbiality. Above all, it is by using the word *prouerbium* that the legislator shows his full awareness of the generic nature of the vernacular phrase. What more evidence is needed? Incidentally, it should be noted that the author uses the past tense (*habebat*), as if he, at the time of writing, is dissociating himself from the Anglo-Saxon (vernacular) past.

Finally, in the Latin laws of Henry I, dating to c. 1125, a passage deals with injuries, even fatal ones, that were inflicted unintentionally. So even though there is no guilt, compensation should still be paid for the victim, a claim that is justified by adducing a proverb that is given the status of a legal rule: *Legis enim est: qui inscienter peccat, scienter emendet, et qui brecht ungewaldes, betan gewealdes.* ("For it is a rule of law that a person who unwittingly commits a wrong shall wittingly make amends, and "he who unintentionally breaks the law, must compensate intentionally").[44] Alliteration is

---

[42] Bruce R. O'Brien, *God's Peace and King's Peace: The Laws of Edward the Confessor* (Philadelphia: University of Pennsylvania Press, 1999), 3.

[43] O'Brien, *God's Peace and King's Peace*, 170-1. Identified as a proverb by Lieberman, *Gesetze*, II, s.v. *spere*.

[44] L.J. Downer, ed. and trans., *Leges Henrici Primi* (Oxford: Clarendon Press, 1972), 90.11a (pp. 282-3); identified as a proverb by Lieberman, *Gesetze*, II, s.v. *brecan* (col. 2). The same proverb, now only in Latin, is also quoted at 88, 6a (pp. 222-3): "Legis enim est, qui inscienter peccat, scienter emendet." The vernacular proverb also seems to underlie article 70, 12b: "Que enim per inscientiam peccamus, per industriam corrigamus" (For the wrongs which we commit unwittingly we must set right by deliberate intention).

present in the vernacular phrase as is repetition. The alliterative combination of *brecan* and *betan* is not original, for Archbishop Wulfstan also used it in his famous *Sermo Lupi*: *we ær þysan oftor bræcan þonne we bettan* ("before this time we more often broke the law than we amended it").[45] The combination of the adverbs *gewaldes* and *ungewealdes* is also found in King Alfred's translation of Gregory's *Regula pastoralis* as well as in a homily attributed to Wulfstan.[46] In other words, the phrase is evidently made up of traditional elements and hence exhales an authority that befits a proverb. The conclusion must therefore be drawn that the vernacular version preceded the Latin one. Furthermore, it bears pointing out that the legislator equates a proverb with a rule of law, an equation that will have been triggered by the imperative infinitive in the vernacular version, as I explained in my introduction. Finally, the conjunction *enim* "for, because," that is used serves the same function as its vernacular counterpart.[47]

Surveying my harvest, the rather extensive corpus of Anglo-Saxon laws contains a mere six, possibly seven, vernacular proverbs. This is admittedly more than the one about the axe that Grimm had identified, but significantly fewer than, for example, those found in the much smaller and later corpus of Frisian laws. Why would this be? Does it suggest that the bulk of Anglo-Saxon legal discourse was not rooted in a popular culture that was still vibrant with features of primary orality? As I have shown in each instance a proverb in the laws is introduced by a causal conjunction, "for," "because." This is because the purpose of their being quoted in all cases is to lend authority to the rule just given. By appealing to common, traditional wisdom, the legislator invites his intended audience to accept the rule he has just stipulated for the full one hundred percent.

Now an important difference between the Anglo-Saxon laws and the Frisian ones is that the latter were drafted by wise men, selected from the assembly of land-owning peasants. Proverbs, as expressions of experienced popular wisdom, were quoted to promote general acceptance of the legal rules enunciated. Most Anglo-Saxon laws, in

---

45 Bethurum, *The Homilies of Wulfstan*, XX, l. 53 (p. 269); cf. *ibid.* XV, ll. 44-5.

46 Henry Sweet, *King Alfred's West-Saxon Version of Gregory's Pastoral Care*, EETS os 45, 50 (London: Oxford University Press, 1871-72), 199, l. 22 (Hatton variant) and Arthur S. Napier, *Wulfstan. Sammlung der ihm zugeschriebenen Homilien*. (Berlin: Weidmann, 1883), 135, l. 30.

47 The frequent appeal in the *Leges Henrici* to the proverb might indicate a growing influence of the legal maxim (variously called *brocarda*, *regula iuris* or *generale*) as found in high medieval treatises of canon law. A discussion of this aspect falls outside the frame of my paper, however. For a succinct account, see Paul Hyams. "Due Process versus the Maintenance of Order in European Law: The Contribution of the *ius communis*," in *The Moral World of the Law*, ed. Peter Coss (Cambridge: Cambridge University Press, 1999), 86-90; on the use of aphorisms in the *Leges*, see Robert L. Keyser, "Agreement Supersedes Law, and Love Judgment:" Legal Flexibility and Amicable Settlement in Anglo-Norman England," *Law and History Review* 30.1 (2012): 37-88.

contrast to the Frisian ones, were issued by kings, often provided by prologues that profiled their legislative powers, an authority that was absent from the Frisian laws. In other words, popular communal wisdom was not really required in Anglo-Saxon laws to lend support to a given rule. Viewed in this light, it is the more remarkable that occasionally a proverb was adduced in order to make a rule acceptable. But then, we all know that blood is thicker than water.

The Cuckhamsley Chirograph

Simon Keynes

It is easy to get the impression from a reading of selected entries in the *Anglo-Saxon Chronicle* that the tenth-century successors of King Alfred the Great pursued and in due course achieved the realization of his political vision: the transformation, against the odds, of the ancient "kingdom of the West Saxons," by one stage after another, into a "kingdom of the English," which itself came by the end of the century to be regarded as a kingdom of "England." The political unification on the surface was real enough, and all that sustained it, reaching across the country, impressive for its time; but much was imposed from above, and the underlying apparatus was barely sufficient to hold it all together in times of stress.

The documentary records which survive from Anglo-Saxon England provide the basis for deeper understanding of all that can be learnt about the period from the available "narrative" sources. Law-codes and royal diplomas, for the most part representing the products of royal assemblies, form the most obviously significant part of this evidence.[1] The surviving charters in the vernacular complement the royal diplomas. They are less formal, more varied in their content, and suffused with circumstantial as well as personal information—throwing light in places that other sources cannot reach. The corpus of charters in the vernacular comprises over 300 texts, ranging in date from the early ninth century to the Norman Conquest (and beyond), and embracing a variety of documentary forms, including records of grants, agreements, leases, and wills, as well as the series of royal writs in the names of Cnut, Edward the Confessor, and Harold. The earliest surviving examples, from Kent and Mercia, date from the early ninth century; it is also from the ninth century that we have evidence for the increasingly widespread (and latterly more disciplined) use of the vernacular on the more formal diplomas in Latin, for boundary-clauses and for other notes added on face and dorse. The extent to which documents in the vernacular came to proliferate, in the tenth and eleventh centuries, is without question an important aspect of the story of the emergence across this period of a versatile and

[1] For Kentish legislation in the seventh century, and the advantage taken by King Æthelberht and his successors of the technology of the written word, see Oliver, *Beginnings*, esp. 18-20.

dynamic documentary culture, as befitted the (seemingly) "unified" kingdom of the English.[2]

If one works systematically through the surviving corpus as a whole, taking all due account of whatever can be added to it from Latin abstracts or translations of vernacular documents which no longer exist in their original form, and bearing in mind how much *more* has been lost, and that some part of what survives was fabricated (before or after the Conquest), one gains a sense of the place that any one document, or group of documents, occupies in the wider context.[3] The corpus can be broken down into five groups, each defined by the nature of the document itself. The first group comprises "royal" charters; many of these prove on closer inspection to be spurious in one sense or another, though a few are seemingly authentic in this form, and for that reason of special interest. The second comprises vernacular records of "private" (non-royal) transactions or agreements, in many cases drawn up at local courts or assemblies, although also at royal assemblies. The third group comprises the well-known and extensively analyzed series of Anglo-Saxon wills, including the wills of King Alfred and King Eadred, though also extending deeper into lay society. The fourth comprises leases of estates by bishops, and other land-owners, to other parties, on specified terms; in this case, the examples in English are complemented by examples in Latin, and by examples making use of both languages. The fifth group comprises the relatively small number of documents which appear to have been drawn up in connection with litigation, and which are of special interest for the light they throw on the maintenance of law and order among the English in the tenth and eleventh centuries.

My concern for present purposes is solely with the fifth group (summarized in Fig. 1), which comprises records generated by the processes of litigation, here further divided

[2] The Latin and vernacular texts included in *The Crawford Collection of Early Charters and Documents now in the Bodleian Library*, ed. A. S. Napier and W. H. Stevenson (Oxford: Clarendon, 1895), set the standards which have guided subsequent scholarship. The greater part of the corpus of charters in the vernacular, with translations and commentary, are accessible in one or other of three volumes: *Select English Historical Documents of the Ninth and Tenth Centuries*, ed. F. E. Harmer (Cambridge: Cambridge University Press, 1914); *Anglo-Saxon Wills*, ed. Dorothy Whitelock (Cambridge: Cambridge University Press, 1930); and *Anglo-Saxon Charters*, ed. A. J. Robertson (Cambridge University Press: Cambridge, 1939), 2nd ed. (1956). These three volumes have been reprinted in paperback (Cambridge University Press, 2009-11), with some additional material. They are complemented by *Anglo-Saxon Writs*, ed. F. E. Harmer (Manchester: Manchester University Press, 1952), reprinted (Stamford, 1989).

[3] A survey of the corpus as a whole formed the basis of Simon Keynes, "Anglo-Saxon charters in the vernacular," given as a Robertson Memorial Lecture, University of Aberdeen, in 2009, with a classified list, publication of which is forthcoming. For the conventions used in citation of particular charters, see Simon Keynes, "Church Councils, Royal Assemblies, and Anglo-Saxon Royal Diplomas," *Kingship, Legislation and Power in Anglo-Saxon England*, ed. G. R. Owen-Crocker and B. W. Schneider (Woodbridge: Boydell, 2013), 17-182, at 180-2.

into three sub-groups (a-c). Sub-group (a) comprises five letters or formal declarations in writing addressed by one "interested" party to another. Letters in *Latin* were commonplace at high levels, to an extent most clearly suggested (for the tenth century) by the varied contents of the "Canterbury Letter-Book."[4] The surviving documents in this sub-group, however, are in English, perhaps the chance survivals of a once much larger body of material. The "Fonthill Letter," directed by Ealdorman Ordlaf to King Edward the Elder (*c.* 920) for use in litigation about land in Wiltshire, is a potent symbol of what could be represented as the "Alfredian" legacy underlying the documentary culture of the tenth and eleventh centuries; the key points being that the letter was addressed by a layman to the king, and that a record of the *outcome* of the lawsuit was added on the dorse, by a different hand, indicating that the letter itself had served its purpose.[5] The "Cooling Letter," directed by Queen Eadgifu to Archbishop Dunstan and the community of Christ Church, Canterbury, was evidently intended to protect their title to land at Cooling in Kent, probably in the 960s, against any challenge that might arise in the future.[6] A letter from Archbishop Dunstan to King Æthelred, in the 980s, describes the circumstances in which three estates in Cornwall had formerly been assigned to the bishop of Sherborne, and explains why in his view they should now be assigned to the bishop of Cornwall.[7] The "Ruishton Letter," directed by Ælfthryth, mother of King Æthelred, to Archbishop Ælfric and Ealdorman Æthelweard, concerns an estate at Ruishton in Somerset (995 x ?998).[8] Finally, a letter directed by Æthelric, bishop of Sherborne, to a certain Æthelmær (*c.* 1010), reports a loss of revenue in respect of ship-scot, evidently seeking action or redress.[9] The first three of these five

4 The principal witness is BL Cotton Tiberius A. xv, for which see *Memorials of Saint Dunstan*, ed. William Stubbs (London: Longman, 1874), 354-404. The collection was put together at Canterbury in the late tenth century; similar collections may have existed elsewhere, which have not chanced to survive.

5 S 1445 (*CantCC* 104), in *Select EHD*, ed. Harmer, no. 18, with Simon Keynes, "The Fonthill Letter," *Words, Texts and Manuscripts*, ed. Michael Korhammer (Cambridge: Cambridge University Press, 1992), 53-97, at 55.

6 S 1211 (*CantCC* 124), in *Select EHD*, ed. Harmer, no. 23, with *The Golden Age of Anglo-Saxon Art 966-1066*, ed. Janet Backhouse, *et al.* (Bloomington: Indiana University Press, 1984), 164. The circumstances as described by Eadgifu, who had suffered loss of her estates in the reign of King Eadwig (955-959), gave particular cause for concern, and the title-deeds might not have been considered enough to ensure security of tenure.

7 S 1296 (*Exet*), in *Crawford Charters*, ed. Napier and Stevenson, no. 7, with *Facsimiles of Anglo-Saxon Charters*, ed. Simon Keynes (Oxford: Oxford University Press, 1991), no. 8. See also *Councils & Synods*, ed. Whitelock, 169-73 (no. 35/II).

8 S 1242 (*WinchOM*), in *AS Writs*, ed. Harmer, no. 108, preserved in the twelfth-century *Codex Wintoniensis*. See also Andrew Rabin, "Anglo-Saxon Women Before the Law: A Student Edition of Five Old English Lawsuits," *Old English Newsletter* 41.3 (2008), no. 4.

9 S 1383 (*Sherb* 13), in *AS Writs*, ed. Harmer, no. 63. For Æthelmær, son of Ealdorman Æthelweard, see *ibid.*, 553, with Keynes, *Diplomas*, 198-9 n. 163 and 209-10.

letters survive in single-sheet form, preserved in appropriate archival contexts; the fourth as a copy, in a twelfth-century cartulary, also in an appropriate context; and the fifth, most interestingly, as a copy entered in a contemporary hand at the back of the Sherborne Pontifical, as if retained for the record.

Sub-group (b) comprises five impersonal or "institutional" statements about the history of particular estates, prepared for the record or for use in litigation. The "Sunbury Statement," on the history of estates at Sunbury and Send, in Middlesex, is connected with a dispute over Westminster abbey's ownership of Sunbury in the 980s.[10] The "Bromley Statement," on the history of an estate at Bromley, in Kent, was drawn up at much the same time, when the bishop of Rochester (Ælfstan or Godwine) was trying to recover the land for the see of Rochester.[11] The "Wouldham Statement," on the history of an estate at Wouldham, in Kent, was prepared for litigation in the 990s, when Bishop Godwine was trying to recover the estate for the see of Rochester.[12] The "Sandwich Statement," featuring King Harold Harefoot, was drawn up in connection with measures taken by the monks of Canterbury to protect their interests at Sandwich, Kent, in the 1040s.[13] Of these, three survive in their original single-sheet form, and the fourth as a later cartulary copy.

Sub-group (c) comprises seven records of the *settlement* of disputes. Significantly (and most appropriately), five of the seven were drawn up as chirographs, on the occasion of the settlement itself, and the component parts entrusted to the parties concerned. Pride of place belongs to the "Cuckhamsley Chirograph," issued from a shire-meeting (*scirgemot*) for Berkshire held at Cuckhamsley in the early 990s.[14] From the same decade is a document which may be called the "Cookham Chirograph," also preserved in its original single-sheet form: drawn up at a royal assembly held at Cookham, on the Thames, in the late 990s.[15] From the same period comes the "Snodland Settlement" (preserved only in a cartulary), which records a settlement (*loc*, or *foreword*) reached in a shire-meeting for Kent, convened at Canterbury under Ælfric, archbishop of Canterbury

[10] S 1447 (*West*), in *AS Charters*, ed. Robertson, no. 44, from a contemporary single sheet.

[11] S 1457 (*Roch* 36), in *AS Charters*, ed. Robertson, no. 59, from a copy in the Textus Roffensis. For discussion, see Simon Keynes, "King Æthelred the Unready and the Church of Rochester," *Textus Roffensis: Law, Language, and Libraries in Early Medieval England*, ed. Bruce O'Brien and Barbara Bombi (Turnhout: Brepols, 2015), 315-62, at 324-5, 333-4 and 343-4.

[12] S 1458 (*Roch* 34), in *AS Charters*, ed. Robertson, no. 41, from a contemporary single sheet. For discussion, see Keynes, "King Æthelred and Rochester," 325-7, 334 and 337-8.

[13] S 1467 (*CantCC* 164), in *AS Charters*, ed. Robertson, no. 91, from a contemporary single sheet.

[14] S 1454 (*CantCC* 133) in *AS Charters*, ed. Robertson, no. 66. See also Rabin, "Anglo-Saxon Women," no. 3.

[15] S 939 (*CantCC* 137), in *AS Wills*, ed. Whitelock, no. 16. ii. For further discussion, see N. Brooks, "Treason in Essex in the 990s: The Case of Æthelric of Bocking," *Royal Authority in Anglo-Saxon England*, ed. G. R. Owen-Crocker and B. W. Schneider, BAR British Series 584 (Oxford, 2013), 17-27. Below, n. 64.

(995-1005).[16] The four other settlements takes us further into the eleventh century. The settlement of a lawsuit over land at Inkberrow in Worcestershire was agreed at a shire-meeting at Worcester, and set down there as a chirograph (1016 × 1023).[17] A record of a law-suit heard at a shire-meeting for Herefordshire was made (most interestingly) not in single-sheet form but by entry in a gospel-book at the see of Hereford (1016 × 1035).[18] The settlement of a dispute between St Augustine's abbey, Canterbury, and a priest called Leofwine, was brokered by Earl Godwine, probably at Canterbury, also set down as a chirograph (1044 × 1045).[19] The settlement of a dispute between Ælfwold (bishop of Sherborne), with Sherborne abbey, and a certain Care, son of Toki, over land at Holcombe (Rogus), in Devon, again brokered by Earl Godwine, was set down as a chirograph in a shire-meeting at Exeter (1045 × 1046).[20]

It emerges that the document here called the "Cuckhamsley Chirograph" is the earliest surviving example of a vernacular charter which originated as a formal record of the settlement of a dispute, representing in this respect a significance advance on the note added to the dorse of the "Fonthill Letter." It is interesting that the earliest should come so late in the tenth century. It could be no more than a hazard of survival; or it may be that there was heightened awareness by this stage of the need to keep better records, in the interests of all concerned.

The Proceedings at Cuckhamsley (990 × 993)

As the pre-Conquest forms of its name suggest, Cuckhamsley (*æt Cwicelmeshlæwe*), on the Ridgeway as it passes through the parish of East Hendred, Berkshire (now Oxfordshire), has long been renowned as the place where a certain Cwichelm was buried, in a mound.[21] The person in question is likely to have been Cwichelm, son of Cynegils, king of the West Saxons (611-41), who features in Bede's *Historia ecclesiastica gentis Anglorum* (ii. 9) as a king, in his own right, who had sent an assassin to deprive Edwin,

---

16 S 1456 (*Roch* 37), in *AS Charters*, ed. Robertson, no. 69, from the *Textus Roffensis*. For discussion and further references, see Keynes, "King Æthelred and Rochester," 333-5 and 341-3 (with observations on its form in the cartulary, which may have raised it above a chirograph).

17 S 1460 (*Worc*), in *AS Charters*, ed. Robertson, no. 83.

18 S 1462, in *AS Charters*, ed. Robertson, no. 78.

19 S 1472 (*CantCC* 169), in *AS Charters*, ed. Robertson, no. 102.

20 S 1474 (*Sherb* 17), in *AS Charters*, ed. Robertson, no. 105.

21 M. Gelling, *The Place-Names of Berkshire*, 3 pts, EPNS 49-51 (Cambridge: Cambridge University Press, 1974-5), pt 2, 481-2. The Ridgeway runs roughly from Avebury in the west, up along the line of the Berkshire Downs (known formerly as "Ashdown": *ibid.*, pt 1, 2-4) past Uffington, Wantage, Cholsey and Wallingford, before heading up along the Chiltern Hills towards Aylesbury and the Icknield Way.

king of the Northumbrians, of his kingdom and his life; and who features also, in the *Anglo-Saxon Chronicle*, as one who had fought alongside his father against the Britons in 614, against the Mercians in 628, and who was baptised, and then died, in 636. It was an impressive record of belligerence, even for a West Saxon.[22] Perhaps the mound had needed a suitable identity, and no doubt Cwichelm was considered worthy of such a resting-place. Whatever the case, the truth would have been far more complicated.[23] It is likely, furthermore, that already by the end of the ninth century "Cwichelm's Barrow" had become a meeting-place for the shire in which it lay.[24] It long remained a prominent feature of the landscape: clearly identified, for example, on John Speed's map of Berkshire (1612), and conspicuous also on the fine historical map devised by Edmund Gibson to accompany his edition of the Anglo-Saxon Chronicle (1692).[25] Indeed, it remains a distinctive feature to this day. One can well believe, therefore, that in 1006, when the Danish army was "lighting its beacons" as it moved up the Thames from Reading towards Wallingford, and then headed west along "Ashdown" towards Cwichelm's Barrow, some among the English were boasting of what lay in store: that if the Danes went to Cuckhamsley, "they would never get to the sea." It was a place, in other words, with associations which raised expectations; according to the chronicler, the Danes went there, waited awhile to see what might happen, and then repaired to their ships by another route.[26]

---

[22] We need not take seriously the statement, which seems to have originated at St Albans in the thirteenth century, that King Edwin (d. 633) contrived to have Cwichelm killed, at the place where he was then laid to rest; see W. H. Stevenson, *Asser's Life of King Alfred* (Oxford: Oxford University Press, 1904), 234-8.

[23] For the Bronze Age tumulus on Cuckhamsley Hill, known also as Skutchamer Knob, in its archaeological and historical contexts as a place of assembly, see Sarah Semple, *Perceptions of the Prehistoric in Anglo-Saxon England: Religion, Ritual, and Rulership in the Landscape* (Oxford: Oxford University Press, 2013), 1-2 and 216-17, with further references.

[24] For references to "Berkshire" in the late ninth century, see the *Anglo-Saxon Chronicle*, s.a. 860, and Asser's *Life of King Alfred*, ch. 1.

[25] J. Speed, *Theatre of the Empire of Great Britain* (1612), with J. Speed, *Britain's Tudor Maps County by County* (London: Batsford, 2016), 24-5; and E. Gibson, *Chronicon Saxonicum* (Oxford, 1692), before the gazeteer of place-names at the end, illustrated in Simon Keynes, "Mapping the Anglo-Saxon Past," *Towns and Topography: Essays in Memory of David H. Hill*, ed. G. R. Owen-Crocker and S. D. Thompson (Oxford: Oxbow, 2014), 147-70, at 162.

[26] ASC C s.a. 1006. For discussion, see Ryan Lavelle, *Æthelred II King of the English 978-1016* (Stroud: Tempus, 2002), 108-11; *Alfred's Wars: Sources and Interpretations of Anglo-Saxon Warfare in the Viking Age* (Woodbridge: Boydell, 2010), 32-4 (boasts) and 222-4 (beacons); and "Royal Control and the Disposition of Estates in Tenth-Century England: Reflections on the Charters of King Eadwig (955-959)," *Haskins Soc. Jnl* 23 (2014): 23-49, at 39-40; with T. J. T. Williams, "Landscape and Warfare in Anglo-Saxon England and the Viking Campaign of 1006," *Early Medieval Europe* 23 (2015): 329-59, at 352-5; and Levi Roach, *Æthelred the Unready* (New Haven: Yale University Press, 2016), 217-18.

The "Cuckhamsley Chirograph" draws us into the midst of this story.[27] It belongs to the small corpus of vernacular charters which illustrate the operation of legal processes in Anglo-Saxon England, giving an account of proceedings at a meeting of the shire-court of Berkshire held at Cuckhamsley in the early 990s. A dispute had arisen between a certain Leofwine and a certain Wynflæd about the ownership of land at Hagbourne (near Wallingford) and Bradfield (near Reading), in Berkshire. The early stages of the story are not known, but if only to judge from what is reported of the later stages, it seems that the two estates in Berkshire had belonged formerly to Leofwine's father Ælfric; that Ælfric had given them to Wynflæd in exchange for her land at Datchet, in Buckinghamshire; and that Ælfric had also given her a certain amount of gold and silver, whether as part of the same arrangement or in some other connection. As his father's son, Leofwine would have had his own interest in the estates, and seems recently to have taken possession of them—an act regarded (in this record) as one of *reaflac*, or robbery. When we join the story, the two estates were in Leofwine's hands; Wynflæd was still in possession of a quantity of gold and silver which had belonged to Leofwine's father; and she was intent upon the recovery of her land. On the occasion of an assembly which took place at the royal estate at Woolmer, in Hampshire, Wynflæd nominated four witnesses (Sigeric, archbishop of Canterbury [990-4]; Ordbriht, bishop of Selsey [*c.* 988-*c.* 1009]; Ælfric, ealdorman of the "Winchester" districts [982-1016];[28] and Ælfthryth, the king's mother [d. *c.* 1002]), who affirmed that she had received the two estates in question from Ælfric (son of Leofwine), in exchange for land at Datchet in Buckinghamshire.[29] One can judge simply from the status of her supporters that Wynflæd was very well connected, and this would have been an early stage in her attempt to recover the estates. The king made known the development to Leofwine himself, through the agency of Archbishop Sigeric and the other witnesses. Doubtless aware of the appropriate procedure in such cases, Leofwine was able to insist that the matter should be referred to a shire-meeting (*to scirgemote*), where his own interests might be better respected.[30] When

[27] S 1454 (*CantCC* 133), edited with translation in *Anglo-Saxon Charters*, ed. Robertson, 136-40 and 379-82 (no. 66), and most recently in *Charters of Christ Church Canterbury*, ed. N. P. Brooks and S. E. Kelly, 2 vols. (Oxford: Oxford University Press, 2013), II, 987-93 (no. 133), with translation and commentary.

[28] For the style "Wentaniensium prouinciarum dux," accorded to Ælfric in a diploma dated 997, from the Old Minster, Winchester, see the discussion of S 891 (KCD 698) below, p. 000.

[29] In the absence of information on the configuration of the estates in the late tenth century, one can but note that in 1066, Bradfield (a few miles west of Reading) was assessed at 9 hides, worth £24, and East and West Hagbourne (further north, a few miles west of Wallingford) were assessed at 15 + 10 = 25 hides, worth £15 + £13 = £28; Datchet, Bucks, was assessed at 13½ hides, worth £12. On the face of it, Wynflæd had the better deal; though much might have changed.

[30] The principle that one should seek justice in the first instance from a local court, and only after that from the king, is implicit in *III Eg.* 2; for later formulations of the principle, see *II Cn.*17 and 19.

the time came, the king "sent his seal, by means of Abbot Ælfhere (of Bath), to the assembly at Cuckhamsley," and greeted all the counsellors who were assembled there, namely Bishop Æthelsige (of Sherborne), Bishop Æscwig (of Dorchester), Abbot Ælfric (probably of Malmesbury), "and all the shire," and ordered them to "reconcile" Wynflæd and Leofwine, "as justly as seemed to them forever most just" (*swa rihtlice geseman swa him æfre rihtlicost þuhte*). The combination of names establishes a date for this shire-assembly in the early 990s (990 × 993).[31] No ealdorman is mentioned as present, suggesting perhaps that none charged with responsibility over Berkshire was in office at the time, and that the secular order was covered none the less by the expression "all the shire," which included Ælfgar, the king's reeve. As a witness to Wynflæd's acquisition of the two estates, Archbishop Sigeric had sent his own declaration (*swutelung*) to the shire-court, presumably in writing, and so too had Bishop Ordbriht. At the meeting itself, Wynflæd made her claim to the disputed lands; and with the particular support of (Queen) Ælfthryth, of an unspecified kind, she was authorised to proceed to her declaration of ownership (*ahnung*).[32] A total of twenty-four men and women are specifically identified in this connection, comprising Abbot Wulfgar (of Abingdon), Wulfstan the priest, Æfic the athelings' discthegn, and eight other men, together with Abbess Eadgifu (of the Nunnaminster, Winchester), Abbess Liofrun (of Reading) and Eadgifu "of Lewknor," and ten other women, as well as "many a good thegn and good lady" who are not named, making a total which must have exceeded thirty. The mention of Wulfgar, abbot of Abingdon (990-1016), in first place, shows again that Wynflæd moved in high circles; the prominence accorded to the priest Wulfstan in such company, in second place, raises the question whether this might have been the Wulfstan appointed bishop of London in 996 (and translated to York in 1002); and the inclusion of Æfic, described as the ætheling's dish-thegn, in third place, reinforces further the sense of a connection to the king and his immediate family.[33] Wynflæd was able in this

[31] The meeting took place after the appointment of Sigeric as archbishop in early 990, and after Wulfgar had succeeded Eadwine as abbot of Abingdon (in the same year). Sigeric's translation to Canterbury had created a vacancy at Ramsbury, and it seems that Æthelsige bishop of Sherborne, and Æscwig, bishop of Dorchester, were providing cover. The vacancy at Ramsbury had been filled, *by* the summer of 993 (S 876), by Ælfric, abbot of St Albans; the Abbot Ælfric who attended the assembly at Cuckhamsley was probably the abbot of Malmesbury, though he might have been Ælfric of St Albans, if by then the prospective bishop of Ramsbury (Brooks and Kelly, *Charters of Christ Church Canterbury*, 991). Bishop Æthelsige was not succeeded at Sherborne until the appointment of Wulfsige in the summer of 993 (S 876).

[32] For *ahnung* as one of the three modes of proof granted to all people (though not allowed to the bishop of Rochester in the late 970s), see S 1457 (*Roch* 36), from the 980s, in *Anglo-Saxon Charters*, ed. Robertson, 122-4 and 365-7 (no. 59), discussed in Simon Keynes, "King Æthelred the Unready and the Church of Rochester," *Textus Roffensis: Law, Language, and Libraries in Early Medieval England,* 315-62, at 324-5 and 329-36.

[33] For Queen Ælfthryth and the athelings, see Keynes, *Diplomas of King Æthelred*, 187, with nn. 115-18; *Atlas of Attestations*, table lix; and Andrew Rabin, "Female Advocacy and Royal Protection in Tenth-Century

way to produce the number required, "including both men and women" (*ge of werum ge of wifum*). At this stage the *witan*, in their wisdom, declared that it would be better to set the oath aside than for it to be sworn, so that "friendship" could be maintained between the two parties, and further (more serious) consequences averted.[34] Accordingly, Leofwine handed the land over to Bishop Æthelsige (of Sherborne), presumably by surrendering the title-deeds, and abandoned his claim. At this point, Wynflæd was instructed to bring all that she had of Leofwine's father's gold and silver. She did so; but Leofwine, evidently aggrieved by the turn of events, refused to accept that all the money was there, and Wynflæd was seemingly evasive. The witnesses for this aspect of the matter are named as Ælfgar "the king's reeve," Byrhtric, and Leofric of Whitchurch,[35] and "many good men beside him." It is conceivable that all of this took place on one and the same day; it may be, however, that Wynflæd's production of the money (in response to a request which might not have been foreseen) took place a day or two later, after the main company had dispersed, and that while the surviving chirograph was drawn up in respect of the shire-assembly at Cuckhamsley, it served also as a record of an extension to that event.

It should be noted that the copy of the chirograph which has survived was preserved among the muniments of Christ Church, Canterbury. It seems, therefore, that if one copy had been given to Wynflæd herself, another (probably *the* other) copy had passed to Archbishop Sigeric.[36] One is reminded of the case of the Fonthill Letter, which also survives from the archives of Christ Church, Canterbury. The evidence is slight; but perhaps there was sometimes reason for the archbishop, or his representative, to take custody of such a document by virtue of his office, and perhaps on behalf of the king.

England: The Legal Career of Queen Ælfthryth," *Speculum* 84 (2009): 261-88. The athelings make their first "public" appearance in the witness-list of King Æthelred's diploma for Abingdon, in the summer of 993; see S 876 (*Abing* 124). In his will, drawn up in June 1014, Æthelstan thanked Ælfthryth, who had brought him up; see S 1503 (*CantCC* 142). The Æfic who served the athelings in the early 990s (designated "Æfic 1" in the online *Prosopography of Anglo-Saxon England*) was possibly the king's "high-reeve," "Æfic 2," killed by Ealdorman Leofsige in 1002, and the "Æfic 3" whose brother Eadric was killed in 1010. See also n. 44.

[34] For payment of a man's wergild to the king, as the highest penalty payable for any offence which was commutable in such a way, see: *III Eg*. 2.2; *III Atr*. 1; and *II Cn*. 63.

[35] Leofric of Whitchurch was evidently the Leofric, former owner of Whitchurch, Oxon., who by 1012 had forfeited his property for acts of treachery and other wrongdoing; see S 927 (*Abing* 136), with Keynes, *Diplomas of King Æthelred*, 97 and 265 (spurious), and "Crime and Punishment in the Reign of King Æthelred the Unready," *People and Places in Northern Europe 500-1600*, ed. Ian Wood and Neils Lund (Woodbridge: Boydell, 1991), 67-81, at 77-8. The "Leofric of Whitchurch" killed in 1001 (ASC 1001A) was probably a different person, holding Whitchurch, Hants.

[36] Brooks and Kelly, *Charters of Christ Church Canterbury*, 987-93 (no. 133), with Wormald, *Making*, 152 n. 118.

The Cuckhamsley Chirograph as a Historical Record

Had the Cuckhamsley Chirograph been an extended annal in the *Anglo-Saxon Chronicle*, it would have been read, and studied intensively, as a record of Æthelred's government in action, from the early 990s, providing an example of how the king at the center communicated his will, by means of his accredited agents, to those gathered at assemblies in the shires, and of how justice was done. Even as a legal instrument, it has long attracted attention. John Mitchell Kemble, writing in the late 1840s, identified the meeting-place, and fastened on Leofwine's insistence, against the king's will, that the case should be heard in the appropriate shire-court.[37] In 1935, J. E. A. Jolliffe took the view (because no title-deeds are mentioned) that the land involved must have been folkland; that for this reason the matter was heard before the shire-court; leaving intact a presumption that disputes over bookland were heard before the king.[38] In 1939 A. J. Robertson provided the first modern text and translation, with commentary serving to locate the action firmly in its appropriate contexts.[39] In 1985 Alan Kennedy took issue with Jolliffe's position, drawing on his own command of a wide range of evidence for the operation of Anglo-Saxon law, and establishing the key point that in the later tenth and eleventh centuries disputes over bookland were often heard before shire-courts.[40] Five years later Arnold Baines accorded the document the singular distinction of a commemoration of its millennium.[41] In a paper first published in 1997, Patrick Wormald showed how the story of Wynflæd and Leofwine animated our understanding of the operation of Anglo-Saxon law as represented by the (surviving) law-codes. He took the view that Leofwine's father, who had given gold and silver to Wynflæd, was the Ælfric with whom she had made the exchange of lands, perhaps as part of a marriage agreement, and suggested that Leofwine was a son of Ælfric by a former marriage. He remarked on the number and identity of Wynflæd's oath-helpers; on the apparently close connection between Wynflæd and Ælfthryth (the king's mother), and through her with the athelings, which might have weighted the scales in her favor; and on the possibility that the report itself, given its preservation at Canterbury, "might be less impartial than at first appears" (given Sigeric's role on Wynflæd's behalf). He stressed its value as evidence of the

[37] J. M. Kemble, *The Saxons in England*, 2 vols. (London, 1849), II. 46-9.

[38] J. E. A. Jolliffe, "English Book-Right," *EHR* 50 (1935): 1-21, at 17-18.

[39] *Anglo-Saxon Charters*, ed. Robertson, 136-9 and 379-82.

[40] A. G. Kennedy, "Disputes about "bocland": The Forum for their Adjudication," *Anglo-Saxon England* 14 (1985): 175-95, at 187-8.

[41] A. H. J. Baines, "Wynflæd v Leofwine: a Datchet Lawsuit of 990," *Records of Buckinghamshire* 32 (1990): 63-5. It has to be said that Baines's identification of Ælfric, putative father of Leofwine, as Ælfric, ealdorman of Hampshire, is hard to sustain. The identification flows from the second sentence, but is rendered improbable by the wider context.

implementation and operation of procedures set out in the law-codes, observing, quite rightly, that proceedings which took place in a shire-court were not taking place outside the sphere of the king's influence; and he drew attention to a respect in which the consequences envisaged for Leofwine, as an alleged perpetrator of *reaflac*, seem to anticipate a provision in Cnut's law-code.[42] In the first volume of his *Making of English Law: King Alfred to the Twelfth Century* (1999), comprising Parts I and II of the whole work, Wormald remarked further that the Wynflæd-Leofwine dispute would be "pivotal in Part III's account of the operation of early English law," no doubt along the lines he had sketched before, but one imagines along other lines as well.[43] Within the same context, Andrew Rabin has explored the role of Ælfthryth as advocate.[44] In their recent edition and translation of the text, Brooks and Kelly provide a comprehensive and measured discussion of the document in every respect, which now becomes the definitive treatment.[45]

In a subject area where evidence of any kind is precious, there is a danger that the commonplace and the unusual cannot easily be distinguished from each other. Royal diplomas, which are relatively plentiful, take us into the assemblies of the king and his counsellors, convened from time to time during the course of a year. The Cuckhamsley Chirograph, on the other hand, draws us into the heart of a shire assembly; and in this way it commands attention as a product of a documentary culture which drove and indeed animated King Æthelred's kingdom.[46] By the late tenth century use of the written word, in Latin and in the vernacular, was well embedded in the routine procedures of royal government, for purposes of communication between the center and the localities, and for purposes of report, publication, and record keeping. Here we encounter an

---

[42] Patrick Wormald, "Giving God and King their Due: Conflict and its Regulation in the Early English State" [1997], reptd in his *Legal Culture in the Early Medieval West* (London: Hambledon, 1999), 333-57, at 343-52 with 356-7. See also *idem*, "A Handlist of Anglo-Saxon Lawsuits" [1988], reptd in his *Legal Culture*, 253-87, at 285-6.

[43] Wormald, *Making*, 12-13 and 151-3; for the second volume of Wormald's work, which remained unfinished at the time of his death in 2004, see the "Early English Laws" website, and search under "Wynflæd." See also Patrick Wormald, "Germanic Power Structures: the Early English Experience," *Power and the Nation in European History*, ed. L. Scales and O. Zimmer (Cambridge: Cambridge University Press, 2005), 105-24, at 116 and 119-20.

[44] Andrew Rabin, "Anglo-Saxon Women," 33-56, at 44-6; "Female Advocacy," 273-8; and "Law and Justice," in *A Handbook of Anglo-Saxon Studies*, ed. Jacqueline Stodnick and Renee R. Trilling (Chichester: Wiley-Blackwell, 2012), 85-98, at 86-91.

[45] Brooks and Kelly, *Charters of Christ Church Canterbury*, 987-93 (no. 133). For more recent discussion, see Tom Lambert, *Law and Order in Anglo-Saxon England* (Oxford: Oxford University Press, 2017), 255-6 and 283.

[46] S. Keynes, "Royal Government and the Written Word in Late Anglo-Saxon England," 226-57, at 245-6 and 249-50.

approved representative of the king, who although recognizable to all as a distinguished abbot, brought with him an impression of the king's "seal," on which basis he was able formally to greet the assembled company on behalf of the king himself, and (perhaps reading from a document) to convey the king's wishes in respect of a particular matter in hand.[47] It is likely that this practice came at a stage in the development of the king's writ when a separate impression of a king's seal guaranteed the origin and authority of the message delivered, and before the seal came to be attached as a matter of course and convenience to the document itself. The chirograph was produced as a record of the settlement reached at the end of the process, at the shire-court, and is all the more important for precisely that reason.[48]

The wider historical context is also of interest. Far from its being a story of steady progression from division towards unification, or from discord towards harmony, the tenth century would be better characterized as a period of upheaval and change, driven by the conflicting or competing interests of those in positions of authority, or with control of resources, and affecting many others at lower levels of the various hierarchies. The death of King Edgar, in 975, had precipitated an outburst of disorder which in its complexity is still little understood, yet which was nothing if not intense, and widespread. The prevalence of disorder seems to have run through the reign of King Edward the Martyr (975-8), and into the early years of Æthelred's reign; and it was compounded further by disruption which followed the death of Æthelwold, bishop of Winchester, in 984. By *c.* 990, King Æthelred himself would have been in his early twenties, entering a period of his reign when the king and those around him took stock of their predicament.[49] Matters were exacerbated in 991 by the resumption of Viking raids on a significant scale, which if nothing else would have concentrated the collective mind, requiring a sustained response until such time as the threat seemed to have passed. We have no idea, alas, what might have been on the agenda when the king, Archbishop Sigeric and others had been together on the royal estate at Woolmer, in Hampshire,

[47] For further discussion, see S. Keynes, "The Use of Seals in Anglo-Saxon England," *Seals and Status: The Power of Objects*, ed. John Cherry, Jessica Berenbeim and Lloyd de Beer (London: Oxbow, 2018), 73-83. T. A. Heslop, "Seals and Sealing in England," *ibid.*, regards "seal" in this context as a "sealed letter," in other words a letter on a strip of parchment which had been folded, tied, and then sealed close, with an impression of the king's seal, which had then been broken so that its bearer could read it to the assembled company.

[48] For the emergence of shire-reeves and shire-courts, in the second half of the tenth century, see Keynes, *Diplomas of King Æthelred*, 197-8, with "Edgar, *rex admirabilis*," *Edgar, King of the English 959-75*, ed. Donald Scragg (Woodbridge: Boydell, 2008) 3-59, at 10-12; see also George Molyneaux, *The Formation of the English Kingdom in the Tenth Century* (Oxford: Oxford University Press, 2015), esp. 155-82.

[49] For the light thrown by Æthelred's diplomas on this period, see Keynes, *Diplomas of King Æthelred*, 193-200; "Re-Reading King Æthelred the Unready," *Writing Medieval Biography 750-1250*, ed. David Bates, *et al.* (Woodbridge: Boydell, 2006), 77-97, at 80-1 and 89-96; and "Councils, Assemblies, and Royal Diplomas," 102-26.

shortly before the shire assembly at Cuckhamsley; but it must have been one of many occasions when the larger issues were discussed, and decisions taken to impose order and make amends. We may imagine that every king, and every archbishop, would have been ever mindful of the three-fold oath sworn by a king on the occasion of his coronation, which in Æthelred's case had been administered by Archbishop Dunstan, on 4 May 979, at Kingston-upon-Thames. The existence of a vernacular version of the king's coronation oath, with an accompanying homily on the duties of a consecrated king, suggests strongly that during the course of his reign Æthelred would have been reminded of the oath he had sworn at Kingston, as a matter of course;[50] and we may assume that Dunstan's successors as archbishop, from Æthelgar and Sigeric onwards, would have taken their own responsibilities to heart.[51] The king had sworn first that the church and the Christian people would observe true peace; second, that he would forbid "acts of robbery and all unrighteous things (*rapacitates et omnes iniquitates* / *reaflac and ealle unrihte þing*)" to all orders; and third, that he would command justice and mercy in all judgements. Under the archbishop's influence, a king might well have been reminded regularly of the undertakings made on the day of his coronation. and reminded also that the continual application of these undertakings would help to ensure God's favor on the king and his people, especially in times of increasing trouble. It was the king's sacred duty to promote the conditions in which religious houses could prosper, and in which the people could live their lives in accordance with Christian teaching; it was imperative also that the king should deal resolutely with acts of *reaflac* (a generic term for the robbery or plundering of another person's property, extending from seizure of moveable goods to the seizure of land); and in every respect justice had to be seen to be done. The response in high circles is now familiar, and increasingly well understood. It found expression in the remarkable series of diplomas issued at royal assemblies from 993 onwards, in which the king took upon himself the misconduct of his youth, explaining that he had been led astray by those who should have known better, and seeking by display of contrition, and good works, to make due amends. Among the religious houses which are known to have benefitted in the 990s from the special attention of the king and his counsellors were Abingdon (993), the see of Cornwall (994), Muchelney (995), Rochester (995, 998), the Old Minster, Winchester (996, 997), and Sherborne (998); others would follow between 1001 and 1005.[52]

---

[50] For this text, see Mary Clayton, "The Old English *Promissio Regis*," *Anglo-Saxon England* 37 (2008): 91-150, with Roach, *Æthelred the Unready*, 82-5, 96 and 155.

[51] For archbishops Sigeric (990-4), Ælfric (995-1005) and Ælfheah (1006-12), see entries in *The Wiley Blackwell Encyclopedia of Anglo-Saxon England*, ed. Michael Lapidge, *et al.*, 2nd ed. (Oxford: Blackwell, 2014), 436 (Sigeric), 9 (Ælfric) and 7-8 (Ælfheah).

[52] For further discussion, see above, n. 49. It would appear that Archbishops Sigeric and Ælfric set an example in orchestrating what amounted to a significant campaign; and that Archbishop Ælfeah, with Wulfstan of York, followed their lead, in different ways.

Within this context, the story told in the Cuckhamsley Chirograph is of interest as perhaps another aspect of the same determination on the part of the king and his counsellors to set the kingdom in order. In itself, of course, the case can have been no more than one among many such incidents; but we must be grateful that such evidence has survived at all. A certain Leofwine had perpetrated an act of *reaflac*, in Berkshire, against a certain Wynflæd, who had the advantage of good connections. It was dealt with in the appropriate manner; and the evidence, it seems, was taken back to the archbishop.[53] The train of thought leads further. King Æthelred's good works towards religious houses, in the middle years of his reign, were complemented by actions, taken at royal assemblies and at shire courts, which were perhaps another part of the same story. It may not be a coincidence that it became a practice, in the 990s, for draftsmen of the king's diplomas to incorporate, in a new diploma, an account of the circumstances in which the land in question had come into the king's possession, if by due operation of the law, as a way of strengthening the new owner's title to the land in the event of a challenge.[54] Records would have been made of the outcome of decisions taken at assemblies which led to the conviction and punishment of particular offenders, leading also to the confiscation or forfeiture of their property, and in certain cases to exile or death. Such reports would have been drawn up probably in English, and retained for the record, whether in the king's archives, or the archbishop's, or an ealdorman's. Precious few such records survive, but in certain cases they seem to have been made available to the draftsman of a diploma, for the production of a new title-deed for the estate in question. In one case, a short extract from a vernacular document was incorporated in the dispositive section of a new diploma, issued in 995;[55] in another, a detailed account of serial (and seriously aggravated) *reaflac*, perpetrated by a certain Wulfbald, evidently taken direct from a document emanating from a royal assembly at London held under the auspices of Æthelgar, archbishop of Canterbury, in 988 × 990, was incorporated verbatim in a diploma issued in 996.[56] Similar records, perhaps also recorded in the vernacular, lie not far behind the accounts in Latin of crimes incorporated in several other diplomas of the same period.[57]

---

[53] In addition to the "Cuckhamsley Chirograph," one should note other instances of *reaflac*, from much the same period, striking much the same chord: S 1457 (*Roch* 36) and S 877 (*WinchNM* 31), in *AS Charters*, ed. Robertson, nos. 59 and 63. A list of 60 occurrences of Old English *reaflac*, in various contexts, can be generated from the Toronto Old English Corpus (online). See also Lambert, *Law and Order*, 89-90, 189, and 324.

[54] Keynes, *Diplomas of King Æthelred*, 97-8, with "Crime and Punishment," 67-81.

[55] S 886 (*Abing* 126), with *Charters of Abingdon*, ed. Kelly, 492-3.

[56] S 877 (*WinchNM* 31), with *Charters of the New Minster, Winchester*, ed. Miller, 149-54, and Richard Abels, "'The crimes by which Wulfbald ruined himself with his lord': the limits of state action in late Anglo-Saxon England," *Reading Medieval Studies* 40 (2014): 42-53.

[57] S 883 (*Abing* 125), dated 995; S 896 (*Abing* 128), dated 999; S 926 (*Roch* 33); S 927 (*Abing* 136), dated 1012; S 934 (*Abing* 137), dated 1015.

Anglo-Saxon Chirographs

The last word belongs to the scribe of the Cuckhamsley Chirograph. Already in the first half of the ninth century certain kinds of document were produced in more than one copy.[58] Clear evidence emerges, by the middle of the century, that documents which were necessarily or usefully issued in duplicate might be written out twice, on a single sheet of parchment, above and below a form of the word "CYROGRAPHUM" (a grecism denoting a "hand-written document").[59] The two copies of the text were then separated from each other by cutting the sheet of parchment through the middle of the letters, and each copy handed to one of the parties involved; the status of either copy as a record of the act could be verified thereafter by matching it to the other. By the early tenth century, examples or variants of this practice begin to proliferate among the leases drawn up in the west midlands.[60] The practice became increasingly widespread during the tenth century, whether for agreements or for wills; there is even a detailed account showing how Byrhtnoth, abbot of Ely, assumed responsibility (*c.* 990) for the making of the will of Siferth of Downham, in the form of a tripartite chirograph.[61] The assignation of copies to specified parties, sometimes including a copy for the king's "sanctuary" (*haligdom*), occurs for the first time among surviving documents in the "Cookham Chirograph," from the late 990s.[62] The practice became increasingly common in the eleventh century.[63]

Set within this wider context of "standard" practices, the legend on the Cuckhamsley Chirograph is seen to be wonderfully idiosyncratic, perhaps as befits a record drawn up on the top of a burial mound in Berkshire. When first working systematically through the surviving corpus of Anglo-Saxon charters on single sheets, I was struck by the row

---

[58] S 1187 (*Worc*), in 804; S 1438 (*CantCC* 69) in 838; and S 1510 (*CantCC* 78), in 845 × 853. For wide-ranging discussion of diplomatic culture in the ninth century, see Susan Kelly, "Anglo-Saxon Lay Society and the Written Word," *The Uses of Literacy in Early Medieval Europe*, ed. Rosamund McKitterick (Cambridge: Cambridge University Press, 1990), 36-62, with Brooks and Kelly, *Charters of Christ Church Canterbury*, 123-32.

[59] S 1273 (*Worc*), in 855, a "lost" single sheet described by Humfrey Wanley in 1705.

[60] S 221 (*Worc*), in 901; S 1281 (*Worc*), in 904; and S 1283 (*Worc*), in 899 × 904.

[61] Keynes, "Royal government and the written word," 254-5, from the early twelfth-century *Libellus Æthelwoldi episcopi*, ch. 12, derived from earlier vernacular records at the abbey.

[62] S 939 (*CantCC* 137), with Brooks and Kelly, *Charters of Christ Church Canterbury*, 1007-8, and Keynes, "Councils, Assemblies, and Royal Diplomas," 136. For the king's *haligdom*, see Keynes, *Diplomas of King Æthelred*, 148-9, and James Lloyd, "The priests of the king's reliquary in Anglo-Saxon England," *Journal of Ecclesiastical History* 67 (2016): 265-87, at 274-5.

[63] For the incidence of chirographs in the context of all surviving single sheets, see "A classified list of Anglo-Saxon charters on single sheets," on the "Kemble" (Anglo-Saxon charters) website. See also K. A. Lowe, "Lay Literacy in Anglo-Saxon England and the Development of the Chirograph," *Anglo-Saxon Manuscripts and their Heritage*, ed. Philip Pulsiano and Elaine M. Treharne (Aldershot: Ashgate, 1998), 161-204.

of cut-letters along the left-hand side of the lower edge of the parchment, which stood out from all other tenth- and eleventh-century examples of spelling variations of the word "CYROGRAPHUM"—and which clearly demanded an explanation. In her edition of the document, first published in 1939, Jane Robertson had ventured no solution.[64] So, in a mixture of fascination and frustration, but presuming that it had to be meaningful, I telephoned Dr Pierre Chaplais, in Oxford, to ask what he might have made of it.[65] He said he would have a look at the facsimile edition, and wrote back to me on the following day (19 September 1984):

> Re. our telephone conversation, here is a wild suggestion for the legend of the chirograph BMF iii. 37:
>
> $$\mathrm{C}_{\mathrm{P}}\mathrm{I}_{\mathrm{L}}\mathrm{R}_{\mathrm{E}}\mathrm{[A]}_{\mathrm{T}}\mathrm{G}_{\mathrm{V}}\mathrm{R}_{\mathrm{M}}\mathrm{A}_{\mathrm{E}}\mathrm{F}_{\mathrm{S}}\mathrm{V}_{\mathrm{T}}\mathrm{M}$$
>
> The trouble is that the seventh letter does not look like O to me, but rather like A. Too bad!

The "wild suggestion" was, of course, nothing short of an inspiration (the capital O is diamond-shaped).[66] Indeed it soon became apparent, on examination of the original in the British Museum (as then it was), that alternate letters, starting with the first and ending with the last, were picked out in "bold" script:

C P **I** L **R** E **O** T **G** V **R** M **A** E **F** S **V** T **M**

This gives the legend (by reading the sequence of emboldened letters first):

CIROGRAFVM PLETVM EST

The intended meaning is clear enough, with reference to the chirograph, once its two halves have been reunited. It has to be said, however, that while an electronic search in the appropriate database for the collocations "COMPLETUM EST" and "IMPLETUM EST" produces hundreds of results apiece, a search for the collocation "PLETUM EST" produces nothing.[67] One can but assume that the scribe realised that for his trick to work he needed a sequence of nine letters to intersperse with a 10-letter form of the key word, and that he would therefore have to abbreviate whichever form of words he had in mind. It remains a pleasant thought that had the need arisen to check the authenticity of one half of the document against the other, those performing the test

---

64 *Anglo-Saxon Charters*, ed. Robertson, 382: "There is no mention at the end of the document of the number of copies made but a series of capital letters, cut in half, runs along the bottom margin which suggests that there was more than one."

65 Richard Sharpe, "Pierre Chaplais," *Biographical Memoirs of Fellows of the British Academy* 11 (2012): 115-50, at 148 n. 97.

66 Keynes, "Royal Government and the Written Word," 250 n. 94; see also Wormald, "Giving God and King their Due," 346 n. 46.

67 I am most grateful to my colleague Dr Rosalind Love for her help in this connection.

would have been delighted to see the separate letters recover their respective forms as they brought them together, and then, on blinking once, would have seen the words themselves become legible before their eyes. One hopes that they might have appreciated, at the same time, the ingenuity of the scribe, on the burial mound, who had sought in this way to encrypt the operative word in what was perhaps an attempt, on his part, to render the agreement so much the stronger.

Fig. 1: Detail from the "Cuckhamsley Chirograph" (London, British Library, Cotton Augustus ii. 15 showing the sequence of cut letters along the lower edge of the parchment. A color image of the whole charter, face and dorse, is available on the British Library website.

Fig. 2: Bronze Age tumulus on Cuckhamsley Hill (Skutchamer Knob), Berkshire

A checklist of vernacular records associated with processes of litigation						
Sawyer	*older edition*	*BAcad. edition*	*archive*	*source*	*date*	*Identification*

(a) *Records of litigation—letters or personal statements generated within contexts of litigation*

S 1445	*SEHD* 18	*CantCC* 104	Canterbury	single sheet	*c.* 920	Eald. Ordlaf (Fonthill)
S 1211	*SEHD* 23	*CantCC* 124	Canterbury	single sheet	959 × 975	[Q] Eadgifu (Cooling)
S 1296	*Crawford Ch.* 7		Cred/Exeter	single sheet	980s	Abp Dunstan (Cornwall)
S 1242	*ASWrits* 108	*WinchOM*	Winchester	cartulary	995 × ?998	[Q] Ælfthryth (Ruishton)
S 1383	*ASWrits* 63	*Sherb* 13	Sherborne	pontifical	1001 × 1012	Bp Æthelric (Sherborne)

(b) *Records of litigation—partisan statements on the history of a disputed estate*

S 1447	*ASChart* 44	*West*	Westminster	single sheet	970 × 988	Sunbury Statement
S 1457	*ASChart* 59	*Roch* 36	Rochester	cartulary	980s	Bromley Statement
S 1458	*ASChart* 41	*Roch* 34	Rochester	single sheet	*c.* 995 ?	Wouldham Statement
S 1467	*ASChart* 91	*CantCC* 164	Canterbury	single sheet	*c.* 1040	Sandwich Statement

(c) *Records of litigation—formal settlements of a case*

S 1454	*ASChart* 66	*CantCC* 133	Canterbury	single sheet	990 × 993	Cuckhamsley Chirograph
S 939	*ASWills* 16.ii	*CantCC* 137	Canterbury	single sheet	995 × 998	Cookham Chirograph
S 1456	*ASChart* 69	*Roch* 37	Rochester	cartulary	995 × 1005	Snodland Settlement
S 1460	*ASChart* 83	*Worc*	Worcester	single sheet	1016 × 1023	Chirograph (Worcester)
S 1462	*ASChart* 78		Hereford	gospel-book	1016 × 1035	Gospel-book (Hereford)
S 1472	*ASChart* 102	*CantCC* 169	Canterbury	single sheet	1044 × 1045	Chirograph (Kent)
S 1474	*ASChart* 105	*Sherb* 17	Sherborne	cartulary	1045 × 1046	Chirograph (Devon)

Legal Terminology in the Anglo-Saxon Glossaries

David W. Porter

The Roman book arts arrived in England with Christianity at the end of the sixth century. When the English first came to make their own original books in the following century, they produced two types of writings, laws and glossaries, and examples of both would be composed straight through to the end of the Anglo-Saxon age.[1] These are very different genres. The laws descend from an ancient oral tradition of customary usage stretching all the way back to northern Europe,[2] while the glossaries represent the earliest interface with an equally ancient but culturally more remote tradition, the Mediterranean writings of Greece and Rome.

Arising from starkly contrasting sources at opposite ends of the oral/literate spectrum, laws and glossaries are thus a constellation of opposites, and for this reason their connections have remained in large part unexamined. For the present essay, I determined to explore their commonalities, specifically those glossary entries that interpret Roman legal terms with Old English words. These glosses invite analysis for their characteristically Anglo-Saxon interpretations of Roman concepts and customs, because they promise a chance to see the Anglo-Saxon mind at a transition point toward a revolutionary new way of thought. Because of the great institutional and cultural divide between Rome and Anglo-Saxon England, I hypothesized, as these terms crossed the language boundary from Latin to Old English the Anglo-Saxon mindset would come into view: the choices—additions, omissions, modifications—might show how Anglo-Saxon scholars

---

[1] Relevant articles ("Laws"; "Glossaries") in Michael Lapidge et al., eds., *The Blackwell Encyclopedia of Anglo-Saxon England*, 2nd ed. (Oxford: Blackwell, 2014) provide basic introductions and give leads into the now extensive scholarly literature. For the laws, Wormald, *Making* offers a survey of both the primary and secondary literature. Oliver, *Beginnings*, studies the earliest laws of the seventh and early eighth centuries. The earliest glossaries (through about 825) are addressed by W. M. Lindsay, *The Corpus, Epinal, Erfurt, and Leyden Glossaries* (Oxford: Oxford University Press, 1921).

[2] The oral-traditional origin of the laws is a logical given. The idea has been much studied in the past by scholars intent on recovering an artifact of oral Germanic culture. See for example Frederick Seebohm, *Tribal Custom in Anglo-Saxon Law* (London: Longmans, 1911), which is representative of the age. For a more modern approach on the subject, see Wormald, "'Inter cetera bona …genti suae': Law-making and Peace-keeping in the Earliest English Kingdoms," *La giustizia nell'alto medioevo (secoli V-VIII)*. Settimane di studio del Centro Italiano di studi sull'Alto Medioevo 42 (Spoleto: Centro Italiano di Studi sull'alto Medioevo, 1995), II, 963-96 and Oliver, *Beginnings*, 34-41.

responded to the laws and legal traditions of their most important cultural benefactor. As a first approach to this sprawling topic, I have limited my scope here to the glossarial vocabulary relating to civil positions, to the officers of Roman government.

The findings which I report in the conclusion, as is so often true when studying our very fragmentary record of Old English writings, give no final answer to our research question, but they do offer, first of all, broad inferences about the Anglo-Saxon take on Roman legal terms and, second, possible avenues of exploration for a broader examination of the Old English vocabulary relating to law and other areas of Roman institutional history.

As a prologue, let me give the briefest of introductions to glossaries, since they are a difficult and not widely understood genre of writing.[3] To clarify a text, readers in ancient times often made brief notations in interlinear or marginal space. These notations, called glosses, were of many sorts, but very common was the writing of a short verbal equivalent, often a simple one-word synonym. In a text with the name "Cicero," for example, an annotator might add a note like "Tullius" or *orator*. A longer note might read something like *orator Romanus* or *scriptor famosus*, or occasionally an even longer phrase or sentence. Accumulating over time and transmitted alongside the main text, such annotations sometimes came to number dozens per page, and in the most densely glossed texts they might fill all the marginal and interlinear space.

In the absence of dictionaries and the other reading aids that modern readers take for granted, text glosses proved so valuable for ancient and medieval readers that they came to be written down as texts in their own right and to circulate independently in lists known as glossaries. Each glossary item typically has two parts, a headword (called the *lemma*) on the left and an annotation (called the *interpretamentum*) on the right. Thus in glossary format our examples above might read *Cicero, orator; Cicero, scriptor; Cicero, orator Romanus;* or *Cicero, scriptor famosus*, with *Cicero* being the headword or *lemma* in each case and the various material on the right being the *interpretamentum.*

So far so good. It is a fascinating experience to look at all-Latin glosses and enter in to the mind of a reader of a thousand or more years ago. But an added element of interest comes with annotations that cross language boundaries. Glosses were an informal type of text, and it was a natural step for readers to write annotations in their own vernacular language. Thus instead of *Cicero, scriptor famosus* an Anglo-Saxon glossator might write *Cicero, hlisful writere*. Latin-vernacular glosses were in fact among the earliest writings in in English, and the same is true in several modern languages. Since the vernaculars tend to be sparsely represented in the earliest phases of their histories,

[3] The following exposition follows Lindsay's narrative in *The Corpus, Epinal, Erfurt, and Leyden Glossaries.*

the Latin context is especially valuable because it allows a nuanced interpretation that would otherwise be impossible. To make this point more concretely, bilingual glosses let us see well-known Latin concepts in the more recently written vernaculars and to examine how these concepts are adapted in them. Let us pursue this thesis with the legal vocabulary offered by the Anglo-Saxon glossaries. We will proceed in two steps, presentation of the relevant material, followed by an analysis of it. Our material, in the present instance, will come from glossary entries produced from Isidore of Seville's *Etymologiae*, an encyclopedic compendium of the seventh century which was much studied by the Anglo-Saxons and especially by Anglo-Saxon glossary makers.[4] Because the twenty books of the *Etymologiae* handle broad individual topics, glosses collected from it fall naturally into semantic categories, among them the category of law and government. Moreover, another factor of Isidorian glosses, their enduring popularity, makes them especially representative of the Anglo-Saxon period as a whole: they were copied from near the seventh-century beginning of written English straight through to the eleventh century. For simplicity's sake, however, this chapter focuses only on those glosses produced during the tenth and eleventh centuries. The relevant glossaries include the following:[5]

- the three Cleopatra Glossaries, early tenth century
- Ælfric's Glossary, late tenth century
- the Harley Glossary, tenth/eleventh century
- the Antwerp-London Class Glossary, early eleventh century

Let us proceed to the category of civil positions.

---

4 The legal vocabulary is in Isidore's Book V, *De legibus et temporibus*. The *Etymologiae* is still most conveniently available in the edition of W. M. Lindsay, *Isidori Hispalensis Episcopi Etymologiarum sive Originum Libri XX* (Oxford: Oxford University Press, 1911). An ongoing project is re-editing and issuing the individual books in bilingual editions (Paris: Belles Lettres, 1982-), with sixteen of twenty volumes completed thus far. The whole work has been translated into English, Stephen Barney et al. *The Etymologies of Isidore of Seville* (Cambridge: Cambridge University Press, 2010). For the Isidorian content of the early glossaries, see David Porter, "Isidore's *Etymologiae* at the School of Canterbury," *Anglo-Saxon England* 43 (2014): 7-44, and for Isidore's enduring popularity, David Porter, "The Antwerp-London Glossaries and Ælfric's *Glossary*: A Record of the Earliest English Scholarship." *Notes & Queries* 57 (2010): 305-10, and L. Lazzari, "Isidore's *Etymologiae* in Anglo-Saxon Glossaries," in *Foundations of Learning: The Transfer of Encyclopaedic Knowledge in the Early Middle Ages*, ed. Rolf H Bremmer, Jr. and Kees Dekker (Leuven: Peeters, 2007), 63-93.

5 Philip Rusche, "The Cleopatra Glossaries: An Edition with Commentary on the Glosses and their Sources," (Ph.D. Diss., Yale University, 1996) henceforth abbreviated Cleo I, II, and III; J. Zupitza, ed. *Ælfrics Grammatik und Glossar: Text und Varianten* (Berlin: Weidmann, 1880); R. Oliphant, ed., *The Harley Latin-Old English Glossary*; David Porter, ed., *The Antwerp-London Glossaries* (Toronto: Pontifical Institute of Mediaeval Studies, 2011), 45-131, henceforth abbreviated ALC.

Civil Positions and Related Terms

Anglo-Saxon government, growing out of traditional ideas of a royal elite, matched imperfectly imperial governance with its basis in the Roman senate and its officers. By comparison, English governance was above all much simpler, since even the idea of a unified English kingdom appeared only in the reign of Alfred, with the decisive foundation arriving only in the following century.[6] And even this relatively unified England was immeasurably smaller and less ethnically complex than the Empire. For these reasons, English had a sparse vocabulary with which to denote the complicated hierarchy of Roman governance, and this sparseness in turn entailed diverse strategies of translation.

Direct Lexical Loan

One obvious translation strategy was direct loan. For the highest offices, those of *imperator*, *augustus*, and *Caesar*, concepts without even remote English equivalents, Anglo-Saxons used the generic loanword *casere*, i.e., Caesar; which, according to the *Dictionary of Old English*, had been in common use by about 900 (though a much earlier date is likely):[7]

Imperator . cesar . ł augustus . **casere** .[8]

Finer gradations of meaning required circumlocution:

A[u]gusti : þa yldestan **caseras**

Augusti, the eldest Caesars (Cleo I 466)

---

[6] See, e.g., George Molyneaux, *The Formation of the English Kingdom in the Tenth Century* (Oxford: Oxford University Press, 2015), 117-94.

[7] Again, Isidorian content is scattered throughout the earliest glossaries (Porter, "The Antwerp-London Glossaries and Ælfric's Glossary").

[8] Repeated three times, at ALC 122 and 1711, and Ælfric 300. The probable source of the present entry is one of two Isidorian passages. *Etymologiae* VII.vi.43:[...] *apud nos Augusti appellantur reges, cum propriis nominibus censeantur,* "Among us kings are called Augusti, though they are listed in their own names." *Etymologiae* IX.iii.16-17: *Augustus ideo apud Romanos nomen imperii est, eo quod olim augerent rempublicam amplificando. Quod nomen primitus senatus Octavio Caesari tradidit, ut quia auxerat terras, ipso nomine et titulo consecraretur. Dum autem idem Octavianus iam Caesar et imperator appellaretur, vel Augustus.[...],* "For the Romans, 'Augustus' is the name of the imperial office, because formerly the emperors "enlarged" (*augere*) the republic by extending its borders. Originally the senate bestowed this name on Octavius Caesar, so that he might be honored in his very name and title for enlarging their territory. Moreover, this same Octavius was now called Caesar and emperor, or Augustus" (Barney et al., trans., *The Etymologies*).

The great importance of Rome and its literature to the Anglo-Saxon intellectual world can be glimpsed in the fact that *casere* has many hundreds of citations in Old English writings of all sorts.[9] Moreover, to use the vocabulary of the *Oxford English Dictionary*, the word has been "endenizened," that is, expropriated for use as a native word, being extended to refer both to native English rulers and to Old Testament kings, as well as being compounded with native elements.[10]

Angulseaxna Eadred cyning & **casere** (S 566)

Eadred, king and caesar of the Anglo-Saxons

Dauid æt wige soð sigecempa, searocyne man, **casere** cræftig (Psalm 50)

David, in battle a victorious warrior bold in arms, a strong king

Þa wæs syxte gear Constantines **caser**domes (*Elene* 7)

Then was the sixth year of Constantine's reign

Loan Translation/Loan Formation

Another frequent Anglo-Saxon translation strategy was what is termed loan translation or loan formation. Using this process, speakers of Old English might recycle an old word or coin a new English word patterned closely after a Latin original word or phrase.[11] The most germane example here is Old English *ealdor* or *ealdorman*, which survives as Modern English "alderman." Although this "term began as an equivalent to a range of Latin titles,"[12] in the glossaries, we also find it as an equivalent to Latin titles relating to the Roman senate.

In the Antwerp-London Glossary, the Roman senate is termed ***ealdormanna duguð*** (ALC 165) and in the roughly contemporary Harley Glossary there is the entry (E 638) *Exspectabiles* ***senatores***, *þa medumestan* ***ealdras***. While elsewhere in Old English *ealdorman* is a quite general term referring to officers, lay or clerical, or to anyone holding a position of responsibility, both glossarial entries make clear they are refering to elites. *Duguþ* in the Antwerp-London entry is a collective noun with strongly positive connotations: "virtue," "excellence," "strength," "salvation," "wealth," "flower of the

[9] *Dictionary of Old English Web Corpus*, http://doe.utoronto.ca.

[10] All the following examples were accessed via the *DOE Web Corpus*: Peter Sawyer, *Anglo-Saxon Charters. An Annotated List and Bibliography* (London: Royal Historical Society, 1968), no. 155; *Elene*, in George Philip Krapp and Elliott V. K. Dobbie, eds. *The Anglo-Saxon Poetic Records*, 6 vols. (New York: Columbia University Press, 1931-1953), vol. 2; Psalm 50, *ASPR*, ed. E.V.K. Dobbie, vol. 6.

[11] Philip Durkin, *Borrowed Words: A History of English Loanwords* (Oxford: Oxford University Press, 2014), 124-6, gives a thorough discussion of the phenomenon, with many examples.

[12] *Blackwell Encyclopedia of Anglo-Saxon England*, *s.v.* "ealdorman."

nation," and so on, hence "assembly of noble retainers." *Medumestan* in the Harley entry has the equivalents "most worthy," "most esteemed," etc., hence, an elite assembly of nobles. The source for the Antwerp-London item is Isidore's *Etymologiae* IX.iv.8: "An age grouping gave its name to the Senate, because they were elderly" (*Senatui nomen ætas dedit, quod seniores essent*). In other words, *senatus* is derived from *senex* "elderly man." Thus here we see a classic loan formation—one of the many instances where Anglo-Saxons rendered a compound or phrase via the most literal translation of its elements.

OE *ealdorman*, based on Old English *ealdor* "elder," is in fact a close and idiomatic semantic equivalent to Latin *senator*, with its base in *senex* "old man." So this is a much more felicitous pairing of Old English to Latin than the many loan formations which turn out to be *hapax legomena* for the simple fact that they never entered general usage (a topic we return to in the conclusion). But despite even this happy match between the Latin and English, there is no evidence of usage that would indicate a wide standardization of the equivalence. When other entries relating to the Roman senate appear even in the same glossaries, translations are various (ALC 295, and 2777):

Senatusconsultum, riccra gesetness

a law of the powerful

Curia . l Senatus . uþwitena spræchus

auditorium of wise men

Native Vocabulary

To designate the many officials of Roman government such as consul, prætor, censor, the Anglo-Saxons used native vocabulary of the most general meaning. *Gerefa* "reeve" and its compounds, which denote any mid-level position,[13] see a great range of application. One Isidorian gloss of the Antwerp-London Glossary, for example, so terms the Roman consuls who replaced the kings and under the republic served one-year terms.[14]

Consul **gerefa** . (ALC 128)

---

[13] R. I. Page, "*Gerefa*: Some Problems of Meaning" in *Problems of Old English Lexicography: Studies in Memory of Angus Cameron,* ed. Alfred Bammesberger, Eichstätter Beiträge: Abteilung Sprache und Literatur 15 (Regensburg: Pustet, 1985), 211-28.

[14] From *Etymologiae* IX.iii.6: *Consules appellati a consulendo, sicut reges a regendo [...] Nam cum Romani regum superbam dominationem non ferrent, annua imperia binosque consules sibi fecerunt,* "Consuls were named from counseling, as kings were named from ruling ... When the Romans could not bear the despotism of the kings, they put in office two consuls who held executive position for a year."

Logically enough, the proconsul, who served on a substitute or pro-tem basis, was termed *undergerefa* "under-reeve," i.e., assistant or subordinate reeve.[15] But again complete consistency is neither expected nor encountered. Another gloss (C 2741) in the same list equates "proconsul" and *gerefa*! And glossators found yet other possibilities. Two text glosses to Aldhelm's *Prosa de Virginitate* which have been transfered to the Cleopatra glossaries (Cleo I, C 512-13) named consuls as "year-kings."

Consulis : géarcininges

Consul : gércining. Heretoga

This is a rather odd choice since, as we saw in the Isidorian quotation above (note 13), consuls were emphatically not kings. But it is likely the glossator chose this inexact equivalent on the basis of phonetic similarity, the /k/ + /n/ in both *consul* and *kyning*. Such simple alliterative pairing is found very frequently in Latin-English glosses of all sorts, and below we will see the phenomenon in several glossary entries.

A rather puzzling Antwerp-London entry pairs *exconsul* ("who left office after their year was done") with the compound *hiredgerefa*, a hapax legomenon (ALC 131). If *hired* is taken here to mean the *comitatus* or *familia* of a prominent individual, the gloss would apparently be a thoroughly Anglo-Saxon superimposition on a Roman concept. Consular rank would indeed denote social prominence, but the implication of formal group affiliation in this case would appear to be an Anglo-Saxon concept. H. D. Meritt, however, rejects this interpretation of the element *hired*--and instead would interpret the whole as "hired reeve,"[16] hardly an accurate rendering of the Roman consul's lofty status. On the other hand, the word *burhgerefa* (literally, "reeve of a city or of a fortified city") never refers to an Anglo-Saxon office, despite the importance of the *burh* in English history, but always to a magistrate of Rome, and in reponse to a Latin headword: in the Antwerp-London glossary it glosses the headwords *prætor*, *prefectus* ("prefect"), *prepositus* ("overseer"), and *questor* in one entry (ALC 133) and the words *curiales* ("curia members") and *decuriales* (read *decuriones* "decuria members") in another (ALC 170). A similar example is

Municeps . portgerefa . ł burhwita. (ALC 169)

Port can mean simply "town," in which case *burhgerefa* and *portgerefa* may be considered equivalent. The same glossary gives a very English interpretation to a Roman office by

[15] ALC 129, "Proconsul . undergerefa," from *Etymologiae* IX.iii.8: *Proconsules suffecti erant consulibus, et dicti proconsules eo quod vicem consulis fungerentur,* "Proconsuls were substituted for consuls, and they were called proconsuls because they functioned in place of consuls."

[16] H.D. Meritt, *Fact and Lore about Old English Words* (Stanford: Stanford University Press, 1954), 107.

pairing *scirgerefa* "shire reeve, sheriff" (a word known primarily from all-English texts such as the versions of the Chronicle) with *praeses* "provincial governor":

Preses . scirgerefa. (ALC 137)

So the glossator here matches, more or less, the English shire to the Roman province, just as earlier, with the word *casere* he equated the English king with the Roman emperor.

The word *wicgerefa* ("reeve of a village or town") is well known in Old English sources, including the laws of Hlothere and Eadric, where they are said to serve as witnesses to transactions.[17] One sole glossatorial entry pairs the word with Latin *publicanus* (ALC 174), from which it is inferred that some tax collecting duties fell to the *wicgerefa.*[18] Another compound of *gerefa* is quite straightforward, for there is a close semantic match between *vilicus*, manager of an estate, and Old English *tungerefa*, reeve of a farm:

Uilicus . ł actor . ł curator . ł procurator . ł rector .
tungerefa. (ALC 175)

In addition to serving as an etymological calque and loan formation to name Roman senators, Old English *ealdor* does wide duty as a title for persons of responsibility, rather in the manner of *gerefa* in the above quotations. A few examples from the Antwerp-London Glossary will illustrate (ALC 127, 138, 139):

Ducatus . ealdor (ALC 127)

Centurio . hundredes ealdor (ALC 138)

Quinquagenarius . ł pentecontarcus . fittiga ealdor

In the first entry, *ducatus* is "military leadership," in the second, *centurio* ("centurion") is "captain of a hundred," and in the last *quinquagenarius* ("captain of fifty") is translated as "elder of fifty." Additionally, Latin *tribunus* (ALC 134) is rendered as "manna ealdor" (elder of persons or of commoners), evidently a reflection of the elite's financial obligation to commoners. The source is Isidore, *Etymologiae* IX.iv.18: , "Tribunes are so called because they give either justice or wealth to the commoners" (*Tribuni dicti quod plebi vel iura vel opem tribuunt*).

---

[17] Accessed via the *DOE Web Corpus*. From F. Liebermann, *Die Gesetze der Angelsachsen,* I, 9-11.

[18] On the subject of taxes, Latin *exactor* "tax collector" (ALC 171, a gloss on *Etymogiae* XX.ix.7) gets a picturesque equivalent derived from French, *kæce[p]ol,* literally "chase-chicken." A serviceable word, it survived well into the modern era, being last cited with this meaning by the *OED* in 1652 (*s.v. catchpole/ catchpoll*). Though French loans are very rare in OE, this one was common enough to be used by Ælfric in the Catholic Homilies, Peter Clemoes, ed. *Ælfric's Catholic Homilies: The First Series,* EETS s.s. 17 (Oxford: Oxford University Press, 1997), 361.

For king and related offices that were longstanding in English and related Germanic societies, native terms naturally came into play, e.g., rex, cyning (Ælfric 300); Basileus . kining (ALC 123); Regillus . undercyning (ALC 124); Regulus, lytel cyning oððe undercyning (Ælfric 16).

But less familiar offices and institutions required creative coining and circumlocution. For example, the glossaries define the Latin term *dictator* as "ælces þinges dihtnere," i.e., one who administers everything or one who is in charge of everything.[19] This is close to the *Oxford Latin Dictionary* definition "a magistrate having plenary powers," but it is only in the glossaries that Old English *dihtnere* is defined as a governmental official: other occurrences refer to clerical offices or to God who organizes the world. In this instance, it is likely that the glossator chose his unusual Old English equivalent on the basis of phonetic similarity to the Latin headword, a fairly frequent Anglo-Saxon glossing strategy, as we noted above. The consonantal shells of the two halves of the present gloss are quite close: /d/ + palato-velar consonant (OE /ç/ or /x/ resembling Latin /k/) + /t/ + /r/. The strategy of phonetic association deserves comment because it has no real validity. Since phonetic similarity across language boundaries is a matter of happenstance, no pedagogical theory recommends matching bilingual pairs on the basis of sound. The limitations are evident. Many Anglo-Saxon glossators paired alliterating words of less happy fit than the present item, as in our earlier example *consul . gércining*.[20] It is likely that sound association is a mnemonic device inherited from a preliterate culture in which orality still played an important role, that the reliance on alliteration and phonetic resemblance reflects traditional manners of learning.

Conclusion

How then to sum up this varied material? First, it is clear that Anglo-Saxon glossing habits had limitations when it came to the task of communicating Latin complexities. The reliance on short one-to-one equivalents left little to no room for nuance. A very early glossing tradition where extended Isidorian paragraphs received English glosses[21] early on yielded to the simplified Latin-Old English entries typified by our examples here. In this format, Old English glosses could hardly tell an Anglo-Saxon scholar the

[19] ALC 130; see also Oliphant, *The Harley Glossary, s.v., "Dictator .i. dictor relator preceptor imperator* ***dihtnere*** *ordinator prescriptor."*

[20] The same process of sound association is found in the reverse, where Classical words are chosen because of their phonetic similarity to OE. In the Colloquies of Ælfric Bata, for example, the rare Grecism *scibalum*, oddly, is used to denote "feces," a surprising lexical choice resulting from the phonetic similarity to Old English "scit-." David Porter and Scott Gwara, *Anglo-Saxon Conversations* (Woodbridge: Boydell, 1997), 138.

[21] Rusche, "Isidore's *Etymologiae* and the Canterbury Aldhelm Scholia," *JEGP* 104 (2005): 437-55.

complicated structure of the Roman senate, for example, or the various types of tribunes, or other such questions. The fondness for alliterating Latin-English word pairs likewise gave little help, and in fact bilingual pairs chosen mainly by sound association could in fact mislead, as in the case "consul=year cyning," and so a useful oral strategy for learning in a mostly non-literate culture might become a stumbling block for learners crossing the boundary from English to Latin. The technique of loan formation, as we noticed, produced some accurate and frequently used equivalents, *dihtnere*, for instance, or Old English *ealdorman*, which comes to mind as the prime example. But even here it is good to keep in mind that the Anglo-Saxons had a very conservative bent, and it is easy to find instances of loan formation that never gained currency—a good number of potentially serviceable Old English words coined in this manner were in fact *hapax legomena* or in use by a single author only, and never saw even a modestly broad usage.[22]

In spite of the limitations enumerated above, Anglo-Saxon glossators accomplished some tasks quite well. They managed to draw clear distinctions between senators and other officers, such as tribunes, for example, and they also were precise about denoting an officer's place in the administrative hierarchy and at least sometimes about defining the extent of his jurisdiction, whether city, region, or province.

A question worth asking, however, is how accurately the Anglo-Saxon conception of "administrator" matched the official Roman positions named in glossed texts. Did the two languages overlap closely enough in their formulation of the concept that Anglo-Saxon readers might gain accurate knowldge, or were there important areas of semantic difference that might lead to confusion?

Let us suppose a major disconnect. By the late Anglo-Saxon period, the senators, tribunes, tax collectors, and others officers of the Empire were a distant memory of a long defunct polity. Moreover, Latin, the language that communicated their functions and bailiwicks, was always a foreign language to every literate Anglo-Saxon, and, by this time, to many it was a difficult and very imperfectly understood foreign language at that.[23] The Anglo-Saxon officers and their Old English titles, on the other hand, would have been intimately familiar not just to the literate but to all the English, even those of the most modest rank. For by this period the civil service of the English royal government had long been a significant presence in the lives of ordinary citizens.[24] Even in the chaotic reign of Alfred, for example, the ealdormen and reeves are depicted as having

---

[22] A famous example is Ælfric's grammatical terminology. Literal loan formations like *foresetnyss* (=Latin *praepositio*) or *betwux-aworpennyss* (=Latin *interiectio*), etc., were picked up by no other writers.

[23] Supporting evidence is frequent. A few examples: Alfred's low estimation of Insular latinity stated in the preface to *Pastoral Care* is of course well known, but we can also mention the shaky Latin of Ælfric's early teacher (Mark Griffith, "How Much Latin Did Ælfric's *Magister* Know?" *Notes and Queries* 244 [1999]: 176-81) and the many errors of the *Chronicle of Æthelweard*, ed. A. Campbell (London, Thomas Nelson, 1962)

[24] James Campbell, *The Anglo-Saxon State* (London: Hambledon, 2000), xxvi.

broad authority in trade, law, and governance at the level of town and shire.[25] And in the eleventh century, these same officials had become a stable bulwark of government and society at large, without whom the relatively smooth accessions of first the Scandinavian king Cnut and then the Norman king William would have been impossible without great disruption.[26]

Anglo-Saxon readers interpreting Roman officers by their Anglo-Saxon counterparts would necessarily introduce considerable misinterpretation, for the actual differences between the two were manifest and many. Late Anglo-Saxon England has been described as a nascent nation state,[27] meaning a polity with natural borders, and one whose citizens feel they are united by a common language and culture. Even if the reality was neither that neat or simple, what a clear contrast with the far-flung, culturally diverse, and polyglot Roman empire. And of course the political cultures of the two entities were widely divergent. Anglo-Saxon civilization was hierarchical but the emphatic hallmark of its management style was collaboration.[28] At the royal level, the king's *witan* shared legislative and policy making decisions, with the corporate spirit being formalized in the long lists of names appended to the charters by churchmen and nobility. Even the selection of king was reached not by a rigidly established custom of primogeniture but by a rather flexible consensus building on the part of the *witan.*[29] The same impetus toward collaboration is reflected in church councils and in local judicial proceedings.[30] The emphasis on consensus is in fact so pervasive that it cannot be the result of any formal statute but must be simply the Anglo-Saxon way of doing things, a deeply rooted pattern of social organization which the culturally insular Anglo-Saxons would consider simply natural behavior.[31] But a projection of these Anglo-Saxon

---

25 David Pratt, *The Political Thought of King Alfred the Great* (Cambridge: Cambridge University Press, 2007), 29-30.

26 James Campbell, *The Anglo-Saxon State,* 24.

27 Ibid., 37-8; Molyneaux, *Formation,* 11. Molyneaux, however, stresses the fact tha the late Anglo-Saxon state, which had borders quite different from those of the later Norman period, included speakers of other languages even while some English speakers lived outside of it.

28 The general thesis of *Kingship and Consent in Anglo-Saxon England, 871-978* by Levi Roach, who prominently cites Patrick Wormald, Simon Keynes, and James Campbell. But the same point is made by F. Liebermann, *The National Assembly in the Anglo-Saxon Period,* and by early scholars who saw the king's *witan* as an embryonic parliament.

29 Liebermann, *National Assembly,* 54-7; Roach, *Kingship and Consent* 151.

30 Patrick Wormald, "Charters, Law, and the Settlement of Disputes in Anglo-Saxon England": "In nearly every text the judging, decreeing or settling verb is plural: the rhetoric of Anglo-Saxon process remained participatory and communal," 305-6.

31 So natural was the collaborative model of governance that one Anglo-Latin writer even pictured God's rule of the universe to profit by the participation of a heavenly *witan* composed of archangels (David Porter, "The Anglo-Latin Elegy of Herbert and Wulfgar", *Anglo-Saxon England* 40 [2011]: 225-47).

traits onto the Roman bureaucracy would leave out of account the absolutism of the Emperor and the governance of a far flung empire whose great distances rendered consultation with the capital slow and difficult. Just as the Anglo-Saxons were able to recast the Christ of *The Dream of the Rood* as a heroic figure almost epic in his self-sacrifice, and routinely to depict Old Testament personages in the guise of Anglo-Saxon nobles, it is entirely likely that the Roman bureaucracy pictured by the Anglo-Saxons had a distinctly English flavor.

In conclusion, the conventions of Anglo-Saxon glossing were something of a mixed bag, offering on the one hand rough equivalents allowing a proximate understanding of Roman institutions but on the other hand lacking the depth and detail to inform those readers for whom Rome was a new and unfamiliar subject. As a result, readers would be expected to fill this void with their personal knowledge and thereby to introduce Anglo-Saxon elements into texts where none were intended. The later writings of the Benedictine Reform of the tenth and eleventh centuries offer a promising place to test this idea because at this period not only was Latin literacy greatly prized, but a great appetite for rare and exotic glossematic vocabulary, much of it evidently derived from Latin-Old English glossaries, became the hallmark of Anglo-Latin.[32] In addition to entries on Roman offices, the glossaries contain legal vocabulary relating to slavery and manumission, to wills and inheritance, and to crime and punishment. If glossaries prompted Anglo-Saxon readers to add their own interpretations of Roman offices, the same influence may be expected in these other areas as well.

[32] The style is described by Michael Lapidge, "The Hermeneutic Style in Anglo-Latin Literature," *Anglo-Saxon England* 4 (1975): 67-111. Rebecca Stephenson, *The Politics of Language* (Toronto: University of Toronto Press, 2015) analyzes the use of hermeneutic (and glossary-based) Latin as a sociological marker of in-group status.

IV. The Reception of Anglo-Saxon Law and Culture

The Reception of Kentish Law in the Eleventh Century: Archbishop Wulfstan as Legal Historian

Andrew Rabin

Scholarship on the laws of the early kings of Kent has largely been shaped by the complicated circumstances of their preservation: although the laws' seventh-century composition places them among the earliest surviving Old English texts of any substance, they survive only in *Textus Roffensis*, a manuscript compiled c. 1124, by which time the Anglo-Saxon period had nearly passed out of living memory.[1] During the almost five centuries that elapsed between their composition and their transcription in *Textus*, only the barest of evidence remains for the laws' transmission and reception. Indeed, between 700 and 1066, there are only two extant references by name to a piece of Kentish royal legislation: Bede famously describes the laws of Æthelberht as being

[1] Dorothy Bethurum, "Stylistic Features of the Old English Laws," *Modern Language Review* 27 (1932): 263; Nicholas Brooks, "The Laws of King Æthelberht of Kent: Preservation, Content, and Composition," in *Textus Roffensis: Law, Language, and Libraries in Early Medieval England*, ed. Bruce O'Brien and Barbara Bombi (Turnhout: Brepols, 2015), 107-9; Carole A. Hough, "Palaeographical Evidence for the Compilation of the *Textus Roffensis*," *Scriptorium* 55, no. 1 (2001): 71-2; Hough, "Numbers in Manuscripts of Anglo-Saxon Law," in *Writing and Texts in Anglo-Saxon England*, ed. Alexander Rumble (Woodbridge: D.S. Brewer, 2006), 128-9; Hough, "The Earliest English Texts? The Language of the Kentish Laws Reconsidered," in *Textus: Roffensis: Law, Language, and Libraries in Early Medieval England*, ed. Bruce O'Brien and Barbara Bombi (Turnhout: Brepols, 2015), 137-53; Lisi Oliver, *The Language of the Early English Laws, Unpublished Ph.D. Dissertation* (1995), 13-23; Oliver, *Beginnings*, 20, 25; Oliver, "Royal and Ecclesiastical Law in Seventh-Century Kent," in *Early Medieval Studies in Memory of Patrick Wormald*, ed. Stephen Baxter, et al. (Aldershot: Ashgate, 2009), 112; Oliver, "Legal Documentation and the Practice of English Law," in *The Cambridge History of Early Medieval English Literature*, ed. Clare Lees, *The New Cambridge History of English Literature* (Cambridge: Cambridge University Press, 2012), 500; Mary P. Richards, "The Manuscript Contexts of the Old English Laws: Tradition and Innovation," in *Studies in Earlier Old English Prose*, ed. Paul Szarmach (Albany: State University Press of New York, 1986), 185; Richards, *Texts and Their Traditions in the Medieval Library of Rochester Cathedral Priory*, Transactions of the American Philosophical Society (Philadelphia: The American Philosophical Society, 1988), 45-6; Richards, "Elements of a Written Standard in the Old English Laws," in *Standardizing English: Essays in the History of Language Change*, ed. Joseph B. Trahern (Knoxville: The University of Tennessee Press, 1989), 5; Wormald, *Making*, 244-5; Wormald, "*Laga Eadwardi*: The *Textus Roffensis* and Its Context," in *Legal Culture in the Early Medieval West: Law as Text, Image, and Experience* (London: The Hambledon Press, 1999), 115-39; Wormald, *The First Code of English Law* (Canterbury: The Canterbury Commemoration Society, 2005).

composed "after the examples of the Romans" (*iuxta exempla Romanorum*) in the *Historia ecclesiastica* and Alfred claims to have drawn inspiration for his laws from "Æthelberht, the first to receive baptism among the English people" (*Æþelbryhtes, þe ærest fulluhte onfeng on Angelcynne*).[2] The effect of this silence has been to significantly limit our understanding of the ways in which Kentish legislation was read and understood by subsequent generations of lawmakers, particularly those of the tenth and eleventh centuries. If, as Mary Richards has argued, pre-Conquest royal law demonstrates, "an emerging self-consciousness [...] of what it meant to be Anglo-Saxon," the role of Kentish legislation in this emergence has yet to be fully explored.[3]

One lawmaker who did acknowledge Kentish influence, however, was Archbishop Wulfstan of York (d. 1023), in whose legal writings can be found several explicit borrowings from the laws of Æthelberht and his successors. The outlines of Wulfstan's biography have grown progressively clearer over the past several decades: during a career that included appointments as Bishop of London (996-1002) and then as Bishop of Worcester (1002-1016) and Archbishop of York (1002-1023), Wulfstan rose to prominence as a homilist, Church administrator, royal counsellor, and ultimately as the principal author of the laws of Kings Æthelred and Cnut.[4] In this latter capacity, Wulfstan composed the most far-reaching corpus of royal legislation since the Alfredian

---

[2] For the passage from Bede, see the *Historia ecclesiastica gentis Anglorum* II.5, ed. Bertram Colgrave and R. A. B. Mynors, *Bede's Ecclesiastical History of the English People* (Oxford: Clarendon Press, 1991), 150. Although it is tempting to speculate that the translator of the *Old English Bede* may have consulted Æthelberht's laws when rendering the relevant passage, his text is not sufficiently similar to Æthelberht's to permit any firm conclusions. For *Alfred*, see *Af. El.* 49.9. Quotations of Old English law are taken from Liebermann, *Gesetze*.

[3] Mary P. Richards, "Anglo-Saxonism in the Old English Laws," in *Anglo-Saxonism and the Construction of Social Identity*, ed. Allen J. Frantzen and John D. Niles (Gainesville: The University Press of Florida, 1997), 42.

[4] On Wulfstan's life and career, see Stephen Baxter, "Archbishop Wulfstan and the Administration of God's Property," in *Wulfstan, Archbishop of York: The Proceedings of the Second Alcuin Conference*, ed. Matthew Townend (Turnhout: Brepols, 2004), 161-206; Dorothy Bethurum, "Wulfstan," in *Continuations and Beginnings: Studies in Old English Literature*, ed. E.G. Stanley (London: Thomas Nelson and Sons, Ltd., 1966), 210-46; Andrew Rabin, *The Political Writings of Archbishop Wulfstan of York* (Manchester: Manchester University Press, 2015), 9-16; Rabin, "Wulfstan at London: Episcopal Politics in the Reign of Æthelred," *English Studies* 97, no. 2 (2016): 186-206; Dorothy Whitelock, "A Note on the Career of Wulfstan the Homilist," *EHR* 52, no. 207 (1937): 460-5; Whitelock, "Archbishop Wulfstan, Homilist and Statesman," in *Transactions of the Royal Historical Society*, 4th Series (London: Butler & Tanner, Ltd., 1942), 25-46; Whitelock, "Wulfstan at York," in *Franciplegius: Medieval and Linguistic Studies in Honor of Francis Peabody Magoun, Jr.*, ed. Jess B. Bessinger (New York: New York University Press, 1965), 214-31; Patrick Wormald, "Archbishop Wulfstan: Eleventh-Century Statebuilder," in *Wulfstan, Archbishop of York: The Proceedings of the Second Alcuin Conference*, ed. Matthew Townend (Turnhout: Brepols, 2004), 9-27.

domboc of the late ninth century.[5] Undergirding this legislation is a fascination with legal history that led Wulfstan to collect and rework earlier law-codes (as he did in the so-called "Compilation on Status"), and in at least one instance to identify a composition of his own as a text from an earlier era (the so-called "Peace of Edward and Guthrum").[6] For Wulfstan, early legal texts, whether authentic or created, provided a necessary precedent for the ambitious program of moral and social renewal he sought to effect with the laws of Æthelred and Cnut. Yet although Wulfstan drew extensively on Anglo-Saxon, Frankish, and Irish materials, he rarely quoted directly from his sources and seldom cited them by name.[7] As Andy Orchard observes, "Wulfstan hardly ever uses direct quotations, even when his source is in Old English [...E]ven when echoing the work of others, he always seems to take pains to alter the words, taking the sense and making it his own by overlaying it with his idiosyncratic style. Where Ælfric adopts, Wulfstan adapts."[8] It is striking, then, that Wulfstan several times quotes directly from Kentish legislation and in one case even calls attention to the fact that he is drawing on "the laws of the Kentish people" (*Cantwara lage*).[9] Passages of this sort have the potential to shed light both of the reception of Kentish law by later Anglo-Saxon legislators and on Wulfstan's own practices as a reader and writer of Old English royal legislation.

This chapter will examine the reception of Kentish law by later Anglo-Saxon legislators with special attention to the writings of Archbishop Wulfstan. If our understanding of the reception history of Kentish legislation prior to the twelfth century is necessarily incomplete, the surviving borrowings by later lawmakers testify both to an ongoing awareness of its significance and to the role played by early precedent in the drafting of royal legislation. In particular, the importance of Kentish law to the legal project of Archbishop Wulfstan illustrates how texts from the earliest generation of Anglo-Saxon lawmakers came to be read once the *Cantware* were fully incorporated into greater *Englalond*. At the same time, Wulfstan's use of this material also offers insight into the ways in which he reshaped legal history in order to support his own ideological ends.

[5] Patrick Wormald has described Wulfstan's legal writings as the "second climax in the story of Old English legislation." Wormald, *Making* 363.

[6] See Andrew Rabin, "Archbishop Wulfstan's 'Compilation on Status' in the Textus Roffensis," in *Textus Roffensis: Law, Language, and Libraries in Medieval England*, ed. Barbara Bombi and Bruce O'Brien (Turnhout: Brepols, 2015), 175-92; Rabin, *Political Writings*, 38-40; Dorothy Whitelock, "Wulfstan and the So-Called Laws of Edward and Guthrum," *EHR* 56, no. 221 (1941): 1-21.

[7] Andy Orchard, "Wulfstan as Reader, Writer, and Rewriter," in *The Old English Homily: Precedent, Practice, and Appropriation*, ed. Aaron Kleist (Turnhout: Brepols, 2007), 334-5; Orchard, "The Library of Wulfstan of York," in *The Cambridge History of the Book in Britain, Volume I: C. 400-1100*, ed. Richard Gameson (Cambridge: Cambridge University Press, 2012), 695-99; Rabin, *Political Writings*, 25-31.

[8] Orchard, "The Library of Wulfstan of York," 695.

[9] *Grið* 6.

Adapting the laws of Kent for an eleventh-century readership, Wulfstan drew upon nostalgia for the Christian kingdoms of the conversion era in order to evoke a sense of moral urgency in his Viking-age audience. If, for Æthelberht and his successors, the drafting of written law served as a means of legislating social order in seventh-century Kent, so Wulfstan returned to their laws as he attempted to impose his own vision of social order on eleventh-century England.

-I-

Although the precise date remains uncertain, the kingdom of Kent was absorbed by Mercia sometime during the reign of King Offa (r. 757-796).[10] By that time, copies of Kentish royal legislation had already begun to circulate elsewhere in the British Isles, but the limited number of surviving legal texts from this period makes it difficult to ascertain the extent to which Kentish practices influenced lawmakers in other Anglo-Saxon kingdoms. A series of clauses shared between the laws of Ine of Wessex and the slightly later laws of Wihtræd of Kent indicates some degree of correspondence between the two courts in the mid-690s, though the nature of this correspondence remains the subject of considerable debate.[11] Likewise, while Bede received his copy of the laws of Æthelberht sometime in the 720s, almost certainly from Abbot Albinus of the monastery of St. Peter and St. Paul (later St. Augustine's) in Canterbury, too little Northumbrian law survives for us to know whether his texts were passed on to the royal court.[12] Given how difficult it is to document the influence of the Kentish laws during this period, it may be tempting to dismiss them as, in the words of Patrick Wormald, "mere clerical fantasies without relevance to the law as it was issued and enforced."[13] Within Kent itself, however, the existence of charters confirming privileges first granted in the laws of Wihtræd suggests that those responsible for producing the legislation did view royal legislation as potentially enforceable and as a model for legal draftsmanship.[14]

---

[10] See Frank M. Stenton, *Anglo-Saxon England*, 3d ed. (Oxford: Clarendon Press, 1971), 206-9.

[11] See the discussion by Stefan Jurasinski elsewhere in this volume.

[12] On Bede's source, see Richard Shaw, *The Gregorian Mission to Kent in Bede's* Ecclesiastical *History: Methodology and Sources* (London: Routledge, 2018), 124-5 as well as Bede's own preface to the *Historia ecclesiastica,* Colgrave and Mynors, *Ecclesiastical History*, 2-3. On the evidence for early Northumbrian law, see Bryan Carella, "The Earliest Expression for Outlawry in Anglo-Saxon Law," *Traditio* 70 (2015): 111-43.

[13] Patrick Wormald, "Æthelred the Lawmaker," in *Ethelred the Unready*, ed. David Hill, B.A.R. British Series (Oxford, England: B.A.R., 1978), 49.

[14] See, for instance, charter S 20, ed. in S.E. Kelly, *The Charters of St Augustine's Abbey, Canterbury, and Minster-in-Thanet*, Anglo-Saxon Charters (Oxford: Oxford University Press, 1995), no. 10, 40-4. On this point, see also Richard Abels, *Lordship and Military Obligation in Anglo-Saxon England* (London: British

Accordingly, although little indication of Kentish influence on non-Kentish lawmakers survives prior to the end of the ninth century, we can conclude with some certainty that the laws were known beyond the boundaries of the Kentish kingdom and that contemporaries would have viewed these texts as legitimate means of expressing the royal will.

The earliest undisputed reference to a Kentish lawcode by a non-Kentish legislator is Alfred's claim in the prologue to his laws that, "Those [laws] which I found—either of my kinsman Ine's time, or of Offa, king of the Mercians, or of Æthelberht, the first to receive baptism among the English people—which seemed to me most just I gathered here, and rejected the others" (*Ða ðe ic gemette—awðer oððe on Ines dæge, mines mæges, oðð on Offan Mercna cyninges oððe on Æþelbryhtes, þe ærest fulluhte onfeng on Angelcynne, þa ðe me ryhtoste ðuhton, ic þa heron gegaderode, 7 þa oðre forlet*).[15] Yet precisely what Alfred meant by "gathered here" (*heron gegaderode*) remains unclear. The problem, as Patrick Wormald noted, is that "no single law of Alfred's was an unaltered rehearsal of one of Æthelberht's [...] Alfred was therefore professing a greater respect for precedent than he actually practiced."[16] The only section of Alfred's *domboc* which does contain echoes of Æthelberht's legislation is the personal injury schedule (clauses 44-77), yet the absence of explicit verbal borrowings or overlapping penalties has led scholars to question whether Alfred truly relied on *Æthelberht*, or if both kings simply drew on a shared oral tradition. As Lisi Oliver demonstrated, however, the sequence of injuries treated in *Alfred* 44-64—though not necessarily the penalties themselves—follows *Æthelberht* 33-71 more closely than it does the personal injury schedules of contemporary continental legislation.[17] Likewise, Carole Hough has argued that the scribal practices used to transcribe these particular clauses in the manuscripts of Alfred's laws bear an especially close resemblance to those of the scribe responsible for Æthelberht's laws in *Textus Roffensis*. She suggests that this unusually high degree of similarity may indicate, "an influence from the way Æthelberht's laws were represented graphically, strengthening the hypothesis that this section of Alfred's laws was based on Æthelberht's."[18] The

Museum Publications, 1988), 50; Nicholas Brooks, *The Early History of the Church of Canterbury* (London: Leicester University Press, 1984), 75, 183-4.

15 *Af.El.* 49.9

16 Wormald, *Making* 279. For similar observations, see also Stefan Jurasinski, *The Old English Penitentials and Anglo-Saxon Law* (Cambridge: Cambridge University Press, 2015), 16; Oliver, *Beginnings*, 38; Oliver, "Legal Documentation and the Practice of English Law," 505; David Pratt, *The Political Thought of King Alfred the Great*, Cambridge Studies in Medieval Life and Thought (Cambridge: Cambridge University Press, 2007), 218-22.

17 Oliver, *Beginnings*, 37-9. For an authoritative account of the Kentish and West Saxon injury schedules, see Oliver, *Body Legal.*

18 Hough, "Numbers," 127-8.

implication underlying both Oliver's and Hough's claims is that Æthelberht's influence on Alfred was more formal than substantive. In other words, Alfred was less interested in replicating specific clauses or provisions than he was in producing a document that, at least in parts, recognizably hearkened back to the earlier lawcode. Doing so enabled Alfred to situate his legislation within a tradition of English Christian lawmaking stretching back to the first king "to receive baptism among the English people" (*fulluhte onfeng on Angelcynne*). Within this context, it may be significant that the *domboc*'s prologue refers to Ine as Alfred's kinsman, thus West Saxon, and Offa as Mercian, but it identifies Æthelberht as a foundational figure for the *Angelcynn* as a whole. It seems, then, that the value of Kentish legislation to Alfred lay less in its character as law than in the *imprimatur* it granted to his own legal project.

Important as the laws of Æthelberht were to Alfred's legislation, they played only a small role in the lawmaking practices of his successors. Over the next century, no legislator explicitly cited the Kentish laws and few clauses show any evidence of Kentish derivation. Of those that do, it remains unclear whether the later clauses borrowed directly from Kentish sources, whether Kentish texts informed the later clauses indirectly, or whether the Kentish and West Saxon clauses were simply analogues that happened to regulate similar practices.[19] Perhaps the most intriguing parallel occurs in the so-called "Andover Code" of King Edgar (*II Edgar*). The clause in question reads,

> 7 healde man ælces Sunnandæges freolsunga fram Sæternesdæges noontide oð Monandæges lihtinge, be þam wite, þe seo domboc tæce, 7 ælcne oðerne mæssedæg, swa he beboden sy.
>
> And every person shall observe the Sunday Sabbath from mid-afternoon on Saturday until dawn on Monday, according to the punishment which the *domboc* prescribes, and every other holy day according to what is commanded for it.[20]

The reference to *seo domboc* appears to link this ruling with the laws of Ine and Alfred, both of which regulate Sunday observance; however, the relevant clause in *Alfred* concerns thefts on the Sabbath rather than labor while the relevant clauses in *Ine* only regulate labor carried out by slaves or by freemen working without their lord's permission.[21] Given these differences in phrasing, subject, and scope, the connections between the Sunday regulations in *II Edgar* and *Alfred-Ine* appear tenuous at best. This tenuousness raises the possibility that Edgar's use of the phrase *þe seo domboc tæce* may not refer to Alfred's lawbook after all: as both Dafydd Jenkins and Mary Richards have observed, post-Alfredian legislation frequently links specific clauses to *seo domboc*, even when no

[19] See, for instance, *II Em.* 1 (*Abt.* 22), *II Em.* 7.3 (*Wi.* 11, 12, and 14), *II Eg.* Pr.1 (Wi. 21.1), *IV Eg.* Pr.1 (Wi. Pr), *II Atr.* 3.4 (*Wi.* 25), and *IV Atr.* 7.1 (*Wi.* 26 and 27).

[20] *II Eg.* 5.

[21] *Ine* 3-3.2, *Af.* 5.5.

analogous clause occurs in *Alfred-Ine*.[22] Rather, Richards suggests, by the early tenth century, the phrase *seo domboc* had come to serve as a general term encompassing any "compendium of judgments."[23] That this might be the case here is suggested by the fact that *II Edgar*'s Sunday clause bears less resemblance to those in *Alfred-Ine* than it does to *Wihtræd* 8-8.2, which regulates Sabbath observance more broadly than its West Saxon contemporary. In these clauses, as in *II Edgar*, labor is forbidden to both slaves and freemen, whether the lord countenances it or not.[24] *Wihtræd* 8 also specifies the period of the Sabbath from "sunset on the eve of Sunday until sunset on the eve of Monday" (*an sunnan æfen æfter setlgange oþ monan æfenes setlgang*), a phrase similar to *II Edgar*'s "from mid-afternoon on Saturday until dawn on Monday" (*fram Sæternesdæges noontide oð Monandæges lihtinge*). Indeed, if the Andover Code did draw on Kentish material, it may be that the clause in *II Edgar* was partially motivated by the need to redefine the legal limits of Sunday observance as first legislated by Wihtræd in order to bring them into line with tenth-century religious practices.[25] Whether or not this was the case, however, the similarities in subject and phrasing between *II Edgar* 5 and *Wihtræd* 8-8.2 indicate that the *domboc* in question was more likely to be a Kentish than a West Saxon compilation, suggesting at least some degree of familiarity with Kentish law at Edgar's court.

The strong likelihood that *II Edgar* 5 derives from *Wihtræd* 8-8.2—along with the possibility that Kentish source material may also have indirectly informed clauses in *II Edmund*, *IV Edgar*, and *II* and *IV Æthelred*[26]—lends credence to the suggestion that the Kentish laws remained within the intellectual scope of West Saxon lawmakers well into the tenth century. Yet even if the laws of Æthelberht, Hlothhere and Eadric, and Wihtræd may have been consulted by later legislators, they appear to have felt little need to cite Kentish law by name or identify it as precedent. In part, this doubtless reflects the fact that by the end of the tenth century, the kingdom of Kent had been defunct for a little more than two centuries. Its laws reflected the needs and practices of a conversion-era regional monarchy, not those of the emerging unified English realm

---

[22] Dafydd Jenkins, "The Medieval Welsh Idea of Law," *Tijdschrift voor Rechtsgeschiedenis* 49 (1981): 343-5; Richards, "Written Standard," 8.

[23] Richards, "Written Standard," 9.

[24] Passage from *Wi* follows Oliver's numbering. On these clauses, see Oliver, *Beginnings*, 170-4.

[25] *II Eg.*'s definition of the Sabbath appears nearly verbatim in a roughly contemporary homiletic version of the so-called Sunday Letter, suggesting either a direct connection or a shared source. See Dorothy Haines, *Sunday Observance and the Sunday Letter in Anglo-Saxon England* (Woodbridge: D.S. Brewer, 2010), 62n. 150; Dorothy Whitelock, "Bishop Ecgred, Pehtred and Niall," in *Ireland in Early Medieval Europe: Studies in Memory of Kathleen Hughes*, ed. Dorothy Whitelock, Rosamond McKitterick, and David Dumville (Cambridge: Cambridge University Press, 1982), 51; Patrick Wormald, *Papers Prepatory to the Making of English Law: King Alfred to the Twelfth Century, Vol. II: From God's Law to Common Law* (London: Early English Laws, 2014), 55.

[26] See above, n. 19.

that replaced it. Moreover, the emphasis on stylistic conservatism rather than specific precedent in legal composition made the specific citation of Kentish law unnecessary. In other words, the authority of royal legislation, reflecting its likely origins as a form of oral literature, rested in large part upon the extent to which it adhered to a series of traditional rhetorical conventions rather than the explicit identification of precedents.[27] For later West Saxon legislators, a formal resemblance between their enactments and the laws of Æthelberht and his successors—perhaps accompanied by an allusion to a *domboc*—was more in keeping with the practices and expectations of legal composition than the citation-heavy style that would come into fashion after the twelfth century. At the same time, though, the vague and allusive nature of tenth- and eleventh-century references to earlier law makes Archbishop Wulfstan's explicit references to "the laws of the Kentish people" in his own legal writings that much more surprising. For Wulfstan, the evocation of conversion-era Kent would come to play an important role in the legal program he mapped out during his early years as bishop of Worcester and archbishop of York.

-II-

More so than any of his predecessors, Archbishop Wulfstan turned to earlier Anglo-Saxon legal history when seeking inspiration and source material for contemporary legislation.[28] His legal writings include explicit borrowings from nearly all the major West Saxon royal enactments of the previous century as well as various regional statutes.[29] Likewise, his legislative style could be deliberately archaic, echoing the minimal conditionals, non-dependent directives, and topicalization more characteristic of the seventh century than the eleventh.[30] Yet if Wulfstan's familiarity with earlier legal material is obvious, less clear are the sources of his knowledge. We may suppose that some texts of royal legislation must have been readily available to him: legal manuscripts likely circulated at Æthelred's court and compilations of West Saxon law formed

---

[27] On the impact of oral composition on the conventions of early written law, see Eric Alfred Havelock, *The Muse Learns to Write: Reflections on Orality and Literacy from Antiquity to the Present* (New Haven: Yale University Press, 1986), 74-5. On the stylistic conservatism of Old English law, see Bethurum, "Stylistic Features," 268; Richards, "Written Standard," 12; Levi Roach, "Law Codes and Legal Norms in Anglo-Saxon England," *Historical Research* 86 (2013): 465-86; J.R. Schwyter, "Syntax and Style in the Anglo-Saxon Law-Codes," in *Verschriftung - Verschriftlichung: Aspekte des Medienwechsels in verschiedenen Kulturen und Epochen*, ed. C. Ehler and U. Schaefer (Tübingen: Gunter Narr, 1998), 190.

[28] On this point, see especially Rabin, "Compilation on Status," 175-92; Rabin, *Political Writings*, 37-40.

[29] See, for instance, Wormald's analysis of the legal sources for *I-II Cn.* in Wormald, *Making* 357-60.

[30] Schwyter, "Syntax and Style," 222.

part of the library at St. Paul's Cathedral in London, where Wulfstan served as bishop from 996-1002.[31] Nonetheless, although the admittedly elliptical references to Kentish material in the earlier West Saxon codes suggests that the seventh-century laws may have been similarly accessible, the circumstances under which Wulfstan first encountered them are unknown, though his close affiliation with Archbishop Ælfric of Canterbury during the early part of his career provides a Kentish connection about which it is tempting to speculate.[32]

However, if the sources of Wulfstan's knowledge cannot be identified with certainty, the intellectual trends that shaped his approach to the Kentish laws are somewhat easier to trace. Perhaps the most significant influence on Wulfstan's view of conversion-era legal history was his affiliation with the second generation of the monastic reform movement, those ecclesiastics who trained with first-generation reformers such as Dunstan and Æthelwold, and whose political views were shaped by the civil disruptions of the 970s and 980s.[33] The prominent place that nostalgia for conversion-era Christianity occupied in reformist thought has long been recognized, although this nostalgia has typically been discussed as centered only on the monastic practices of Bede's Northumbria.[34] Less recognized, though, has been the role of seventh-century Kent in reformist accounts of the English past, particularly in those of Wulfstan's contemporaries. Ælfric, for instance, builds his homily on Pope Gregory I around an extended account of

---

31 The great twelfth-century anthology, C.C.C.C. 383, was compiled at London based on earlier materials. Wulfstan's association with the sources employed by the later scribe remains ambiguous, however the compilation does include several works attributable to the archbishop and at least one text, the so-called "Shipman's List," was likely commissioned during his London tenure. Baxter, "Archbishop Wulfstan," 164-5; Wormald, *Making* 228-36.

32 On Wulfstan's relationship with Archbishop Ælfric, see Rabin, "Wulfstan at London," 192-8.

33 On Wulfstan's affiliation with the monastic reform, see Joyce Hill, "Monastic Reform and the Secular Church: Ælfric's Pastoral Letters in Context," in *England in the Eleventh Century: Proceedings of the 1990 Harlaxton Symposium*, ed. Carola Hicks (Stamford: Paul Watkins Publishing, 1992), 103-17; Hill, "Reform and Resistance: Preaching Styles in Late Anglo-Saxon England," in *De L'homélie Au Sermon: Histoire De La Prédication Médiévale*, ed. Jacqueline Hamesse and Xavier Hermand (Louvain-La-Neuve: Institut d"Etudes Médiévales de l'Université Catholique de Louvain, 1993), 15-46; Hill, "Archbishop Wulfstan: Reformer?," in *Wulfstan, Archbishop of York: The Proceedings of the Second Alcuin Conference*, ed. Matthew Townend, Studies in the Early Middle Ages (Turnhout: Brepols, 2004), 309-24; Rabin, *Political Writings*, 25-31; Rabin, "Wulfstan at London," 186-206.

34 See Simon Coates, "Perceptions of the Anglo-Saxon Past in the Tenth-Century Reform Movement," in *The Church Retrospective: Papers Read at the 1995 Summer Meeting and the 1996 Winter Meeting of the Ecclesiastical History Society*, ed. R.N. Swanson, Studies in Church History (Woodbridge: Boydell, 1997), 61-74; Antonia Gransden, "Traditionalism and Continuity During the Last Century of Anglo-Saxon Monasticism," *Journal of Ecclesiastical History* 40 (1989): 159-207; Joyce Hill, *Bede and the Benedictine Reform*, Jarrow Lectures (Jarrow: St. Paul's Church, 1998).

Æthelberht's conversion, largely based on that in Bede's *Historia*.[35] Likewise, the anonymous author of the *Vita sancti Dunstani*—like Wulfstan, a member of the circle of Archbishop Ælfric of Canterbury[36]—highlighted that it was "to this part of the country" (*has patriae partes*, referring to Kent) that God, through Pope Gregory, chose to send Bishop Augustine.[37] Most notably, Wulfstan himself (also drawing on Bede) turned to the early Archbishops of Canterbury when seeking models of ecclesiastical independence from external interference: as he noted in a letter to the pope (likely Benedict VIII, although the date is uncertain), "Augustine was followed by Laurence, whom he had consecrated while still living, according to the example of the blessed Peter, prince of the Apostles, who is reported to have consecrated Clement as his aide and successor" (*Augustinus successorem sibi Laurentium, adhuc vivens, ordinavit, exemplum sequens beati Petri, principis apostolorum, qui Clementem adiutorem et successorem sibi consecrasse perhibetur*).[38] Wulfstan and his contemporaries' reliance on Bede as their primary source for conversion-era history meant that seventh-century Kent inevitably took second place to eighth-century Northumbria—and indeed, was understood largely from a Northumbrian perspective—in the reformist historical narrative; nonetheless, as a foundational moment in the history of English Christianity, it still provided a useful set of precedents for those seeking to promote a return to religious orthodoxy. For Wulfstan in particular, early Kent appears to have served as a means of establishing the historical justification for his views concerning ecclesiastical rights and prerogatives.

Borrowings from Kentish law occur even in Wulfstan's earliest legislative efforts. Particularly in the law-codes *V-VII Æthelred*, Wulfstan introduces terminology and themes drawn from seventh-century legal enactments as a way of evoking the theological orthodoxy of conversion-era England. *V Æthelred*, for example, decrees that "each Christian man is to zealously avoid illicit intercourse and faithfully adhere to the laws of the Church" (*æghwilc Cristen man unriht hæmed georne forbuge 7 godcunde laga rihtlice healde*).[39] The significance of this clause is indicated by its near-*verbatim* repetition in

[35] Ælfric's homily on Pope Gregory is edited in M.R. Godden, *Ælfric's Catholic Homiles, the Second Series: Text*, EETS s.s.5 (London: Oxford University Press, 1979), 72-80.

[36] See Michael Winterbottom and Michael Lapidge, *The Early Lives of St. Dunstan*, Oxford Medieval Texts (Oxford: Oxford University Press, 2012), lxxiii.

[37] See the *Vita sancti Dunstani* 2.2 in Winterbottom and Lapidge, *Early Lives*, 8-9.

[38] Wulfstan's so-called "letter of protest" is edited in Dorothy Whitelock, ed., *Councils and Synods with Other Documents Relating to the English Church: 871-1066*, vol. I, part 1 (Oxford: Clarendon Press, 1981), 441-7. The passage in question appears on p. 445. For a general discussion of this text, see Dorothy Bethurum, "A Letter of Protest from the English Bishops to the Pope," in *Philologica: The Malone Anniversary Studies*, ed. T.A. Kirby and H.B. Woolf (Baltimore: The Johns Hopkins University Press, 1949), 97-104. A discussion of this particular passage and its relevance to Wulfstan's views on episcopal independence occurs in Gareth Mann, "The Development of Wulfstan's Alcuin Manuscript," in *Wulfstan, Archbishop of York: Proceedings of the Second Alcuin Conference*, ed. Matthew Townend (Turnhout: Brepols, 2004), 263.

[39] *V Atr.* 10.

both *VI Æthelred* and *I Cnut*.[40] Although provisions forbidding adultery and other forms of extramarital sexual activity had been a regular feature of ninth- and tenth-century legislation, these clauses identify the crime with the nouns *æwbryce* or *hæmedþing* and the verbs *forlicgan* or *hæman*.[41] Wulfstan, however, employs the collocation *unriht hæmed* ("illicit intercourse"), a phrase drawn from the laws of Wihtræd, where it appears as the compound *unrihthæmed*: "Men committing illicit intercourse shall take up a righteous life through the repentance of sins or be cast out from the communion of the Church" (*Unrihthæmde mæn to rihtum life mid synna hreowe tofon oþþe of ciricean g[m] a[n]an ascadene sien*).[42] In a similar instance of borrowing, *VII Æthelred* rules that slaves guilty of breaking a fast shall "suffer the lash" (*corio [...] componat*), while poor freemen must pay 30 pence and royal thegns 120 shillings.[43] Earlier West Saxon law had penalized the violation of religious fasts, yet the punishments set by Wulfstan—whipping for the enslaved and fractional wergild payments for the free—are drawn from the laws of Wihtræd, which likewise require a slave guilty of breaking a fast to "pay with his hide" (*gebete [...] his hyde*) and a freemen with his *healsfang* (a fraction of his wergild).[44] In each of these cases, Wulfstan bypasses West Saxon antecedents in order to resurrect the language or practices of Kentish law. Doing so provides him with the precedent necessary to magnify the moral consequences of the crimes proscribed by each clause. Thus, Wulfstan's revival of the collocation *unriht hæmed* draws on the theologically-informed language of Wihtræd's legislation to restore a sense of moral condemnation to a term that had, by the eleventh century, been reduced to a generic euphemism for "marriage" or "cohabitation."[45] As Shari Horner has argued, Wulfstan's reframing of the legal language of sexual transgression in religious terms marks a transition between "literal [...] proscriptions of sexual violence and moral injunctions, couched in a language of both sexual and spiritual danger."[46] Similarly, in restoring the original Kentish penalties for the violation of a fast, Wulfstan signals the enhanced significance of what had been relatively minor infraction. Much like the penitential processions mandated elsewhere in the same text—which Simon Keynes has shown to have their roots in the

[40] *VI Atr.* 11 and *I Cn.* 6.3.
[41] See, for instance, *Af.* 10, 11.1-2, 18.1; *I Em.* 4.
[42] *Wi.* 3.
[43] *VII Atr.* 2.4. Similar provisions occur in *EGu.* 8.
[44] *Wi.* 14-15. On *healsfang*, see Oliver, *Beginnings*, 171-2.
[45] On the evolving definition of *hæmen*, see Julie Coleman, "Sexual Euphemism in Old English," *Neuphilologische Mitteilungen* 93 (1992): 94; Andreas Fischer, *Engagement, Wedding, and Marriage in Old English* (Heidelberg: Carl Winter, 1986), 67; Shari Horner, "The Language of Rape in Old English Literature and Law: Views from the Anglo-Saxon(ist)s," in *Sex and Sexuality in Anglo-Saxon England: Essays in Memory of Daniel Gillmore Calder*, ed. Carol Braun Pasternack and Lisa M. C. Weston (Tempe: Arizona Center for Medieval and Renaissance Studies, 2004), 157.
[46] Horner, "The Language of Rape," 162.

ritual practices of Augustine of Canterbury and his companions[47]— reviving conversion-era practices here serves to emphasize the necessity of returning to a more orthodox form of religious practice in the face of the increasing Viking threat. Taken together, clauses such as these suggest that Kentish legislation initially functioned for Wulfstan as a source of moral and legal precedent upon which he could draw in the course of his emerging project of social regeneration. Framing conversion-era legislation as a model of moral rigor thereby provided Wulfstan with a degree of historical justification for his increasingly orthodox approach to the composition of royal legislation.

Wulfstan's most direct engagement with Kentish royal legislation occurs in a short tract titled *Be griðe 7 be munde* (*Concerning Sanctuary and Protection*) preserved in London, British Library, Cotton Nero A.i. Likely composed sometime between 1006 and 1008, *Grið* (as it has been designated by modern editors) catalogues past and present sanctuary practices in order to emphasize the inviolability of ecclesiastical authority.[48] In the course of its catalogue, *Grið* explicitly cites Kentish law:

> [6] 7 on Cantwara lage cyning 7 arcebiscop agan gelicne ana efen dyrne mundbryce.
> [7] 7 on þam lagum is arcebiscopes feoh endlyfangylde 7 cynges is nigongylde.
> [8] 7 Christes cyrican mundbyrd is efne swa cynges.
>
> [6] And in the laws of the Kentish people, the king and archbishop are owed an equal and likewise costly penalty for the violation of their protection.
> [7] And according to those laws, elevenfold compensation is due for the archbishop's property and ninefold for the king's.
> [8] And the penalty for violating the protection of Christ's church is the same as that [for violating the protection] of the king.[49]

Rather than quote directly from Kentish legislation, Wulfstan here constructs something of a legal pastiche based primarily on prescriptions found in *Æthelberht* 1-2 and *Wihtræd* 2.[50] This adaptive approach allows Wulfstan to reframe his Kentish sources according to his own priorities: whereas *Grið* decrees that king and archbishop are to receive equal compensation for the violation of their protection and that damage to archiepiscopal property is to be compensated at a higher rate than damage to royal property, *Æthelberht* only lists compensation rates for violations of ecclesiastical protection,

---

47 Simon Keynes, "An Abbot, an Archbishop, and the Viking Raids of 1006-7 and 1009-12," *Anglo-Saxon England* 36 (2007): 181-2.

48 On *Grið*, see Dorothy Bethurum, "Six Anonymous Old English Codes," *JEGP* 69 (1950): 449-63; Rabin, *Political Writings*, 76-81; Wormald, *Making*, 394-5.

49 Translation based on that in Rabin, *Political Writings*, 77-8. The clause numbers were added by later editors.

50 It should be noted that although this is the only passage in which Wulfstan cites Kentish law as his source, similar stipulations regarding sanctuary privilege do occur elsewhere in his legal corpus. See *VIII Atr.* 2 and 3; *I Cn.* 2.3-5, 3a.2.

while elevenfold compensation is listed as the penalty for damage to episcopal property only.[51] The rights of king and archbishop remain unspecified. Dorothy Bethurum has suggested, surely correctly, that Wulfstan's revisions were "aimed at elevating the status of the upper clergy"[52]; however, it should be emphasized that a crucial element of this elevation involved, not merely establishing the status of the archbishop, but defining the rights of the Church as superior to those of the king. Much as he does elsewhere—perhaps most famously in the chapter on divine authority which begins the later versions of the *Institutes of Polity*[53]—Wulfstan here acknowledges the legitimacy of royal authority even as he asserts the primacy of ecclesiastical privilege. In so doing, Wulfstan remakes early Kentish law in the image of the late Reform, in which a suspicion of secular governance replaced the close partnership between *rex* and *ecclesia* promoted by Bishop Æthelwold and his contemporaries.[54] Attributing his revisions to the "the laws of the Kentish people" provides a necessary legal context for Wulfstan's revisions. Simultaneously citing and rewriting Kentish law thus offers Wulfstan a means of championing ecclesiastical prerogatives by grounding those prerogatives in historical precedent.

The three Kentish clauses are not *Grið*'s only gesture towards regional specificity: clauses 9-12, based on sections of *Alfred-Ine*, are attributed to "the laws of the Southern English" (*Suðengla lage*) and clauses 13-13.2, for which sources do not survive, are identified as "laws of the Northern English" (*Norðengla lage*). Similar examples of regional cataloguing occur elsewhere in Wulfstan's work, most notably in *II Cnut* 12-15 and the "Compilation on Status," but this is the only instance of him including Kentish law in such a grouping.[55] Typically, Wulfstan employs such passages to emphasize the subordination of local jurisdictions to royal authority. In the case of *Grið*, however, the cataloguing of sanctuary practices appears to be directed towards a more ambitious end. *Grið* is a

---

[51] Liebermann hypothesizes that the difference between the two passages might also be partially accounted for by the fact that the laws of Æthelberht were preserved in a manuscript from Rochester (an episcopal see) while *Grið* survives in a manuscript associated with Canterbury (an archiepiscopal see). See Liebermann, *Gesetze*, III: 265.

[52] Dorothy Bethurum Loomis, "*Regnum* and *Sacerdotium* in the Early Eleventh Century," in *England before the Conquest: Studies in Primary Sources Presented to Dorothy Whitelock*, ed. Peter Clemoes and Kathleen Hughes (Cambridge: Cambridge University Press, 1971), 140. On this point, see also Wormald, "*Laga Eadwardi*," 132.

[53] Rabin, *Political Writings*, 103n. 2, 192; Renée Trilling, "Sovereignty and Social Order: Archbishop Wulfstan and the *Institutes of Polity*," in *The Bishop Reformed: Studies of Episcopal Power and Culture in the Central Middle Ages*, ed. John Ott and Anna Trumbore Jones (Aldershot: Ashgate, 2007), 69.

[54] Christopher A. Jones, *Ælfric's Letter to the Monks of Eynsham*, Cambridge Studies in Anglo Saxon England (Cambridge: Cambridge University Press, 1998), 42-51; Andrew Rabin, "Holy Bodies, Legal Matters: Reaction and Reform in Ælfric's *Eugenia* and the Ely Privilege," *Studies in Philology* 110, no. 2 (2013): 228-30; Rabin, "Wulfstan at London," 196-8.

[55] On such passages, see Rabin, "Compilation on Status," 183.

curiously hybrid text, the opening clauses of which (1-5) adopt an explicitly nostalgic tone documenting how "it once was" (*hwilom wæran*) in the "capital cities" (*heafodstedas*) and how "it stood in those days among the English" (*hit stod in ðam dagum inne mid Englum*). The retrospective clauses are followed by a series of legal stipulations—including the regional catalogue—composed in the conditional "if/then" syntax familiar to readers of Old English royal legislation (6-18). Beginning with clause 19, though, the text abruptly shifts from law to homily, introducing Biblical citations (from *Psalms*, *Proverbs*, and *Matthew*), assurances that "we all have one heavenly father and one spiritual mother" (*Ealle we habbað ænne heofonlicne fæder 7 ane gastlice modor*), and interjections (*la!*) typical of oral performance.[56] The integration of diverse genres is characteristic of Wulfstan's prose, but *Grið* does not so much integrate genres as combine seemingly distinct historical, legal, and homiletic texts into a tripartite whole. Wulfstan's purpose in constructing his text in this fashion becomes clear in its concluding sentence: "Therefore, every church sanctuary is Christ's own sanctuary, and every Christian has a fundamental responsibility to hold that sanctuary in great reverence" (*Forðam ælc cyricgrið is Cristenes agen grið, 7 ælc Cristen man ah micle þearfe, þæt he on ðam griðe mycle mæþe wite*).[57] The aim of the text, in other words, has been to define the inviolability of ecclesiastical sanctuary, not as a privilege granted by secular authority, but as a feature of divine law which "every Christian" (*ælc Cristen man*), king and subject, is bound to observe. The account of historical and regional sanctuary practices in clauses 1-18 thus serves to establish sanctuary as a central tenet of English law, while clauses 19-31 ground English practice in Biblical precedent, thus linking it to a form of universal authority transcending the traditions of individual regions and the decrees of individual kings. Within this context, Wulfstan's summary of Kentish sanctuary practices provides a useful bridge between his historical account in clauses 1-5 and the subsequent discussion of contemporary law in clauses 6-18. Drawing on the laws of Æthelberht thereby evokes reformist nostalgia for the religious orthodoxy of the seventh century even as it acknowledges the different legal traditions that shaped his eleventh-century present.

In the years following 1016, borrowings from Kentish legislation occur less frequently in Wulfstan's legal writings. In part, this reflects the shift towards the more explicitly homiletic register characteristic of what Wormald has called his "mature legislative style,"[58] though it also reflects Wulfstan's increasing reliance on his own work as source material for his legislative efforts. Accordingly, although several clauses in *I-II Cnut* seem—albeit tenuously—to draw on Kentish source material,[59] only one

---

[56] See *Grið* 23, 23.1, 26, 29, and 30.

[57] *Grið* 31.1.

[58] Wormald, *Making* 352.

[59] See *I Cn.* 6.3 (*Wi.* 3), *II Cn.* 45.1 and 46 (*Wi.* 11), and *II Cn.* 59 (*Abt.*18).

quotes directly from a piece of seventh-century legislation. Serving as the final clause in a small cluster devoted to sexual crimes, *II Cnut* 55 reads, "Foreigners, if they will not make their unions legal, are to depart from the land with their possessions and their sins" (*Ælðeodige men, gif hig heora hæmed rihtan nellan, of lande mid heora æhtum 7 synnan gewitan*), a *verbatim* rendering (with orthographic variations) of *Wihtræd* 4.[60] This clause most likely indicates an attempt to encourage the conversion of Scandinavian immigrants by invalidating marriages not conducted in proper Christian fashion. Significantly, though, as was the case with Wulfstan's earlier borrowings from Kentish law, the ruling set out in this clause is without analogues in earlier West Saxon legislation. Indeed, *II Cnut* 55 marks the only attempt by a later Anglo-Saxon lawmaker to mandate the regularization of foreign marriages; however, any implication of legal novelty is contradicted by the clause's origin in a resurrected seventh-century prohibition. It seems plausible, then, that Kentish law here fills much the same role for Wulfstan that it did earlier in his career: as precedent justifying the reassertion of religious orthodoxy. Borrowing from the Kentish laws once again enables Wulfstan to ground what may have appeared as legislative innovation in the legal traditions of the conversion era.

The recurrence of Kentish borrowings in Wulfstan's legal writings indicates that the seventh-century laws remained within his intellectual orbit throughout his career. Although they cannot be considered among Wulfstan's most influential sources—their importance to his work is dwarfed by that of contemporaries like Ælfric or the Carolingian reformers of the previous generation—the laws of Æthelberht and his successors nonetheless provided him with a useful instrument as he developed his vision of eleventh-century England as a Christian society. Yet if Wulfstan's interest in legal history led him to avail himself of early materials to a greater degree than did his predecessors, his use of Kentish law was not in any sense a rediscovery: rather, Kentish legislation had been consulted by West Saxon lawmakers—regularly, if not necessarily frequently—for well over a century. As such, Lisi Oliver was surely correct in writing that the kings of Kent "set a precedent that would cast a long shadow." [61] It was one under which Archbishop Wulfstan still labored four hundred years later.

[60] The version quoted above is taken from London, British Library, Cotton Nero A. i. Troubled by the clause's archaic syntax, the later scribe of Cambridge, Corpus Christi College 383 revised it to read, "Foreigners, if they will not make their unions legal, shall be driven from the land with their possessions and depart their sins "Ælðeodige men, gif hig heora hemed rihtan nellað, driue hi manof lande mid heora æhtum 7 on synnan gewitan." See Stefan Jurasinski, "The Old English Penitentials and the Law of Slavery," in *English Law before Magna Carta: Felix Liebermann and die Gesetze Der Angelsachsen*, ed. Stefan Jurasinski, Lisi Oliver, and Andrew Rabin (Leiden: Brill, 2010), 112; Wormald, *Making,* 353n. 422.

[61] Oliver, "Royal and Ecclesiastical Law," 112.

English Legal Discourse in *Quadripartitus**

Jay Paul Gates

From the time the English began writing their laws, they wrote them in English, unlike Continental counterparts such as the Franks or Normans, who wrote in Latin.[1] As such, the laws have been taken as an especially strong expression of Anglo-Saxon identity. Commenting on the drafting of the earliest lawcode, Æthelberht's, Lisi Oliver posits an underlying logic for the choice:

> Two possible motivations can be hypothesized for Æthelberht's commission of his laws in the vernacular: first to reproduce as nearly as possible the orally transmitted version of legal stipulations in a language accessible to his people; and second, to separate himself and his people linguistically and thus politically from the dominance of Francia (where laws were composed in Latin).[2]

Similarly, Mary Richards has shown that the drafters of law drew on vernacular poetic traditions and that the choice of English as the language of law allowed for the preservation of Germanic legal traditions preceding the conversion.[3] Indeed, Lisi Oliver's *The Body Legal in Barbarian Law* demonstrates overwhelmingly the continuity of legal traditions and concepts embedded in the language of law among the English and other barbarian peoples. Yet Patrick Wormald finds that there was space for innovation within the legal tradition; moreover, issuing legislation was often ideological, meeting an expectation that kings would promulgate laws at certain intervals in their role as king.[4] While there is no question that law remained important to English identity throughout the

* Support for this project was provided by a PSC-CUNY Award, jointly funded by The Professional Staff Congress and The City University of New York.

[1] Patrick Wormald, "*Lex Scripta* and *Verbum Regis*: Legislation and Germanic Kingship from Euric to Cnut," in idem, *Legal Culture in the Early Medieval West: Law as Text, Image and Experience* (London: Hambledon Press, 1999), 1-43.

[2] Lisi Oliver, "Legal Documentation and the Practice of English Law," in *The Cambridge History of Early Medieval English Literature*, ed. Clare A. Lees (Cambridge: Cambridge University Press, 2013), 499-529, at 500.

[3] Mary Richards, "Elements of a Written Standard in the Old English Laws," in *Standardizing English: Essays in the History of Language Change in Honor of John Hurt Fisher*, ed. Joseph B. Trahern (Knoxville: University of Tennessee Press, 1989), 1-22, at 11-12; eadem, "Anglo-Saxonism in the Old English Laws," in *Anglo-Saxonism and the Construction of Social Identity*, ed. Allen J. Frantzen and John D. Niles (Gainesville: University of Florida Press, 1997), 40-59, at 40.

[4] Wormald, "*Lex Scripta* and *Verbum Regis*," 11-13.

Anglo-Saxon period, between the seventh-century Kentish laws that introduced written English law and the late tenth- and early eleventh-century laws of Æthelred and Cnut, the status of written law and of legal language had most certainly shifted.[5] Yet the two purposes for composing law in English that Oliver posits, accessibility and creating a distinct national and political identity, clearly persisted. Components of what would later be recognizable as a distinctly English legal vocabulary are already recognizable as such in the earliest Kentish laws, and Lisi Oliver demonstrated a recognizable, standard, technical English legal vocabulary minimally influenced by Latin by the ninth century.[6] Moreover, as Catherine Cubitt has shown, there was a "pragmatic literacy" among the laity in the tenth and eleventh centuries and technical legal language pervades Old English literary texts that engage with issues of English identity.[7] English legal tradition also survived the Norman Conquest. In his London Charter, issued in English shortly after his coronation (1066x1075), William I states, "I make known to you that it is my will that both of you [English and French] heed all the laws which existed in the time of King Edward."[8] Although several Norman kings found it useful to maintain this politically convenient fiction,[9] evidence in some twelfth-century compilations of pre-Conquest law indicates some scholars were thinking about the practical and symbolic value of a living Anglo-Saxon tradition.

Bearing in mind these issues, I began puzzling over some words occurring in the twelfth-century Latin translation of the law code *IV Æthelred* and what they may indicate about the continuing role of pre-Conquest legal discourse in English. The first of these, *ouerhyrnessam meam* ("[the fine for] insubordination to me") is used twice:

> And we order that no one refuse money that is pure and of correct weight, coined in whatever town in my kingdom, or incur the fine for insubordination to me (*ouerhyrnessam meam*). (*IV Æthelred* 6)[10]

---

[5] Oliver, "Legal Documentation."

[6] Lisi Oliver, "The Development of West Saxon Legal Language." Paper presented at the 48th International Congress on Medieval Studies, Western Michigan University, Kalamazoo, Michigan, May 9, 2013.

[7] Catherine Cubitt, "'As the Lawbook Teaches': Reeves, Lawbooks and Urban Life in the Anonymous Old English Legend of the Seven Sleepers," *EHR* 124 (2009): 1021-49.

[8] The dates are from Liebermann. The writ's most recent editor prefers a date "shortly after William's coronation on Christmas Day 1066." David Bates, "William I's Writ for London," *Early English Laws* <http://www.earlyenglishlaws.ac.uk/laws/texts/wl-lond/>.

[9] George Garnett, *Conquered England: Kingship, Succession, and Tenure, 1066-1166* (Oxford: Oxford University Press, 2007), 1-17.

[10] All references to the laws refer to Liebermann, *Gesetze*. All references to the rubrics of *Quadripartitus* are to Felix Liebermann, *Quadripartitus, ein englisches Rechtsbuch von 1114* (Halle: Max Niemeyer, 1892). Unless otherwise noted, all translations are my own.

> And those who are in charge of towns shall execute this, or incur the fine for insubordination to me (*ouerhyrnessam meam*), that every weight is marked at the weight to which my money is guaranteed; and thus on each will be stamped that 15 ores make a pound. (*IV Æthelred* 9.2)

As a Latinization rather than a translation of an English phrase, the seemingly technical *ouerhyrnessam meam* is interesting because it indicates a special kind of fine that was personal to the king, and because it is used without explanation. It is possible the term was so recognizable that there was no need to translate, or, conversely, it was so technical that translation would have distorted its meaning. *Ouerhyrnessa* is not unique; by my count, there are seventeen other English terms retained or Latinized in *IV Æthelred*, of which two are repeated, for a total of twenty-one examples in the text. Among these, *ouerhyrnessam meam* stands out as a distinct legalism. The *Dictionary of Old English: Old English Corpus* (hereafter, *DOE Corpus*) lists only seventeen occurences of *oferhyrness* and one of *oferhirness*. Although there are more varied uses of words derived from the verb *oferhiran* "to disregard, disobey,"[11] *oferhyrness* is used substantively only in laws and always in passages concerned with maintaining the correct functioning of law.[12] As such, it appears to carry a specific legal meaning, and its persistence in the Latin version of *IV Æthelred* perhaps suggests a living English-language legal discourse survived in twelfth-century England.

Yet another example from *IV Æthelred*, does not permit quite the same conclusion:

> Women who deal in dairy produce (i.e. cheese and butter) (*Smeremangestre [que mongonant in caseo et butiro]*) pay one penny fourteen days before Christmas, and another penny seven days before Christmas. (*IV Æthelred* 2.12)

The purpose for retaining English *smeremangestre* here is not clear, especially since the translator renders its meaning in Latin. Moreover, the word does not have nearly the same kind of focused presence as *oferhyrness* in the corpus. The compound of *smeoru* "fat or grease" and the feminine *mangestre* "monger, merchant" appears only in *IV Æthelred*; in fact, *mangestre* is only attested in *IV Æthelred*, or so both Bosworth and Toller's *Anglo-Saxon Dictionary* and the *DOE Corpus* indicate.[13] While the word's rarity may be more indicative of the limited need to record a term for women who deal in

---

[11] Translations of individual Old English words are drawn from Joseph Bosworth and T. Northcote Toller, *An Anglo-Saxon Dictionary* (Oxford: Oxford University Press, 1898) and Antonette di Paolo Healey, ed., *Dictionary of Old English: A-G Online* (Toronto: University of Toronto Press, 1998-).

[12] Antonette di Paolo Healey, ed., *Dictionary of Old English: Old English Corpus* (Toronto: University of Toronto Press, 1998-), s.v. *oferhyrness, oferhirness*. Although the *DOE Corpus* does not record every use of every word, it gives reasonable and reliable impressions of how words were used in Old English.

[13] *DOE Corpus*, s.v. *smeorumangestre, mangestre, smeoru*; Bosworth-Toller, s.v. *smeorumangestre, mangestre, smeoru*.

dairy produce than of any lack of currency in Old English, its presence in *IV Æthelred* raises questions about the translator's purpose in retaining English vocabulary.

IV Æthelred survives only in Latin translation in *Quadripartitus*, a twelfth-century compilation of Anglo-Saxon laws, and this context raises several questions about the status of English tradition, custom, and law for the translator and the audience he wrote for.[14] Although there had long been a tension between English and Latin, one of the most dramatic and immediate changes to English law after the Norman Conquest was that it started being written in Latin.[15] Yet *Quadripartitus* is a compilation and translation of Anglo-Saxon laws, and as Bruce O'Brien observes:

> The preservation of law through translation reveals attitudes toward the past and toward English culture. It can tell us perhaps a good deal about royal power. It goes to the heart of Norman rule in general.[16]

Much has been made of the professionalization of legal culture over the course of the twelfth century and Anglo-Saxon law's role in that process.[17] In the early twelfth century, a coterie of Anglo-Norman legal authors took an interest in compiling Anglo-Saxon laws and translating them into Latin. *Quadripartitus*, the *Leges Henrici Primi*, the *Instituta Cnuti*, and the *Consiliatio Cnuti* were all produced at about the same time, albeit with distinctly different approaches. The efforts to compile and translate the laws imply they held some degree of authority, even if merely symbolic, and the preface to *Quadripartitus* states clearly that the laws of Cnut and Edward the Confessor were still relevant[18]; however, the compilers' intended uses for their texts, the status of Anglo-Saxon

---

[14] L. J. Downer, ed. and trans., *Leges Henrici Primi* (Oxford: Clarendon Press, 1972), 12-28; Patrick Wormald, "'*Quadripartitus*,'" in idem, *Legal Culture in the Early Medieval West: Law as Text, Image, and Experience* (London: Hambledon Press, 1999), 81-114, at 103-5. There are nine extant manuscripts of *Quadripartitus* and their relationships are complex. For a complete discussion of the manuscripts, see Wormald, "'*Quadripartitus*.'" Richard Sharpe, "The Dating of *Quadripartitus* Again," in *English Law Before Magna Carta: Felix Liebermann and Die Gesetze der Angelsachsen*, ed. Stefan Jurasinski, Lisi Oliver, and Andrew Rabin (Leiden: Brill, 2010), 81-93.

[15] Alexander R. Rumble, "*Interpretationes in latinum*: Some Twelfth-Century Translations of Anglo-Saxon Charters" in *Early Medieval English Text and Interpretations: Studies Presented to Donald G. Scragg*, ed. Elaine Treharne and Susan Rosser (Tempe: Arizona Center for Medieval and Renaissance Studies, 2002), 101-18, at 103.

[16] Bruce O'Brien, "The *Instituta Cnuti* and the Translation of English Law," *Anglo-Norman Studies* 25 (2003): 177-97, at 182.

[17] Patrick Wormald, "Law Books," in *The Cambridge History of The Book in Britain, Volume I, c. 400-1100*, ed. Richard Gameson (Cambridge: Cambridge University Press, 2012), 525-36; Nicholas Karn, "*Quadripartitus, Leges Henrici Primi* and the Scholarship of English Law in the Early Twelfth Century," *Anglo-Norman Studies* 37 (2014): 149-60.

[18] Liebermann, *Quadripartitus*, 83; Richard Sharpe, "The Prefaces of 'Quadripartitus,'" in *Law and Government in Medieval England and Normandy: Essays in Honour of Sir James Holt*, ed. George Garnett and

legislation under Norman rule, and how much Norman compilers truly understood about the Old English laws they translated are all unclear. A brief glance at these texts' translations of common source material makes clear that among them *Quadripartitus* overwhelmingly retains English terminology, the *Instituta* retains select terms but favors translation, and the *Consiliatio Cnuti* retains almost none.[19] Although the existence of these compilations implies the Anglo-Saxon legal tradition was important to the current state of law in early twelfth-century England, the compiler-translator of *Quadripartitus*, commonly known as Q, seems to have valued legal diction as an important means of understanding the language of the tradition. Therefore, I focus on Q's treatment of English terms in *Quadripartitus*.

Although Q's frequent use and attempted translation of English words has been observed, no full, systematic examination of *Quadripartitus* has been conducted to see what Q's choice of words may indicate about his argument concerning the place of Anglo-Saxon law in the twelfth century. This scholarly lacuna stems from the fact that no complete edition of *Quadripartitus* exists. Liebermann's edition consists of his commentary, the prefatory material, and the rubrics, but is often inconsistent and unclear in what it records. Otherwise, the entire text appears in his *Gesetze* where it is disintegrated and placed alongside the English law codes, often merely in support of the English text. While a comprehensive study will have to await a complete and much-needed edition of *Quadripartitus*, the present essay attempts to identify every rubric that retains English vocabulary from Liebermann's edition of *Quadripartitus*, whether Latinized or in its original form. I examine the body of the text accompanying those rubrics for their treatment of English vocabulary. Wherever possible, I draw comparative examples from the body of the laws that do not necessarily fall under an English rubric, but without discussing every instance of a retained English word.

Q seems to have identified as English. He wrote *Quadripartitus* in England and in speaking of Henry I as "our lord" and of "our people," he speaks of those living in England, not just the Normans.[20] However, he was not a native English speaker, and scholarly opinion of his competence in English has been low. A summary of Liebermann's conclusions represents the consensus. Q is often ignorant of English vocabulary, frequently confusing Anglo-Saxon terms similar in sound and appearance. When he translates phrases or individual morphemes, Q clearly relies on a glossary since he rarely

---

John Hudson (Cambridge: Cambridge University Press, 1994), 148-72, at 162-3 and 169; Karn, "*Quadripartitus*," 150; Bruce O'Brien, "Translating Technical Terms in Law-Codes from Alfred to the Angevins," in *Conceptualizing Multilingualism in Medieval England, c. 800-c. 1250*, ed. Elizabeth M. Tyler (Turnhout: Brepols, 2011), 57-76, at 59-60.

[19] I exclude the *Leges*, which draws on *Quadripartitus*'s translations and was probably by the same author.

[20] Liebermann, *Quadripartitus*, 17; Wormald, *Making*, 473.

grasps legal concepts as a whole. He divides compounds into their constituent simplexes before translating both together. If given two meanings for a word, Q often chooses the nonsensical one. Still, he translates word for word, even syllable for syllable, indicating a seriousness of purpose and method. Q often gets translations right, though errors occur, presumably because some meanings were already obsolete by the time he translated. And as the above examples attest, Q retains the English on some occasions, sometimes inserting a Latin translation, but with no recognizable pattern in these decisions. Still, this may reflect a process whereby he deferred a gloss until a word's meaning became clear from another context. Finally, Q improved as he worked.[21]

While much of Liebermann's assessment is accurate, he overstates Q's linguistic struggles. Q's treatment of retained English vocabulary suggests that he faced two primary challenges. First, he had to adapt legal traditions to a new context. Second, he had to make that tradition's technical vocabulary meaningful for an early twelfth-century Anglo-Norman context. According to Nicholas Karn, Q "believed that there was a ready potential audience for the work, which would be motivated to read it, that there would be at least some capable of making use of a written text in Latin, and that it would fit into existing debates such that it elicited some kind of response from the assumed readership."[22] Concerned as he is with the question of a professional legal class in the early twelfth century, Karn does not venture into the assumed readership's vernacular competencies. Yet Bruce O'Brien notes that the English had a long history of multilingualism and translation, well before the Norman Conquest, because of their interactions with the Britons, the Scandinavians, and with the Latin of Christianity.[23] They had established techniques for translation into Latin, and they were aware of when and how to deploy those: transcription, whether copying the original or Latinizing it; etymological translation; or substituting a cultural equivalent.[24] Moreover, with the Conquest, "stuffed Latin" was introduced to England, a French habit which David Trotter describes as "the incorporation of vernacular elements in Latin documents [including] isolated words, or more importantly, phrases, and also proper names."[25]

Accounting for the multilingual contexts and audiences for these translation practices reveals a systematic pattern of usage. It is clear that the English-language vocabulary that is retained in *Quadripartitus*, with only a few anomalies, falls into just five semantic

---

21 Liebermann, *Quadripartitus*, 17-24.

22 Karn, "*Quadripartitus*," 156.

23 O'Brien, "Translating Technical Terms," 58.

24 O'Brien, "Translating Technical Terms," 63. O'Brien provides examples and a thorough discussion of each of these.

25 David Trotter, "'Stuffed Latin': Vernacular Evidence in Latin Documents," in *Language and Culture in Medieval Britain: The French of England c. 1100-c. 1500*, ed. Jocelyn Wogan-Browne et al. (York: York Medieval Press, 2009), 153-63, at 153. My thanks to Jocelyn Wogan-Browne for drawing my attention to this article.

fields that represent traditional Anglo-Saxon legal concerns: social status and structure; penalties, fines, and judicial procedure; categories of crime; taxes and other payment obligations; property and jurisdiction; treaties. While these fields often overlap, they offer a useful means of structuring my discussion.

Social Status and Social Structure

aldremannus (OE *ealdormann* "a nobleman of the highest rank, between king and thegn; the official who presided over shire courts"[26])
thainus/tainus (OE *þegen* "retainer, officer, minister")
syðcundus homo (OE *gesiðcund man* "companion or follower of a king")
ceorlus (OE *ceorl* "churl, peasant, free man of the lowest status"[27])
twyhyndus homines (OE *twihynde* "a person of a rank for which the wergild was 200 shillings")
VIhindus homines (OE *sixhynde* "a person of a rank for which the wergild was 600 shillings")
XIIhindus homines (OE *twelfhynde* "a person of a rank for which the wergild was 1200 shillings")
bondus (OE *bonda* "householder")
gavelgildus (OE *gafolgylda* "rent-payer")

The English words Q retains in the semantic field of social status and structure interweave terms defining rank, wergild, and property ownership. The degree of translation Q applies to each seems to relate to how traditional or legally technical each is. *Aldremannus*, *thainus/tainus*, *ceorlus*, and the adjectival *syðcundus* and *cyrliscus* supply the ranks of men, and their English counterparts, *ealdormann*, *þegen*, *gesið*, and *ceorl*, are all well attested in the Old English homiletic, legal, and poetic corpus. Q's use of these terms, along with *weregyldus* (OE *wergild*), suggests his audience was familiar with them. However, Q offers more guidance for *twyhyndus homines*, *VIhindus homines*, and *XIIhindus homines*, restricted terms confined to laws and charters that may be taken as technical legal equivalents for traditional status terms.[28] Similarly, *bondus* is overwhelmingly legal. The *DOE Corpus* lists eight uses of *bonda*, five appearing in law codes, one in a charter, and two in homilies associated with Archbishop Wulfstan that draw on or adapt royal laws.[29] Only Old English *gafolgylda* does not appear to have a restricted legal meaning, but Q may have understood it as technical, as I discuss below.

---

26 But see *DOE*, s.v. *ealdormann*, for fuller ranger of definitions, especially the range of positions it glosses. Cf. O'Brien, "Translating Technical Terms," 67.

27 But see *DOE*, s.v. *ceorl*, for fuller range of definitions, especially legal definitions I.B.1.a.

28 *DOE Corpus*, s.v. *twihynde*, *sixhynde*, *twelfhynde*.

29 *DOE Corpus*, s.v. *bonda*. *VI Atr.* 31, *II Cn.* 8, 72, 72.1, 76; *Rect.* 1.8, Napier 35 and 50. Napier 35 is an adaptation of *VII Atr.* and Napier 50 draws on the laws of Cnut. Andrew Rabin, ed., *The Political Writings of Archbishop Wulfstan of York* (Manchester: Manchester University Press, 2015), 130 and 143.

Traditional English vocabulary for rank gets minimal intervention. Q never translates *thainus/tainus*.[30] *Syðcundus homo*, *ceorlus*, *bondus*, and *aldremannus* each receive a single accurate translation and Q is otherwise free in his choice to use English or a Latin translation. The rubric for *Ine* 50 gives "Concerning the composition of a *gesiðcund* (*syðcundi*) man, that is, a noble (*id est nobilis*)," but the body of the text uses just the Latinized English. Moreover, all subsequent uses retain only the Latinized English. *Ceorlus* is directly translated in the *Treaty of Alfred and Guthrum* as *id est rusticus* ("that is, a peasant") (2). The rubric for *II Cnut* 72 gives the Latinized *De bondis* ("Concerning a householder") and the body of the text gives the English and translates: "*bonda*, that is, the head of the household (*id est paterfamilias*)." Earlier, Q simply uses *paterfamilias* without the English (*II Cnut* 8) and, in a later passage, he translates *ne mæg nan wif hyre bondan forbeodan* as "a wife (*uxor*) cannot prohibit her husband (*sponsum*) anything" (*II Cnut* 76.1b). These examples imply that Q understood English *bonda* sufficiently to distinguish between the meanings "householder" and "husband" and expected his audience to be familiar enough with the Latinized *bondus* to understand the rubric. Similarly, the rubric for *II Cnut* 58 gives: "One who breaks his pledge to the king (*regis*), whether an archbishop (*archiepiscopi*) or the son of the king (*filii regis*) or a bishop (*episcopi*) or an *ealdormann* (*aldremanni*)." Q then translates in the body of the law: "aldremanni (id est comitis)" (*ealdormann*, that is, a count).[31] He uses *aldremannus* six more times in his rubrics and seems comfortable alternating between English and Latin in the text's body. In one rubric he uses *comes*, and there he retains the untranslated *thainus*: "Concerning the heriots of counts (*comitum*) and of high-ranking thegns (*thainorum provectorum*) and of others" (*II Cnut* 71). Q appears to use the most traditional English terms for social rank interchangeably with and alongside their Latin counterparts with no concern for lost meaning.

But Q does not anticipate complete familiarity with all English vocabulary or the Anglo-Saxon legal system. When dealing with the technical legal vocabulary of wergild and social status, Q offers more guidance for his audience:

> De weregildo twelfhindes. Twelfhyndes hominis iusiurandum contraualet sex uillanorum iusiurandum; quia, si twelfhynde man (-dus homo) uindicari deberet, plene uindicaretur in VI ceorlis, et eius weregildum est VI ceorlorum weregildum. (*Að* 1)
>
> Concerning the wergild of a *twelfhynde* man. The oath of a *twelfhynde* man is worth the oath of six villeins; thus, if a *twelfhynde* man (*douze* man) must be redeemed, he will be fully redeemed in six churls, and his wergild is the wergild of six churls.

---

30 But see *Rect.*

31 R.E. Latham, D.R. Howlett, and R.K. Ashdowne, eds., *DMLBS.*, s.v. *comes* 2. Subsequent entries distinguish between pre-Conquest *comes* as "king's minister or nobleman (AS *gesiþ*, *ealdorman*, or *eorl*)" (3) and post-Conquest *comes* as "feudal earl (equivalent to count)" (4).

Here Q anticipates varying degrees of familiarity with English vocabulary. *Wergild* is Latinized but receives no translation, implying Q thought his audience understood it.[32] In spite of using *ceorlus* both in rubrics and in the body of the text, Q uses it interchangeably with the Latin *villanus* "peasant, villein," indicating both were already familiar. Yet the retention of the English *twelfhynde man* and its translation into French (*-dus*) and Latin (*homo*) suggest that the English technical system of wergild-based rank and the associated terms were not immediately familiar to Q's French-speaking audience. Nonetheless, Q's translation shows he understands the meaning and functioning of the English system of valuing oaths based on social status, and the English legal vocabulary retained in the rubric indicates that he expected his audience to recognize it sufficiently to find the fuller description in the body of the text.

Although the examples above show a fairly consistent approach and seem to indicate Q expected his audience to understand English legal terms, there are curious or confusing examples that deserve particular attention. *Ine* 6 addresses the penalties for those who fight. The rubric reads: "Concerning fighting in the house of the king (*regis*) or in a church (*ecclesia*) or in the house of an *ealdormann* (*aldremanni*) or of a baron (*baronis*) or in a *gafolgylda*'s (*gavelgilda*), or in the home of a neighbor (*vicini*), or in the middle of a field or while drinking." In the body, Q translates the English in fairly straightforward fashion, but with a notable quirk. *Ine* 6.2 in English and Q's translation read:

> Gif hwa on ealdormonnes huse gefeohte oððe on oðres geðungenes witan, LX scill. gebete he 7 oþer LX geselle to wite.
>
> Si quis in domo aldermanni uel alterius sagibaronis pugnet, LX sol. emendet et alios LX emendet pro wita.
>
> If anyone fights in the home of an *ealdormann* or another *sagibaron*, make amends with 60 shillings and make amends with another 60 shillings as a fine.

Q retains the traditional English word for an official in *aldremanni* but translates his source's *oðres geðungenes witan* (another excellent wise man/counsellor) to *alterius sagibaronis* (another wise-baron). The *Dictionary of Medieval Latin from British Sources* (hereafter, *DMLBS*) records *sagibaro* as a Latin term, defining it as "class or official or officer (prob. w. judicial function or responsibilities)," but it cites this very example from *Ine* 6.2. The *Glossarium mediae et infimae latinitatis* records *sagibarones*, citing *Lex Salica* 56.2, and defines it as *Causarum iudices, qui in mallis publicis jus dicebant* ("judges of cases who render justice in public disputes") and as *quasi Senatores* ("resembling

[32] It is translated once in the body of *Ine* 15 as "id est natalis sui pretio" (that is, his birth price), but the frequent use of *weregyldus* and *wera* without translation encourages the assumption that wergild was a familiar term.

senators")[33] However, *sagibaronis* appears to me to be an example of both etymological translation and stuffed Latin, aimed at Q's French-speaking audience. Q apparently created a new compound out of French words and put a Latin genitive ending on it. This peculiar translation may be indicative of Q's accurate sense of the English here. *Oðres geðungenes witan* probably gestures to a general category rather than any specific official—something like "or another man of standing comparable to the *ealdormann*." Elsewhere, Q does take English *wita* as the technical "counsellor to the king," but in those cases, he translates it by the Latin *sapiens* (e.g., *Alfred* Prol. 49.9, *I Æthelred* Prol., *I Cnut* Prol.). Although it is possible that Q looked to Salic law, it is likelier that he strove for a way to express the generic English for a French-speaking audience by compounding *sage* "wise" and *baron*, a term that in French can mean variously "man, worthy man, baron, lord," and mostly expresses a general sense of high status.[34] If my reading is correct, Q created a vernacular term, *sagibaron*, that he believed a French-speaking audience would read as comparable to the generalization of the English rather than taking it as a specific office.

A second example raises questions about intention and audience. In the rubric for *Ine* 6, Q retains *gavelgilda*. As noted above, the English *gafolgylda* "rent-payer" does not appear to carry a strict legal meaning, and, so, like *smeremangestre* in *IV Æthelred*, does not seem to fit a clear pattern of translation. Q does offer a translation for *gavelgilda* in the body of the text: "that is, one who pays *gablum*." *Gablum* is a Latinization of the English *gafol* that appears as early as *Domesday Book*.[35] Although not uniquely a legal term, *gafol* was widely used in the Anglo-Saxon period, perhaps most familiarly as the word for tribute paid to the Vikings,[36] and it does appear in Middle English and Anglo-Norman as *gavel* "land tax" from the late twelfth century.[37] Q clearly understands it in such a context in the *Treaty of Alfred and Guthrum*, where he has "*gafulland*, that is, in the decreed/rented land (*terra censaria*) (2).[38] However, at other times, Q does not seem to know what to do with it. In *Ine* 44.1 he has "*Gafolhwitel* and *hiwisce* will be valued at five pennies." It is safe to say in this case that Q, probably with good reason, does not have a clear sense of the meaning of either English term he retains.[39] Based on these consistent examples, it seems Q recognized *gafol* as an important legal term since he

---

[33] Charles Du Fresne Du Cange *et al.*, *Glossarium mediæ et infimæ latinitatis* (Niort: L. Favre, 1883-1887), s.v. *sagibarones*.

[34] *Anglo-Norman Dictionary*, s.v. *baron*.

[35] Du Cange, *Glossarium*, s.v. *gablum*.

[36] For example, see Anglo-Saxon Chronicle CDE, s.a. 991, 994, 1002, 1006, 1007, 1011, 1012, 1018.

[37] *Anglo-Norman Dictionary*, s.v. *gavel*. Cf. *DMLBS*, s.v. *gavella*, "family holding" being used in the late thirteenth century.

[38] *DMLBS*, s.v. *censaria*.

[39] See F. L. Attenborough, *The Laws of the Earliest English Kings* (Cambridge: Cambridge University Press, 1922), 190 n. 44.2.

retains it both as the Latin *gablum* and in English compounds, but when he is unsure of its technical function, he leaves it untranslated.

The impression left by these examples is that Q was quite consistent, retaining the core English vocabulary of rank and status central to the Anglo-Saxon legal system. He transcribed or transliterated traditional and familiar terms, indicating their enduring currency. He clearly valued outdated technical legalisms enough to keep the words in his rubrics, but found it necessary to make them comprehensible to a French-speaking audience—and he did so with a certain degree of nuance. Finally, though he recognized and retained some technical terms of significance, he was not always able to discern or convey their nuanced meanings.

Penalties, Fines, and Judicial Procedure

lada (OE *lad* "defense against a charge")
laga (OE *lagu* "law")
utlaga (OE *utlaga* "outlaw")
wera (OE *wer* and *were* "wergild, the price set for a man according to his degree")
wergyldus (OE *wergild* "wergild, the price set for a man according to his degree")
wita (OE *wite* "punishment, fine")
ordalium (OE *ordal* "judicial ordeal")
forfangio (OE *forfang* "rescuing of stolen property")
ceapgildo (OE *ceapgild* "market price for stolen property; indemnity for stolen property")
weretihla (OE *wertihtle* "accusation of a crime where the crime requires the payment of wergild")
fihtewita (OE *fihtwite* "a fine for fighting")
congildo (OE *gegilda* "a guild brother, companion)
fridgildo/friðgildo (OE *friþgild* "a peace-guild, a society for the maintenance of peace and security)
frumgild (OE *frumgyld* "a first installment of payment of a wergild")
furigildum (OE *þeofgyld* "compensation paid by one convicted of stealing")
flima (OE *flyma* "one who flees from justice; an outlaw, exile; a man whose flight was equivalent to conviction")
weregyldo-fur (OE *wergild-þeof* "a thief whose wergild was paid as a punishment for his crime")
manbota (OE *mannbot* "the fine to be paid to the lord of a slain person)
ouerhyrnessa (OE *oferhyrness* "fine for insubordination")
haderunga (OE *haderung* "*personarum acceptio*, the subjective preference for certain persons as opposed to judgment based on merit")
wytaseruus (OE *witeþeow* "a man who has been sold into penal slavery or has sold himself into slavery to cover a debt")

In turning to the category of judicial procedure, penalties, and fines, it is unsurprising to find terms associated with rank such as *wera* and *wergyldus*. Moreover, several terms left untranslated can readily be taken as traditional and unproblematic: *lada*, *laga*, *utlaga*, *manbota*, *wita*.[40] These examples aside, the clearest evidence that Q considered terms current and comprehensible is when he retained an English word in the rubric and either silently translated it into Latin in the text's body or alternated between English and Latin as he did with *ceorlus* and *villanus*. The most common of these is *ordalium*, by my count appearing thirteen times in rubrics.[41] Although the English word is favored in both rubrics and the body of the text, Q comfortably alternates between the English and Latin *iudicium*, as is evident in *II Æthelstan* 23:

> Concerning those who undergo ordeal (*ordalium*). If one will undergo the *iudicium* of iron or of water, let him go three nights earlier to a priest who must consecrate it, and let him eat bread and salt and water and herbs, and let him hear Mass on each of the three days, and let him make offering and attend holy communion on that day that he is obligated to be examined at the ordeal (*ordalium*), and he will swear an oath in public that he is innocent of the accusation before he comes to the ordeal (*ordalium*).

The alternation between English and Latin and his accurate translation of process indicate he fully understood English *ordal*, and his frequent use of the Latinized *ordalium* suggests the word was current enough to be understood by his audience.

Other less-frequent terms have comparable claim to be understood. Like *ordalium*, Q uses *forfangio* in the rubrics, but on each occasion he silently shifts to Latin in the text's body, twice translating the verb as *intercietur* "be claimed," and once as *capiatur* "be seized" (*Ine* 53, 75, and 72). Similarly, the rubric for *Ine* 71 reads *De weretihla* ("Concerning the accusation of a crime for which wergild is due"), but the body of the text says simply "If a man is accused of homicide and, being required to swear an oath, he confesses to that which he previously denied, payment of the fine (*wite*) shall be delayed until he has paid the wergild (*wera*)." These examples presume that a reader would readily understand the English words since they occur in rubrics designed to be skimmed. Yet, in the body the author goes directly into Latin.

Several English words—notably *ceapgildo* and *fyhtwita*—are retained in rubrics and directly translated in the body of the text. Hence they require little discussion.[42] Where variant terminology is adopted—as with *ouerhyrnessa* and *flima*—it becomes obvious Q

---

[40] On the intentional use by Norman kings of *laga* rather than *lex*, see O'Brien, "Translating Technical Terms," 74.

[41] This word was clearly a legal term in Old English. The *DOE Corpus* lists 67 uses of *ordal*, all in laws and two homilies associated with Wulfstan, Napier 23 and 43.

[42] *VI As.* 6; *II Em.* 3.

was aware of multiple meanings for the English and was attempting to discern between them.[43] Perhaps more telling about what Q understood as traditional and valuable in this field appears in examples of "stuffed Latin" compounds. Standing out in the rubrics is *wytaseruus* (*Ine* 48). As one would expect, the English *witeþeow* is overwhelmingly legal in tone, but Q's translation is a strange collocation: it retains English *wite* "punishment, fine" but translates the term for servitude or slavery into Latin. On its own, this makes little sense. Yet, it is not the only example of a mixed-language compound. In the body of the text of *II Cnut* 30.1, Q renders English *þeofgyld* "compensation paid by one convicted of stealing" as *furigildum*. Taken together, these compounds indicate that the retained English simplex carried a technical resonance for Q while the translated portion did not. In the case of *wytaseruus*, slavery would have been a straight-forward concept in Latin or English. However, as Daniela Fruscione has demonstrated, *wite* was bound up with centralized political authority and royal claims on the right to punish and to use force.[44] Similarly with *furigildum*, the Latin *fur* "thief" would have conveyed the necessary category, but *gild* Q associated with payments for transgressions. This conclusion is supported by his other compound, *weregyldo-fur* (OE *wergild-þeof* "a thief whose wergild was paid as a punishment for his crime") (*Ine* 72).

Another set of terms shows a similar interest in English word elements, but given their shared context and linguistic interplay, they deserve to be discussed as a group. *VI Æthelstan*, the obligations of pledged members of a peace-guild, probably comprised of the bishops and reeves of London,[45] contains *congildo* and *friðgildum* in its rubrics. The body of the text gives:

> We declare also that all of those men who have pledged themselves to our guild (*gildscipam*), that if any one should die, every guild-member (*congilda*) shall give one loaf and accompanying food for his soul, and sing or cause to be sung fifty psalms within thirty nights.

The retention here of related terms shows Q's sensitivity to the significance of linguistic morphemes and vocabulary. He retains the whole of the English compound *friðgildum*. He gives the transliterated *gildscipam* (OE *gegyldscipe*), where *-scip* indicates a condition or kind of relationship.[46] He also translates the English prefix of *gegilda* with a comparable Latin one: *gegilda* > *congilda*. As Bosworth-Toller notes, *ge-* as a prefix means "with" and "in accordance with this meaning, it often gives a collective sense to

[43] *II As.* 20, *III Atr.* 10; *II As.* 20.8, *II Ew.* 5.2, *II As.* 2.1 and *II Cn.* 13.2.

[44] Daniela Fruscione, "Beginnings and Legitimation of Punishment in Early Anglo-Saxon Legislation from the Seventh to the Ninth Century," in *Capital and Corporal Punishment in Anglo-Saxon England* (Woodbridge: Boydell, 2014), 34-47, at 36 and 46.

[45] Wormald, *Making*, 296-9.

[46] *Oxford English Dictionary*, s.v. *-ship*.

nouns to which it is prefixed."[47] Q's treatment of these terms implies he understood and considered sufficiently current the simplex *gild* to retain it in several words in close succession, but he also understood the significance of the affixes in the English words. On the one hand, *-scip* was clear enough to be retained completely; on the other hand, Q translates the English prefix *ge-* to highlight the implicit sense of collectivity in the vernacular.

In this field, Q treats his English vocabulary much as he did terms of social status and structure. The most obviously traditional terms are retained and go untranslated and unexplained while more technical terms are retained and translated. However, Q here shows a particular attention to linguistic resonance and historical relevance in his translations.

Categories of Crime

æbere morð/eberemorde (OE *æbere morð* "manifest murder")[48]
hamsocna (*hamsocn* "attack on a man's house")
husbrece et bernet (OE *husbryce et bærnet* "housebreaking and burning")
blaserus (OE *blasere* "an incendiary")
open thiefþe/ openthiefþe (OE *open þifþ* "manifest theft")
reaflacus (OE *reaflac* "robbery, spoliation")
here/herege (OE *here* "a hostile army")
hloþ/hlothe (OE *hloþ* "a body of robbers, the crime of taking part in *hloþ*")
hlafordswice/lafordswike (OE *hlafordswice* "betrayal of the lord")
mundbrece/mundbryce (OE *mundbryce* "the violation of protection")
griþbrece (OE *griðbryce* "breach of the peace, violation of protection granted by the king")
wealref (OE *wælreaf* "robbing the slain")
liblacus (OE *lyblac* "sorcery, witchcraft")

Unlike the first two fields, Q's treatment of the vocabulary for crime suggests that he did not consider it to carry sufficient traditional or technical significance. Retained terms fit into a group of traditional concerns: violence against individuals, or a district, violations against property, betrayal of one's lord, and witchcraft. However, many of the terms seem to have been retained incidentally. Of the terms listed, four

---

47 Bosworth-Toller, s.v. *ge-*.

48 The terms *morð* and *murdrum* have received extensive discussion: Bruce O'Brien, "From *Morðor* to *Murdrum*: The Preconquest Origin and Norman Revival of the Murder Fine," *Speculum* 71 (1996): 321-57; idem, *God's Peace and King's Peace: The Laws of Edward the Confessor* (Philadelphia: University of Pennsylvania Press, 1999), 73-84; Stefan Jurasinski, "*Reddatur Parentibus*: The Vengeance of the Family in Cnut's Homicide Legislation," *Law and History Review* 20 (2002): 157-80, at 161-2.

do not appear in rubrics (*hlafordswice*, *griþbrece*, *morð*, and *thiefþe*), and six appear only once (*hlafordswice*, *husbrece*, *mundbrece*, *reaflac*, *thiefþe*, *wealreaf*). All of these are translated except *mundbrece*. Five terms appear repeatedly (*blaserus*, *liblacus*, *here*, *hloþ*, *hamsocn*, *griþbrece*). Of these, *blaserus* and *liblacus* go untranslated; *here* appears frequently but is only tranlated once (*Ine* 15); *hloþ* appears twice in rubrics and is translated in one of those (*Ine* 14 and *Pseudo-Alfred-Guthrum* 2); *hamsocn* and *griþbrece* are translated repeatedly, but not always. Many of these terms are usually silently translated from the English source (e.g., *here* > *exercitum*, *reaflac* > *robaria* or *rapina*, *thiefþe* > *fur*).

The overwhelming impression is that the language for crime did not strike Q as sufficiently important to retain widely and Q clearly believed his audience needed help understanding those terms he did retain. In fact, the three terms that go untranslated give little information about what was understood. He almost certainly understood *mundbrece* since he translates the simplexes correctly elsewhere and in the sole use of it, it appears untranslated together with *hamsocn*, which we know he understood (*II Edmund* 6). It is unclear if he understood *blaserus* since it appears twice in the law of the same title, again at *II Æthelstan* 6.2, and there is no context in either to make sense of the word. He almost certainly did not understand *liblacus*. It appears in *II Æthelstan* 6 and *I Edmund* 6 and goes untranslated in both. Moreover, it is recorded as *liblatum* in *I Edmund*.

Taxes, Obligations, Lordship

chyricbota (OE *cyricbot* "church repair")
brigbota (OE *brycgbot* "obligatory bridge repair or maintenance")
burhbota (*burhbot* "obligatory maintenance of a fortification or town")
ferdfare (OE *fyrdfaru* "obligatory military service")
Romfeoh (OE *Romfeoh* "Peter's Pence")
cyricsceattis (OE *cyricsceat* "church-scot")
dryncelean (OE *drynclean* "drink-reward")[49]
handgrið (OE *handgrið* "peace, protection, security")
ciricsocna (OE *cyricsocn* "church privilege, right of sanctuary, territory belonging to a church")
hlafordsokna (OE *hlafordsocn* "right to seek the protection of a lord")
socna taini (not attested as an Old English word)

[49] This particular term is unclear. It appears rarely, only in legal codes, only in late or Latin sources. See Bosworth-Toller, s.v. *drincelean*; (*DOE*, s.v. *dryncelean*; A. J. Robertson, *The Laws of the Kings of England from Edmund to Henry I* (Cambridge: Cambridge University Press, 1925), 359 n. 81.2.

Most of the technical terms in this field get direct "id est" translations, but Q's handling of them suggests they were already familiar to his audience. *II Cnut* 65-65.1 alone covers most of these terms. The rubrics read "If one withholds fortification repair (*burhbotam*) (or bridge repair (*brigbotam*) or military service (*ferdfare*)" and "Concerning church repair (*chyricbota*)." The body of the text then reads:

> If anyone withholds fortification-repair (*burhbotam*) or bridge-repair (*brigbotam*), that is fortification- (*burh-*) or bridge repair (*pontis emendationem*) or *fyrdfare*, that is, to go into the army (*exercitum*) [...] The whole nation must assist in church repair (*refectionem ęcclesię*), as is proper.

The accuracy of Q's translations implies understanding. He uses all three again in *Rectitudines Singularum Personarum*: "This is the law of the thegn, that he be worthy of his book-right[50] and that he do three things for his land, these are campaigning, fortification-repair (*burhbotam*) and bridge-repair (*brugbotam*)." Elsewhere, he translates *fyrdunga* "military service, a military expedition" and *fyrdwite* "fine for neglect of military service" with *expeditio* (*II Cnut* 12 and 15). Based on these examples, the obligations of *bricgbot*, *burhbot*, and *fyrdfaru* must have been widely familiar, but still sufficiently technical to warrant at least one translation.

Similarly, *cyricsceat* and *Romfeoh*, are both provided with "*id est*" translations in their first appearance at *I Cnut* 9 and 10 but not thereafter, suggesting that, while technical, they were already widely familiar as terms for taxation. However, Q adds a comment beyond mere translation that may be indicative of the argument that he advances in *Quadripartitus*: "*Romfeoh*, that is Rome's tax (*Romę censu*), which the plentiful kindness of our king decided always to be paid to Saint Peter each year to the praise and glory of God" (*I Cnut* 9). With his supplementary explanation of *Romfeoh*, Q appears to link good kingship with Christian virtue and the fulfillment of Christian duty (major concerns expressed in his prefaces to *Quadripartitus*).

The remaining terms have to do with privileges and protections, and, taken together, these show not only Q's familiarity with the vocabulary, but the assumption that his audience could distinguish subtle differences in meaning since he comfortably oscillates between English and Latin terms. The rubric for *Edward-Guthrum* 1 reads "And concerning the church's peace (*pace ęcclesię*) and the king's peace (*handgrið*)." The body of the text then reads: "And here is the first decree, that the peace of the church (*ecclesie pax*) and the king's peace (*handgrið*) always remain inviolable within their walls." Elsewhere, he gives "the peace of the church (*ęcclesię pax*) within its walls and the peace (*pax*) of the Christian king, which he gives with his own hand, will remain always inviolable" (*I Cnut* 2.2).

---

[50] This seems to be a word-for-word translation of the Old English *his bocrihtes wyrðe*.

Indeed, it is with the retention of *handgrið* that we may best be able to understand Q's nuanced understanding of three other terms that we might assume his audience could confuse. Three "soke" terms appear in the rubrics: *ciricsocna*, *socna taini*, and *hlafordsokna*, and only the first is translated. The rubric for *Ine* 5 gives *De ciricsocna* ("Concerning *ciricsocn*") and he translates without comment in the body *ad ecclesiam confugiat* ("seek refuge in a church"). In fact, two of the manuscript witnesses have a Latin rubric rather than the English: *De confugio ad ecclesiam.*[51] *III Æthelred* 10 has the Latin rubric *De flima; de socna taini* ("Concerning a fugitive; concerning the *socn* of a thegn"). The reference to *socn* of a thegn appears under *III Æthelred* 11. The English text says *nan man nage nane socne ofer cynges þegen buton cyng sylf* ("no one will have jurisdiction over the king's thegn but the king himself"), which Q translates *nemo socnam habeat super tainum regis nisi solus rex* ("no one will have *socn* over the thegn of the king except the king alone"). To this point, it appears that Q is comfortable retaining English *socn* both for the specific "sanctuary" and for the general "jurisdiction." But with *hlafordsokna* we may see Q's assumptions about the technical meanings of *socn* and his audience's competence in nuances of English legal vocabulary. The *DOE Corpus* does not attest *hlafordsocn* and both Bosworth-Toller and *DMLBS* cite the Latin *hlafordsoknam* from *Quadripartitus.*[52] In fact, the word appears twice in *Quadripartitus*, both times in *III Æthelstan*. *III Æthelstan* 4.1 reads: *et etiam ne dominus libero homini hlafordsoknam interdicat, si eum recte custodierit.* F. L. Attenborough translates this: "And a lord also shall not prohibit a free man from seeking for himself a [new] lord, if he has conducted himself rightly"[53]; however, based on the meaning of *ciricsocn* as "church sanctuary," it should plausibly be able to mean "And a lord shall also not forbid sanctuary to a free man, if he has conducted/defended himself rightly." But written over the prologue to *III Æthelstan* is a passage claiming to be a letter from the bishops and thegns of Kent to the king, which reads: *ne iniuste quis alterius hominem recipiat, nec libero homini dominus iniuste hlafordsocnam interdicat* ("no one shall unjustly receive another man, nor a lord unjustly forbid *hlafordsocn* to a free man"). Given the first clause, in which a man may be received, presumably into service, the meaning of *hlafordsocn* in the second clause is apparently "to seek a new lord." *Hlafordsocn* must mean to seek service rather than sanctuary with a lord because the latter was covered by *handgrið*. It would seem that Q presumed his audience could distinguish between the kinds of *socn* based on their context.

---

[51] See Liebermann, *Quadripartitus*, 106.

[52] *DOE Corpus*, s.v. *hlafordsocn*, *hlafordsokn*; Bosworth-Toller, s.v. *hlafordsocn*.

[53] Attenborough, *Laws*, *III As.* 4.1.

Property and Jurisdiction

Angliæ lagam (OE *Engla lagu* "English law, law in an English district")
Denalaga (OE *Dena lagu* "Danish law, the law in a Danish district")
Mircna laga/Mercenorrum laga (OE *Mircna lagu* "Mercian law")
hida (OE *hid* "a hide of land, quantity of land sufficient to support a household")
hundretus (OE *hundred* "hundred, a territorial division, the assembly of the men in such a division")
burgus (OE *burh* "fortification, fortified dwelling, estate")
burgimotus (OE *burhgemot* "meeting of the men of a town or city")
scyremotus (OE *scirgemot* "meeting of the men of the shire")

The language of property and jurisdiction appears largely untranslated, supporting Nicholas Karn's suggestion that this aspect of English law was part of a living legal tradition and still very much in use.[54] The territories under specific legal traditions go under *laga*, although the peoples associated with them appear in either English or Latin: e.g., *Denalaga* (*II Cnut* 15), *Anglorum et Danorum laga* (*II Cnut* 15.2), *Angliæ lagam* (*I Æthelred* Prologue), *Mercennorum laga* (*Mircna laga* Inscription) *Mircenorum laga* (*Mircna laga* 1). The divisions of land and associated jurisdiction generally go untranslated. The hide as land measurement is Latinized to *hida* but is not explained (e.g., *Ine* 64, 65, 66). The hundred is similarly Latinized but not translated (e.g., *II Cnut* 17, 30; *I Edgar* 1, 3, 5, 7). The *burh* goes untranslated (e.g., *II Cnut* 34; *II Æthelstan* 13), and as seen above, it is retained even when it is in a translated compound (*II Cnut* 65). Shire is consistently translated to *comitatus* (*Alfred* 37; *Ine* 36.1; *II Æthelstan* 8). Interestingly, *burgimotus* is always untranslated, and when it appears in a pair with *scyremotus* the latter goes untranslated (e.g., *III Edgar* 5). However, when *scyremotus* appears on its own, it tends to be translated.[55]

Treaties

friðmannus (OE *friðmann* "one who is under special protection, one who is under special protection of a peace agreement")
unfriðmannus (OE *unfriðmann* "one who is not under special protection, one who is not under special protection of a peace agreement")
eahta men (OE *eahta men* "eight men")
landesmannus (OE *landes mann* "man from this land or country")
sceidmannus (OE *sceiðmann* "an enemy, one who causes harm")

---

[54] Karn, "*Quadripartitus.*"
[55] Compare *II Cn.* 18 and 19-19.1.

steoresmannus (OE *steormann* "helmsman, steersman, pilot, captain")
unfriðland (OE *unfriðland* "a hostile country, a country where hostilities are being carried on")
ungilden (OE *ungilde* "not entitled to wergild")

This final field is a small one. There are only three treaties included in *Quadripartitus*—*Alfred-Guthrum*, *Edward-Guthrum*, and *II Æthelred*. Much of the English vocabulary retained in these has already been discussed under other fields. However, two examples from rubrics are worthy of discussion since they explain Q's treatment of English vocabulary in treaties. Only two English words are retained in the rubrics for *II Æthelred*: *De friðmanno regis* ("Concerning a *friðmann* of the king") (3) and *Et si eahta men occidantur* ("And if *eahta men* are killed") (5.2). *Friðmannus* is used three times in the body of the text and is translated "that is a man covered by the treaty (*homo pacis*)" on the third occasion (3.4). *Eahta men* goes untranslated and is repeated twice more in the body of c. 5.2. Apparently, these registered for Q as technical categories of men under the terms of the truce, but he seems to misunderstand *eahta men*, since it really means "eight men."[56] Yet his mistake makes sense and his pattern of retaining English vocabulary becomes clear if other terms in the treaty are considered. In addition to *friðmannus* in c. 3 Q gives *unfriðmannorum* "that is, those who are not covered by the treaty (*pacem*)," *unfriðland* "that is, in a region not covered by the treaty (*in hostilem terram*)," *ungilden* "that is, uncompensated (*insolutus*)." These are all clearly linguistically related to one another (like the *-gild-* words discussed above) and he retains the English to show the relationships: *frið* relates to the treaty, and *un-* puts someone or something outside of the treaty. Elsewhere Q retains *steoresman* "that is, captain (*gubernator*)" (4). And he translates c. 7 as follows:

> If a man of our country (*compatriota*) is accused of having been a thief or killed a man, and one seafaring Dane (*sceidmannus*) and one landsman (*landesmannus*) makes it, then he may not make any denial.

The overwhelming retention of *-mann* terms indicates that Q thought that they carried technical meanings specific to the treaty's terms, although he may not have understood all of them, as is suggested by *eahta men* and *sceidmannus* not being translated. A similar pattern attends the retention of terms specific to the treaty in *Alfred-Guthrum* and *Edward-Guthrum*.

It does not appear that Q assumed his audience would understand these English words, or at least not all of them. But the pattern of retention seems systematic and

[56] On Q's misunderstanding and handling of this term in *Leges Henrici Primi*, where it renders this same clause), see Stefan Jurasinski, "Scribal Malpractice and the Study of Anglo-Saxon Law in the Twelfth Century," in *Textus Roffensis: Law, Language, and Libraries in Early Medieval England*, ed. Bruce O'Brien and Barbara Bombi (Turnhout: Brepols, 2015), 83-104 at 91-2.

suggests that Q considered these to carry technical meaning under the terms of the treaty, and the linguistic patterns from the English significant and recognizable enough to retain them for his audience.

Conclusion

Examining Q's systematic retention of English vocabulary according to semantic fields demonstrates a far greater competence in English on his part than Liebermann recognized. The language that appears to have been self-evident or in minimal need of translation tends to be traditional or fundamental to the operation of the judicial system. Terms that get retained but translated tend to be technical. There is a category of terms that show creative approaches, possibly because the terms were not readily understood by a Norman audience, because they did not refer to contemporary legal practice, or because Q recognized them as important but struggled to know how to treat them. Finally, there is a small group of words that Q clearly did not understand and so merely transliterated or simply got wrong in his translation. If Q's approaches are indicative of his audience's interests and competencies, it would appear that the major concerns of traditional Anglo-Saxon law remained valid in Norman England and would even have translated to Norman concerns without serious conflict. The Normans were at least as concerned with social status and social order as the English, and there is no question about their emphasis on property. Moreover, Q seems to assume that his audience could recognize much of the vocabulary that he retains, even if they needed help on occasion. But this does not explain why the Anglo-Normans would have been interested in highlighting those traditions.

Q retained English vocabulary in *Quadripartitus* much more insistently than the translators of the *Instituta* and *Consiliatio Cnut.* If Q could recognize the English terms as traditional and technical, it is reasonable to believe they were part of a recognizable legal discourse in Anglo-Saxon England, albeit one open to innovation. I posit that he was striving for goals similar to those of the first drafters of English law who chose to write in English: they were interested in representing participation in a continuing legal tradition and, through it, claiming a distinct national identity. A set discourse may have given the impression of a central English state bureaucracy and certainly gave the king a patina of customary authority to go with his practical legislative authority. William I had recognized this when he insisted that he was Edward the Confessor's chosen successor, heir not only to the English throne but to England and its traditions. By the early twelfth century, Q looked to English law as a part of a larger process of legitimation, especially in the transition between William Rufus and Henry I. Continuing to use it indicated continuity. Whether or not it was in force in the same way was not relevant.

The *idea* that English legal custom was still in force was what mattered. The Norman kings adopted and exploited the fiction that they held the laws as they were held *in tempore Edwardi regis*. And to an extent, this is a fair claim. The Anglo-Saxon laws were flexible and living. English kings used the idea of an English legislative tradition to advance their own ideological agendas. Making use of a familiar and traditional legal vocabulary would have been a particularly useful way of appearing to operate within English norms. But it also allowed those participating in the legal tradition to claim an English identity.

Briefly returning to *IV Æthelred* and to the terms *ouerhyrnessam meam* and *smere-mangestre*, I think that these terms do prove illustrative of Q's translation choices. The fine for insubordination to the king is easily recognizable as both traditional and technical. It stands out as a valuable example because it emphasizes the importance of the king's judgment in enacting the law and the king's special status within the law. The women who sell dairy products, however, are also important. The term is invoked in relation to a particular (low) social status and in relation to taxes to be paid. Retaining it, even if it is necessary for Q to translate, indicates that English legal tradition and English identity continue for all.[57]

[57] On the effects of law, tradition, and the ways of handling cases on all levels of society, see Karn, "Scholarship of English law." On Q's possible roles in local courts, see Karn, "Rethinking the *Leges Henrici Primi*," in *English Law Before Magna Carta: Felix Liebermann and Die Gesetze der Angelsachsen*, ed. Stefan Jurasinski, Lisi Oliver, and Andrew Rabin (Leiden: Brill, 2010), 199-220.

King Cnut and his Laws in Early Modern English History and Drama

Rebecca Brackmann

It has been a truism for some time that Anglo-Saxon studies in the first half of the seventeenth century focused on uncovering support for claims of "Saxon liberties"—constitutional principles that Parliamentarian opponents to the first two Stuart monarchs cited against royal absolutism.[1] This essay examines the reception of King Cnut, the Viking invader who became king of Anglo-Saxon England, to demonstrate how other discourses motivated and shaped seventeenth-century scholars of Anglo-Saxon England and even of Anglo-Saxon laws. *I* and *II Cnut* are the largest and most comprehensive of the Old English codes, and many early scholars wanted the laws of this Viking invader to be brought into the discourse of English liberties, and indeed English identity. However, the episcopal components of Cnut's laws grew increasingly at odds with the Presbyterian convictions of many common lawyers such as John Pym. As we now know (but early scholars did not) Cnut, after his successful conquest, engaged Archbishop Wulfstan of York, one of the best legal minds of the day, to draw up his laws. Even though they did not know the laws' author, early modern readers certainly recognized what modern legal scholars have also observed: Cnut's legislation, in its compendious nature, its originality, and its portrayal of the relationship between the crown and the Church in building a holy society, represented something new in Old English law. Patrick Wormald observes that in *I* and *II Cnut* "The English Church was buttressed by a remarkably full system of legal support. There was corresponding reinforcement for the morality of a Christian society"—and bishops had a substantial role.[2] Early modern readers, no less than their modern counterparts, recognized this exceptional coherence and episcopal emphasis. However, the strength of Cnut's codes became their weakness, and depictions of Cnut himself more negative, as the episcopal vision of Archishop Wulfstan became increasingly unpalatable to English Presbyterians and Calvinists.

---

[1] For a fairly recent example, see Janelle Greenberg, *The Radical Face of the Ancient Constitution: St. Edward's "Laws" in Early Modern Political Thought* (Cambridge: Cambridge University Press, 2001).
[2] Wormald, *Making*, 363.

HOLINSHED'S *CHRONICLES*

Early seventeenth-century writers knew Cnut's story primarily from the exploration of English history overseen and partially written by Rafael Holinshed, which is usually referred to by his name. Holinshed's *Chronicles* first edition appeared in 1577; ten years later a revised version was printed, largely overseen by Abraham Fleming. Both versions drew on William Lambarde's 1568 *Archaionomia*, an edition of Old English laws with a Latin translation. The *Chronicles* publication stemmed from nationalist desires in the wake of the English Reformation. Its presentation of medieval history served those desires; as Alexandra Gillespie and Oliver Harris write, "the break with Rome reoriented the nation's idea of history: it made the medieval past determinedly "other," while at the same time locating in the Middle Ages an emergent story of the development of an independent and imperial English realm."[3] This is not to say that *Holinshed* presents a monolithic view of the "medieval" past. Harriet Archer notes some differentiation between the discussions of pre-Norman invasions: "Danish rule is altogether leaner and meaner than the oscillations between British and Saxon, savagery and erudition, paganism and Christianity seen in the previous book." [4] Overall Cnut comes off well:

> Cnut proves an enlightened ruler, repairing abbeys and reforming "all such things as he and his ancestors had doone amisse" [...] While restoring religious houses, he exercises a proto-Henrician control over the Church, bringing spiritual matters under "the lawfull authoritie of the temporall prince"—the prescience of which is highlighted by demoting the pope to "bishop of Rome" [...][5]

Making Cnut a proto-Henry requires a fairly positive portrayal. When Cnut mutilated his English hostages, the text does what it can to exculpate him. According to Holinshed, Cnut acted in a rage born from grief and loyalty: "sore greeued in his mind to remember what mischeefe was fallen and chanced to his friends and subiects of Lindsey, onelie for his cause."[6] As a conqueror, Cnut treated the English with "bountifulness and courteous dealings" to retain their loyalty. After Ironside's death, Cnut effected his "wise and politike" marriage to Æthelred's widow, Emma of Normandy, who gave him good counsel.

---

[3] Alexandra Gillespie and Oliver Harris, "Holinshed and the Native Chronicle Tradition," in *The Oxford Handbook of Holinshed's "Chronicles,"* ed. Paulina Kewes, Ian W. Archer, and Felicity Heal (Oxford, Oxford University Press, 2013), 137.

[4] Harriet Archer, "Holinshed and the Middle Ages" in *The Oxford Handbook of Holinshed's Chronicles*, ed. Kewes, Archer, and Hall, 171-86, at 174.

[5] Archer, "Holinshed," 174.

[6] 1578 7.7. All quotations from Holinshed are from "The Holinshed Project," http://english.nsms.ox.ac.uk/holinshed/texts

"Then rested the whole rule of the realme in [Cnut's] hands, wherevpon he studied to preserue the people in peace, and ordeined lawes, according to the which both Danes and Englishmen should be gouerned in equall state and degree."[7]

Holinshed's Chapter 7.13 is devoted to praising Cnut's imperial power, his godliness, and his legislation. The highest praise is reserved for his law-giving:

> Diuerse lawes and statutes he made for the gouernment [of] the common wealth, partlie agreeable with the lawes of king Edgar, and other the kings that were his predecessors, and partlie tempered according to his owne liking, and as was thought to him most expedient: among the which there be diuerse that concerne causes as well ecclesiasticall as temporall. Whereby (as maister Fox hath noted) it maie be gathered, that the gouernment of spirituall matters did depend then not vpon the bishop of Rome, but rather apperteined vnto the lawfull authoritie of the temporall prince [...]

Praise for good laws is not a standard trope in this section of *Holinshed*; the *Chronicles* do not so much as mention the legislation of Cnut's predecessors except in this passage. *Holinshed's Chronicles* makes plain that Cnut's legal accomplishments were not only visible to early modern readers, but key to his initial reception.

The seventeenth century inherited this version of Cnut: an invader whose laws paradoxically represented a key moment in English legal history. The need to claim those laws encouraged Cnut's positive portrayal as a proto-Henry VIII in his religious independence and his imperial ambitions. However, the episcopal slant to his laws would ultimately prove a liability, outweighing the potential for constitutional arguments to be found in pre-Conquest England's most comprehensive codes.

Seventeenth-Century Histories: John Speed, Nathaniel Bacon, and William Prynne

By the early years of the Stuarts, rifts grew within the reformed Church of England. Anti-episcopal sentiment increased, as did the desire for church doctrine and practice to more explicitly embrace the extreme Calvinism of theologians such as Theodore Beza, highlighting (among other things) the need for stricter Sabbath-keeping and the making of sermons, not sacraments, the focal point of worship. These hopes were disappointed when James I not only refused to abolish episcopacy, but published a work allowing and encouraging sports and games on Sunday after church attendance. James was, however, doctrinally Calvinist; he believed in predestination and the primacy of grace as opposed to works. In contrast, the so-called "Arminian" belief gained ground

[7] *Holinshed* 1587 7.11.

in Protestant Europe, arguing that works, especially participation in ritual, could and should play a role in an individual's salvation. This camp, ultimately associated in England with Charles I and his Archbishop of Canterbury William Laud, emphasized churches as beautiful sacred spaces, the locus of rituals and sacraments. Laudian Anglicans had no objection to subsequent participation in worldly activities, even on Sundays. Debates over how to keep the Sabbath, the validity of episcopacy, and the kind of legislation a king should pass regulating religious action compelled scholars to re-examine Cnut's codes as examples of "English" precedent and history. The ground-breaking legislation of *I* and *II Cnut*, reflecting Wulfstan's archiepiscopal perspective, became increasingly distasteful to many Presbyterian English readers. The popular perception of Cnut, as seen in his depiction on the stage, also reflected the difficulty of claiming Cnut as fundamentally English during the decades when Englishmen fought bitterly amongst themselves about their own national and religious identity.

John Speed, "The Historie of Great Britaine Vnder the Conqvests of the Romans, Saxons, Danes, and Normans"

John Speed hoped his book would "replace [Holinshed] in the vernacular history market" —and in the public consciousness as the "true" story of England's history.[8] The first edition appeared in 1611, the second in 1623; both contain an introductory poem by Speed's fellow antiquary, John Davies, claiming that in Speed's work:

> Time and Place, like friendly foes doe warre
> Which should shew most desir'd Particulars;
> But Place gives place, sith Time is greater farre
> Yet Place, well rang'd, gets glory by these warres[9].

Although in Davies's text Time takes precedence, Place argues for the importance of geographic location in establishing the foundation of contemporary identity. By extension, Speed's Cnut, who lived and ruled in England, can be claimed as "English." Speed also asserts that the Vikings ultimately came from the same place that the "Saxons" did, implying that their shared geography and Germanic heritage tie them together, making Cnut a validly "English" king.

Speed's narrative of the Danish invasions, however, diverges from Holinshed's *Chronicles* treatment. Anti-episcopal notes begin to sound in Speed's discussion of the Viking incursions; consequently he portrays Æthelred fairly sympathetically, as a king

[8] Glyn Parry, "Berosus and the Protestants: Reconstructing Protestant Myth," *Huntington Library Quarterly* 64 (2001): 7.

[9] John Speed, *The Historie of Great Britaine Vnder the Conqvests of the Romans, Saxons, Danes, and Normans.* 2nd ed. (London, 1623).

struggling with both foreign invaders and the opposition of the clergy and episcopacy. Speed objects to the traditional view of Æthelred:

> His youth was spent in idleness, feeding his senses with all voluptuous baites; his middle yeeres with a carelesse gouernment, maintaining ciuill dissensions; and his latter end deseruingly in continuall resistance of the bloud-thirsty *Danes*. With these imputations by Writers hee is taxed, though wee find no such iust cause in recording his life [...][10]

Speed indicates that Æthelred's susceptibility to bad press rises from "malignant reporter[s]" and began during his life: "And that this King lay lyable to such mens humors, the working of *Dunstan* euer against him, is a sufficient witnesse, who not onlely did refuse to act his Coronation, but would haue preferred Lady *Edgith* a bastard before him to the Crowne [...]"[11] Æthelred's openness to clerical marriage and "iust indignation conceived against the Bishop of *Rochester*" divided first the church, then the people from him; the Danes, Speed says, were quick to seize the opportunity: "perceiuing the hearts of the subiects to bee drawne from their Soueraigne, they thought it a sufficient occasion to forward their intendments" and invade England.[12] Æthelred's failure to hold them off arose not only from the nobility, many of whom "were allianced into the *Danish* bloud," but also from the churchmen who, "as backward as any, denyed the King their assistance, pleading their exemptions from warre, and priuiledge of the Church, when the land lay bleeding and deploring for helpe, and scandalized all his other proceedings for demanding their aide [...]"[13] After Æthelred's death, Speed claims that although the Archbishop of Canterbury crowned Ironside, "a great part of the Clergy" favored Cnut and swore fealty to him.[14] Speed's portrayal of Dunstan's and the churchmen's obstruction of Æthelred tacitly counters James I's famous comment, "No bishop, no king." [15] Against James's view that hierarchy in the church reinforced hierarchy in the polity, Speed's history argues that bishops could just as well undermine monarchs, especially in time of unrest.

Speed's Cnut, when he takes the throne, understands that a wise monarch does not rely on popular support:

> He called a Counsell of the *English* Nobility at *London;* wherein was propounded, whether, in the agreement betwixt Edmund and him, any claime of title to the Crowne had beene reserued for King *Edmunds* brethren or sonnes. The English [. . .] not daring now to buy,

[10] Speed, *Historie*, 7.414.
[11] Speed, *Historie*, 7.414.
[12] Speed, *Historie*, 7.414.
[13] Speed, *Historie*, 7.414.
[14] Speed, *Historie*, 7.425.
[15] See the discussion of James's statement and position on episcopacy in James Doelman, *King James I and the Religious Culture of England* (Cambridge: D.S. Brewer, 2000), 14-16.

> with too late repentance, the wrath of this *Dane*, absolutely answered, No, and hauing learned to appease Princes with flattery, offered their swords against any such claimes, and tooke themselues the Oath of alleaiance vnto *Canutus;* who being a very wise and politike Prince, thought neuer the better of them for such their doings; whose truths thus failing towards their naturall Princes, could neuer (hee well know) stand firme for him or his forreine posteritie.[16]

Cnut's "wise and politic" nature not only taught him not to rely on popular support, but to seek out those whose influence and advice could most aid him. He married Emma, who, although reluctant to marry her husband's opponent, know that by doing so she could stabilize the succession: "the issue of her body by him, should inherite the English Crowne … hoping also, if that failed betwixt them, to establish her other sonnes by King *Ethelred*." A marginal note observes "*Emma* a very prudent Lady"—and Canute was wise enough to realize it. Speed claims that her measures for stability "drew the hearts of the *English* vnto *Canutus*, and their loue vnto *Emma*," especially after she convinced Cnut to relocate the "*Danes*, that lay lazie and idle, as drones in the hiue, who at her instigations were sent into *Denmark*."[17] Cnut, although an invader, understood good council when he saw it and used Emma as a bridge between himself and his new subjects.

For Speed, however, Cnut's legislation most clearly proved his regnal success in England. Unlike Holinshed, Speed had mentioned the codes of Æthelred and other earlier kings, but his extended discussion of Cnut's law highlights their particular importance and applicability:

> Canutus his next care for the maintenance of his owne safety, and the continuance of his new got Empire, was the establishment of good lawes [(]which if duly executed, are the very sinewes and strongest guards of all States) to be administred and practised both on the English and Dane alike [...] [He] established many wholsome Acts both for the Clergy and Laitie to obserue, some of which were divulged by the praise-worthy care of a studious Antiquarie, and a few, as touching Religion, as a relish of the rest, we thinke it not amisse to giue the Reader a taste of.
> And first, for the celebration of Gods most diuine Seruice, it was ordained, that all decent ceremonies tending to the encrease of reuerence and deuotion, should be vsed, as need required.
> That vpon the Lords Sabbath, publike Faires, Markets, Synods, Conuenticles, Huntings[18], and all secular actions should not be exercised, vnlesse some weighty and vrgent necessity required it.

[16] Speed, *Historie*, 8.398. The page numbers erroneously revert from 429 to 392 in book 8.
[17] Speed, *Historie*, 8.399.
[18] Perhaps an error for "Hustings."

> That euery Christian should thrice in the yeere addresse himselfe to the receiuing of the blessed Sacrament of the Lords Supper.
> That if a Minister of the Altar killed a man, or else committed any notorious crime, hee should be depriued both from his order and dignity [...][19]
> These and many other were made, whereby sin was much restrayned, and this realme peaceably and iustly gouerened.[20]

Speed, who clearly had a copy of Lambarde's *Archaionomia* (and often cites it), does not expand so on the laws of any other pre-Conquest king. His interest here is not in "Saxon liberties," but instead in Cnut's religious legislation. He approvingly notes that Cnut's laws mandated "decent" ceremony and periodic sacraments, while also forbidding commerce and "all secular actions" on the Sabbath except in dire need. Cnut's laws provide a middle way between Laudian and Calvinist extremes, and Speed observes that such sound legislation both united and protected the nation. The fact that this was a commonplace in early modern discussions of law's role in society make it no less sincere on Speed's part.

Having held Canute up as a model of royal concern for godly legislation and political acumen, Speed faced one final challenge: making Cnut's trip to Rome palatable to his audience. Cnut first has a change of heart:

> But being at length ouerburdened as it were with his owne greatness, and surfeited with glory [...] hee resolued on a more placable course of life, and to affect a higher and heuenly glory, which hath neuer satiety or end. And therefore his deuotion being great vnto God-ward, on a zealous intent (such as *S. Paul* commended in the deuout Israelites) hee tooke a iourney to *Rome*, to visite the sepulchers of *S. Peter* and *Paul* [...][21]

Zeal and devotion motivate Cnut's journey, which conforms with the advice of the Apostle Paul; in Speed's version, Cnut's interactions with the Pope are secondary to his main purpose. Cnut writes from Rome to his clergy, expressing his intent to devote "the whole remainder of his life and reigne, to the onley seruice of God, and due administration of *Iustice* to his people [...]."[22] Piety and justice are Cnut's main concerns, which Speed explicitly notes have present relevance:

> By this his great care of his owne saluation, and his peoples tranquility, we may see the zeale of those darke daies, to haue beene accompanied with the workes of true pietie;

[19] This must have had a particular resonance in the *Historie*'s 1623 edition, as in 1621 Archbishop of Canterbury George Abbott had accidentally killed one of his companions while hunting, but had retained his office amid much controversy.
[20] Speed, *Historie*, 8.399-400.
[21] Speed, *Historie*, 8.400.
[22] Speed, *Historie* 8.400.

> whose carnall applications of the sprituall texts, may well condemne these cleerer times, and daies of more brightnesse [...][23]

Cnut's "conversion" from glory-seeking to piety mimics hagiographic narratives from late antiquity on, but it also chimes with Calvinist autobiographical writing, much of which narrates an author's spiritual journey from worldly concerns to spiritual ones, from doubt to certainty, and from unthinking compliance with religious mandates to embracing them with an internal "zeal" that conveyed one's elect status.[24] Speed's use of the word "zeal" to similarly describe Cnut is perhaps a coded reference to these narratives. The narration of Cnut's life displays his laudable inner state, which manifested in outer deeds—especially legislation: "And surely, howsoeuer this King is taxed of ambition, pride and vaine-glory, for which some haue not stucke to say, that he made his iourney to *Rome*, rather to shew his pompe and riches, then for any humble deuotion or religious intent, yet by many his intercurrent actions and lawes of piety enacted, hee may iustly be cleared of that imputation [...]"[25] Cnut's legislation provides a moderate path for Church practices while his personal life shows him compatible with Calvinist spiritual narratives. Cnut's virtues ultimately lift him not only above other English kings, but all European monarchs: "he was a Prince of such temperance and iustice, that no other in this West of the World was so highly renowned, or might be compared vnto him in heroicall vertues, or true humility."[26]

Sir Nathaniel Bacon, "An Historical Discourse of the Uniformity of the Government of England"

Speed's middle ground between "decent" ceremonial observance and the Calvinist insistence on prayer (preferably spontaneously composed) and preaching was much harder to hold in the divisive years of the latter 1640s. Nor was Nathaniel Bacon the religious moderate that Speed was. Bacon, a member of the Long Parliament, directly engaged constitutional concerns and "Saxon Liberties" in his discussion of English history. He strove to demonstrate that the past, and in particular the pre-Norman past, could not only provide evidence of ancient rights but heal a war-torn England: "For as in all other cures, so in that of a distempered government the originall constitution of the body is not lightly to be regarded [...]"[27] The most salutary period was the time of the

---

[23] Speed, *Historie* 8.401.

[24] For example, see Simonds D'Ewes, *The Autobiography and Correspondence of Sir Simonds D'Ewes*, 2 vol. (London: Richard Bentley, 1845) and discussion in Sears McGee, *An Industrious Mind: The Worlds of Sir Simonds D'Ewes* (Stanford: Stanford University Press, 2015).

[25] Speed, *Historie,* 8.401.

[26] Speed, *Historie,* 8.401-2.

[27] Sir Nathaniel Bacon, *An Historical Discourse of the Uniformity of the Government of England* (1647), [A4r].

Anglo-Saxons since subsequent centuries "were times of force, and can give little or no evidence against the customes rightly setled in the Saxon times, which I have more particularly insisted upon, that the original constitution of this government may the better appeare."[28] As he lays out his arguments, he regularly cites Cnut with other Anglo-Saxon kings as evidence for this constitution. However, his text ultimately presents a conflicted image of Cnut and his legislation. Bacon's difficulty with Cnut is precisely what attracted Speed (and perhaps Holinshed) in the first place—Cnut's extensive legislation of religious obligations and church duties.

Bacon doubts that ceremony is even relevant to divine worship; he dryly observes that "the rude Saxons [. . . w]ere content to come to Church onely to pray and heare the word, and so went away; this is noted by that ancient writer [Bede] in nature of an imputation, as if somewhat else was to be done which they neglected."[29] In Bacon's view, the Saxons' apparent "rudeness" was actually a proto-Calvinist stance and contrasts with contemporary Laudianism. According to the godly, preaching and prayer were the only beneficial elements in a church service. Bacon claims that the common Saxons shared this conviction, even in the face of a Roman Catholic establishment, represented by Bede, who thought otherwise.

Bacon also sees the roots of his and his fellow Calvinists' concern with Sabbath-keeping in Saxon, or indeed even pre-Saxon, history. Laws for Sabbath-keeping combined the power of the state to that of the church in order to create a holy society:

> I am the rather induced to conceive charitably of those times in regard of their exceeding zeale for the honour of the Lords day; which sheweth, that so farre as their knowledge would maintaine them they had zeale to make it into action [...B]ecause they would not allow their secular affaires to trench too nigh that daies devotion, they made the Lords day to begin upon Saturday at three of the clocke in the afternoon, and to continue till Munday morning. No pastime, no not their beloved sport of hunting, was allowed during all that time: nor no works were to be done, but such as concerned the worship of God; and those laws they bound with a penalty of fine [...] Nor were these the Laws of one King, or age onely, but of the whole currant of the Saxon government, and may, although darke times they were, yet put us in these daies of light to the blush, to enter into compare with them for their devotion.[30]

The religious legal mandates of Anglo-Saxon England are held up as a positive example of their "zeal" (which as we have seen was a charged term). Bacon cites Cnut's along with other codes for this "Saxon" trait and does not mention Cnut's non-Saxon origin. Shortly after this passage, Bacon includes Cnut as a "Saxon" king in his

[28] Bacon, *Historical Discourse*, "Preface" [np].

[29] Bacon, *Historical Discourse*, 40.

[30] Bacon, *Historical Discourse*, 98.

discussion of the laws pertaining to the Fifth Commandment: "It would be too tedious to recite all the particular Laws, with their changes, and therefore they shall be left to the view in the severall Laws of *Alfred, Edmond, Canutus,* and *Edward*, the Saxon Kings."[31] Here Cnut is unequivocally "Saxon"; nothing differentiates him from the other rulers.

However, at other moments in his book Bacon rejects Cnut as a model for contemporary England. The Danes, as relatively (and opportunistically) new converts to Christianity, were more "susceptible" to the Roman Catholic clergy than the Saxons:

> The worst effect [Danish conquest] had was upon the Church in the decay of the power of Religion and worship of God. For after much toile and losse both of sweat and blood, the Danes (finding that [...] the Clergy at the least was the side-wind in the course of all affaires) laid aside their Paganisme, and joined with the Clergy; and as their converts and pupils gained not onely their quiet residence, but the favour of the Clergy to make Trial of the Throne, and therein served the Clergy so well as they brought the people to a perfect Idolatry, with times, places, and persons, and subjection of their estates to Church tributes. And as at Tenis the Dane and Bishop served each other with the fond Countrey man, that whether Lord Dane or Lord Bishop was the greater burden, is hard to be determined. Thus became ambicious Prelacy in its full glory [...][32]

Unlike Speed's version of events, in which the Anglo-Saxon Æthelred was more vulnerable to episcopal influence, Bacon argues that the origin of bishops' ascendancy over the English polity came with Danish rule. This was more lasting than any legal changes, for ultimately "nor did any monument of the Danish government remain, saving a few customes in some places which shew rather that the Danes were there then ruled there."[33]

Bacon's text displays perhaps most strongly of all "non-fiction" narratives a curious double-vision of Cnut. On the one hand, Bacon cites Cnut's codes marginally throughout his discussion as evidence of the Anglo-Saxon history of laws, courts and criminal proceedings. Cnut's codes were, of course, written in Old English, and to that extent Bacon needed—even wanted—to claim them, and him, as authentically "Saxon." On the other hand, however, Bacon was astute enough to recognize *I Cnut*'s strongly episcopal bias. A staunch Presbyterian, he wished to reject as "foreign" the code's emphasis on the role of bishops in ensuring a holy society. Cnut and his legislation shows the seams between Bacon's aims and his sources more clearly, perhaps, than any other aspect of the *Historical Discourse.*

---

[31] Bacon, *Historical Discourse*, 100.

[32] Bacon, *Historical Discourse*, 111-12.

[33] Bacon, *Historical Discourse*, 112.

William Prynne: A Seasonable, Legal, and Historical Vindication 165[6]

The title of William Prynne's volume spells out its ideological purposes: *The Third Part of a Seasonable, Legal, and Historical Vindication of the good old Fundamental Liberties, Franchises, Rights, Properties, Laws, Government of All English Freemen with a Chronological Collection of their strenuous Defences, by wars, and otherwise: of all Great Parliamentary Councills, Synods, and chief Laws, Charters, Proceedings in them: of the publike revolutions of State, with the sins and vices occasioning them; and the exemplary Judgements of God upon Tyrants, Oppressors, perjured perifious Traitors, Rebels, Regicides, Usurpers, during the reigns of our Saxon and Danish Kings* [...] *With brief usefull observacions on and from them.*[34] While Bacon wished primarily to use the past as evidence for present constitutional arguments, Prynne's aim was minatory. He wished to show that God had often ordained social and political turmoil (even in defense of English rights) as a direct response to public sin. God had also directly struck down those unlawfully holding power as a result of such upheaval. Should any of his readers have missed the thrust of the book's title, Prynne's preface reiterates his aims in examining the pre-Norman past:

> yet notwithstanding wise intelligent Christians by a serious trutination, and comparing of the Judgements of God, expresly threatned against, and usually inflicted upon *Nations* or *Persons*, for such and such transgressions, in precedent generations *may probably conjecture & predict*, what severe exemplary punishments our late present transcendent wickednesses, & outragious crimes, are like to draw down upon our impenitent, secure perjured *sinful Nation* [...][35]

Prynne saw sin everywhere, from the lifestyle of the English people to the actions of those currently in power, and firmly believed that God would punish these ills unless immediate action was taken. He does not specify which action, although since he opposed the regicide, presumably in his mind the Restoration would have been a good start. Prynne also claimed—and seems to have actually believed—that the regicide and the downfall (in his view) of the Long Parliament's efforts toward securing English liberty had been caused entirely by the Jesuits, who had managed to suborn MPs to act as their unwitting agents. By taking this view, Prynne could, at least in his own mind, absolve himself of any responsibility for the direction the Parliament (of which he had been an influential member for most of the 1640s) had ultimately taken.

However things might have looked to him in the 1650s, however, Prynne had been one of the firebrands of the early Long Parliament. As Mark Kishlansky observes, "There were many moderate puritans in Caroline England, but William Prynne was

[34] William Prynne, *The Third Part of a Seasonable, Legal, and Historical Vindication*, London: 165[6].

[35] Prynne, *Third Part*, Preface [np].

not among them."[36] He conceived that his conviction and judicial mutilation by the judges in Star Chamber had come about due to a personal vendetta against him by Archbishop Laud (a view that Kishlansky believes was mistaken). When Prynne had a chance to retaliate, he took it; he was a prime mover in the legal case against Laud that led to the Archbishop's execution in 1645. Given Prynne's implacable opposition to Laud and to episcopacy in general, it comes as some surprise that his view of Dunstan is far more positive than Speed's or Bacon's. Dunstan's appeal to Prynne probably rose from the former's reputed role as a prophet of doom (a role which Prynne himself embraced). Dunstan supposedly prophesied that Æthelred and the whole kingdom would suffer invasion and conquest due to the murder of Æthelred's annointed brother Edward, and Prynne explicitly links Dunstan's word to the present: "let all others whom it concerns most nearly, with our whole English Nation now seriously reminde it."[37] Prynne continues, "I cannot but take special Notice of Gods admirable retaliating Justice inflicted upon some of our Saxon usurping Regicides and their Posterities, worthy our saddest contemplation." [38] Prynne saw Dunstan as a kindred spirit in decrying the sins of his age and threatening God's vengeance for them.

Divine retaliation had arrived in the form of the Danes and especially Cnut, whom Prynne depicts as a savage, lawless figure. In contrast to *Holinshed*'s exculpating depiction of Cnut's mutilation of hostages, Prynne states that Cnut acted "by way of revenge **humano et divino Jure contempto** in insontes grassatus."[39] Cnut, with the help of Eadric Streona, ultimately convinced Edmund Ironside to split the kingdom with him, providing Prynne with an example of the dangers of counsellors who have been suborned by the enemy. Prynne no doubt expected his readers to connect Cnut's and Eadric's actions to his prior discussion of the Jesuits' supposed role in the regicide. Cnut remains a scourge worthy of Dunstan's predictions, at first leading the conquered English into even greater sins than the ones for which God had sent him as punishment.

Prynne's need to show Cnut as first and foremost a punishment sent to the English shades his narration of Cnut's lawgiving. For Prynne, Cnut's legislation has an entirely self-serving purpose. Having married Emma in order to pacify the English, "because they much honoured and affected her for her manifold vertues, of which they had long former experience,"[40] he follows some of her suggestions, including one to placate his new subjects "by ratifying all their former good old fundamental Laws, Rights, Liberties, Privileges,

---

36 Mark Kishlansky, "A Whipper Whipped: The Sedition of William Prynne," *The Historical Journal* 56 (2013): 604.
37 Prynne, *Third Part*, 142.
38 Prynne, *Third Part*, 142.
39 "proceeding, in disregard of human and divine law, against the guiltless." Bold type here represents a shift in the original to blackletter, which Prynne used for emphasis. Prynne, *Third Part*, 202.
40 Prynne, *Third Part*, 226.

which they used, enjoyed under their Saxon Kings, by enacting other good wholesom Laws, repealing all unjust Laws, and redressing all exactions and grievances."[41] It is only after Emma suggests it that Cnut agrees to honor the ancient rights of the English, and Cnut's legislation is at the same time the only evidence for his reform. Prynne (predictably) views the pilgrimage to Rome with suspicion: "King *Cnute*, *Anno* 1031, (to palliate his Usurpations of other mens Crowns with the shew of Devotion) travelled to *Rome* in very great pomp, where he offered very great gifts in gold, silver, rich vestments, and pretious stones [...]"[42] Prynne's dismissive use of "pomp" to describe the "shew" indicates that Cnut's journey had no real spiritual motivation. By contrast, the only evidence that Cnut could perhaps have mended his ways is found in his subsequent legislation:

> King *Cnute* in the year 1033 on the Feast of Christs Nativity, held a Parliamentary Council at *Winchester*, where, **Venerando Sapientum eius Consilio**, by the venerable Counsel of his Wisemen, he made and published sundry excellent Ecclesiastical and Civil Laws for the good government of the Church and Realm, *to the praise of God, the honour of his Regality, and common good of the People*, being 103 in the *Saxon* and 110 in the *Latine* Copies. His 61 Ecclesiastical Law thus resolves, against the Anti-Magistratical opinion of this licentious age, *Christiano Regi jure pertinet,* **ut injurias Deo factas vindicet**, *secundum quod accederit.* [43]

If even the Viking ruler whose primary function was to serve as a punishment from God could reform enough to legislate proper religious devotion, Prynne observes, how can anyone excuse the wrongdoings of his own day:

> If this Forein Danish *Conqueror* and Usurper of the Crown of *England* ... Was at last so just and equal to the *English*, as to reform all his former extravagant acts of Injustice, Exactions, Oppressions, to release all unjust Taxes, Exactions. Oppressions, and not to exact or raise any monies unjustly on the people, upon any real or pretended necessity, without their common consent in Parliament, by any of his Officers, should not our own English Conquerors & domineering Grandees now much more imitate this his laudable Example, who pretend not only to equal but exceed him in Saintship [...][44]

Cnut here is used as a warning to Cromwell's government, but Prynne's view of Cnut never really grants him the status of "English," however much Prynne approves of Cnut's legislation. He remains a foreign outsider, sent by God as a punishment to the Anglo-Saxons and a warning to Cromwell and his fellow regicides. God's chosen foreign invader must by necessity remain foreign.

---

[41] Prynne, *Third Part*, 230.
[42] Prynne, *Third Part*, 237.
[43] It pertains in law to a Christian king, to punish injuries done to God, according to which he was summoned. Prynne, *Third Part*, 241.
[44] Prynne, *Third Part*, 238-9.

Cnut on Stage: Anthony Brewer, *The Love-Sick King*

From Speed to Prynne, the general trend of Cnut's reception in seventeenth-century histories is downward. Cnut goes from *Holinshed's* and Speed's supreme example of English legislation to a dupe of bishops and a Divine scourge only barely kept from crushing the English entirely. Anthony Brewer's 1617 play *The Love-Sick King* stands at the midpoint of this trajectory, and shows the pull in both directions: the need to claim Cnut as part of English history and to reject him as a foreign outsider. Cnut's popular reception, if Brewer is an indicator, mimics the trends in polemical texts from the heart of the nation's struggles.

The Love-Sick King strikes most modern readers as enigmatic, if not downright weird. Its plot is (by our understanding) absurd, and its "history" is a jumbled mess of characters from different time periods. It cheerfully brings Cnut together with King Alfred the Great, who had ruled some two hundred years previously, and Thornton of Newcastle, who died in 1430. Randall Martin, the play's modern editor, speculates that the play was perhaps first performed as a "Lord Mayor's Show" in Newcastle, perhaps with King James in attendance. The chronological mash-up, Martin observes, is not due to lack of knowledge on Brewer's part, but is a deliberate—and usual—aspect of many such Lord Mayor's shows. *The Love-Sick King* "does not aim to show the causes of [historical] events but rather to gather the chief associations of their names into a thematic ancestry in which James, and any mayor, can place themselves as most recent heirs."[45] Curtis Perry, in one of the few extended treatments of the play in recent years, argues that the play also goes against modern notions of centralized national identity based on a sharp divide between Us and Them. Perry suggests that the *Love-Sick King*, in comparison to sixteenth century plays about early medieval history, depicts "Englishness" as local, land-based, and inclusive.[46] I find Perry's arguments about the play's national interests persuasive, and his discussion shows how nuanced and interesting the play is; however, in the context of previous and ongoing depictions of Cnut, I argue that *The Love-Sick King* undermines its own attempts at forming a national identity that stems from inclusive, welcoming notions of Englishness as grounded in geography and character. First, the play's potential desire for a fluid national identity is strictly limited to the male characters in contrast with the historical sources; unlike Emma,

---

[45] Anthony Brewer, *Edmond Ironside and Anthony Brewer's The Love-sick King*, ed. Randall Martin (New York: Garland, 1991), 192.

[46] Curtis Perry, "'For They are Englishmen': National Identities and the Early Modern Drama of Medieval Conquest," in *Shakespeare and the Middle Ages*, ed. Curtis Perry and John Watkins (Oxford: Oxford University Press, 2009), 172-95; see also Gordon McMullan, "The Colonization of Early Britain on the Jacobean Stage," in *Reading the Medieval in Early Modern England*, ed. Gordon McMullan and David Matthews (Cambridge: Cambridge University Press, 2007), 119-40.

the female characters in Brewer's play all die after aligning themselves with a member of the other nation. The play does not allow women to actively interface between invader and English. Canutus himself, whom the play at times wants to claim as "English," is not seamlessly absorbed after his defeat—if indeed he becomes in any way "English" at all.

Brewer's play is not well known, so a brief summary is in order. The play's action begins as Canutus completes his invasion of England by defeating the English forces at Winchester. Canutus orders the slaughter of the nuns of Winchester, but is captivated by the beauty of Cartesmunda, one of the nuns, and she is spared and taken prisoner. Cartesmunda, after initially resisting Canutus's advances, finally gives in and agrees to be his mistress. Meanwhile, Alured, younger brother of the slain English king, disguises himself as a commoner when he is captured by the Viking Erkinwald. Canutus's sister Elgina sees the captured Alured, and falls in love with him. When Elgina expresses her love to Alured, the eavesdropping Erkinwald rushes in to kill him, but instead fatally stabs Elgina when she tries to intervene. Alured then kills Erkinwald and escapes. After several scenes in which we see Thornton of Newcastle's rise from poverty to wealth and position, Alured visits Newcastle with an army of English and Scots which he has raised to attack Canutus. The Newcastle characters immediately pledge to serve in his army. Canutus, meanwhile, has been utterly neglecting his duties in favor of entertaining Cartesmunda, to the despair of his Viking lords who recognize the danger Alured poses to them. Finally one of his men attempts to forcibly remove Cartesmunda from Canutus's side, and in the ensuing fight Canutus accidentally runs her through. Canutus then immediately takes up his arms to fight the English. During the battle, he and Alured fight, and Alured gets the upper hand but spares Canutus for Elgina's sake. Canutus is ultimately captured by the Newcastle characters, and Alured pledges that, once Canutus has returned to his kingdom in Denmark, the two will be sworn brothers and friends.

Perry argues that this play shows an English nationalism that is inclusive, rather than relying entirely on "exclusionary logic."[47] Although the "Saxons" are "the key to something like a national character," the invading Danes are ultimately absorbed into the matrix as "brothers." Ultimately, Perry argues, "the play's nationalism is designed to appeal to King James and to respond to the need for a specifically British history compatible with the idea of Saxon liberties."[48] The British history includes the Saxon and Scottish characters, but it also includes the noble Danes—as in fact many northern English in the seventeenth century had Danish ancestors, and James's wife Anne was a Danish princess. Gordon McMullan's analysis agrees with Perry's that "through Elgina's

[47] Perry, "For They are Englishmen," 177.
[48] Perry, "For They are Englishmen," 191.

example, Englishness and Danishness have begun in fact to merge by the close of the play."[49]

Perry and McMullan are no doubt right about the play's intent, and the interest in "Saxon liberties" which motivated Brewer's desire to integrate Canutus. However, the value of Cnut's codes for showing these liberties was increasingly outweighed in the wider discourse by the need to reject Wulfstan's episcopal focus. Accordingly, the play's attempt at depicting an Englishness that can include Cnut is neither entirely comfortable, nor successful. First, the play is nervous about the female role in boundary-crossing, in that neither Elgina nor Cartesmunda, two characters with the most claim to breaking down borders between English and Danish, survives the play. Elgina openly claims a trans-national identity:

> If all the English perish, then must I
> For I [...] in England here was bred,
> Although descended of the Danish blood,
> King Hardiknut my Father, thirty years
> Governed the one half of this famous Kingdom,
> Where I that time was born an English Princess.[50]

Elgina claims that geography, not descent, makes one "English," and Perry rightly points to these lines as among the play's most broad-minded in terms of national identity. Playgoers who had read Speed would have recognized Emma's shadow in Elgina's proclamation that national identity is not governed exclusively by one's descent; the notion that geography influences identity also resonates strongly with Davies's prefatory poem to Speed's work. However, in the next act Elgina is killed by Erkinwald. The play poses the notion of geographic Englishness, expressed by a female character embracing multiple national identities, but Elgina is not allowed to be the Emma who bridges two nationalities.

Canutus similarly envisions his amorous relationship with Cartesmunda in terms of transcending national boundaries: "In thee we have all good that England holds / All Conquest in these Arms Canutus folds."[51] He continues:

> [...] Come Cartesmunda kiss me:
> Go bid our Souldiers hang their Arms up;
> Fold up our Ensigns, and unbrace our Drums,
> England is conquer'd, all Wars are done,
> And all in this, that Cartesmunda's won.[52]

---

[49] McMullan, "Colonization," 126.
[50] Brewer, *Edmund Ironside*, 1.3.242-7.
[51] Brewer, *Edmund Ironside*, 2.4.56-7.
[52] Brewer, *Edmund Ironside*, 2.4.70-4.

In Canutus's view, England and Cartesmunda are parallel; joining himself to her completes a merger of the two nations. While she lives, Canutus refuses to engage in warfare against the English; while perhaps not depicted as a "union" between English and Danish, he ceases the atrocities he has been inflicting on the country. His Vikings criticize his lack of military action, but Canutus refuses to arm himself and fight until Cartesmunda is dead. Again, a female character dies who could have ultimately served as a bridge between Danish and English. Once she is dead, Canutus goes immediately back to war against the English.[53]

The climactic battle in Act 5 continually highlights English and Danish interactions through dead female characters. When Alured gets the upper hand over Canutus, he declines to kill or capture him: "for your fair sisters sake, whose love was to me / So high and potent, that it did attract / Her Virgin-thoughts to dart Loves joyes into me." Once Canutus has been captured by the Newcastle characters, he asks to be slain and buried with Cartesmunda: "Let me be buried with her, that's all the mercy / I now will beg of thee from all thy Conquests."[54] Canutus himself prefers death with Cartesmunda to mercy from the Anglo-Saxon victors, but Alured again refuses to harm him, for Elgina's sake:

> I call to mind thy Royal Sisters love,
> Beauteous Elgina, worthier then thy Nun,
> Whose loving heart was once unbosom'd here,
> And for her sake Ile like a brother use thee [...][55]

Alured then offers to send Canutus home with pledges of fellowship: "you shall return unto your State in Denmark, / and henceforth even as brothers wee wil live, / Exchanging Embassies of Love and Honor."[56] Canutus does not, in Brewer's play, get to rule half of England at the end of his military conflicts as the historical Cnut did. Alured, finally, encourages Canutus to "Let Cartesmunda dye in our new love" making explicit women's potential role as an interface between nationalities, but also highlighting that this (at least in Brewer's play) requires their death. Homosocial male bonds are formed through women, but in this play the women themselves must be removed from the equation before the bonds can be cemented and the love can be described as familial. Nor are these bonds equal by the end, for Canutus never responds to Alured's offers of brotherhood. After his lines asking for death and burial, he is silent for the rest of the

[53] Brewer's source for this plot was *Hiren, or The Faire Greeke*, a narrative poem about Mehmet II and his love affair with Irene, a nun of Constantinople. Robert Dent, "The Love-Sick King: Turk Turned Dane," *Modern Language Review* 56 (1961): 555-7.

[54] Brewer, *Edmund Ironside*, 5.2.67-8.

[55] Brewer, *Edmund Ironside*, 5.2.70-3.

[56] Brewer, *Edmund Ironside*, 5.2.73-7.

play—a situation reminiscent of the treatment of Isabella at the end of Shakespeare's *Measure for Measure*. His consent, like hers, is never given, and his lack of verbal acceptance and his expulsion back to Denmark undermine Alured's claims about their new-found "brotherhood." The conjoining and adaptation of Danish identity to English does not proceed smoothly nor is it complete at the play's end.

The play's attempt at claiming brotherhood, and coopting Canutus as "English" stems (as Perry points out) from a desire to showcase the "Saxon liberties" that both the historical Cnut and Alfred the Great represent. Like Cnut, Alfred's early modern reputation rested largely on his legislation.[57] Choosing Alfred for Canutus's opposite explicitly places the two best-known and most comprehensive vernacular legislators of pre-Conquest England on stage together and declares them brothers. The simultaneous erasure of that familial bond, qualifying it heavily based on gender (and so metaphorically deleting Emma of Normandy and her influence) and finally leaving Cnut's "Englishness" in question, perhaps stems from the increasing difficulty, in the climate of the seventeenth century's second decade, of conceiving of "English" as anything but an exclusive identity. However, the fact that Cnut's legislation promulgates a cultural and legal system in which episcopacy plays a key role also would have made him difficult for many English Presbyterians to absorb into "English" history.

That difficulty would have been even more apparent to the play's readers after its publication in 1655; readers of Bacon and (after 1656) Prynne who perused Brewer's work would be primed to reject any notion of Cnut as an "English" king and consider Alfred's victory a national triumph of English of Dane. The publication of the play gave it a new audience who had lived through civil wars and regicide and would be even less likely to embrace the notion that English identity could be achieved merely by geography, or that savage conquerors could suddenly soften under a woman's wise influence to become astute legislators. In the histories which they had read, Cnut was first an embarrassingly malleable puppet of bishops, and then a foreign scourge—a mere historical plot point. Cnut, and his role in the "Saxon liberties" narrative, would be reduced to silence and departure from the record, like Canutus in Brewer's play.

Early-modern English discussions of Cnut offer new insight into medievalism's potential to reveal otherwise indiscernible aspects of a culture's dynamics. Rather than being seamlessly absorbed into the discourse of "Saxon liberties" by the Parliamentary and Presbyterian party, Cnut's image was shaped and reshaped based on a multitude of conflicting desires for the contemporary English church and state. The historical texts' depiction of Cnut also gives us necessary insight to understand the character of Canutus in Brewer's play, which otherwise remains enigmatic. There is more work to be done

[57] Simon Keynes, "The Cult of King Alfred the Great," *Anglo-Saxon England* 28 (1999): 225-356.

here, of course, especially in tracing the understanding of early medieval England's royal women, which have only been touched on in this essay. This much, however, is clear: "Anglo-Saxon England," largely an invention of the early modern period, refused to be monolithic even in its original conceptions. Even in the seventeenth century, narratives of early medieval history shifted rapidly based on contemporary desires. Attempts to reduce the history of pre-Conquest England to little more than an instrument of polemic or an overly simplified account of national and racial origins failed utterly, and have continued to do so ever since.

Dream on? Alfred's Vision of Cuthbert in Reformation-era Historiography

Susannah Brietz Monta

To contemporary scholars of Anglo-Saxon England, Alfred the Great is known as a military leader, a religious reformer, a sponsor of vernacular literature, a translator, and a focal point for nationalist sentiment and creative historiography from his own time to ours.[1] To the early modern English Jesuit and controversialist Robert Persons (1546-1610), he was a king who had a great dream, one in which St. Cuthbert encouraged him and predicted his victory at Edington. To be sure, the dream put Alfred in good company: the biblical David, Jacob, and Joseph had wondrous dreams, as Persons eagerly points out. But Persons had little time for Alfred's other accomplishments. The dream was the thing wherein to catch the conscience of his Protestant rival, John Foxe, whose influential martyrology, the *Actes and Monuments*, Persons was determined to bury once and for all.

At issue in the quarrel between Foxe and Persons was Alfred's role as an historical forebear whom polemicists could deploy as they forged narratives of religious continuity. Scholars have traced the uses and reshapings of Alfred's legacy from the ninth to the twentieth centuries.[2] This essay revisits Alfred's portrayal, not from the vantagepoint of popular culture or English nationalism, as others have done, but of Reformation historiography. My focus is Alfred's dream of St. Cuthbert, or rather the ways that dream's content, contexts, and credibility changed in Reformation writing. The dream does not appear in the earliest Alfredian biography, that of Asser.[3] Asser's work was

[1] See, *inter alia,* Richard Abels, *Alfred the Great: War, Kingship, and Culture in Anglo-Saxon England* (London: Longman, 1998); David Pratt, *The Political Thought of King Alfred the Great* (Cambridge: Cambridge University Press, 2007); and Simon Keynes, "The Cult of King Alfred the Great," in *Anglo-Saxon England* 28 (1999): 225-356.

[2] These include Barbara Yorke "Alfred the Great: the Most Perfect Man in History?," *History Today* 49:10 (1999); "Alfredism: The Use and Abuse of King Alfred's Reputation in Later Centuries," in *Alfred the Great,* ed. T. Reuter (Aldershot: Ashgate, 2003), 361-80, David Horspool (*King Alfred: Burnt Cakes and Other Legends* (Cambridge: Harvard University Press, 2006), and, above all, Simon Keynes "The cult of King Alfred the Great".

[3] The episode does not occur in either Asser's *De gestis Alfredi* or the *Anglo-Saxon Chronicle.* Its earliest appearance seems to be in the eleventh-century *Historia de sancto Cuthberto*; see Ted Johnson South, ed.,

known to early modern historians primarily through Archbishop Matthew Parker's edition of 1574, which silently interpolated material from other texts (including the infamous burnt cakes episode, taken from the *Vita prima sancti Neoti*).[4] But the dream featured in other sources widely used in the period, most importantly William of Malmesbury's twelfth-century histories *Gesta Pontificum Anglorum* and *Gesta Regum Anglorum*. The ways early modern authors handle the dream—ranging from passionate endorsement to creative redirection to willful suppression—illuminate the complexities of early modern thought about reported wonders in historical writing. The dream makes for an especially interesting case study: it is neither a spectacular miracle (an external occurrence witnessable by others), nor, for its Catholic defenders, simply a product of Alfred's own wishful thinking. It exists in a middle space between spectacle and perception, precisely the space that early modern historiographers found both important and challenging to define.

Those early modern sources that include the dream evince some defensiveness. Protestant attacks on medieval hagiographic excess certainly matter here. Still, the dream persists longer, even in some Protestant accounts, than one might predict. The dream's uneven durability reveals that the reformation of historiography cannot be characterized as a clean break with medieval precedent, nor do historiographical approaches to reported wonders sort neatly along confessional lines. That the dream should have come under some suspicion is unsurprising: post-Reformation Protestant and Catholic writers alike undertook the purging of miracles and wonders from their medieval sources—noisily if sometimes unevenly, in the case of writers like John Foxe, and cautiously, in the case of Catholic figures like Laurentius Surius or Caesar Baronius. Perhaps more surprising are the ways the dream endures in both Catholic and some conservative Protestant sources. Yet during the late sixteenth and seventeenth centuries, wonders and miracles were by no means easily or readily discarded. Statistically, the seventeenth century is the age of miracles; no other century rivals it in the establishment of miracle-commemorating saints' shrines.[5] Reports of saints' miraculous activities were

---

Historia de sancto Cuthberto (Woodbridge: D. S. Brewer, 2000), 90. Alfred Smyth notes the similarities between this story and that of Alfred's two visions of St. Neot, who also predicted victories over the Danes (*King Alfred the Great*, [Oxford: Oxford University Press, 1995] 334-5).

4 *Aelfredi Regis res gestae* (London, John Day, 1574); on the burning cakes, see Smyth, *King Alfred*, 325-8. Parker's source, the anonymous *Vita prima sancti Neoti*, contains both the cake-burning episode and a dream vision of Neot (similar to that of Cuthbert); Parker ignored the dream and lifted only the burning cakes episode.

5 See Craig Harline, *Miracles at the Jesus Oak: Histories of the Supernatural in Reformation Europe* (New York: Doubleday, 2003), prologue; Harline's sources include Philip Soergel, *Wondrous in His Saints* (Berkeley: University of California Press, 1989); Jean Delumeau's *Rassurer et protéger: Le sentiment de sécurité dans l'Occident d'autrefois* (Paris: Fayard, 1989); and H. Platelle, "Mirakels in de Zuidelijke Nederlanden,"

numerous in France and in the Spanish Habsburg-controlled areas of the Low Countries, where English Catholic exiles had intellectual and educational centers. As Anne Dillon has shown, English Catholic martyrologists tended to downplay miracles in favor of a humanist emphasis on martyrs' heroism.[6] Still, they usually defended historical miracles as necessary for the establishment of Catholicism during the Anglo-Saxon period, and some English Catholics were keen—especially in manuscripts and printed texts intended primarily for English Catholic consumption—to stress the continuity of wonders (admittedly, often relatively sober ones) into the present.[7] Nor was Protestant England entirely averse to marvelous tales. John Foxe included some wonders, albeit chastened, in his martyrological work, and firm distinctions between providential wonders (acceptable to godly Protestants) and miracles (supposedly the purview of papist superstition) proved difficult to draw.[8]

That distinction proved even more challenging in the case of Alfred's dream, a sort of borderline wonder hovering between witnessable miracle and hopeful individual perception. It is tempting to read the shifting status of Alfred's dream as a microcosm for the broad Protestantizing of history in England, as it slowly and unevenly pulls away from Counter-Reformation attempts to revise late medieval hagiography as decently respectable *historia sacra*.[9] Yet English Catholic writers worked to maintain the dream as reported in their preferred medieval sources, despite (and indeed partly because of) Protestant criticisms. And some Protestants held onto Alfred's dream, though with adjustments to its theology. Early modern treatments of Alfred's dream raise critical theological questions concerning the means of divine intervention in human affairs, the typological reenactment of biblical precedent in human lives, and the role of the saints as mediators and guides. Prolonged historiographical differences over Alfred's dream suggest that these questions were not easily resolved.

Foxe's *Actes and Monuments* represented a concerted effort to compose an ecclesiastical history supportive of Protestantism. Foxe's project traces the continuous presence of a

---

Spieghel Historiael (1973): 175-7. Mary Lee Nolan and Sidney Nolan in *Christian Pilgrimage in Modern Western Europe* (Chapel Hill: University of North Carolina Press, 1989) support Harline's claim that the seventeenth was "the biggest shrine-establishing century ever" (Harline 254).

6 Dillon, *The Construction of Martyrdom in the English Catholic Community, 1535-1603* (Aldershot: Ashgate, 2002), 68, 85, 209.

7 See for instance John Geninges, *The life and death of Mr. Edmund Geninges priest* (St. Omer, 1614).

8 Alexandra Walsham, *Providence in Early Modern England* (Oxford: Oxford University Press, 1999); I discuss chastened marvels and wonders in English Protestant and Catholic martyrologies (*Martyrdom and Literature in Early Modern England* [Cambridge: Cambridge University Press, 2005] ch. 3).

9 Simon Ditchfield has argued that the distinction between hagiography and history in Italian historiography only became firm in the nineteenth century ("'Historia Magistra Sanctitatis'? The relationship between historiography and hagiography in Italy after the Council of Trent (ca. 1564-1742)," *Studies in Medieval and Renaissance History* 18:3 (2006): 159-84).

true—if sometimes scattered and persecuted—church. Alfred first appears in its second edition (1570). In this edition, Foxe expanded his English martyrology by beginning not with the Lollards (as in the 1563 first edition) but the earliest days of Christianity. Foxe used many sources for his story of Alfred; these include the chronicles and histories of Roger of Hoveden, Henry of Huntington, Robert Fabian, Ranulf Higden, and William of Malmesbury (Foxe admits that he cannot read the Saxon tongue). Still, he had little use for one of the most famous anecdotes about Alfred's life, one missing in Asser but present in several of Foxe's other sources, as he acknowledges: a prophetic dream Alfred had at a critical moment.[10] In Foxe's version, Alfred is forced to withdraw to the island of Athelney after disastrous battles with invading Danes. He lodges with a swineherd, Dunwolfus, and his wife; both are ignorant of Alfred's identity. During this low point, Alfred has a wondrous dream. Foxe reports the dream, but hedges it with a naturalistic explanation and uncertainty about his sources' reliability:

> certaine stories recorde of a poore beggar, which there came and asked hys almes of the kyng. And the night folowing he appeared to the king in his sleepe: saying hys name was Cutbert, promising (as sent from God, unto him for his good charitie) great victories agaynst the Danes. But to let these dreaming fables passe, although they bee testified by dyvers authors, both Wilelmus lib. de Reg. Polychronicon Rog. Heueden, Iornalensis, and other mo. Notwithstanding the king in proces of tyme, was strengthened and comforted more and more, through the providence of God.[11]

In Foxe's rendering of these "stories," the dream's content stays slightly out of focus. Foxe omits some details as Malmesbury recorded them, such as Cuthbert's indication that God would look with favor on Alfred thanks to the merits of earlier English saints (*sanctorum meritis super eam misericordiae oculo respicit*).[12] While Malmesbury does not mention a beggar or poor man, Higden's *Polychronicon* does.[13] By including this detail, Foxe implies that the dream of the beggar-as-Cuthbert may be motivated by Alfred's earlier generosity, and that Alfred's promised victories will reward his generosity ("for

[10] Foxe refers to William of Malmesbury's *Gesta Regum Anglorum* (elsewhere he draws also on Malmesbury's *Gesta Pontificum Anglorum*), Roger of Hoveden's *Chronica*, Ranulf Higden's *Polychronicon,* and "Iornalensis," a fourteenth-century manuscript known as the *Chronicon* and erroneously attributed by John Bale and others to John Brompton; see V. J. Goodman, "Brompton, John, fl. 1436-c.1464, abbot of Jervaulx and supposed chronicler," *Oxford Dictionary of National Biography*, and Matthew J. Philpott, *Rectifying the "ignoraunce of history"*: "John Foxe and the Collaborative Reformation of England's Past," Vol. 1, Ph.D. thesis, University of Sheffield, 2009, 171-2.

[11] Foxe, *Actes and Monuments* (London, John Day, 1570), 201. Henceforth *A&M.*

[12] As cited in Persons, *A Treatise of Three Conversions* (St. Omer, 1603-4), part 2, 145. See also Malmesbury's *The Deeds of the Bishops of England = Gesta Pontificum Anglorum,* ed. David Preest (Woodbridge: Boydell, 2002), 180.

[13] *Polychronicon Ranulphi Higden monachi Cestrensis* (London: Longman, 1865-6), Vol. 6, 373-4.

his good charitie"). Foxe treats the story with some suspicion: he mentions but then undercuts this "dreaming fable." His procedure allows him both to acknowledge his sources and to distance his history from what he sees as their foolish credulity. While the episode has its medieval champions—whom Foxe duly lists—Foxe concludes that Alfred benefited from divine providence, not so much in a temporally discrete wondrous intervention but "in proces of tyme."[14]

Like the godly Calvinists Alexandra Walsham has studied, Foxe tends to substitute providence's guiding care for miracles, though the line between providential wonder and miraculous intervention is, in his and others' hands, a wavering one.[15] Foxe doubles down on providence in his narrative following the dream: it is due to providence that Alfred defeats the Danes in the battle of Edington and captures their raven standard. And providence chose its champion well: for Foxe, Alfred is an ideal king. Like other early modern historians, Foxe saw in Alfred's godliness, generosity, and work ethic an example with which to admonish contemporary monarchs. To find many "heroyical properties, joyned together in one prince" is "a thing most rare, & seldome seene in Princes now adaies"; contemporary princes should aspire "to hys imitation."[16] Those princes could, presumably, imitate Alfred's charitable deeds and hope for providence's guidance, if not for prophetic visionary visitations by important English saints.

The Jesuit Robert Persons's account of Alfred aims to redeem what Foxe saw as "dreaming fables." In the early seventeenth century, Persons undertook the most systematic Catholic response to Foxe's martyrology. Persons's *A Treatise of Three Conversions*, published in 1603-4, traces England's three Christian conversions (under the apostles, Pope Eleutherius and King Lucius, and Pope Gregory the Great and King Æthelberht) in order to link each one firmly to Rome. It also undertakes lengthy, detailed refutations of Foxe's work, including Foxe's handling of Alfred's dream. Persons first recounts Alfred's visit to Pope Leo IV with his father, during which he was confirmed, Persons claims, with the Pope as his godfather. He thus stresses connections between the papacy and Anglo-Saxon Christianity.[17] After attacking Foxe's account of Pope Joan, Persons returns to Alfred, focusing almost entirely on historiographical questions about the credibility of wondrous dreams and the role of the saints in history. Persons argues that Foxe spends little time on Anglo-Saxon England because of the problems Anglo-Saxon saints present for Foxe's narrative. At issue is the witness of miracles: Foxe cannot show,

[14] Here, Foxe cites Henry of Huntingdon's *Historia Anglorum* in a marginal note. Foxe's reference to providence adds a Protestant gloss to Henry's statement that after Alfred's withdrawal into hiding "the Lord looked down on the remnants of His people" (Henry, Archdeacon of Huntingdon, *Historia Anglorum: The History of the English People,* ed. and trans. Diana Greenway [Oxford: Clarendon Press, 1996] 288-9).

[15] Walsham, *Providence*; Monta, *Martyrdom*, ch. 3.

[16] Foxe, *A & M* (1570), 200.

[17] Persons, *A Treatise of Three Conversions*, 1603-4, part 2, 394-5.

Persons writes, "that any one of these, that wrought so infinite miracles both alive and dead, (as the former authors do testifie) had byn of his religion."[18] Persons notes that when Foxe discusses Anglo-Saxon kings, he does not speak of religious matters but instead censures the kings "for their beleefe, actions and doings in religion" such as building monasteries, giving privileges and lands to abbeys and churches, going on pilgrimages, offering alms for their sins, and ordaining masses to be said for their souls. These kings "beleeved so easily miracles, went to shrift, humbled themselves to Priests, and other such like religious actions."[19] Such actions were, of course, contentious in the Reformation. In the *Treatise of Three Conversions*, Alfred's story provides an historical English witness for religious practices that Persons claims as distinctively Catholic.

Those practices include reverence for English saints like Cuthbert. Persons recounts the dream as William of Malmesbury reported it in the *Gesta Regum Anglorum*. The story is rich in biblical echoes, as Persons highlights. In this account, Alfred flees with his mother to "Adaling" (Athelney), a little island in the midst of marshland. Pressed by hunger and fear, they send some of their men to fish at night to avoid detection, while they sleep. Cuthbert appears to Alfred in a dream, and tells him that the Danes act as chastisements for sin. But God has not abandoned Alfred's beleaguered, all-but-disbanded Anglo-Saxon army, because of the virtues of Anglo-Saxon saints: in the dream Alfred learns that God "would not extinguish them, in respect of so many Saincts that had byn of that Nation; and from this day foreward [God] would sett them up againe."[20] It is not hard to see a subtle message of encouragement to contemporary English Catholics: pressed by reformers who may also serve as scourges of sin, they will be rescued for the sake of the saintly forebears whose histories Persons traces. Cuthbert next promises a sign to confirm the restoration of Alfred's kingdom: "that albeit that night was a very contrary tyme to Fishers, both for that all ryvers were frozen, and a litle rayne being fallen upon the same, had made it unfitt for men to travayle in that arte: yet his men should come home all loden with incredible abundance of fish." In Luke 5, Jesus calls to Peter (then Simon), James, and John, encouraging the three fishermen to let down their nets for fish. They reply that they have fished all night with no luck; still, they comply, and catch so many fish that their nets begin to break. Similarly, despite bad weather Alfred's men return with loads of fish "sufficient to satisfie the hunger of never so great an army."[21] The wonder is linked to biblical precedent and Alfred's future military success.

---

[18] Persons, *A Treatise*, 384.
[19] Persons, *A Treatise*, 405.
[20] Persons, *A Treatise*, 419.
[21] Persons, *A Treatise*, 420.

Persons also insists that the dream supports his vision of the English nation as historically Catholic. Persons claims that "both [Alfred] & his mother were wont to recount" the dream and its aftermath "all dayes of their life after, & the events themselves did evidently declare the truth of the miracle, recorded as hath byn said by our best historiographers."[22] Foxe is not one of those historiographers. He is instead "perfidious" for dismissing this dream as a "*dreaminge fable*" when it is one of many "important miracles shewed by God for testification of his love and providence towards our countrey and the savinge and restoringe therof."[23] Persons highlights what he sees as the *Actes and Monuments'* internal contradictions: while undermining Alfred's dream, Foxe credits the visions and dreams of his co-religionists, such as Martin Luther or the Marian martyr Cuthbert Simpson (the contrast with St. Cuthbert is left implicit). At issue for Persons are the standards of evidence upon which to build a history of religious continuity. The similarities between Alfred's dream and biblical precedents should shore up claims of miraculous occurrences in Anglo-Saxon England; these tales of miracles and saints should in turn reveal the Catholic Church as the true heir to the early medieval church and encourage English Catholics that they, like Alfred, might emerge from their internal exile to triumph over their enemies. Persons bolsters his argument for continuity and the credibility of wondrous dreams with biblical precedent: David, Jacob, Saul, Daniel, Joel, Joseph, and Mary were given "visions by sleepe" that offered important revelations. To doubt dreams is to "bringe in doubt and contempt, most of the principall misteries and miracles of the old and new testament."[24] For Persons, the standards for biblical and historical credibility are shared and mutually dependent.

Persons' narrative was influential for other English Catholics. One of them was William Blundell (1560-1638), a landowner, antiquarian, and committed Catholic—or in the words of the authorities, one of Lancashire's most "bloody" recusants.[25] Blundell suffered fines and imprisonment during Elizabeth's reign, and witnessed the death of his father in prison, put there for sheltering a priest.[26] In roughly 1610, Blundell enclosed some of his land for use as a burial ground for Catholics denied burial in the

---

22 Persons, *A Treatise*, 421-2.
23 Persons, *A Treatise*, 422.
24 Persons, *A Treatise*, 422.
25 *Crosby records; a chapter of Lancashire recusancy. Containing a relation of troubles and persecutions sustained by William Blundell, of Crosby hall, Lancashire, esq. (1560-1638), and an account of an ancient burial ground for recusants, called the Harkirke, and of coins discovered there ...*, ed. Thomas Ellison Gibson, introd. Alexander Goss (Manchester: Printed for the Chetham society, 1887), x.
26 D. R. Woolf, "Little Crosby and the Horizons of Early Modern Historical Culture," in Donald R. Kelley and David Harris Sacks, eds., *The Historical Imagination in Early Modern Britain: History, Rhetoric, and Fiction, 1500-1800* (Cambridge: Cambridge University Press, 1979), 98-9.

local parish church.[27] The first burial occurred on 7 April 1611. The next day, a servant boy found several silver coins in a pile of dirt displaced by the burial. Eventually, according to Blundell's written account, fourscore coins were found, most of Anglo-Saxon origin. His grandson suggested that the finding of coins "stamped in the reigns of Catholick Saxon Kings" was part of a providential plan: "The valew of the whole sum seemed equal as possible to the expence of fencing, and of converting that smal parcel of land to that particular use. So he had a tymely payment for all, and, as we have reason to hope, an eternall."[28] In his account of the coins, Blundell thus used these "Catholick Saxon Kings" to portray his religion as, in the words of one of his poems, "Ancient truthe," the "ould Religion" that "Austin [St. Augustine of Canterbury] planted here most sure."[29]

Like Persons, Blundell is interested in continuity: the coins link his actions in establishing a Catholic burial ground to the faithful devotions of early kings. Using these coins, he aims to oppose the current "tym" in which "each man may/ See newe Religions coynd each day."[30] Blundell wrote short descriptions of the coins, offering details about the figures whose names appear on them. Most of the narratives concern Saxon kings; many relate their devotions to saints or assert their own status as saints. Thus Blundell records Æthelstan's devotion to St. John of Beverley, who helped him win a decisive victory against the Scots. King Edmund (r. 940-946) was counseled by the future St. Dunstan (as, Blundell notes, Stowe and others attest). King "Edered" (Eadred) "humbled himselfe to the feete of holy men" and "devoted his lyfe to God and St. Dunstan."[31] Miracles figure prominently: the wife of King Edmund was canonized thanks to "Miracles wrought at her tombe," while "St. Eadmund, king and martir" also had "greate miracles [...] wroughte after his death [which] yow may see in his lyfe written by Surius in his sixte Tome."[32] Blundell's allusion to Surius's work suggests his up-to-date knowledge of Counter-Reformation hagiography.

Given Blundell's interest in miracles, it is unsurprising that Alfred's dream makes a prominent appearance. Alfred's is the longest narrative, and Blundell has done his homework: he cites Foxe, Polydore Vergil, Richard Verstegan (whose antiquarian text

[27] Blundell suffered for his makeshift graveyard: in 1629 he was summoned before Star Chamber for this and other offenses, and set a ruinous fine of 2000 pounds. In 1631 Charles I reduced the fine to a more manageable 250 pounds (*Calendar of State Papers,* Vol. 194, 22b, p. 81; Woolf, "Little Crosby," 101; see also the *Chronicle of the English Canonesses Regular of the Lateran, at St. Monica's in Louvain,* ed. Dom Adam Hamilton, O.S.B., London, 1904, 153).

[28] *Crosby records,* 43.

[29] *Crosby records,* 25.

[30] *Crosby records,* 28.

[31] *Crosby records,* 58.

[32] *Crosby records,* 58, 59-60.

had been published in 1605), and, most of all, Persons, whose rendering of Malmesbury's account he incorporates almost verbatim, though without the vituperation against Foxe that frames the Malmesbury account in Persons's text. Blundell notes the monastery built at "Adelinge, or Ethelinge, where St. Cudberht, appearinge unto him, encoraged and Comforted him, beinge in greate distresse and heavines. This monasterie, saithe Polidore, hee gave to the monks of Sainte Benett."[33] The "notable storie" of Alfred's comforting by St. Cuthbert dominates Blundell's account of Alfred. For Blundell, the dream links the greatest of Anglo-Saxon kings with the early English saint. The story also quietly encourages the contemporary recusant Catholics whom Blundell's burial ground was to serve.[34]

Where for Persons the dream helps refute Foxe's historiography, Blundell emphasizes Alfred's religiosity and virtue (themes also stressed in his less detailed portraits of other Anglo-Saxon kings). The close connection between Alfred and Cuthbert is, Blundell, believes, inscribed on one of the coins: it has "AELFRED REX" on one side and "CUDBERHT" on the other (this is Blundell's preferred spelling for Persons's "Cuthbert"; Blundell's choice of "Cudberht" may underscore the coin's influence on his thinking). Blundell sees the coin as evidence of the miraculous encounter between king and saint:

> I thinke it moste lyke and probable that K. Ælfred caused the Coine so to be made in memorie of the fore saide miracle, for althoughe there was an Archbishoppe of Canturburie named Cudberht, whoe dyed aboute the yeare 798, a man of greate renowne for learninge and vertue, yet can I fynde written no espetiall cause or reason why this kinge shoulde set him in his Coyne, who dyed a longe tyme (as the former Cudberht did also) before hee was made kinge, and gave not anie occasion of such spetiall memorie to be made of him by the saide kinge as did the other St. Cudberht, whoe was Bishoppe of Lindesfarne aboute the yeare 689, of whose holy lyfe and deathe yowe maye reede in St. Bede.[35]

Blundell is determined to find persistent, material evidence for a "miracle" connecting an admired Anglo-Saxon king, an early English saint, and his own beleaguered Catholic community. Blundell's account is to participate in the project of the coins as he sees it: to prolong the "memorie of the fore saide miracle."

Alfred's dream persisted in later English Catholic arguments for religious continuity, though its content sometimes underwent revision. In 1655 in Paris, a volume entitled *Meditations upon the Marks of the True Church of Christ: or, Motives of Credibility in behalf of the True Religion* proclaimed Roman Catholicism's antiquity. The author's

[33] *Crosby records*, 49.

[34] Phebe Jensen, "Religious Identity and the English Landscape: William Blundell and the Harkirk Coins," in *Religious Diversity and Early Modern English* Texts, ed. Arthur F. Marotti, et al. (Detroit: Wayne State University Press, 2013), 65; Woolf, "Little Crosby."

[35] *Crosby Records,* 53.

initials, H.W., possibly belong to Fr. Henry Wilkinson, S.J., not to be confused with two Protestant ministers of the same name.[36] (Next to the initials "H.W." on the title page of the British Library's copy of *Meditations,* someone has helpfully added a disambiguating annotation: "Papist.") In the eighteenth meditation, H.W. argues that the Roman Catholic church has always been favored by "temporal blessings"—especially of the military sort—bestowed "in a miraculous way" on its defenders, and that England boasts its fair share of these:

> Venerable *Bede* recounts a famous victory [...] which King *Oswald* got against the Pagan King *Cadwallus,* in the battell, he had for his Ensigne, the sign of the Crosse; and the victory was so much attributed to a heavenly assistance; as that the place was called *Heavens field*; now corruptly *Haden field. Alfred* King of the west Saxons, got so miraculous a victory over the *Danes, Anno* 880. by means of Saint *Cuthbert* (who bid him encounter with the enemy, notwithstanding his forces were small; and told him when, how and in what place he should fight them) that many of the nobler sort of the Danish Army were Baptized and Converted upon it: yea, the same Saint *Cuthbert* told *Alfred,* that his posterity should rule over all *England*: which in *Athelstane,* and King *Edward* was fulfilled.[37]

Cuthbert has gone beyond encouraging Alfred to come out of hiding, foretelling a successful fishing trip, and predicting the kingdom's restoration: here, Cuthbert offers precise military advice. H.W. does not connect Alfred's encounter with Cuthbert to biblical precedent, as Persons did, but to ecclesiastical and military history. H.W.'s changes align Alfred and Oswald before him with the Christian emperors Constantine and Theodosius. Sources from Eusebius to Baronius credited Constantine's victory at the Battle of the Milvian Bridge to a vision of a cross under which he should conquer (*in hoc signo vinces*). According to St. Augustine in chapter 26 of *De Civitate Dei,* Theodosius defeated the forces of Eugenius with the assistance of a strong wind that blew their weapons back into them.[38] Historical precedent again establishes truth in religion; as H.W. bluntly puts it, "since the forementioned Princes, and their Armies (on which God bestowed these victories) were Roman Catholicks; as all history evidently shews: and [...] the victories bestowed on them were above the forces of nature, or humane endeavours, and pollicy; and none such were ever obtained by any other sect: it evidently follows, that the religion of these Roman Catholicks is the true

---

[36] Born in Yorkshire in 1595, Fr. Henry Wilkinson, S.J., entered the Society in 1619 and was professed in 1633. He was imprisoned in 1640 for refusing the oath of allegiance. Brought to trial in 1641, he again refused the oath and was condemned to life in prison but was liberated by about 1644. He was with the College of the Immaculate Conception in 1655 and died in 1673. Jesuit records do not mention publications. See *Records of the English Province of the Society of Jesus,* vol. 2, ed. Henry Foley (London: Burns and Oates, 1877), 309-10.

[37] H.W., *Meditations upon the Marks of the True Church of Christ* (Paris, 1655), 219, 222, 225-6.

[38] These miracles are discussed in *Meditations,* 222-4.

religion."[39] The language of "sect" may target not only Protestantism but also the Cromwellian regime, whose military victories must, in H.W.'s view, not be "above the forces of nature, or humane endeavours, and pollicy." Alfred's triumphs witness to supernatural intervention; Cromwell's do not.

For Catholic writers like Persons, Blundell, and H.W., Alfred's encounter with Cuthbert makes the cut for respectable historiography. For Foxe, it remains a "dreaming fable"; providence's guidance, not saintly intervention, shapes the redemptive turns and twists of historical narrative. As Foxe's account shows, Alfred's life presented challenges for Protestant writers. One of those challenges concerned Alfred's habit of endowing monasteries.[40] In her work on Blundell, Phebe Jensen writes that Catholics like Persons and Blundell emphasize "saints and monasteries as demarcating sacred sites," an emphasis she calls "definitively Catholic."[41] In the chorographies of Speed and Camden and in Foxe's account of Alfred, on the other hand, she claims that "English land was reconceptualized to erase the traces of medieval sacred sites." Yet that erasure is not total: Foxe does record Alfred's founding of "divers houses of religion" as well as the "religious house at Ethelynge" (and Blundell relies on Foxe as a source for Æthelstan's monastic foundations).[42] While Speed does not mention the abbey at Athelney, Camden draws reluctantly on Malmesbury—*"(whose words these are and not mine)"*—to acknowledge that Alfred *"founded a little Monasterie,"* before moving on to focus on its architectural features.[43] Given arguments like Jensen's, one might be tempted to draw sharp confessional distinctions with respect to Alfred's dream. Certainly in the years following Foxe's account, the dream of Cuthbert—that "dreaming fable"—fades from many Protestant sources. Thus Speed's chorography omits the dream in favor of the famous anecdote about burning cakes.[44] Similarly, in Francis Godwin's 1601 *A catalogue of the bishops of England*, burning cakes appear but the dream of Cuthbert does not; we are told simply that "At last" the king's friends gathered and defeated the Danes.[45]

---

39 H.W., *Meditations*, 230-1.

40 The notion that Alfred supported monasteries may have descended to early modern authors from West Saxon royal propaganda; there is some historical evidence that "Alfred's extension of West Saxon power into Kent and Mercia involved large-scale confiscation of ecclesiastical estates" (South, *Historia*, 93).

41 Jensen, "Religious Identity," 69.

42 Jensen, "Religious Identity," 69-70; Foxe, *A & M* (1570), 201; *Crosby records*, 58; cf. *A& M* (1570), 210, where Foxe includes the founding but criticizes its purpose. Though I quibble here, I learned much from Jensen's work.

43 John Speed, *Theatre of the Empire of Great* Britaine (London, 1612); William Camden, *Britain, or A chorographicall description of the most flourishing kingdomes ...* (London, 1637), trans. Philemon Holland, 224.

44 The anecdote is taken from Parker's edition of Asser.

45 *A catalogue of the bishops of England, since the first planting of Christian religion in this island together with a briefe history of their lives and memorable actions, so neere as can be gathered out of antiquity* (London, 1601), 164.

While Godwin's text fits the pattern Jensen describes, there was room for intra-confessional variation on the historiographical questions that Alfred's dream raised. In 1621, William Slatyer published *The history of Great Britanie from the first peopling of this island to this present raigne of or [sic] happy and peacefull monarke K: James.* Slatyer was a Church of England clergyman who served, at one point, as a chaplain to Anne of Denmark, James I's queen; he was deprived of his ecclesiastical post in 1645, in the midst of the English civil wars.[46] His poetic history nearly deifies Alfred: "A crowne of thornes then *Alfred* ware,/ Whose head from care, nor hands from bloud,/ Or he from toyle, ere vacant stood."[47] The Christ-like Alfred suffers due to an ally who has fled to Rome; the religious point is subtle but clear. Alfred is left exposed to the Danes and retreats to "Athelney the Nobles Ile." While there, "holy Cuthbert" somehow cheers him—the means are left vague—and persuades him to "take armes in hand." This Cuthbert, like H.W.'s, offers military advice as well as comfort. In gratitude, Alfred "Had *Cuthberts* lands vow'd, and in fine/ Dedicate to him *Chesters* sumptuous shrine."[48] The dream is not mentioned *per se.* But Slatyer does not shy away from Alfred's religious endowments. And unlike Foxe, Slatyer praises and even glorifies "holy" Cuthbert, crediting an encounter with him for effecting a change in Alfred's story. For Slatyer, the turning point is a saintly intervention.

By contrast, the seventeenth century's first book-length treatment of Alfred's life, Robert Powell's *The Life of Alfred[...] with a parallell of our soveraigne lord, K. Charles* (1634), omits the dream of Cuthbert altogether. Yet Powell, a conservative Protestant, is invested in aspects of Alfred's religious practice that some Protestant writers, including Foxe, downplay. Powell was a Gloucestershire solicitor interested in the history of law, though admittedly his work verged on the fanciful: one treatise traces the frank-pledge to Alfred and then beyond him to Moses.[49] Still, in Keynes's view, Powell's life of Alfred "must be accorded pride of place (after Asser) in the long line of Alfredian biography."[50] Powell's dual biography compares Alfred, a model Christian king, with Charles I.

[46] Slatyer wrote an extension of this poem that traced James I's descent from Adam, a set of poems on Anne of Denmark in Hebrew, Greek, Latin, and English, a catechism entitled *The Compleat Catechism,* and *The Psalmes of David in 4 languages and in 4 parts.* He got in trouble for the last publication, perhaps because it included a list of popular secular tunes to which psalms might be sung; see "Slatyer, William (c. 1587-1647), Church of England clergyman and author," E.I. Carlyle, rev. Vivienne Larminie, ODNB.

[47] Slatyer, *The history of Great Britanie from the first peopling of this island to this present raigne of o[u]r happy and peacefull monarke K: James* (London, 1621), 205.

[48] Slatyer, *The history*, 205.

[49] See Powell's *A treatise of the antiquity, authority, uses and jurisdiction of the ancient Courts of Leet, or view of franck-pledge* ... (London, 1642), written in the early 1630s, though its publication was delayed by decree of the Star Chamber (Keynes, "The cult," 253).

[50] Keynes, "The cult," 253.

A royalist for whom obedience to the king is a religious duty, Powell nevertheless expresses some dissatisfaction with Charles I's conduct. He both advises his king through his portrait of Alfred and insists on a high royalist doctrine: "It is most expedient that the lives of good and gracious Princes, being gods on earth, should be set forth unto their people as *specula*, a *super*-eminent watch-Tower whom their subjects every where might behold afar off, and learne to obey their supreme power; and as *speculum*, a mirrour wherin they might gaze on, and strive to imitate their Soveraigne in vertue and goodnesse."[51] Powell's book is an Erastian masterpiece, uniting church and state in the person of the ruler: in lieu of the continuity of saints it offers the continuity of god-like kings. There is no Cuthbert, no dream, not even any Foxean providence; Alfred simply withdraws to Athelney under duress. Powell does note that Alfred built a monastery at the site out of "a locall gratitude."[52] He praises Alfred's religious endowments, his "strict and severe Lawes" against those who refuse paying tithes to support clergy, and his "zealous" enlargement of "the immunities and priviledges of his Churches."[53] Powell also takes a relaxed attitude towards the paying of Peter's pence; Foxe would have been appalled.[54]

Despite Powell's conservative Protestantism, however, there is no wondrous dream. What is miraculous, in his account, is the power of common prayer. While Charles was not, like Alfred, "forced into the field in the very infancy of his raigne," he did go to the far west of his kingdom—a "toilesome journey"—and prepared a defensive war against "the most potent and mightiest Christian Princes of *Europe*" (characterizing Charles's difficulties with France and Spain as a defensive war is a stretch).[55] Facing these challenges, Charles put his trust in God and common prayer. After a "sudden and miraculous deliverance from the Pestilence" brought about by the "incense" of Charles's prayers, the king prescribed a public "forme of prayer" and general fasting, a practice Powell supports by pointing to Alfredian precedent.[56] Charles's efforts were, it seems, successful: "God heard him … he made warres to cease, hee broke the bow and knapped the speare in sunder. He blessed our *Alf.* [Charles] and those two great neighbour

[51] Powell, *The life of Alfred, or, Alured: the first institutor of subordinate government in this kingdome, and refounder of the University of Oxford Together with a Parallel of our Soveraigne Lord, K. Charles until this year, 1634* (London, 1634), sig. a4v.
[52] Powell, *Life of Alfred,* 49.
[53] Powell, *Life of Alfred,* 54.
[54] Powell, *Life of Alfred,* 67.
[55] Powell, *Life of Alfred,* 96, 99.
[56] Powell, *Life of* Alfred, 100, 103. While fasting was a less prominent practice for early modern English Protestants than for Catholics, it remained an important "pious discipline" (Alec Ryrie, *Being Protestant in Reformation Britain,* [Oxford: Oxford University Press, 2013] 196).

Princes with a gratious issue of truce and peace."[57] In case the message is not clear enough, Powell gets explicit: "the best armour of a Christian Prince is prayer and humiliation; the strength and sinewes whereof, doe consist in the uniformity of religion and conformity of the ministry; upon both these the peace and quiet of the Church … doe principally depend."[58] Like Alfred establishing the peaceful practice of Christian religion through his treaty with Guthrum, leader of the Danish army defeated at Edington, Charles too established peace, this time within his church.[59] In this comparison, Puritan attempts to weaken the established church are tantamount to Danish pagans' behavior. Powell praises Charles, "our now *Alf.*," for publishing his "utter dislike of all those, who did or should adventure to stirre or move any new opinions, contrary and differing from the sound and orthodoxall grounds of the true religion here professed and established," noting that Alfred too endorsed regularity and "conformity of the Ministry."[60] While the dream of Cuthbert is gone, its redemptive power has not so much disappeared as it has been dispersed to the practice of common prayer, led by a king justified in his religious practices not by saintly but monarchical precedent. Alfred becomes a precocious Erastian.

John Milton, of course, would have none of this. His *History of Britain,* not published until 1670, was written earlier, in the 1640s and early 1650s, amid the heat of the civil wars, the regicide, and its immediate aftermath. In the *History,* Milton gives Alfred his due: he is a bright spot in the otherwise dismal Anglo-Saxon period, when the English suffered the scourge of Danish invasions as punishment for their sins. In the manuscript of Milton's poetry and notes held at Trinity College, Cambridge, Milton proposed that one might write "A Heroicall Poem" on some episode in Alfred's reign, "especially at his issuing out of Edelingsey on the Danes," where his actions were "wel like those of Ulysses"—who returned from seeming oblivion to effect a slaughter on uncouth usurpers.[61] In the *History,* Milton shows knowledge both of Asser (who does not have the Cuthbert dream) and Malmesbury (who does). But he does not include the cake-burning story (interpolated into Parker's edition of Asser), the founding of a religious house, or the Cuthbert dream. Instead, we see hints of Milton's later vision of the heroic in his Alfred, a man remarkable for devotion, unafraid of solitude (his time with Dunwulf is a sojourn "with a small Company" and "for some time all alone"), brave in battle, and quick-witted.[62] No saintly military advice is required: while Milton

---

[57] Powell, *Life of Alfred,* 101.
[58] Powell, *Life of Alfred,* 102-3.
[59] Powell, *Life of Alfred,* 103.
[60] Powell, *Life of Alfred,* 104, 106.
[61] Trinity College MS R.3.4, 38.
[62] Milton, *The history of Britain, that part especially now call'd England from the first traditional beginning, continu'd to the Norman conquest* (London, 1670), 206.

must have known of the dream as Malmesbury recounts it, he chose to omit it, silently. Perhaps for Milton (as was not the case for Foxe) it was simply not worth contesting.

The 1630s might seem, then, to be the point at which Alfred's dream of Cuthbert drops out of Protestant history: despite the obvious religious differences between Powell and Milton, neither finds the dream worth preserving (though Powell does relocate its transformative import in the established church's prayers, structures, and rituals).[63] Yet the dream makes an emphatic and roughly contemporaneous reappearance in the most significant work of Alfredian scholarship of the seventeenth century: John Spelman's *The Life of Alfred the Great.* Complete by 1643, the work was first published in 1678 in a Latin translation as *Alfredi magni Anglorum regis invictissimi vita.* In 1709, Spelman's English text appeared in an edition prepared and heavily annotated by Thomas Hearne.[64] John Spelman was the son of Henry Spelman, an antiquarian best known for his *History and Fate of Sacrilege,* a treatise detailing the evil fates that befell those who received secularized properties after the dissolution of the monasteries.[65] John Spelman was a friend and advisor of Charles I, a defender of conformist orthodoxy, and a critic of root-and-branch reform.[66] His Alfredian life was dedicated to the future Charles II, then Prince of Wales; its suggestions of kingly suffering followed by triumph would have been timely in the early 1640s, to say the least, as Charles I's conflict with Parliament erupted into civil war.[67] Spelman's biography evinces a royalist, conservative Protestant perspective. The 1678 Latin translation demonstrated loyalty to the restored monarchy in its dedication to Charles II and sported notes by Obadiah Walker which, in Keynes's words, "displayed the tendencies which made him notorious as a closet Catholic."[68] A hint of Blundell's work to forge connections between Alfred and recusant Catholicism appears in the life of a king Spelman tried to render as a moderate, tolerant, high church proto-Protestant: the 1678 edition included Blundell's

---

[63] The same is true of Richard Baker, whose brief account of Alfred in his *Chronicle of the Kings of England* (London, 1643) omits the dream (11).

[64] *The Life of Alfred the Great, By Sir John Spelman Kt[...] with considerable additions, and several historical remarks by the publisher Thomas Hearne, M.A.* (Oxford, 1709).

[65] Henry Spelman worked on the treatise through at least 1633. Scheduled to be printed in 1663, delayed in press, and then temporarily lost, it was finally printed in 1698 (Stuart Handley, "Spelman, Sir Henry (1563/4-1641), historian and antiquary," *ODNB*).

[66] See his 1642 treatises *A Protestants Account of his Orthodox Holding in Matters of Religion, Certain considerations upon the duties both of prince and people,* and *A View of a Printed Book Entitled "Observations upon His Majesties Late Answers and Expresses"* (a reply to Henry Parker's *Observations*); see also David L. Smith, "Spelman, Sir John (1594-1643), royalist author," *ODNB.*

[67] See Keynes: "we may suppose that it was conceived by its author as a way of conveying to the reigning king, and to his heir, a picture of one of their most illustrious forebears, from whose experience they would be able to take comfort, and from whose example they might be able to draw inspiration" ("The cult," 254).

[68] Keynes, "The cult," 265.

coin engravings as one of its illustrations, and a description of the Alfred/"Cudberht" coin repeats Blundell's claim that Alfred's devotion to Cuthbert inspired him to put Cuthbert's name on the coin.[69] Thomas Hearne, editor of the 1709 edition of Spelman's *Life*, was a nonjuring Jacobite who stood out even in conservative Oxford.[70] In these three incarnations of Spelman's work is evidence for the ongoing vitality of conservative Protestant and (in the case of Walker) subtly Catholic readings of Alfred. The dream is retained.

Spelman's meditation on the dream of Cuthbert offers a providentialist reading different in tone from Foxe's. Where Foxe worked to distinguish (albeit incompletely) the wondrous from the providential, Spelman seeks to reconcile them, both theologically and historiographically. Spelman first notes that "the Religious of those Times" thought that Alfred must have deserved his period of suffering, that God was for some reason "greatly offended by him." Still, God mercifully called him to "severe Account" here on earth before facing a worse accounting "in the world to come."[71] In the view of these "Religious," Spelman claims, Alfred was too interested in literature (a terrible fault indeed), knowledge, hunting, and hawking. The future St. Neot warned him, to no effect; Neot's dismay distilled into "a Spirit of Prophesy" as he foretold "what Crosses and Afflictions [Alfred] should for that Cause certainly encounter: That he should be deprived of his Kingdom, and live as it were an Exile in his own Country."[72] The parallel to Charles I's struggles with his Parliament is implicit. Spelman then proposes a providential perspective on temporary afflictions:

> But howsoever presented in the Shew of Punishments, yet (as God's Chastisements ever prove in the upshot) they rather became so many real Blessings, not only in a spiritual Consideration, as they mould them, that suffer in them, into a fitter Temper for receiving the renewed Impressions of the Divine Image once Defaced: but even in human Respects also; clearing the Understanding; sharpening the Wit; taking off the Mind from hurtful and unprofitable Affections; disposing the Will resolutely to undertake what only now remained to be done; and strengthening both the Heart and Hands to struggle with all obstacles of the Difficult work.[73]

Both spiritual and practical benefits redeem suffering. In Alfred's case, one year of suffering seems to have been enough: at the end of that period, God let Alfred know

---

[69] See the "Tabula Tertia" and its description in *Alfredi Magni Anglorum Regis*, trans. Christopher Ware (London, 1678), sigs. c2r-v; the description of the table's eleventh coin reads "Cum Aelfredus noster maxima versus Sanctum Cuthbertum veneratione ferebatur, verisimile est nummi undecimi parte altera Sancti istius nomen inscribi" (c2v).

[70] Theodor Harmsen, "Hearne, Thomas (bap. 1678, d. 1735), antiquary and diarist," *ODNB*.

[71] Spelman, *Life of Alfred*, 55.

[72] Spelman, *Life of Alfred*, 55.

[73] Spelman, *Life of Alfred*, 56.

that "he was pacified towards him, and had determined his Restitution."[74] Spelman is content to let a visionary encounter with Cuthbert serve as a means for God to communicate this change of plan.

For Spelman, as for Persons, biblical precedent is critical, albeit for different ends. In Spelman's telling, a poor man knocks at the door of the cowherd's hut while everyone other than Alfred and his mother is out fishing. (Hearne can hardly contain himself at this, pointing out that Alfred's mother was long dead and that his mother-in-law was in France.)[75] The poor man asks for food, but as they have only one loaf between them Alfred's mother advises Alfred to reject the request. Alfred reminds her of the story of loaves and fishes in the gospels, wherein Jesus fed 5,000 with little more than a five loaves and two fish; he instructs her to give bread to the poor man, and she does so.[76] The king soon falls asleep. He dreams that Cuthbert has come to tell him that the sufferings of the English for their sins have moved God to compassion, and that God has determined to restore Alfred's crown. (Importantly, Hearne does not quibble with the dream itself, only with those who have argued that the dream was of St. Neot instead.)[77] As a sign or "Token" of this change, Alfred's servants would return from their fishing trip with so many fish that it would be "wonderful" to behold. When Alfred wakes, he tells his mother of the dream; she has dreamed the same thing. Soon his servants return "with so incredible a Quantity of Fish, as were in their Seeming sufficient to have fed an Army."[78] Again, the gospel echoes are intertwined with militancy; an army does indeed need to be provisioned in order to ensure Alfred's victory.

Spelman then offers several possible readings of the dream, hedging its interpretation in mystery:

> Whether we shall think the Dream to have proceeded from a natural Cause only, as presented by the Fancy according to the Current of Thoughts precedent; or whether we shall believe it a supernatural and immediate Revelation from God, it is not here very much material. The one as well as the other serves at God's Appointment, by raising or dejecting of the Mind with Hopes or Fears, to lead Man to the Resolution of those Things whereof he has before ordained the Event.[79]

---

[74] Spelman, *Life of Alfred*, 57. (The internal exile was shorter, likely a little less than half a year; see Smyth, *King Alfred*, 73-86).

[75] Spelman, *Life of Alfred*, 58, n. 1.

[76] The feeding of the 5,000 appears in all four Gospels; the feeding of the 4,000, a similar story, appears in Matthew and Mark.

[77] See his note to Spelman, *Life of Alfred*, 59.

[78] Spelman, *Life of Alfred*, 59.

[79] Spelman, *Life of Alfred*, 59.

In Spelman's irenic treatment, neither the natural workings of the mind's imaginative capacities nor supernatural immediacy need be dismissed, nor, indeed, distinguished; both serve divine ends. While more rigid Protestants might attribute miraculous stories to overheated fancy, Spelman conceives of "Fancy" as a potential site of divine intervention. Spelman allows for the possibility that Alfred's encounter with the poor man triggered his dream, but argues that such natural workings of the mind are also at God's disposal. He blurs the lines Foxe began to establish between reliable visions (those of Protestant martyrs like Cuthbert Simpson) and dreaming fables (Alfred's dream of Cuthbert), using the principles of divine guidance and design to ground both imaginative fancy and "supernatural and immediate" intervention. Dreams *and* imaginative fancy —both halves of Foxe's "dreaming fables"?—have a role in God's workings.

One must not be too quick, then, to see the secularized history of, say, David Hume as the inevitable outcome of Protestant historiography. Though he relied heavily on Spelman, Hume includes nothing about Cuthbert or the dream in his account of Alfred.[80] But while Hume has his early modern precedents in the omission of the dream (Speed, Godwin, Camden, Powell, Milton), conservative Protestant writers like Slatyer, Spelman, and Spelman's editor Hearne were reluctant to give up the dream. It's admittedly tidier to accord more polemical Reformation-era Protestants pride of place: their points of difference from Catholicism are stark. It's neater, too, to sideline English Catholic historiography, although that historiography was both varied and influential within and beyond Catholic circles (even influencing the 1678 Latin translation of Spelman's text via its illustrations and Walker's notes). As the wavering fortunes of Alfred's dream in early modern historiography suggest, the lines we often draw to demarcate the intra- and extra-confessional boundaries of early modern Protestantism and Catholicism can be too hard, inadequate to the complex texture of historiographical contest. Reports of saintly wonders did not disappear from English history at the Reformation's early blows. As far as some writers were concerned, for reasons ecclesiastical, historical, theological, controversial, and biblical, Alfred was free to dream on.

[80] David Hume, *The history of England, from the invasion of Julius Caesar to the accession of Henry VIII* (London, 1762), vol. 1, 56-7; Keynes, "The cult," 282.

Index

PRINTED ON PERMANENT PAPER • IMPRIME SUR PAPIER PERMANENT • GEDRUKT OP DUURZAAM PAPIER - ISO 9706
N.V. PEETERS S.A., WAROTSTRAAT 50, B-3020 HERENT